Cambridge Imperial and Post-Colonial Studies Series

Series Editors
Richard Drayton
Department of History
King's College London
London, UK

Saul Dubow
Magdalene College
University of Cambridge
Cambridge, UK

The Cambridge Imperial and Post-Colonial Studies series is a collection of studies on empires in world history and on the societies and cultures which emerged from colonialism. It includes both transnational, comparative and connective studies, and studies which address where particular regions or nations participate in global phenomena. While in the past the series focused on the British Empire and Commonwealth, in its current incarnation there is no imperial system, period of human history or part of the world which lies outside of its compass. While we particularly welcome the first monographs of young researchers, we also seek major studies by more senior scholars, and welcome collections of essays with a strong thematic focus. The series includes work on politics, economics, culture, literature, science, art, medicine, and war. Our aim is to collect the most exciting new scholarship on world history with an imperial theme.

More information about this series at
http://www.palgrave.com/gp/series/13937

Reuben A. Loffman

Church, State and Colonialism in Southeastern Congo, 1890–1962

palgrave
macmillan

Reuben A. Loffman
School of History
Queen Mary University of London
London, UK

Cambridge Imperial and Post-Colonial Studies Series
ISBN 978-3-030-17379-1   ISBN 978-3-030-17380-7   (eBook)
https://doi.org/10.1007/978-3-030-17380-7

This book is dedicated to the memory of Chris Bayly

The original version of the book was revised: Belated corrections have been incorporated. The correction to the book is available at https://doi.org/10.1007/978-3-030-17380-7_9

ACKNOWLEDGEMENTS

Writing this book has been tough. Its completion was in no small measure down to the huge contributions and encouragement of a number of dear colleagues. It is no exaggeration whatsoever to say that without them (as well as perhaps the omnipresent pressures of the Research Excellence Framework [REF]) this book would not have seen the light of day. This is my attempt to try to thank those who have given their time and expertise—I owe them all a great deal. My profound apologies if you have helped and your name is not here.

David Maxwell was the most patient of supervisors. If I have written coherently here, it is down to his diligence as a supervisor. Numerous other scholars read chapters of this book and commented on them. I am therefore very grateful to Giacomo Macola, Miles Larmer, Ashley Leinweber, Piet Clement, René Lemarchand, Dunja Hersak, Kate Skinner, Harry Verhoeven and Eyal Poleg. Not only that, but Colin Jones and Saul Dubow read through the entire manuscript before submission and I am very grateful to them for this. Needless to say, though, if there are errors in this manuscript they are mine alone. I would also like to thank Richard Drayton for all his support as well as that of my Head of School as this book was being completed, Julian Jackson. James Ellison was also a vital source of advice and encouragement. At Palgrave, I would like to express my profound gratitude to Molly Beck and Maeve Sinnott for their unwavering commitment to and belief in this manuscript. I would also like to thank my anonymous readers for their time and insightful comments. I would also like to thank Hemapriya Eswanth at Springer for all her help.

During the time in which I was really struggling with this manuscript, Miri Rubin, who has been a constant source of inspiration during this project, suggested that I set up a group of early career scholars who were at a similar stage of book writing. I am grateful to her for this suggestion and note it here as I can think of no better way of making the book writing process less painful. I am therefore grateful to Chris Moffat, Simon Layton, Nick Beech, Charlotte Faucher and Chloe Ward for their insightful comments and suggestions. I also want to thank my colleague Ed Oliver, in Queen Mary's School of Geography, for doing the maps for me. The African reading group at QMUL, which included, among others, Clive Gabay and Sophie Harman, was another important source of support as were my many conversations with Robert Saunders who kept up my belief that this book could indeed see the light of day.

Another thing that made this book less painful to write were the archivists from across the world, specifically the late Father Vieria of the Spiritans, the White Fathers' archivists in Rome, Rafael Storme, Pierre Dandoy and Alain Gérard in the Ministry of Foreign Affairs in Brussels and Hancko Musinde in the Democratic Republic of the Congo. I would also like to especially thank Hein Vanhee and Donatien Dibwe Dia Mwembu who have been constant sources of inspiration and support throughout. Michel Lwamba Bildona provided me with invaluable local knowledge about Kongolo during this project. Thanks, also, to all those who welcomed me into their homes for interviews and even short stays on occasion. Thanks especially to my tireless research assistant Juvenal Paipo who was phenomenal throughout. Moreover, I would like to express my gratitude to the United Nations for carrying me safely to Kongolo and back three times. This was above and beyond the call of duty and I appreciate them allowing me on board.

Thanks to all my family and close friends for all their support: my wife Claire Bryony Loffman who is the light of my life; Carolyn and Bruce Douglas, Jeff and Marion Loffman, my brother Matt and my sister Anna have always been there for me as have my parents-in-law, Colette and Mike Williams; Joy Loffman provided crucial support when I was studying for the early phase of this project and my conversations with Rod Farningham were also important at this time.

A year or so before I finished this monograph, Chris Bayly died. Although I had only known him for a very short time, Chris' mastery of the discipline and generosity of spirit made a great impression on me and I was greatly saddened by his passing. He dealt with unconventional histories such as this one and it is to Chris' memory that this book is dedicated.

CONTENTS

Abbreviations

AFAC	Association des Fonctionnaires et Agents Coloniaux
AIMO	Affairs Indigènes et du Main-d'œuvre
ANC	Armée Nationale Congolaise
ATCAR	Association Sociale et Culturelle des Tshokwe du Congo, de l'Angola et de la Rhodésie
Balubakat	Association des Baluba du Katanga
BJI	Bulletin des Juridictions Indigènes et du Droit Coutumier Congolais
BSAC	British South Africa Company
BSBEC	Bulletin de la Société Belge d'Etudes Coloniales
BTK	Bourse du Travail du Katanga
CA	Cercle d'Albert 1
CAF	Central African Federation
CAM	Central African Mission (formally the Congo Evangelistic Mission)
CAPS	Centre Agricole pour la Production des Semanciers
CEC	Centre Extra Coutumier
CEHC	Comité d'Etudes du Haut Congo
CEM	Congo Evangelistic Mission
CFL	Compagnie des Chemins de Fer des Grands Lacs Africains
CFS	Congo Free State
CIE	Conseil Indigène d'Entreprise
CK	Compagnie du Katanga
COLOMINES	Société Coloniale Minière en Abrégé
Colonat	European settlers
Conakat	Confédération des Associations Tribales du Katanga

CRA	Congo Reform Association
CSK	Comité Spécial du Katanga
CSSp	Congrégation des Pères du Saint–Esprit, Chevilly la Rue, Paris
DC	District Commissioner
DRC	Democratic Republic of the Congo
EAP	Ecole d'Apprentissage Pédagogique
Febaceka	Fédération des Baluba Centraux du Katanga
Fédéka	Fédération des Associations des Ressortissants de la Province du Kasaï
FTYP	First Ten-Year Plan (1949–1959)
HAV	Hommes Adultes Valides
HGF	Holy Ghost Fathers and the Immaculate Heart of Mary (Spiritains)
IAA	Association Internationale pour l'Exploration et la Civilisation de l'Afrique Centrale
INEAC	Institut National pour l'Etude Agronomique du Congo Belge
Interfina	Société Commerciale et Financière du Congo Belge
Jebakat	Jeunes Baluba du Katanga
MAE	Mission Antiérosive
MNC	Mouvement National Congolais
MOI	Commission de la Main-D'œuvre Indigène
MPNC	Mouvement pour le Progrès National Congolais
PPK	Parti Progressiste Katangais
PSC	Parti Social-Chrétien
RJK	Revue Juridique du Katanga
SAL	Station d'Adaptation Locale
SBEC	Société Belge d'Etudes Coloniales
SCK	Syndicate Commercial du Katanga
SDA(s)	Seventh Day Adventist(s)
SEJK	Société d'Etudes Juridiques du Katanga
SF	Congregation of the Immaculate Heart of Mary, better known as the Scheut Fathers
SMA	Society of Missionaries of Africa (Société des Missionnaires de l'Afrique) (N.B. commonly known as the 'White Fathers')
SOC	Sisters of the Holy Cross
SOREKAT	Société de Recherches et d'Exploitations Aurifères au Katanga
STYP	Second Ten-Year Plan
TC	Territorial Council
Texaf	Compagnie des Textiles Africains
TYP	Ten-Year Plan
UMHK	Union Minière du Haut Katanga
UNO	United Nations Organisation

LIST OF FIGURES

GLOSSARY

By referring to these words by using the languages of the peoples that originated them, such Hêmbá, I do not mean to suggest that other social groups do not use them. Many of these terms are shared between many linguistic groups. For ease of reference, though, I have alluded to them according to the language that they are most associated with. Secondly, when I write 'Luba' I mean KiLuba, as spoken in the former Katanga province, as opposed to TshiLuba, as spoken in Kasai.

Agulu-Abuti (Hêmbá) 'Prediction mound,' where a number of *Kibangile* witch-trials took place.

Hêmbá (Hêmbá) The social group that inhabits much of eastern Kongolo. The word *Hêmbá* is sometimes translated as 'east' as in the 'eastern Luba.'

Bena (Swahili) 'People of,' e.g. the Bena Mambwe are 'people of Mambwe.'

Bilolo (Luba) A vassal of a Luba king, or *Ngoy*, or sacred ruler, *Mulopwe*.

Bula Matari (Kongo) 'Breaker of rocks.' The term was used to describe Henry Morton Stanley's attempts to build roads using dynamite in the 1870s and was then appropriated by the territorial service to mean the colonial state itself. The phrase also is used to indicate a port in Lower Congo by some social groups there.

Les Blue(s) (French) 'Fresher(s),' a reference to the colonial officials who came to the Congo after the Second World War.

Bruges-Saint-Donat (Belgian) The White Fathers' mission outstation in Sola, named after the patron Saint of Bruges.

Bulamba (Hêmbá) A dance that had been part of the Báhêmbá tradition before the incursion of European missionaries in 1909.

Chabo (Hêmbá) A Báhêmbá age-set.

Chicote (French) The hippopotamus-hide whip used widely across the Belgian Congo.

Dawa ya Mvita (Swahili) War medicine used by a number of African communities. Protestant missionaries associated this with Luba groups during decolonization.

Elisabethville The current province of Katanga during the Great Depression (it was changed back to Katanga in 1947). This is also the name given to the city that is currently Lubumbashi (1971–).

Hata(s) (Songye) Sacred groves in which the *Sultani Ya Miti* reside.

Kibangile (Hêmbá) A witch-finding movement Katore and Sindano adopted.

Kibangule (Swahili) The (possible) town in which *Kibangile* originated in Maniema/Manyema.

Kongolo (Luba) The name of the territory in which the chieftainships of Bena Mambwe and Bena Nyembo were situated. Kongolo is named after one of the founders of the Luba ethnic group, *Nkongolo*, the 'drunken king.'

L'intérieur (French) The internal Congolese hinterland, which signifies remoteness to urban centres.

Lisala (Luba) A Luba king.

Lozi/mlozi (Hêmbá) 'Evil.' *Mlozi* means a witch.

Maniema/Manyema (Swahili) The province in which *Kibangule* is situated, whose etymology derives from a word for 'slave.'

Mkubwa (Swahili) A local power broker.

Mucheza wa tambour (Hêmbá) A tambourine dance that was popularised in Kíhêmbá-speaking regions of Kongolo, probably by missionaries at the turn of the twentieth century.

Mudiavita (Songye) A chief of war or war advisor.

Mulopwe (Luba) A title for a sacred Luba ruler.

Mulopwe wa Mudilo (Luba) 'Fire king' or someone given the ashes of a Luba monarch as a signifier of their noble status.

Mungeni (Luba) A word for foreigner.

Muti (Hêmbá) A term meaning 'medicine' in Bemba and that Catholic missionaries ascribed to Báhêmbá as well.

Mwavi (Hêmbá) The concoction likely drunk by suspected witches under the *Kibangile* witch-finding regime.

Mwana (Hêmbá) A term used widely across cultures in Kongolo for the head of a lineage group.

Mzee (Swahili) A respected (male) elder used as another Swahili term for a local big man.

Ngoy (Luba) A title for a Luba noble, slightly less senior than *Mulopwe* (see note on Mulopwe above).

North Katanga/Lualaba Province The quasi-autonomous states that conferred its loyalty to the Lumumbist administration in Leopoldville rather than to the separatist Elisabethville administration.

Ntambwe Bwanga (Luba) This was a closed association of Luba who mobilized to fight Conakat during 'decolonization.'

Politique indigène (French) 'Native' politics, this was, in colonial parlance, Belgian rule as it referred to Africans. Often *politique indigène* was associated with rural government in particular though there were exceptions to this trend.

Population Flottante (French) Africans who clandestinely resided in urban areas without a job.

Shauri (Swahili) A council for local nobles associated with the East African slave trade but incorporated into local governance in the early years of the Belgian Congo.

Sola, Bena Nkuvu (Hêmbá) The headquarters (*chef-lieu*) of Bena Nkuvu wherein the White Fathers' out-station was situated (*Nkuvu* is a Kíhêmbá word for tortoise).

Sultani Ya Miti (Songye) 'Tree sultans,' these were rulers of the Songye before the Swahili invasions who survived by hiding in forested groves subsequently known as *hatas.*

Tambwe (Hêmbá) 'Lion,' also forms a part of a number of Báhêmbá peoples' names, particularly those in authority.

Twite (Songye) A chief's second-in-command, the head of the local judiciary and the president of the chief's council.

Ukanga (Tetela) 'Charm' and also adopted as the name for an iteration of a closed association of hierarchical merchants selling these charms to peoples across eastern Congo.

Vilinyambi (Hêmbá) Word for God.

Wali (Swahili) Governor, a title granted to Tippu Tip by the Congo Free State in the 1890s.

Wanyampara (Swahili) A courtier.

Yamina (Swahili) A mound in Bena Nkuvu that Europeans called Mount Dhanis.

CHAPTER 1

Introduction: Church and State in Southeastern Congo

Scholars have traditionally assumed that the Catholic Church had an *exceptionally* close and collaborative relationship with the colonial administration of the Belgian Congo. Crawford Young, writing in his influential book *Politics in Congo*, argued that, along with business enterprises, the Church formed part of a 'seamless web' in tandem with colonial officialdom.[1] Wamu Oyatambwe reached a similar conclusion in his book *Eglise Catholique et Pouvoir Politique au Congo-Zaire* in that he argued that the Latin phrase *do ut des* ('I give so that you will give') essentially captured the essence of the Church–state relationship in the Congo.[2] These authors are representative of the wider literature on the Church–state relationship in the Belgian Congo in that they see an *unusually* collaborative relationship between the state and missionaries. Scholars working in other imperial contexts have not emphasized such a close relationship between Church and state. Hugo Hinfelaar, writing on Catholic missionary activity in Zambia, was careful to elucidate the significant struggles between the interests of the state and those of the Church.[3] And Andrew Porter did not even suggest that the Anglican Church, part and parcel of the British state, had such a hand-in-glove relationship with British imperialism.[4]

The original version of the book was revised: Belated corrections have been incorporated. The correction to the book is available at https://doi.org/10.1007/978-3-030-17380-7_9

© The Author(s) 2019
R. A. Loffman, *Church, State and Colonialism in Southeastern Congo, 1890–1962*, Cambridge Imperial and Post-Colonial Studies Series, https://doi.org/10.1007/978-3-030-17380-7_1

1

This study challenges the idea that the Church had an exceptionally close relationship with the colonial state in the context of the Belgian Congo. To do so, it examines the history of southeastern Congo. Specifically, this book looks at the Church–state relationship in the Congolese territory of Kongolo, in what is now the Tanganyika province, which has largely been ignored by authors hitherto. Kongolo was of vital importance to the Catholic Church in southeastern Congo and to two mission orders in particular: the Spiritans and the White Fathers. It played host to a vital Spiritan out-station in the north of the territory, for example, which became so famous for its educational facilities that Africans walked from many, many miles away to attend classes there. Kongolo town centre also hosted a major seminary meaning that Catholics not only from the Tanganyika province but across the Belgian Congo as a whole deemed it to be an extremely important site. Kongolo was important not just as a Catholic centre in and of itself but also as a bulwark against the Protestant expansion that had occurred during the early phase of Leopoldian rule. American Presbyterians, for example, had been working tirelessly in Kasai since the 1891 and so Catholic missionaries wanted a strong Catholic presence to counter what one Catholic missionary referred to as the incoming Protestant 'invasion.'[5] While Kongolo was not the only place that developed a significant mission infrastructure, few other territories in rural southeastern Congo boasted the same intense Catholic mission presence.

Not only did Kongolo develop an impressive mission infrastructure, but the history of Tanganyika (see Fig. 1.1) as a whole is pertinent for a number of reasons. First, the leader of the White Fathers, Cardinal Lavigerie, wanted to establish a Christian kingdom in Central Africa and he believed that what is now the Tanganyika province could be that polity. Lavigerie's desire for a theocratic polity to emerge in southeastern Congo, coupled with the state's initial neglect of it, meant that there was a substantive Church presence in the region. The Church in Tanganyika therefore developed relatively independently from the colonial state and so it is a good litmus for what missionaries did when they had more leeway to disagree with the Belgian administration. Secondly, that Tanganyika was a centre for the Spiritans as well as the White Fathers means that this is one of the first studies of a Spiritan mission encounter in the Belgian Congo. Unlike the White Fathers, the Spiritans were initially prohibited from working in the Congo by the Belgian king, Léopold II, because he believed that they could be a fifth column for French imperial interests given they were a French order. The Spiritans, therefore, perhaps exemplify this book's thesis that a close, collaborative

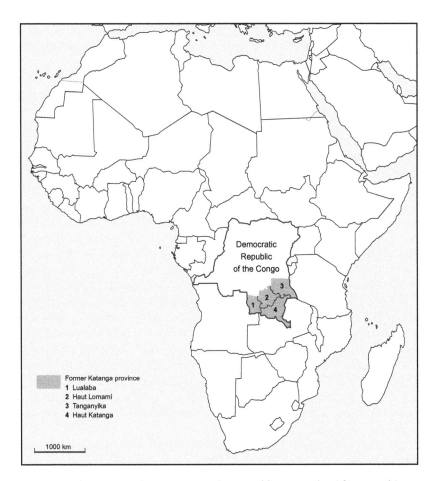

Fig. 1.1 The Tanganyika Province and its neighbours in the African and international context, present borders

relationship between the Church and the state was not the inevitable product of Belgian colonialism. Rather than enjoying a consistently cordial and co-dependent relationship with the state, there were a number of occasions in which missionaries clashed with colonial officials working in Kongolo. So, while surveying the times when the Church did facilitate the colonial state's work, and vice versa, this study focuses more on the episodes in which the two institutions clashed. Instead of allies working seamlessly with each other, this study suggests the Church and state were in fact *competitive* collaborators. That is to say that while they did collaborate on a number of occasions they retained demonstrably different agendas and these often clashed with each other.

Some authors have already drawn attention to Church-state conflicts in the context of the Belgian Congo. Marvin Markowitz is the most notable of such scholars. He examined the Church's relationship with the colonial state in a lucid, sustained and detailed way. But, in his book *Cross and Sword*, he tended to approach the Church–state relationship in the Belgian Congo very much from a 'top down' as opposed to a 'bottom-up' perspective.[6] In a similar vein, Jean-Pacifique Balaamo Mokelwa, in a book about the influence of the Church on the formation of Congolese law, focused on the state–Church relationship from a metropolitan vantage point.[7] In his comprehensive and masterful account of the White Fathers' operations in the Belgian Congo, as well as those of other Catholic missionaries, Marchal/Delathuy took a similar approach.[8] He pointed to a number of clashes between the state and the White Fathers in a local context, for example over their use of their own currency: the *pesa*.[9] In a similar vein, Bruce Fetter, in his book *The Creation of Elisabethville*, notes that 'In Elisabethville... [the] colonial trinity was not solidified into its final form until the 1930s.'[10] Yet this book differs from Fetter's and Marchal/Delathuy's, as well as Mokelwa and Young's, in two key respects. First, as already noted, it focuses on the local, territorial scene more than the above-mentioned authors who adopted a largely metropolitan perspective. And, secondly, it brings African intermediaries, such as chiefs and nobles, much more meaningfully into its analysis of the Church–state relationship.

To bring Africans into the story of Church–state relations in the Belgian Congo, this book examines the Church–state relationship largely through the individual mission stations themselves as well as through the prism of *chieftainship*. Chieftainship, or the rule of a geographically defined territory by a single chief, was the lowest level of colonial administration. Such polities constituted territories, such as Kongolo, that in turn constituted provinces, such as Katanga. Catholic missionaries tended to have significant influence on the colonial construction of chieftainship and sometimes even more than that of the colonial administration. The Belgian versions of chieftainship were generally weak in Kongolo due to its initial neglect by the colonial state, local revolts against chiefs, and depopulation from disease and colonial recruitment. So, missionaries exerted a great deal of influence over colonial government there. It used its greater staff, defined as its affiliated missionaries and African converts, as well as its built infrastructure, to shape societies in the territory and often in ways that contradicted state policy. For example, Chapter 4 discusses, in part, how one missionary believed that he could impose his own version of canon law even outside his out-stations and in a manner that directly contradicted state policy. Similarly, Chapter 5 deals with a witch-finding movement in which the White Fathers successfully petitioned the state to put two of its most trusted African intermediaries on trial. The Church, then, exercised a great deal of control over the politics of the Katangese hinterland.

Although it could and often did help to shape local societies in the Belgian Congo, this book stops short of suggesting that the Church's influence was *hegemonic*. European Catholic missionaries may have developed strict codes of conduct for those who came to and stayed in their out-stations, which they enforced obsessively at times, but Victor Roelens, who led the White Fathers in Tanganyika, and his followers in Kongolo, such as Joseph Van den Tillaert and Louis Verstraete, frequently could not control nor even fully convert many of the peoples living in villages outside of these out-stations. If conversion, or the process of changing someone's spirituality from one theology to another, is defined along Catholic lines and so involves the complete rejection of other forms of ritual then the missionaries were only partly successful. Rather than a culturally hegemonic force, the Church experienced many struggles. And Roelens and his missionaries frequently expressed concern in their writings about the depth of the piety and devotion of its followers.[11] Even as they *claimed* to amass hundreds of followers—and mission statistics are hardly unknown to exaggerate—Roelens and Emilio Callewaert, who led the Spiritans in Kongolo, always worried that their African converts would go 'back' to following the old ways of their pre-existing traditions that the next chapter outlines. For all their infrastructural achievements, and much as Nicholas Creary observed in Zimbabwe, Catholic missionaries did not gain cultural hegemony in Kongolo.[12]

This is not to say that Catholic missionaries did not strive for cultural supremacy in the Congolese bush. In their attempts to create pristine Catholic communities, and in so doing to thwart Protestant advances, Roelens and Callewaert's approach to proselytizing was more dogmatic than that of Placide Tempels, for example, who worked primarily in southern Katanga.[13] Tempels, also a Catholic missionary, became so frustrated by what he saw as the Church's inability to inspire devotion among its followers that he created what he called the *Jamaa* or 'family' movement in Katanga in 1953.[14] Jamaa, broadly speaking, sought to create Christian fellowships in the context of groups that largely eschewed hierarchies and pursued Christ-centric forms of worship—yet it never made it as far as Kongolo however close it came to the territory.[15] Rather than attempting to dialogue with African expressive cultures, Catholic missionaries in Kongolo tended to learn local languages and about African cultures oftentimes solely as a means of imposing their own worldview on local societies. As Valentine Mudimbe has observed, Victor Roelens wanted to destroy what he described as paganism in his 'republic.'[16] Correspondingly, Allen Roberts argued that: 'The portrait [Roelens] drew of the black man... is particularly negative.'[17] So, although Roelens was keen to inspire and facilitate the creation of an African clergy, he did not want, and neither did the Propaganda Fide, who oversaw 'missionary activity throughout the world with the territories where there is no established hierarchy,' any innovations on the liturgy or the credo.[18]

Unsurprisingly, given Roelens and Callewaert's theological and even racial views, no idiosyncratic African Catholicism emerged in Tanganyika as it did, say, in some parts of Ghana.[19] The influential debates about inculturation that took place within the wider Catholic Church certainly had an impact on Catholicism in Kongolo, of course, not least when the question of extra-European clergies arose and Benedict XV's *Maximum Illud* was published in 1919. And both Roelens and Callewaert accepted the idea of an African clergy with Roelens even sponsoring Stefano Kaoze's passage through seminary to become the first Congolese priest.[20] But Roelens and Callewaert's approach to their work nonetheless provided a stark contrast to that of Tempels. They worked within very hierarchical out-stations and placed a large emphasis on a universalizing Catholic culture that would, they hoped, eventually supersede practices such as ancestor worship, the veneration of elders and polygamy. Few authors in recent times have written about areas in which African thought was so marginal to Catholic thought during the mission encounter and this is another area in which this book innovates. Instead, the trend has overwhelmingly been to write about the ways in which African thought was incorporated into Catholic theological discourses.[21]

The debates surrounding the extent to which Africans adopted Catholicism in their own theological and epistemological frameworks are important and interesting—not least in foregrounding African agency within the colonial mission encounter. Unfortunately, however, they do not speak directly to the kind of uncompromising Catholicism Roelens, Callewaert and their successors, such as Urbain Morlion, proffered. Although unfashionable of late, Jean and John Comaroff's conception of the 'long conversation' in which the London Missionary Society and Wesleyan Methodists encountered the Tswana in South Africa is relevant to this study.[22] It is true that unlike the case in the Comaroff's work, *Of Revelation and Revolution*, Roelens and Callewaert never succeeded in colonizing the consciousness of the African communities that surrounded their out-stations. But the crucial point was that that was what the Spiritans and the White Fathers *wanted* to do. Their attempt at the colonization of Congolese consciousness was made manifest in the strict surveillance of African thought on the part of the European missionaries in their out-stations. Some missionaries, such as the White Father Joseph Van Den Tillaert, would go to the villages outside their out-stations on a daily basis to administer sacraments such as the last rites.[23] At the same time, the stark moralistic intentions behind the White Fathers' neo-Gothic out-stations cannot be ignored.

By the time that they began to map out Kongolo for their own purposes, Belgian colonial administrators in Kongolo, such as René Wauthion, were faced with a strident Church that saw itself very much as having created its own polity replete with an imposing civic infrastructure. What is more, the Church's presence had evolved relatively separately from the state. To all intents and purposes, the Church *was* the state in the early twentieth century in Kongolo. What is more, given their considerable connections to their superiors in Europe, as well as to the Propaganda Fide, Roelens and Callewaert had significant political clout in the Belgian Congo. So, despite its failures, the Church successfully pushed back against certain key state policies—notably the permissibility of violence for its chiefs and the permitted limits of Church expansion. Before explaining *how* it did this, though, it is worth saying a little more about *why* the state struggled to dominate Tanganyika's hinterland during crucial initial phase of colonial rule given that scholars such as Young frequently allude to its transformative power.[24]

WHERE WAS THE SECULAR ADMINISTRATION?

While Belgian colonization of the Congo as a whole began with King Leopold's infamous Congo Free State (CFS) it is not at all clear that this administration exerted much influence in Kongolo. The CFS was founded in the midst of a brutal yet haphazard and unevenly spaced series of conquests.[25] It is possible that the Free State army, known as the *Force Publique*, may have *briefly* passed through what is now Kongolo in its attempt to annex eastern Congo. But again the scale of colonial violence in what would become the territory of Konglo was less than in places such as Kasongo in the north. Similarly, when the Katanga Company (KC) was formed in 1891 to prospect and exploit mineral resources, ivory and, occasionally, undertake agricultural work in south-eastern Congo, it did precious little administrative work in Kongolo.[26]

Given that the KC was predominantly interested in minerals, and Kongolo had very few of them, its presence in the region ended up being particularly sparse. Instead, it concentrated its resources on the central and the southern parts of the province wherein mineral resources were to be found. The lack of secular state coverage in Kongolo continued when the assets of the KC were transferred to its successor, the Special Committee for Katanga (CSK). Like the KC, the CSK concentrated mainly on the central and southern parts of Katanga in order to best exploit the mineral resources there. And, like the KC, the CSK enjoyed near autonomous status, first, within the Free State and, after 1908, within the Belgian Congo.[27] Even after the founding of the Free State and the incorporation of the CSK territory into the central administration of the Belgian Congo in 1910, the secular colonial *postes* in what was to become Kongolo and its neighbouring territories played a minor role in their history.

Rather than transmitters of a crushingly powerful and transformative administration, encapsulated by the term Bula Matari ('Breaker of Rocks' in Kikongo), the few existing bureaucratic posts struggled to collect taxes and co-opt African leaders and their subjects. The lack of a strong state presence in Kongolo left plenty of room for the Church to build a large number of out-stations and other facilities with little concern about what their secular counterparts' plans were. The administration became more significant once the railway, which had brought most Catholic missionaries to Kongolo, was installed in territory's town centre in 1909. The arrival of the railway also meant that a workers' camp was built to house those who worked for the firm that built it: the Great Lakes Railway Company (CFL). It was from the workers' camp, and the

economic demands of the workers there, that a thriving town centre—
also called 'Kongolo'—emerged in the eponymous territory. Yet despite
the smattering of workers and the emerging market in the town centre,
the secular state still only consisted of a handful of buildings with very
few Belgian staff housed in them. Although even this small staff was able
to venture out into rural Kongolo and organize some polities along colonial lines, the costs of occupying the territory were not recouped in taxes
before the First World War. Indeed, relatively few Africans in the territory were actually paying anything at all to the Belgian administration
during the interwar period.

After the War ended in 1918, Belgian officials redoubled their efforts
to map out the hinterland and co-opt African leaders in Kongolo.
However, these efforts largely failed. Few of the state's African allies were
looked upon with the kind of unthinking respect that colonial officials
believed Africans had always reserved for their chiefs. Although the *poste*
in Kongolo did eventually become the main colonial headquarters of the
Tanganyika district, this was not really saying very much given the sparse
amount of Belgian infrastructure in the region as a whole. The Great
Depression only served to reinforce the state's skeletal nature. The lack
of administrative funds meant that the gospel of indirect rule, in which
Africans were promoted to positions of power within the colonial administration, was important during this time. Even if some Belgian officials disagreed with the *theory* of indirect rule, and even if indirect rule
took on a more 'direct' nature if the administration believed that allies
without pre-colonial claims to legitimacy were more loyal to it, colonial finances were such that they had to agree with governing through
African intermediaries in *practice*. In short, the skeletal Belgian presence in Kongolo was a feature of the colonial regime until the end of the
Second World War and this presented Catholic missionaries with more
than enough opportunity to develop and expand their infrastructure.

The period after the Second World War was one in which the state
expanded for the first time since the turn of the century and had arguably as much presence, both in terms of staff and resources, as the
Church. Yet the administration grew in such a way as to coincide with
some of the Church's most important plans. First, the state expanded
its agricultural programmes in order to boost its profitability but
retained the mobility controls on its subjects it had imposed during
the Depression to prevent rural–urban migration. That rural enclaves
were protected from depopulation meant that the pristine communities

that Roelens and Callewaert had initially envisaged were still possible to engineer. Much like the state, though for different reasons, the Church wanted to survey the hinterland of the Belgian Congo. The state feared revolts of the kind that Kitawala adepts had inspired during the Depression and so frequently relied on Church information about rural Congo. For its part, the Church feared reversions to pre-existing traditions. Indeed, the only major competitor to the Church, at least in its own view, was what Jan Vansina called the Equatorial African tradition.

The tradition refers to the ways in which African societies were organized previous to European colonialism. This book argues that the pre-colonial Equatorial political tradition remained—distorted in places but largely intact—due to the emphasis the colonial state places on indirect rule and its corresponding dependency on local potentates. Congolese societies, for example, were organized hierarchically. As the next chapter will explain, the lowest unit was the 'house,' which was constituted of an extended family together with their slaves. Polygamy was central to amassing enough followers to constitute a viable 'house.' Houses could ally with each other to form villages which in turn could ally with each other to form districts. Many of the alliances were held together through a shared veneration of ancestors and food taboos, both of which missionaries regarded as 'pagan' practices. In most respects, and contrary to Vansina's claims, missionaries never entirely broke down these traditions during the colonial period.[28] Rather, they in fact often colluded in localism by attempting to preserve rural community life not least in their attempts to convert chiefs and in their lobbying against urban migration and the wealth workers gained from it. Likewise, because there were different iterations of the tradition, the Church was never faced with unified opposition from people who understood themselves as being part of a monolithic and shared culture. Instead, it was faced with people with local loyalties and split between social dividing lines, such as gender and generation, as well as a number of cultural ones, not least ethnicity.

The Geographical Setting

The Church's encounter with local peoples in Kongolo was facilitated in no small measure by the territory's geography. European Catholic contacts with African societies in Kongolo took place in a large territory even if it was not uncommonly so in the context of the Belgian Congo (see Fig. 1.2). Kongolo's geography challenged historical actors and societies

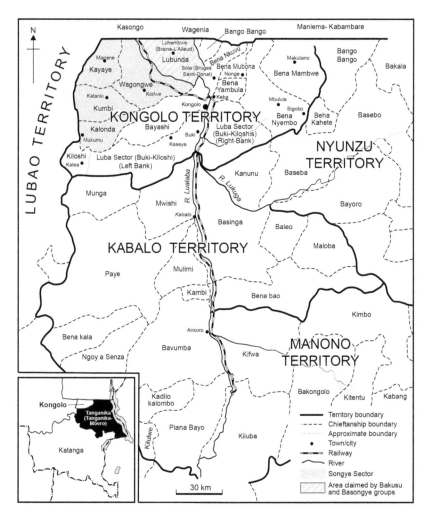

Fig. 1.2 Administrative divisions in the present Tanganyika Province

in this part of the colony but, contrary to a range of general misconceptions about Central Africa, it also gave them opportunities. The Congo's environment has often been stereotyped, particularly by Victorian authors, as one of dark, foreboding jungles shrouding the sunlight and enveloping the whole territory in darkness.[29] Although Kongolo could indeed be very difficult to live in at certain times and in some places, this section dispatches the Victorian stereotype of the Congo—and Kongolo in particular—as *consistently* dark and uninhabitable.[30]

Kongolo contains little if any jungle. In the dry season, which usually occurs from June to August, the territory is actually very light. Rather than being constantly impeded by it, the Church and their colonial counterparts were at times able to benefit from Kongolo's physical geography. After the Second World War, for example, the territory's fertile environment allowed Belgian agents and their African subjects to fashion Kongolo into a productive and innovative agricultural powerhouse that fed much of the former Katanga province. This was in part due to the fact that the territory's lands are well-watered most of the year, with the rainy season lasting as long as eight months in some cases. Kongolo is also on the Lualaba River bank and so most of its plots benefitted from ready access to freshwater.[31] Kongolo's fecundity led a number of migratory groups, not least the Hêmbá, the Luba-Katanga (hereafter simply Luba) and the Bango Bango to settle there during the seventeenth and eighteenth centuries.[32] When they arrived in what would become Kongolo in the late nineteenth century, colonial officials therefore benefitted from access to a pool of labour that was relatively large by the standards of the Katangese hinterland.

Historians have often remarked on the strength of Belgian colonial administrative presence in the Congo—with some even suggesting it was the densest in Africa.[33] Whether it was or not, Kongolo's size, around 7000 square kilometres, meant that any institution wishing to shape the lives of its inhabitants would need to invest heavily in personnel and infrastructure. And the nine or so Belgian agents who were responsible for the territory at any one time between the two world wars were simply unable to survey the territory in its entirety. Although more Belgians arrived after the Second World War, this did not equate to their being able to enforce colonial hegemony in the hinterland. Instead, the majority of the Belgian administration remained concentrated in mining centres— not least those to the south of Kongolo in the Upper Katanga district of the southeastern Congo (see Fig. 1.1). Rather than relying on sheer numbers, therefore, local colonial administrations in the Congo were obsessed with what they called 'prestige.' Prestige in this context meant a process whereby colonial officials would tour with all the pomp and circumstance they could muster to give the impression of the legitimacy and strength of themselves and the potentates whom they had enthroned.[34]

The application of the prestige principle had some success but also some notable failures in Kongolo as we shall see in Chapter 4.

Given the paucity of colonial surveillance in the hinterland, there were multiple spaces for potential rebels to meet in—even if freedom of assembly was supposed to be tightly regulated under Belgian rule. While cars and motorcycles were used towards the very end of the colonial residency to try to close down these areas, for the most part Belgian agents had to cycle, walk or, in some cases, be carried by African porters on what were known as a *Tipoyi*.[35] The slow moving nature of their transportation only added to the gaps in colonial coverage of Kongolo's hinterland. Some Africans did use these spaces to resist Belgian rule but most did not. Instead of using sparsely policed places to turn themselves into proto-nationalists, social imaginaries in Kongolo dealt far more with other preoccupations, such as farming, kinship obligations, healing and, importantly for our purposes, spirituality. Rather than avowedly subversive nationalist movements dominating the hinterland, it was the Catholic Church that constructed significant networks of out-stations in Kongolo in the gaps in secular state coverage. As opposed to the secular state, the White Fathers and the Spiritans were prepared to invest considerable finances and labour to turn the territory into one of the main centres of Catholicism in the Belgian Congo.

Although the Church built up a substantial presence in Kongolo, it could not always prevent the execution of colonial policies that it believed undermined the pristine Christian communities it sought to create. One of the most important examples of such a policy centred on Belgian recruitment of Africans for work in mining centres outside Kongolo. Belgian agents and their European and African allies transported many Congolese people to the mines in the Upper Katanga (see Fig. 1.2) after the arrival of the railway in 1909. These recruitment drives were only briefly interrupted by the Great Depression in the 1930s. Victor Roelens consistently opposed mining recruitment, claiming that they led to the depopulation of his 'republic.'[36] Yet when the rewards of cash wages came to be known, some made the journey to the southern mines mostly out of their own volition—especially during bad harvests. Although a number of people were attracted to mining work outside the territory, others remained inside Kongolo's boundaries to work the land and even in times of relative scarcity.

Farming grew most intense on the very fertile right bank of the Lualaba River, where the Hêmbá ethnic group specialized in producing palm products for themselves and well as for consumers in the burgeoning network of markets that sprung up under colonial rule. Palm products were occasionally sold to concession companies—but Kongolo was outside the now infamous Lever plantations that emerged in the colony in the early twentieth century.[37] Unlike many other crops, therefore, palm production in Kongolo was not a culture imposed by Belgian officials onto local peoples but instead was one that was freely produced by both European and African peoples alike. Palm oil's high status was also derived from the fact that it was a highly versatile commodity that could be used to lubricate machinery, manufacture soap and to producing cooking oil and so it was very profitable. Forced cultivation may have been a grim reality for many in Kongolo, but it was not consistently imposed in the territory over time and space therefore.

Yet disease as well as agriculture has been an important factor in shaping Kongolo's modern history. Sleeping Sickness was very important in the territory even if it later became less significant after the rapid expansion of healthcare following the Second World War. As a number of authors have already suggested, the disease was spread in part by the colonial conquests in the nineteenth and early twentieth centuries. The villages that were dislocated by conflict had previously been able to beat back the bushes on which the main vector of the Sleeping Sickness parasite—the Teste Fly—lived yet could not do this so efficiently during the colonial conquests and so sleeping Sickness flourished.[38] As opposed to elsewhere in the Belgian Congo, colonial efforts to combat this deadly disease in Kongolo only began in earnest just before the Great Depression and were subsequently hampered by the economic downturn. The proliferation of trypanosomiasis had many important consequences. It led to a far more pronounced degree of interference in the daily running of chieftainship on the part of colonial officials with such interference often carrying overtones of 'political expediency or coercion.'[39] And, aside from Belgian efforts to combat it, in parts of Kongolo many believed that Sleeping Sickness was a spiritual evil and so they sometimes fought it using anti-witchcraft practices as we shall see in Chapter 5.

But we must be careful not to overstate the historical significance of biological factors in Kongolo's past. The territory's subjects were not—to borrow a phrase from Tim Marshall—prisoners of biology or geography.[40] Although the various peoples that converged in the territory naturally made the most of the geographical and biological materials available to them, as well as suffering from them in the case of Sleeping Sickness, a glance at Kongolo's landscape emphasizes a wide range of distinctly human footprints. Many if not most of the crops that have come to form such indelible parts of Kongolo's cultural and political life were not actually grown in the area before the nineteenth century. Some examples of foreign imports that stuck are, first, the palm trees that are now so important to the Hêmbá peoples but were introduced by Zanzibari slavers at the end of the nineteenth century. Rice was another Zanzibari import. The third major example of an outside crop imposed on Kongolo was cotton, the cultivation of which was imposed by the colonial regime during the Depression. Humans thus impacted on Kongolo's terrain every bit as much as natural forces. In short, people involved in Kongolo's early modern and modern history and were not simply the products of their environment—they shaped their environment on numerous occasions.

METHODOLOGY

To shed light on the competitively co-dependent relationship that developed between the Church and the state in Kongolo during the colonial period, I will examine a series of historical episodes. To excavate these flashpoints, this book draws heavily on the Manchester School of anthropology founded by Max Gluckman in 1947. In particular, it uses Gluckman's extended-case method, which examines 'a series of specific incidents affecting the same persons or groups through a period of time and showing how these incidents, or cases, are related to the development and changes of social relations among these persons and groups, acting within the framework of their social system and culture.'[41] However, rather than showing how cases related solely to the development and changes of social relations among a group, it also keeps the idea of statehood very much in mind. In other words, it looks at how relations between individuals and institutions in fact formed as much as were formed by the broader social framework, or state, in which they acted. It situates historical episodes within a chronological framework in the hope of showing how larger patterns of change and continuity impacted—and themselves were impacted by—the local milieu.

Just as this study examines a trinity of institutions, it is based on a traditional trinity of Africanist sources, namely: archives pertaining to the activities of the Belgian administration, mission documentation and oral history interviews including individuals from the full gamut of institutions that existed in colonial Kongolo. Taken in its totality, the evidential basis of this book is based on original yet episodic sources. There are moments when a flurry of evidence appears in the oral and written records but, unfortunately, they are punctuated by pronounced periods of relative silence. These gaps in the historical record are frustrating as they potentially relate to some important information such how conversion happened away from the out-stations, out of the sight of European missionaries, and how chiefs recruited labourers to work for European commercial interests. It is unlikely we will ever have comprehensive answers to these fundamental questions, at least as far as Kongolo is concerned. Likewise, the second chapter is based far more on secondary readings than original sources given that, first, many of those who could recall the mid-nineteenth century have now died and, secondly, the archival record is particularly sparse in relation to this period.

Very few of the people with whom I spoke with could recount the history of their community's lineage before the 1880s, the time that the Zanzibari slave trade violently intruded into the political life of Kongolo. Societal trauma has evidently affected the collective memory of what happened. Many of the chiefly elites I spoke to may not have wished to have gone too far back in time in their narratives, either, as this might have exposed their tenuous claims to genealogical legitimacy. Put another way, they could have been related to political upstarts who owed their position to the violent slavers and who were so unpopular across Kongolo. The untitled people I spoke to could not recount the history of Tanganyika since before the late nineteenth century either but this did not stop them from having strong opinions about it. The legitimacy of pre-colonial and early colonial leaders was questioned on occasions and even flatly contested at times. Even given the existance of colonial documentation and recorded oral sources, there was still a noticeable paucity of journals and/or diaries written by Africans themselves that would have allowed insights into their motives, actions and beliefs. This lacuna, added to the usual problems associated with the subjective and incomplete memories of oral informants means that this book charts an episodic path through Kongolo's colonial history.

As the book moves beyond the nineteenth century, the evidential basis for it changes. The KC was formed to govern southeastern Congo in 1890 and began to create a documentary trail, albeit a fragmented one. Many of the KC's activities were referred to only after the fact by its successor organization, the CSK, which took over its territory in 1900 and whose archives are now stored in Brussels in the Ministry of Foreign

Affairs. Frustratingly, KC agents are only referenced by CSK officials in the relevant and surviving documentation. The CSK reports that cite the actions of their KC predecessors arrived in Kongolo at least a generation *after* the KC first occupied the territory. While we have elements of an institutional memory of decisions, and even events on some occasions, we do not know much about the experiences of those Europeans who first began to organize colonial polities in the territory. We can infer that the first European efforts to establish chieftainships were based on geographically determined regions, using rivers and forests as natural boundaries, and relied on installing hereditary chiefs; but we cannot concretely conclude this was the case. The gaps in the early record are also important because it is difficult to know when the KC first set up a poste in Kongolo and what their initial plans were for the area. Kongolo appears in the remaining administrative record as the name of a poste just at the end of the lifespan of the CFS but without an explanation of why it was created and who staffed it.

Thankfully the evidential record gets considerably thicker with the arrival of European Catholic missionaries in 1909. Not only did they keep diaries, which included varying degrees of detail, but they also wrote a plethora of annual reports and in-house publications allowing their headquarters and home congregations to know how they were getting on.[42] Much of this material is unabashedly triumphalist; telling an overarching story about the inevitable victories of faith in the face of considerable 'pagan' adversity to convince home congregation to keep on funding them—but not all take this form. The mission diaries in particular are often subtle, multilayered texts that give very personal accounts of the hardships associated with being isolated in a foreign location and having to learn about cultures while trying to convert the very people who partake in them.[43] Mission documents are indeed, therefore, 'records of uncertainty and doubt.'[44] Missionaries were attentive to local events, to be sure, but they naturally had their own opinions. It would be tempting to suggest that they had a distinct view of the African cultures with which they interacted. But it would be wrong to suggest all missionaries viewed Africans simply as 'backward and uncivilized.'[45] Later generations strove to understand the workings of the groups they sought to proselytize and documented their findings. Some missionaries learnt local and regional languages and, at least according to the remaining oral sources, hardly needed local translators.[46] The mission record is therefore extremely useful even if it overwhelmingly gives the European side of the mission encounter at the expense of African voices.

The third part of the Belgian colonial 'trinity,' European concession companies, also contributes to the archival basis of this study. Some of the archives of the firms involved in Kongolo in the first half of the twentieth century are only just now being catalogued and so were largely unavailable for this study. Yet some were available, and among these were the papers of the CFL. The CFL sources were grouped largely towards the end of the colonial period as opposed to the beginning, which is a shame given how important a number of contemporary commentators suggest their encampment was to the life of Kongolo's town centre. Much of what we know about the organization of the CFL camp comes from other, oral and written sources. However, there is a large volume of CFL material for the period leading up to and including decolonization. Many of these are in the form of memos written by the director of the company in the district of Tanganyika, who was based in Albertville (Kalemie), to his superiors in Brussels. Like the European colonial and mission documents, CFL sources are inflected with a deeply ethnocentric, even racist, bias. But they allow us to document in detail a number of the important meetings and events that occurred as the district of Tanganyika erupted into violent political tumult in the early 1960s.

Although this study makes use of African voices, the recent warfare in eastern Congo has hit elders among the hardest of all and so when I first arrived in Kongolo there were few people with a comprehensive memory of the colonial period. Likewise, when people did remember Belgian rule, they tended to remember it episodically. Many only experienced colonialism as children and so have a hazy memory of the events that are the subject of the present book. Aside from these difficulties, there is a large and productive literature on the use of oral sources for historical purposes in Africa and elsewhere. For example, one of the main criticisms levelled at positivist historians such as Jan Vansina is that oral sources do not in fact shed much light on the past but are stories geared to forward present agendas in a phenomenon Johannes Fabian described as 'historiology.'[47] Inevitably each narrative of the colonial past has to be taken on its own merits but this study attempts to tread a middle ground between skepticism and positivism vis-à-vis oral sources. Bound up in stories about the past are facts upon which these tales tend to hang their arguments. And historiologies can tell us a great deal about what certain facts and events meant to the people that experienced them.

Chapter Summary

The second chapter fashions a historical baseline. It surveys politics in Kongolo before the arrival of Europeans in the late nineteenth century and argues that African politics in Kongolo before the formation of the Belgian Congo was crisscrossed by a number of diverse local political institutions undergirded by tenuous political allegiances. Many—though not all—of these were later co-opted by Belgian agents once they arrived in Kongolo but not all. The Church would define itself against many of the practices of the social groups in Kongolo before its arrival but particularly the Zanzibari slave-merchants. Missionaries believed that they were fighting, at least in part, against polygamy, slavery and ancestor worship yet these practices would not be easy for them to expunge. Indeed, local traditions lived on to influence the work of the Church in later years.

The third chapter argues that while Kongolo was incorporated into the CFS network, the intensity of its incorporation was actually relatively slight. Colonial officials enter our story not as masters of all they surveyed, therefore, but rather as one of a number of interlopers jockeying for position among powerful local and regional potentates. The skeletal administration sought alliances with those they believed to have been in positions of authority on the eastern savannah. Under the aegis of the KC, European sought those who could distribute their orders. One ally who was to become a long-term fixture in Kongolo was a Luba headman called Bùki. The KC's relationship with Bùki was based on a number of false assumptions—not least that Kongolo was Bùki's uncontested Luba fiefdom. The reason the KC understood Kongolo as a hierarchical Luba polity with Bùki as its paramount chief was because it wanted to—and evidently did—believe in a reductive feudal model of African society that it had imported from Europe.

This Belgian quasi-feudal model was expedient because it meant that orders could be distributed cheaply and quickly by chiefs who could expect blind loyalty from their subordinates. Likewise, the resulting system would be presided over by a series of scholar-administrators who had been schooled in the classics and sought to translate this knowledge in a completely different context. In reality, proto-colonial politics in Kongolo was not organized by a series of overlords but more by lineage heads who were simply firsts among equals. These lineage heads had differing attitudes to Luba culture if they had even been exposed to it at all. Yet as colonial rulers sought to promote a Luba leader in Kongolo, they effectively gave someone on the fringes of society in the territory a valuable set of allies with which he could reinforce his fragile grip on power. Like him, those outside Bùki's sphere of influence in Kongolo, from which the KC attempted to project their power into the hinterland, had to deal with the incursion of the Zanzibari slavers. The Zanzibari were the first to bring the violence of global capitalism into the savannah *not* Belgian colonial forces—though they would not be far behind.

While Bùki had attempted to ally himself with the Zanzibari, other leaders across Kongolo fought them with varying degrees of success. Some chiefs defeated the slavers but others were unseated and replaced with *sultanis* whose positions were often supported by the KC and the CSK. Although Zanzibari colonization had been brutal and had centralized chieftainship to a far greater degree than before, a number of political traditions that pre-dated it survived to feature in political life under the colonial administration. Chapter 2 examines how Belgian colonial agents sought to co-opt local political traditions to legitimize their rule. Yet state efforts to co-opt African leaders were overshadowed by the First World War. Many Belgian officials were eventually reduced to conducting night-time raids to kidnap African porters for the infamous allied East African Campaign. Administrators, pressed hard by wartime concerns, lost tax money and even had to delay delineating chieftainships until after the War. Far from an all-powerful state, the secular administration looked enormously fragile.

Rather than state agents, the most significant organization during the early colonial period, aside from local African ones that had survived the proto-colonial period, as I have argued above, was the Catholic Church. Mission out-stations soon became the most important European feature of Kongolo's hinterland, taking their place among the hotchpotch of different kinds of polities that were ruled by a bewildering array of potentates. While the Church's efforts to establish a viable presence in the hinterland outshone those of the state, like the administration, its power was still compromised by the War. The Church could not offer African communities protection from the nightly raids that Belgian functionaries launched to gain troops to fight for their cause during the First World War. So, they too became unpopular in Kongolo.

Missionaries would have to labour hard to regain their hard-won relationships with their surrounding communities if they were to succeed in their goal of creating theocratic Christian communities. The Church expanded rapidly in the 1920s and so much so that it, rather than any particular African revolt, exposed the underdevelopment of the secular administrative architecture in Kongolo. The Church's power in its relationship with colonial officials was manifested, first, in its challenging of the power of the Belgian administration's chiefly allies by building on their land against their expressed wishes. Secondly, the Church's expansion undermined the very basis of colonial authority specifically by ignoring its legal codes and in following its own ones instead. Such was the Church's power across the Congo that it caused much debate in the corridors of power in Brussels as more secular-minded politicians, such as Louis Franck, the Belgian Minister of the Colonies, sought to rein it in.

Chapter 4 discusses how metropolitan disagreements between the Church and statespeople like Louis Franck impacted on Kongolo. After the War, some in Brussels favoured explicitly challenging Church authority by consolidating the myriad of sub-chieftainship that had emerged in the early colonial era into a small number of 'great' ones. Franck led an ultimately unsuccessful struggle with the Church but his influence was felt to some extent in Kongolo. To further Franck's aims, colonial agents built on the alliance they had already formed with Bùki and tried to create a larger ethno-polity, or 'great' chieftainship, based on his rule. For his part, Bùki was more than happy to reprise his relationship with a state that already protected his tenuous claims to local legitimacy. He used state-sanctioned authority to extort from and intimidate his subjects. Yet, like his relations with those he ruled, Bùki's relationship with the state was deeply precarious. He felt badly undermined by the state's unilateral intervention in his chieftainship to prevent serious episodes of Sleeping Sickness. He did not want to be beholden to administrators' orders anymore. Even then, though, Bùki's tumultuous relationship with Belgian officials held out, just.

Chapter 4 focuses on how the Belgian administration entrenched its rule by shifting its focus from southeastern Kongolo to the east of the territory. It argues that rather than being subsumed by Watchtower, the most common form of protest movement in southeastern Congo during the late 1920s and 1930s, the political situation in Kongolo was different. Instead, the chapter focuses on two chiefs who had been co-opted into the administration during the 1920s and who ruled polities on the right bank of the Lualaba, in eastern Kongolo. They had no pre-existing claims to authority and owed their entire position, first, to the missionaries who had trained them and, secondly, to the colonial state that

had originally employed them as clerks. Because their claims to local
authority rested entirely on the foreign colonial state and not local traditions, these chiefs, namely Rasaci Katore and Kilamba Sindano, resorted
to undertaking a witch-hunt to rid their polities of evil. The evil that
they confronted was in fact most likely an outbreak of Sleeping Sickness
that was particularly threatening to the local population given that they
could not easily leave their chieftainships due to the mobility restrictions
imposed on them by the colonial occupation. Belgian administrators
were reluctant to depose their former allies but were pressured to do so
by the Church that found the chiefs' activities distasteful. Rather than
having stirred anger and resentment on the part of their subjects, local
memories of Katore and Sindano suggest that they were in fact held in
high regard as people who confronted evil and succeeded in doing so. As
opposed to Watchtower, which targeted chiefs as colonial collaborators,
in eastern Kongolo chiefs cemented their legitimacy among their subjects even if they alienated themselves from the Belgian administration by
doing so.

Despite the increasing power of the secular administration in eastern
Kongolo, the Church exercised a considerable influence on the relationships between the Belgian territorial service and their chiefly allies.
For example, it consistently pressed officials to take action again Katore
and Sindano. Belgian officials, such as Reymenans, the then head of the
administration in Kongolo, were reluctant to take action because it was
not clear who would be best to replace the two witch-finding chiefs. Yet
the immense pressure that the Church exerted on Reymenans and his
subordinates resulted in Katore and Sindano's arrests. Far from being
superseded as the state grew, therefore, the Church remained a powerful
element in its construction and character.

Chapter 6 examines the administration when it was at its most powerful; when it came the closest they ever got to mirroring Crawford
Young's all-powerful 'Bula Matari' model after the Second World War.
As the secular state reached its apogee, it moved closer to the Church.
The Church trained many of those involved in state efforts to inten-
sify agriculture in the hinterland. Church communities in the bush also
benefitted from the state's emphasis on keeping as many Congolese as
possible away from the cities as they did not experience rapid depopulation. Although the improved relationship the Church had with the
colonial state helped them in the short term, militant African nationalists would later associate missionaries with the Katangese secession later

on—which they saw as the continuation of colonial rule by other means. The association of the Church with the outgoing colonial state ended up meaning that European missionaries began their relationship with the newly independent Congolese state in a distinctly hostile atmosphere.

Chapter 7 focuses on politics in Kongolo from the first local elections in the Belgian Congo in 1957 to the instillation of the violent Lualaba province. It argues that the Luba ethno-polity, the Lualaba Province, which emerged as a counter to the Katangese secession in the early 1960s was not in fact the expression of an organically popular movement in Kongolo. Rather, it was an imposition from without. In fact, Conakat, the party advocating Katangese secession, attained by far the most votes in the territory. Many of those pupils who did get a mission education in the late colonial period took up activist roles within this party. Although some in the Luba areas of Kongolo voted for a more socialist version of nationalism, they were far more the exception than the rule. Indeed, one of the more discomforting processes that occurred during the last days of Belgian rule was that politics quickly became ethnicized with the Hêmbá being closely identified with Conakat and the Luba with more left-leaning political parties. However, as with so many stereotypes, this was not uniformly the case and it was unfortunate and many innocent people died in the wake of this inaccurate representation that would endure to haunt the region until the present day.

This book's last chapter focuses on the Church as an important indirect contributing factor in the politicization of ethnicity. Because of their relatively more successful encounter with the Church than the Luba, the Hêmbá were generally far less willing to see the colonial regime in its entirety swept away by a violent socialist revolution of the kind espoused by the leaders of the Lualaba Province. The last chapter, therefore, foregrounds religion as an important factor in the violence that spread across northern Katanga in the early 1960s. The book ends in 1962 with the Massacre of twenty Spiritan priests in Kongolo's military camp by a group of militant nationalists. The Massacre is in many ways the culmination of the political processes described in the book, notably the fact that the Church had become politicized because of its competitively co-dependent relationship with the colonial state. At the same time, the invasion of the Lualaba revolutionaries was in part the result of the fact that Church-trained activists helped to swing Kongolo towards secession. In the end, the secession severely ruptured the complex but considerable relationship between the Church and the state in Tanganyika.

Following the Massacre the Church had to rebuild its relationship with the newly independent state in a process worthy of its own monograph.

NOTES

1. Crawford Young, *Politics in Congo: Decolonization and Independence* (Princeton: Princeton University Press, 1965), p. 10.
2. Wamu Oyatambwe, *Eglise Catholique et Pouvoir Politique au Congo-Zaire* (Paris: L'Harmattan, 1997), p. 16.
3. Hinfelaar, *History of the Catholic Church in Zambia*, p. 120.
4. Andrew Porter, *Religion Versus Empire? British Protestant Missionaries and Overseas Expansion, 1700–1914* (Manchester: Manchester University Press, 2004), p. 330.
5. Robert Benedetto, *Presbyterian Reformers in Central Africa* (Amsterdam: Brill, 1996), pp. 5, 11; Archives du Saint-Esprit, Chevilly-Larue, Val de Marne (hereafter CSSp), 7J1.1a4, 'Emilio Callewaert to Père Sebire,' 3 mai 1918, p. 6.
6. Marvin Markowitz, 'The Missions and Political Development in the Congo,' *Africa: Journal of the International African Institute*, 40, 3 (1970), pp. 234–247; Marvin D. Markowitz, *Cross and Sword: The Political Role of Missionaries in the Belgian Congo, 1908–1960* (Stanford: Hoover Institution, 1973); and Ruth Slade, *English-Speaking Missionaries in the Congo Independent State, 1885–1908* (Bruxelles: Académie Royale des Sciences Coloniales, 1959).
7. Jean-Pacifique Balaamo Mokelwa, *Eglises et Etat en République Démocratique du Congo: Histoire du Droit Congolais des Religions (1885–2003)* (Paris: L'Harmattan, 2008).
8. Delathuy, *Missie en Staat, 1880–1914: Witte Paters, Scheutisten en Jezuïeten*, pp. 29, 31.
9. Ibid., pp. 80–89.
10. Bruce Fetter, *The Creation of Elisabethville, 1910–1940* (Stanford: Stanford University Press, 1976), p. 166.
11. Delathuy, *Missie en Staat, 1880–1914: Witte Paters, Scheutisten en Jezuïeten*, p. 93.
12. Nicholas M. Creary, *Domesticating a Religious Import: The Jesuits and the Inculturation of the Catholic Church in Zimbabwe, 1879–1980* (Fordham: Fordham University Press, 2011), p. 2.
13. Willy De Craemer, *The Jamaa and the Church: A Bantu Catholic Movement in Zaire* (Oxford: Clarendon Press, 1977); Willy de Craemer, 'The Jamaa Movement in the Katanga and Kasai Regions of the Congo,' *Review of Religious Research*, 10, 1 (1968), p. 11.

14. Johannes Fabian, 'Popular Culture in Africa: Findings and Conjectures. To the Memory of Placide Tempels (1906–1977),' *Africa*, 48, 4 (1978), p. 318.
15. Willy De Craemer, *The Jamaa and the Church: A Bantu Catholic Movement in Zaïre* (Oxford: Clarendon Press, 1977), p. 102; Johannes Fabian, *Jamaa: A Charismatic Movement in Katanga* (Evanston: Northwestern University Press, 1971), p. xi; and Adrian Hastings, *The Church in Africa, 1450–1950* (Oxford: Oxford University Press, 1966), p. 602.
16. V. Y. Mudimbe, *Tales of Faith: Religion as Political Performance in Central Africa* (London: Bloomsbury, 2016), p. 91.
17. Allen F. Roberts, 'History, Ethnicity and Change in the "Christian Kingdom" of Southeastern Zaire,' in Leroy Vail (ed.), The Creation of Tribalism in Southern Africa (Berkeley: University of California Press, 1991), p. 201.
18. Mudimbe, *Tales of Faith: Religion as Political Performance in Central Africa*, p. 110; F. L. Cross and E. A. Livingstone (eds), *The Oxford Dictionary of the Catholic Church* (Oxford: Oxford University Press, 2005), p. 1344; and Peter Guilday, 'The Sacred Congregation de Propaganda Fide, 1622–1922,' *The Catholic Historical Review*, 6, 4 (1921), pp. 478–494.
19. J. Pashington Obeng, *Asante Catholicism: Religious and Cultural Reproduction Among the Akan of Ghana* (Amsterdam: Brill, 1996).
20. Roberts, 'History, Ethnicity and Change in the "Christian Kingdom" of Southeastern Zaire,' p. 201.
21. Ludovic Lado, *Catholic Pentecostalism and the Paradoxes of Africanization: Processes of Localization in a Catholic Charismatic Movement in Cameroon* (Leiden: Brill, 2009); Joan F. Burke, *These Catholic Sisters Are All Mamas! Towards the Inculturation of Sisterhood in Africa: An Ethnographic Study* (Leiden: Brill, 2001).
22. Jean and John Comaroff, *Of Revelation and Revolution: The Dialectics of Modernity on a South African Frontier* (Chicago: Chicago University Press, 1997).
23. Archives des Missionnaires de l'Afrique, Rome (AGM), 'Joseph Van Den Tillaert,' *Petit Écho des Missions d'Afrique*, Année N°, p. 46.
24. Young, *Politics in Congo*, p. 10.
25. Jean-Luc Vellut, 'La Violence Armée dans l'Etat Indépendant du Congo: Ténèbres et Clartés dans l'Histoire d'un Etat Conquérant,' *Cultures et Développement*, 16, 3 (1984), pp. 671–707.
26. Jean-Claude Willame, *Patrimonialism and Political Change in the Congo* (Stanford: Stanford University Press, 1972), p. 87.
27. Piet Clement, 'The Land Tenure System in the Congo, 1885–1960: Actors, Motivations and Consequences,' in Ewout Frankema and Frans Buelens (eds), *Colonial Exploitation and Economic Development: The Belgian Congo and the Netherlands Indies Compared* (London: Routledge, 2013), p. 92.

28. Reuben Loffman, 'On the Fringes of a Christian Kingdom: The White Fathers, Colonial Rule, and the Báhêmbá in Sola, Northern Katanga, 1909–1960,' *Journal of Religion in Africa*, 45 (2016), pp. 1–28.
29. Henry Morton Stanley, *In Darkest Africa: Or the Quest, Rescue and Retreat of Emin Pasha, Governor of Equatoria* (New York: Charles Scribner's Sons, 1891).
30. Joseph Conrad, *The Heart of Darkness* (London: Blackwoods Magazine, 1899).
31. The Lualaba River is the name for the Congo River as it passes through Katanga.
32. Alison LaGamma, *Heroic Africans: Legendary Leaders, Iconic Sculptures* (New Haven: Yale University Press, 2011); Thomas Q. Reefe, *The Rainbow and the Kings: A History of the Luba Empire to 1891* (Berkeley: University of California Press, 1984).
33. Crawford Young and Thomas Turner, *The Rise and Decline of the Zairian State* (Madison: Wisconsin University Press, 1985), p. 10.
34. Marie-Bénédict Dembour, *Recalling the Belgian Congo: Conversations and Introspection* (New York: Berghahn Books, 2001), pp. 154–156.
35. Osumaka Likaka, *Naming Colonialism: History and Collective Memory in the Congo, 1870–1960* (Madison: University of Wisconsin Press, 2009), p. ix.
36. Victor Roelens, 'Les Abus du Recrutement de la Main-d'oeuvre au Congo. Une Protestation des Chefs Religieux Catholiques de la Colonie,' *Le Flambeau* (1923), pp. 129–130.
37. Jules Machal, *Travail Forcé Pour l'Huile de Palme de Lord Leverhulme: L'Histoire du Congo, 1910–1945: Tome 3* (Borgloon: Editions Paula Bellings, 2001).
38. Maryinez Lyons, *The Colonial Disease: A Social History of Sleeping Sickness in Northern Zaire, 1900–1940* (Cambridge: Cambridge University Press, 2002), pp. 8–24.
39. Lyons, *The Colonial Disease*, p. 217.
40. I take the phrase 'prisoners of geography' from: Tim Marshall, *Prisoners of Geography: Ten Maps That Tell You Everything You Need to Know About Global Politics* (London: Eliot and Thompson, 2015).
41. Max Gluckman, 'Introduction,' in A. L. Epstein (ed.), *The Craft of Social Anthropology* (London: Tavistock, 1967).
42. René Lamey, 'Les Archives de La Société des Pères Blancs,' *History in Africa*, 1 (1974), pp. 161–165. Although some features of this article will doubtless be out of date now, it is still useful to consult.
43. Carol W. Dickerman, 'On Using the White Father's Archives,' *History in Africa*, 8 (1991), p. 319.
44. Ann Laura Stoler, *Along the Archival Grain: Epistemic Anxieties and Colonial Common Sense* (Princeton: Princeton University Press, 2010), p. 4.

45. Stoler, *Along the Archival Grain*, p. 4.
46. Interview with Muganza Walunga Augustin, 1 August 2015, Makutano.
47. Johannes Fabian, *Remembering the Present: Painting and Popular History in Zaire* (Berkeley: University of California Press, 1996), pp. 269–277.

BIBLIOGRAPHY

Benedetto, Robert, *Presbyterian Reformers in Central Africa* (Amsterdam: Brill, 1996).

Burke, Joan F., *These Catholic Sisters Are All Mamas! Towards the Inculturation of Sisterhood in Africa: An Ethnographic Study* (Leiden: Brill, 2001).

Clement, Piet, 'The Land Tenure System in the Congo, 1885–1960: Actors, Motivations and Consequences,' in Ewout Frankema and Frans Buelens (eds), *Colonial Exploitation and Economic Development: The Belgian Congo and the Netherlands Indies Compared* (London: Routledge, 2013), pp. 88–108.

Cleys, Bram, and De Meulder, Bruno, 'Imagining a Christian Territory: Changing Spatial Strategies in the Missionary Outposts of Scheut (Kasai, Congo, 1891–1940),' in Fassil Demissie (ed.), *Colonial Architecture and Urbanism in Africa: Intertwined and Contested Histories* (London: Routledge, 2016), pp. 201–238.

Comaroff, Jean, and Comaroff, John, *Of Revelation and Revolution: The Dialectics of Modernity on a South African Frontier* (Chicago: Chicago University Press, 1997).

Conrad, Joseph, *The Heart of Darkness* (London: *Blackwood's Magazine*, 1899).

Creary, Nicholas M., *Domesticating a Religious Import: The Jesuits and the Inculturation of the Catholic Church in Zimbabwe, 1879–1980* (Fordham: Fordham University Press, 2011).

Cross, F. L., and Livingstone, E. A. (eds), *The Oxford Dictionary of the Catholic Church* (Oxford: Oxford University Press, 2005).

De Craemer, Willy, *The Jamaa and the Church: A Bantu Catholic Movement in Zaïre* (Oxford: Clarendon Press, 1977).

Delathuy, A. M., *Missie en Staat in Oud-Kongo: Witte Paters, Scheutisten en Jezuïeten, 1880–1914* (Berchem: EPO, 1992).

Dickerman, Carol W., 'On Using the White Father's Archives,' *History in Africa*, 8 (1991), pp. 319–322.

Eggers, Nicole, 'Mukombozi and the Monganga: The Violence of Healing in the 1944 Kitawalist Uprising,' *Africa*, 85, 3 (2015), pp. 417–436.

Emmerson, Barbara, *Leopold II of the Belgians: King of Colonialism* (London: Weidenfeld and Nicolson, 1979).

Fabian, Johannes *Jamaa: A Charismatic Movement in Katanga* (Evanston: Northwestern University Press, 1971).

Fabian, Johannes, *Remembering the Present: Painting and Popular History in Zaire* (Berkeley: University of California Press, 1996).

Fetter, Bruce, *The Creation of Elisabethville, 1910–1940* (Stanford: Stanford University Press, 1976).

Fields, Karen, *Revival and Rebellion in Colonial Central Africa* (Princeton: Princeton University Press, 1985).

Gluckman, Max, 'Introduction,' in A. L. Epstein (ed.), *The Craft of Social Anthropology* (London: Tavistock, 1967).

Hastings, Adrian, *The Church in Africa, 1450–1950* (Oxford: Oxford University Press, 1966).

Heremans, Roger, *L'Éducation dans les Missions Des Pères Blancs en Afrique Centrale (1879–1914): Objectifs et Réalisations* (Bruxelles: Éditions Nauwelaerts, 1983).

Hochschild, Adam, *King Leopold's Ghost: A Story of Greed, Terror and Heroism in Colonial Africa* (London: Pan Books, 1998).

Jewsiewicki, Bogumil, 'Belgian Africa,' in A. D. Roberts (ed.), *The Cambridge History of Africa, Volume 7, c.1905–c.1940* (Cambridge: Cambridge University Press, 1986), pp. 460–493.

Knighton, Ben, 'The Determination of Religion in Africa,' *African Affairs*, 109, 435 (2010), pp. 325–335.

Koren, Henry, *The Spiritans: A History of the Congregation of the Holy Ghost* (Pittsburgh: Duqesne University Press, 1958).

Lado, Ludovic, *Catholic Pentecostalism and the Paradoxes of Africanization: Processes of Localization in a Catholic Charismatic Movement in Cameroon* (Leiden: Brill, 2009).

LaGamma, Alison, *Heroic Africans: Legendary Leaders, Iconic Sculptures* (New Haven: Yale University Press, 2011).

Lamey, René, 'Les Archives de La Société des Pères Blancs,' *History in Africa*, 1 (1974), pp. 161–165.

Le Roy, Alexandre, *The Religion of the Primitives* (London: Macmillan, 1922).

Likaka, Osumaka, *Rural Society and Cotton in Colonial Zaire* (Madison: University of Wisconsin Press, 1997).

Likaka, Osumaka, *Naming Colonialism: History and Collective Memory in the Congo, 1870–1960* (Madison: Wisconsin University Press, 2009).

Loffman, Reuben, 'On the Fringes of a Christian Kingdom: The White Fathers, Colonial Rule, and the Báhêmbá in Sola, Northern Katanga, 1909-1960,' *Journal of Religion in Africa*, 45 (2016), pp. 1–28.

Longman, Timothy, *Church and Genocide in Rwanda* (Cambridge: Cambridge University Press, 2010).

Lyons, Maryinez, *The Colonial Disease: A Social History of Sleeping Sickness in Northern Zaire, 1900–1940* (Cambridge: Cambridge University Press, 2002).

Machal, Jules, *Travail Forcé Pour l'Huile de Palme de Lord Leverhulme: L'Histoire du Congo, 1910–1945: Tome 3* (Borgloon: Editions Paula Bellings, 2001).

Macola, Giacomo, *The Occupation of Katanga: The Personal Correspondence of Clément Brasseur, 1893–1897* (Oxford: Oxford University Press for the British Academy, 2016).

Markowitz, Marvin D., 'The Missions and Political Development in the Congo,' *Africa: Journal of the International African Institute,* 40, 3 (1970), pp. 234–247.

Markowitz, Marvin D., *Cross and Sword: The Political Role of Missionaries in the Belgian Congo, 1908–1960* (Stanford: Hoover Institution, 1973).

Marshall, Tim, *Prisoners of Geography: Ten Maps That Tell You Everything You Need to Know About Global Politics* (London: Eliot and Thompson, 2015).

Mokelwa, Jean-Pacifique Balaamo, *Eglises et Etat en République Démocratique du Congo: Histoire du Droit Congolais des Religions (1885–2003)* (Paris: L'Harmattan, 2008).

Mpia Bekina, Jacques, *L'Évangélisation du Mai-Ndombe au Congo-Kinshasa: Histoire, Difficultés Présentes et Inculturation* (Paris: L'Harmattan, 2010).

Mudimbe, V. Y., *Tales of Faith: Religion as Political Performance in Central Africa* (London: Bloomsbury, 2016).

Northrup, David, 'A Church in Search of a State: Catholic Missionaries in Eastern Zaïre, 1879–1930,' *Journal of Church and State,* 30, 2 (1988), pp. 309–319.

Nzongola-Ntalaja, Georges, *The Congo from Leopold to Kabila: A Peoples' History* (London: Zed Books, 2002).

Obeng, J. Pashington, *Asante Catholicism: Religious and Cultural Reproduction Among the Akan of Ghana* (Amsterdam: Brill, 1996).

Omasombo, Jean, Kasyulwe, Désiré Kisonga, Léonard, Guillaume, Zana, Mathieu, Simons, Edwine, Krawczyk, Joris, and Laghmouch, Mohammed, *République Démocratique du Congo: Tanganyika: Espace Fécondé par le Lac et le Rail* (Tervuren: Musée Royale de l'Afrique Centrale, 2014).

Oyatambwe, Wamu, *Eglise Catholique et Pouvoir Politique au Congo-Zaire* (Paris: L'Harmattan, 1997).

Porter, Andrew, *Religion Versus Empire? British Protestant Missionaries and Overseas Expansion, 1700–1914* (Manchester: Manchester University Press, 2004).

Reefe, Thomas Q., *The Rainbow and the Kings: A History of the Luba Empire to 1891* (Berkeley: University of California Press, 1984).

Roberts, Allen F., 'History, Ethnicity and Change in the "Christian Kingdom" of Southeastern Zaire,' in Leroy Vail (ed.), *The Creation of Tribalism in Southern Africa* (Berkeley: University of California Press, 1991), pp. 193–214.

Roes, Aldwin, 'Towards a History of Mass Violence in the Etat Indépendent du Congo, 1885–1908,' *South African Historical Journal,* 62, 4 (2010), pp. 634–670.

Roelens, Victor, 'Les Abus du Recrutement de la Main-d'oeuvre au Congo. Une Protestation des Chefs Religieux Catholiques de la Colonie,' *Le Flambeau* (1923), pp. 129–130.

Slade, Ruth, *English-Speaking Missionaries in the Congo Independent State, 1885–1908* (Bruxelles: Académie Royale des Sciences Coloniales, 1959).

Stannard, Matthew, *Selling the Congo: A History of European Pro-Empire Propaganda and the Making of Belgian Imperialism* (Nebraska: University of Nebraska Press, 2012).

Stengers, Jean, *Belgique et Congo: L'Elaboration de la Charte Coloniale* (Paris: Renaissance du Livre, 1963).

Stengers, Jean, 'Western Equatorial Africa, B: King Leopold's Congo, 1886–1908,' in J. D. Fage and Roland Oliver (eds), *The Cambridge History of Africa, Volume 7, 1870–1905* (Cambridge: Cambridge University Press, 1986), pp. 315–358.

Stengers, Jean, and Vansina, Jan, 'King Leopold's Congo,' in J. D. Fage and Roland Oliver (eds), *Cambridge History of Africa, Volume 6: From 1870 to 1905* (Cambridge: Cambridge University Press, 1985), pp. 315–358.

Stengers, Jean, *Congo: Myths et Réalités* (Paris: Racine, 2007).

Stanley, Henry Morton, *In Darkest Africa: Or the Quest, Rescue and Retreat of Emin Pasha, Governor of Equatoria* (New York: Charles Scribner's Sons, 1891).

Stoler, Ann Laura, *Along the Archival Grain: Epistemic Anxieties and Colonial Common Sense* (Princeton: Princeton University Press, 2010).

Sundkler, Bengt, and Steed, Christopher, *A History of the Church in Africa* (Cambridge: Cambridge University Press, 2000).

Vangroenweghe, Daniel, *Rood Rubber: Leopold II en Zijn Congo* (Leuven: Elsevier, 1985).

Vellut, Jean-Luc, 'La Violence Armée dans l'Etat Indépendant du Congo: Ténèbres et Clartés dans l'Histoire d'un Etat Conquérant,' *Cultures et Développement*, 16, 3 (1984), pp. 671–707.

Weisbord, Robert G., 'The King, the Cardinal and the Pope: Leopold II's Genocide in Congo and the Vatican,' *Journal of Genocide Research*, 5 (2003), pp. 35–45.

Willame, Jean-Claude, *Patrimonialism and Political Change in the Congo* (Stanford: Stanford University Press, 1972).

Young, Crawford, *Politics in Congo: Decolonization and Independence* (Princeton: Princeton University Press, 1965).

Young, Crawford, and Turner, Thomas, *The Rise and Decline of the Zairian State* (Madison: Wisconsin University Press, 1985).

CHAPTER 2

Pre-colonial Politics in Kongolo to 1890

This chapter examines one of the first major attempts to colonize the eastern savannah that took place before that inspired by Leopold II and his *Force Publique*. It was organized by a series of slaver-merchants from Zanzibar and/or who had Zanzibari heritage. The White Fathers and the Spiritans would subsequently define themselves *against* many of the core tenants of this brutal but patchy invasion, notably in their anti-polygamy, anti-Islam and, perhaps most importantly, anti-slavery stances. But, as the Zanzibari conquest of what would become Kongolo was incomplete, the Church also had to navigate pre-existing forms of local governance that remained in place. What Jan Vansina described as the Equatorial African political tradition, in which a loose hierarchy of local social institutions governed societies, became important in encounters with the both the Church and the Belgian bureaucracy later on not least since the colonial administration sought to co-opt local African leaders into it.

Unfortunately, not much is known with any certainty about the territory's history before the arrival of Europeans in the 1890s. Most of the oral evidence for the late pre-colonial period is bound up in origin myths, from which scholars are increasingly pessimistic positivist histories can ever be reconstructed. Nearly all documentation about Kongolo's pre-colonial

The original version of the book was revised: Belated corrections have been incorporated. The correction to the book is available at https://doi.org/10.1007/978-3-030-17380-7_9

31

R. A. Loffman, *Church, State and Colonialism in Southeastern Congo, 1890–1962*, Cambridge Imperial and Post-Colonial Studies Series, https://doi.org/10.1007/978-3-030-17380-7_2

past refers to it only in retrospect. What evidence we have of pre-colonial Kongolo suggests that no one overarching institution or mode of sovereignty had gained political hegemony in the region by the latter quarter of the nineteenth century. Instead, a broad cluster of African elites struggled to amass followings in difficult and sometimes violent circumstances. In trying to attract supporters, local leaders deployed a range of sophisticated social mechanisms, including the promotion of foundation myths, food taboos and, occasionally, the acquisition of political authority through victory in battle. None of the groups that converged in Kongolo before the period of colonial rule uniformly imposed fundamental sociopolitical changes there. Instead, the political modalities migratory elites brought with them eventually sat atop a series of autochthonous lineages that continued to form the basis of social and political government in the region. Outside forms of political thought and ritual did percolate into kinship politics but only to varying extents.

THE EQUATORIAL AFRICAN POLITICAL TRADITION

This book focuses on the southern part of the Congo River basin, which eventually became the colonial territory of Kongolo in 1912. The region hosts a series of rapids on the Congo River (called the Lualaba as it passes through Katanga) that are widely known as *Les Portes d'Enfer* (The Gates of Hell) and these impeded onward travel to the south by boat for many years.[1] A number of fishing cultures grew up along the 'Gates of Hell' and upriver. One of these riverine groups came to be known as the 'Genya' or 'fisherpeople' in Swahili. The Genya perhaps demonstrate more than most just how integral labour has sometimes been to the formation of identities and ethnicities in and around Kongolo.

Yet as much as the River was a source of sustenance, its presence also ensured that its environs were and still are immensely fertile. Consequently, a range of people were attracted to the bountiful farmland in Kongolo throughout the pre-colonial period. The existence of a ready supply of fresh water, alongside the temperate climate that proliferated in the territory, meant that the amount of food supply that depended on farming probably exceeded the 40% that Jan Vansina suggested was common across the Congo River Basin before colonial rule.[2] Oil palm and groundnuts were two of the most important crops, but there were a number of others, such as bananas and maize. Alongside subsistence and commercial agriculture, trapping, hunting and rearing animals was very important. In addition to the food they provided, animals played a vital role in mediating social relationships, much as they were in many other parts of sub-Saharan Africa.[3] Peoples exchanged

chickens and goats for dowry payments upon the marriage of their daughters, for example, as well as using them to pay fines to resolve disputes.

The combination of hunting, rearing, fishing and agriculture represented the material foundations of what Jan Vansina has described as
the equatorial African political tradition that influenced peoples in the
entire Congo River Basin.[4] The tradition that he outlined consisted of
a series of loose but hierarchical arrangements between different peoples
and sociopolitical institutions and, according to Vansina, it lasted until
the mid-nineteenth century.[5] At the bottom of the political pyramid was
the 'household' or the 'house.'[6] The house cultivated the crops outlined
above and consisted of an extended kin-group living in one or several
actual homesteads. It 'was always competing for membership with other
establishments' and 'was the unit of food production … usually comprised from 10 to 40 people … a labour force close to the optimum
for the collective labour requirements in agriculture (clearing bush),
trapping, and hunting.'[7] Nearly all houses were patriarchal and the 'big
men' who headed them were polygamous and usually gave 'some of
their wives as consorts to young clients in order to attract men to the
house.'[8] Above the house, in political terms, was the village, which was
formed by '[aggregates] of houses' and usually led by the big man who
had founded it. The village big man received tribute, which usually came
in the form of proceeds from hunts, such as leopard skins. Big men from
other houses, who acted as local councilmen, assisted the headman in
governing the village.[9] Jan Vansina suggests that terms that eventually
became part of Belgian colonial government later on, such as 'palaver'
and 'to pay a fine,' emerged from these self-same local councils.

Far from being static settlements, villages and their councils sometimes moved for a number of reasons, such as to maintain their access
to fertile lands if their original location became infertile, even if their
movements 'were more or less circular over a stable territory.'[10] Villages
could also be destroyed in wartime or move *en mass* to avoid unpopular
regimes, colonial or otherwise. Yet, as much as they could change their
location, the village was the foundation of many central African societies. When two or more villages chose to form an alliance they created a
district.[11] The district was not as hierarchical as Belgian colonial administrators believed it to have been. It was not arbitrarily run by a paramount
chief and did not even need to have a headquarter settlement. To bor-
row John Iliffe's conception of honour in pre-colonial Africa, authority
was very much a matter of negotiation, with big men being first among
equals, rather than ruling arbitrarily through a top-down process of

government.[12] It was not always true, either, that village big men met to discuss pertinent measures affecting the district. Rather, 'cross-cutting bilateral alliances [usually] sufficed' to resolve disputes or problems.[13] Moreover, the largest village in a district did not have de facto control over others therein, even if it might have been the most alluring in terms of fertile land and access to other resources, such as water.

The alliances of houses within districts have traditionally been described as 'clans,' and there were plenty of them in Kongolo. Clans usually developed shared origin stories as well as a common food taboo(s) with 'all the clan's members ... thought to be the progeny of one person.'[14] Clan ideology was very important as all members were presumed to be equal siblings, with their membership to the clan being irrevocable given their shared ancestry.[15] Clans were the social glue that bound districts together, even if their membership to them could shift. While clans, like houses, were not alliances predicted on defence; the district, like the village, clearly was.[16] When different houses or villages were threatened, they called on the social institution 'above' them in the political hierarchy outlined above to intervene to protect them. A house would call on a village, for instance, just as a village might call on a district. Clans could crosscut supposedly 'ethnic' boundaries and many survived the colonial period.

Clans, houses, villages and districts were and still are evident in Kongolo today and they were the predominant ways in which the groups that inhabited the region in the early–mid-nineteenth century were organized. The political basis of the equatorial tradition promoted intellectual and technological innovation. As Jane Guyer suggests, the loose constellations of houses, districts and clans frequently gave rise to new kinds of rituals and beliefs.[17] Likewise, the traditional gave rise to a host of different local and regional variants. Given that Kongolo and its environs were and still are thought to be dominated by a cultural variant of that tradition known as 'Luba-Katanga,' hereafter simply 'Luba,' I will first examine how this culture used and innovated the equatorial political tradition in southeastern Congo.[18]

THE LUBA: HISTORY, MYTH AND POLITICS

Rather than being organized into a centralized and powerful empire, as missionaries, colonial officials and historians alike first thought, the political organization of the Luba peoples of Kongolo as well as those in what is now the province of Tanganyika largely conformed to Jan

Vansina's model of the tradition.[19] Given their lack of a standing army, Luba rulers placed a heavy premium on symbolism, political allegiances and ritual displays of power as opposed to outright conquest.[20] The Luba culture first emerged in the Upemba Depression in central Katanga, which has sometimes been referred to as the 'core' of the central polity.[21] Objects of regalia served to mark Luba territory and simultaneously denoted where the culture's boundaries were.[22] However, Mary Nooter Roberts and Allen Roberts suggest that this 'core' was often more mythical than real, with it having been evoked by frontiersmen who claimed to have had a relationship with it as a means of supporting their own claims to power.[23] Yet, in so doing, the mythical 'core' provided the foundation for cultural integration because these emissaries spread Luba culture beyond their 'home' societies, even if it was not actually real.

The Luba societies of the Upemba Depression and beyond were generally organized into corporate patrilineages, with, as Jan Vansina states, 'clients linked by contact to the lineage and by domestic slaves.'[24] Yet, there were divergences from the patrilineal model the further away one went from the Upemba Depression. For example, there were some matrilineal Luba groups in Kongolo and these were likely to have been those who had developed closer relationships with other cultures in the region. One or several of Luba lineages, be they patrilineal or matrilineal, constituted a village, exactly in accordance with Jan Vansina's model of the 'tradition.' Each village was directed by a headman known as a *kilolo kyà mulopwè*.[25] When several villages conjoined, they were known as a 'chiefdom' and were headed by a collective chief known as a *kilo-lo*.[26] Sometimes, several chiefdoms grouped together to form a supra-polity, though these were rare. Some chiefs were appointed on a hereditary basis, and were said to 'own the land,' while others 'were governed by chiefs appointed by their immediate superiors.'[27] All chiefs who were not 'owners of the land' were known as *balopwè* (*mulopwè* in the singular) or a 'king of the sacred blood,' with the blood itself supposedly belonging to the mythical founder of the Luba, (N)Kongolo, or his vanquisher, Kalala Ilunga.[28] Usually, the royal blood was transmitted only through the male line in an attempt to replicate the patrilineal structures of the central Luba polity, mythical as it may have been.[29]

Luba polities were governed according to an orally transmitted political charter outlined in a genesis myth, which was remembered and deployed by a group of courtiers known as the 'men of memory' or the *Bánà Báluté* in Luba.[30] Given its importance as, among other things, *the* political charter for pre-colonial Luba peoples, scholars have given it a good deal of attention. Yet, anthropologists and historians have long puzzled over the extent to which the myth could also serve to outline a genuinely historical king list, which could in turn be used in a positivist historical fashion. Alternatively, they wonder if the myth is in fact more a rendering of a cosmological belief system that has informed the repro-duction of Luba kingship than an attempt to faithfully reconstruct the Luba past.[31] Initially, historians accepted most of the myth as fact and so reconstructed pre-colonial Luba societies mostly in accordance with it.[32] Subsequent to archaeological and material investigations, though, they are now more likely to accept only some parts of it as fact and most other parts of it far more as cosmological ephemera.[33]

But the latter parts of the genesis myth, along with late pre-colonial Luba history as whole, can be cross-checked with the documentary record and may provide some clues as to what a positivist history of pre-colonial Luba societies might look like. The works of the famed Victorian explorers David Livingstone and Verney Cameron provide some important checks on the latter parts of the myth, for example.[34] This chapter will therefore bor-row largely from the later sections of the Luba myth to reconstruct their history in the mid to late nineteenth century. But, this particular section of the chapter will survey the earlier parts of the myth to give the reader some indication of the context in which important Luba terms, such as 'sacred' kingship, emerged—even if the historical detail of their genesis as outlined in oral traditions might be more symbolic than real. There are a number of different versions of all of the episodes that together comprise the Luba genesis myth, with these differences in part explained by the lived reality of political schisms that emerged as village and district big men sought to promote their own claims to authority.[35] Thomas Reefe suggested that there could be as many as thirteen different versions of the genesis myth, all including and excluding different episodes of it.[36] Rather than rehearsing all the variants of the Luba myth here, I will summarize only the most per-tinent episodes of it only in as much as they relate to Kongolo's history.[37]

The Luba genesis myth begins by following the traditional African trope of a foreign frontiersmen arriving in an unfamiliar land, or the 'internal frontier,' now familiar to scholars working across sub-Saha-ran Africa's oral 'epic belt.'[38] Nkongolo, someone endowed with super-natural powers, arrived among a community in southeastern Congo around 1500 and began to unify peoples there shortly afterwards.[39] Yet Nkongolo is the antagonist of the Luba genesis myth. So, it is not a 'conquest by invitation' narrative of the kind that Igor Kopytoff observed were typical of internal frontier African histories.[40] Instead, Nkongolo violently subdued the villages 'and tiny chiefdoms ... and built his capital at Mwibele near Lake Boya,' close to the present-day town of Kabongo.[41] According to Thomas Reefe, Nkongolo killed those in Mashyo, a salt producing region near Lake Boya, out of frustration because his salt marsh building project had failed.[42] Having settled at Mwibele, Nkongolo was approached by another immigrant called Mbidi Kiluwe, 'a hunter from somewhere east of the Congo River,' who Jan Vansina argued was in fact a real person.[43] Mbili was initially well received, both by Nkongolo and his two half-sisters, Bulanda and Mabela, but he eventually fell out with Nkongolo for reasons that are still unclear.

Most versions of the myth suggest that Mbili attempted to teach Nkongolo what the anthropologist Luc de Heusch described as 'kingly manners' and the disagreements occurred during or shortly after this period of tutelage.[44] Jan Vansina theorized that Mbili likely came from a more sophisticated polity and therefore knew better than Nkongolo how a chief should comport himself for chiefs were usually men.[45] While teaching Nkongolo 'kingly manners,' Mbili fathered children with his two half-sisters. Bulanda gave birth to Kalala Ilunga while Mabela mothered Kisulu Mabele. Kalala Ilunga eventually became a very important warrior who later helped Nkongolo subdue the southern parts of his kingdom.[46] However, Nkongolo began to see Ilunga as a rival and tried to kill him, thereby forcing Ilunga's temporary exile.

After an undefined period of time, Kalala Ilunga mobilized an army and defeated his estranged uncle. Writing in 1936, Edmond Verhulpen suggested that the Luba 'empire' split into two after Nkongolo's defeat, with one lineage following Nkongolo and the other Kalala Ilunga.[47] The idea of two Luba 'empires' forming at this point has stuck in the minds of those, like Jan Vansina, who have tried to reconstruct the pre-colonial Luba past. If the oral record is to be believed, Nkongolo was captured and killed leaving the Kalala Ilunga as the preeminent potentate in central Katanga from around the sixteenth century.[48] Most subsequent Luba monarchies trace or at least try to trace their lineage back to Kalala Ilunga, though the fact that the territory of Kongolo is named as such suggests that Luba monarchs there attached themselves instead to Nkongolo's line. Ilunga expanded his kingdom across the Lualaba River, with it eventually extending as far east as Lake Tanganyika. Upon his death, therefore, the Luba kingdom had 'achieved its basic organization.'[49]

According to the myth, Ilunga's kingdom included a hierarchical monarchy at the centre but with different and less hierarchical political systems emerging further away from the central court. The balopwè chiefs/kings typically claimed that their blood was linked to Ilunga's or Kongolo's and so they had some sort of supernatural authority and legitimacy to rule. As well as human beings endowed with supernatural powers, the balopwè were supported by a caste of priests known as the *vìdyê*.[50] Given the supernatural authority that the vìdyê argued they possessed, there were few mechanisms, either secular or sacred, which could be used to hold the balopwè to account. The only realistic way of deposing a mulopwè was if his half-brothers from his mother's patrilineage, whose claim to authority could rally a following, rose against him.

It is likely that, even if some individuals involved in the Luba foundation myth were real, the main Luba kingdom, at least in its early manifestation was, in Vansina's words, 'first and foremost a construction of the mind.'[51] The centre, and the myth sustaining it, was in many senses designed to legitimate Luba power on what were supposedly its peripheries. Nonetheless, even if we overlook the granular detail of the political accounts of the origin of the Luba polity, the material evidence suggests that African societies had become more centralized on the Upemba Depression by the early 1700s in any case.[52] This material evidence, incidentally, comes to us in the form of pottery, ironwork, coinage, beads and the remains of agricultural activities.[53] The society that produced this evidence may not have been called 'Luba' by others, or even have described itself as such, but it began to engage with and/or conquer other groups. Likewise, the notion of a central polity did indeed probably crystallize in this period as did its concept of sacred kingship, which was embodied in the institution of the balopwè.[54]

This first part of the genesis myth, which describes the Luba state's formation and consolidation, broadly ends with the reign of a mulopwè called Ngoi Sanza (c.1665–c.1685).[55] In Sanza's reign, the central kingdom fragmented, with another three separate Luba kingdoms emerging as well as a host of other peripheral yet independent Luba polities. Luba culture percolated into Kongolo through conquest and other groups adopting the culture only after Sanza's reign, yet it took over a century for this to happen. Ann Wilson argued that the Luba 'empire,' if the word 'empire' is appropriate in this context, began to expand during the reign of Kadilo (c.1720–c.1750).[56] Kadilo's expansionist program was continued by his successors, namely Kekenia (c.1750–c.1780) and Ilunga

Sunga (Sungu) (c.1780–c.1810).[57] It is likely that more of the individuals and events described by the foundation myth after Kadilo's campaigns were indeed real and, at this stage, we begin to move, even if slowly, into more concentrate historical reality. The implantation of various aspects of Luba culture in Kongolo can be attributed to a particular Luba frontiersman, who looms large in the next section.

THE LUBA AND THE SONGYE

A strain of Luba culture, later identified as Luba-Katanga, made its way into Kongolo in the form of a mulopwè named Kumwimba Ngombe (c.1810–c.1840).[58] Ngombe 'led military conquests northeast and north across the Luvidjo River and its tributary, the Kadiabilongo. Later, according to Edmund Verhulpen who was one of the first administrators to be educated at the colonial university in Belgium in the 1920s, Ngombe withdrew to leave his son, Ilunga *Bùki* ('divine'), in charge of a kingdom that extended as far West as the Lomami River.'[59] Along with his father, Bùki was what the historian Thomas Reefe has described as a 'fire king' (or *Mulopwè wa Mudilo* in Luba), meaning that he was endowed with embers that came from a ruler of the 'core' Luba polity, whose capital is said to have been called *Kitenta*.[60] Fire kings were so named because they carried the Luba rulers' cooking embers as a sign that they were close to the 'core.'

Only the Luba kings' inner circle would be allowed to see them eat, and so know for sure that they was mortal rather than divine. This is why the ashes from his cooking pot were so highly prized. The cooking embers, as well as the concept of the fire king, were very important in articulating the Luba concept of perpetual kingship to those outside the Luba cultural sphere. And, like all fire kings, Bùki extended the cultural reach of the Luba monarchy by promoting its rituals and institutions, which had crystallized by the seventeenth century. He was an unusual fire king, though, in the sense that his ashes did not belong to those of a Luba monarch from the 'core' kingdom but to a frontiersman— something that undermined the legitimacy of his progeny in the colonial period and even beyond. Nevertheless, having attained Ngombe's ashes, he proceeded up the Lualaba River recruiting supporters and warriors from the villages through which he passed. One of these villages was called Kansimba, on the western side of the Lualaba River, and so Reefe has suggested Bùki thereafter came to be known as Bùki Kansimba.[61]

When he finally arrived in Kongolo, he encountered a range of different groups among the most important was the Songye.[62]

The Songye were organized into small polities governed by councils of notables. Much like the Luba, the origins of this group are the subject of patchy speculation. Some historians, such as Jan Vansina and Thomas Turner, speculate that the Songye came from what are today the territories of Manono and Kabalo to the south of Kongolo and originated as an off-shoot of the Luba.[63] Thomas Turner observed that some of the Songye he met, when quizzed by a colonial official called M. Lood who was working in the Kabinda area at the time, suggested that their origins related to the arrival of a Luba hunter named *Piwe a Ntoshi Kwi Boloba*.[64] According to Lood's informants, Boloba and his wife, Zibu a Ntoshi, produced two sons: Kusu na Kankumba, the Tetela ancestor, and Biki na Kankumba, the Songye one.[65] However, Thomas Turner believes that the Piwe origin story pertained only to the origins of a *particular* local Songye group and not to the culture as a whole. Altogether, it is unlikely that there ever was any 'original' founder ancestor for the Songye or at least one that is recorded in a more comprehensive Songye genesis myth of the kind that has been produced by their Luba counterparts. Correspondingly, Dunja Hersak has argued that there is no 'singular Songye tradition.'[66] Instead, she suggests that the 'Songye' identity was 'a dynamic, ephemeral phe-nomenon' that probably expanded from a localized series of polities via the incoming Belgian Free State administration that used the word to refer to those who were 'faithful' to it, while contrasting them with the 'Tetela,' who revolted.[67] Indeed, the model of the Songye identity as one indicating a localized series of cultures that expanded during the Free State era (1885–1908), is the most convincing at present.

The Songye likely came to Kongolo from places situated to the east of the territory. Verhulpen suggested that the Songye used Kongolo as an early staging post from which to diffuse their culture further into the eastern savannah.[68] So, when he reached the territory, Bùki Kansimba ran into a series of localized polities that lived in the east of what became Kongolo. But how were these city-states ordered? François Nyet has suggested that: 'the political organization of the Songye [rested] on the authority of a chief, a sacred and benevolent figure … enjoying great magical-religious powers, the chief [was] linked to two "secret societies," one practicing witchcraft (*buci*) and sorcery (*masende*), and the other, under the control of the first, was based on the *Bwadi Bwa Kifwebe* dance society.'[69] Unlike Jan Vansina's decentralized model of the district,

François Nyet suggests that there were in fact supreme chiefs among the Songye, who resided in Kabinda 'in a residence called *Epata*.'[70]

The Songye in what would eventually become the territory of Kongolo operated with an elective system of rule, in which supreme chiefs only ruled for around three to five years each. This elective system, often described as 'rotating chieftainship,' did not always sooth political wrangling and actually inspired it on occasion.[71] The Bwadi Bwa Kifwebe dance group emerged in part to adjudge competing claims to the chieftainship that emanated from different clans, though it could take on different forms depending on the requirements of the local context in which it functioned. The Bwadi Bwa Kifwebe was what Douglas Johnson saw as a closed association because its existence was not secret, and so the colonial term 'secret society' was not appropriate, but their operation and membership was 'closed' to all but a select few.[72] Closed associations, such as the Bwadi Bwa Kifwebe, were, in Jan Vansina's words, generally 'important for the social organization as a whole [and particularly] their role in public government, the maintenance of order, and the reproduction of culture.'[73] They will reappear in our discussions of the colonial period in later chapters.

Like a number of other ethnic groups, the Songye were constituted of a wide range of different subsets, or kinship groups, which farmed particular areas of land that were later named after them. Among the most prominent of these Songye subsets were the Ekiye (Beneki), the Ikalebwe (Bekalebwe), the Ilande (Belande), the Milembwe (Bamilembwe) and the Nsapo (Sappo-Sap).[74] One of the most important of the Songye polities as far as Kongolo was concerned was that ruled by the Kwizimu line, where the 'protective spirit, Lenge, was worshipped at a sacred hill of the same name.'[75] The lineage-based system of government that proliferated among the Kwizimu allowed Bùki Kansimba to intervene in its politics by choosing to collaborate with one of its eligible males, Kibambaleya. He demanded that Kibambaleya collect tribute from the Kwizimu villages but he was unsuccessful because no potentate in this area had done this before. Thereafter, Bùki Kansimba gave Kibambaleya the derisory praise name of Musinga, literally meaning 'tribute collector,' though in this context it meant 'one who was refused tribute.' He deposed Kibambaleya and thereafter installed Kitenge Matembe as his representative instead.

We do not know how successful Matembe was, but it is likely that he was more successful than Kibambaleya because for a long time the Kwizimu chiefs have been known as *Musingalenge*, a name that evokes Bùki's influence as well as the Kwizimu ancestral spirit. Bùki eventually established a court among the Kwizimu villages, recruiting followers of local chiefs who would later identify themselves as Songye into his steadily growing band of warriors. The chief of the nearby Bayazi villages, Lupembwe, enjoyed good relations with Bùki's court and even provided warriors for him on occasion. He established similar arrangements with the Songye polities of Wangongwe and Kayaye to the west of what is now Kongolo's town centre. The Genya fisherpeople, mentioned at the start of the present chapter, also submitted to Bùki soon after his arrival. Reefe tells of an island in the River in which the Genya and other peoples began to worship the ancestral spirit of *Nkongolo* (The Rainbow), one of the mythical founders of the Luba culture (see Fig. 2.1).[76] Bùki even left one of his own representatives as a permanent resident on this island to ensure the spirit of Nkongolo was constantly placated.[77] And it would be after this spirit, that of Nkongolo, that the territory of Kongolo itself was named in 1912.

Fig. 2.1 Photo of Kongolo Island by Author (3 August 2015)

Bùki's fire kingdom expanded eastwards as well as westwards.[78] In the eastern parts of Kongolo, Bùki Kansimba become involved in local conflicts much more at the behest of the autochthonous people there than as a result of his own campaigns of conquest. For example, two Hêmbá chiefs were supposed to have had a disagreement in the ruling Muhiya (Muhona) matriclan, which was not a Luba one, with one chief, Tubula, later appealing to Bùki Kansimba for intervention. Bùki Kansimba ended up intervening on behalf of Tubula and 'destroyed Mwamba's followers.' However, the people of Muhona's ruling matriclan later defeated him under the leadership of someone known as Lutabuka. Undeterred by his initially unsuccessful foray into eastern Kongolo, Bùki Kansimba again became embroiled in its politics when Makenge sent an emissary to him and he recognized *this* emissary as chief rather than Makenge. The dispirited headman then went to Bùki Kansimba's court to try to convince him that he, and not his emissary, was the true chief but Makenge ended up dying there in circumstances that are still unclear. Whatever the truth of Makenge's death was, Bùki Kansimba's influence had spread well beyond the boundaries of his Songye followers' polities even if they did not extend too far eastwards by the time he died.

After his death, one of Bùki's sons, Kekenya, became the main Luba headman from around 1840 to 1870.[79] Confusingly, Kekenya was also referred to as 'Bùki' because it became a Luba aristocratic title, one which each 'Bùki' passed down to their progeny through successive generations.[80] We know that a number of different warriors acting on behalf of the fire kingdom of Bùki Kansimba continued to expand their power bases largely unimpeded. Unfortunately, it is unclear exactly how Bùki Kansimba's heirs interacted with their surroundings and what their relationship with the polities that their father had conquered was. Unfortunately, Alexandre Bùki, Kekenya's great, great grandson, could not talk in any detail about his ancestor's reign beyond saying—somewhat unsurprisingly—that it was 'peaceful' and 'prosperous.'[81]

However, we do know that there was not much Luba expansion in Kongolo after Kekenya's death, with successive leaders seeking instead to cement the gains that he had made earlier in the nineteenth century. Even in the period of Luba consolidation, though, the Songye in Kongolo were not wholly subsumed under Luba stewardship and maintained their fidelity to pre-existing leaders, such as chief Lumpungu in the 1880s. Rather, the Songye developed an ambiguous relationship with the incoming Luba culture. They would sometimes play on it during the period of colonial rule, first, to try to distance themselves from any Luba chiefs they disliked or, alternatively, to attach themselves to those Luba chiefs they liked and/or from whom they sought patronage.

INVADERS FROM THE EAST

Given the overall history of fragmentation and conflict that proliferated as Luba culture was spread in the territory, it is incorrect to see Kongolo as a wholly or even mostly 'Luba-ized' by the late nineteenth century. Rather, the power that Luba kingship ideology had over the tradition of lineage government was not the most important as the twentieth century dawned. Instead, another series of protagonists from what is now the state of Tanzania was on the ascendancy. This group was known as the *Zanzibaris*, with the term referring to a biracial series of warrior merchants who hunted for slaves and ivory to bring back to fast-developing and profitable markets on the east African coast. By the 1830s, there were already Zanzibari groups in Ujiji, on the Tanzanian side of Lake Tanganyika.[82] However, it took them longer to reach Kongolo. It was not until the 1870s that 'Zanzibari traders established a commercial empire' in eastern Congo.[83] To explain the patterning of Zanzibari presence in Kongolo, it is first necessary to detail the ways in which they moved across the eastern savannah.

Zanzibari traders tended to travel in what were known as 'caravans,' much like merchants did in the Middle East at this time. These caravans consisted of a series of peoples, typically young men, responsible for keeping captured slaves with the rest of the group and, also, for hunting for ivory.[84] Some of these young men were from the interior and had taken on some aspects of Zanzibari culture, such as the dress, and were described as *waungwana* by their peers.[85] By the late nineteenth century, with the help of their *Waungwana* allies, the Zanzibari caravan networks had expanded markedly across the east and central Africa.[86] Tippu Tip, a nickname that he interpreted to mean the sound his guns supposedly made, was the foremost of these Zanzibari slavers. His first independent journey into the interior took place in either 1860 or 1861. At this time, he had few men and his volume of trade was slight.[87] From 1864–1869, though, he made a second voyage into the eastern savannah in which he eventually found his way to Lungu. There, Tippu Tip found someone who told him that two of his relatives had been defeated by a local chief from a subset of the Tabwa ethnic group known as the *Nsama*.[88] Thereafter, he defeated the Nsama in battle along with his local allies, the Cungu, who were the erstwhile enemies of the Tabwa. The use of local alliances to advance his trading interests was something that defined Tippu Tip's slaving network, as they proved essential in helping him purchase ivory or copper to procure slaves at minimal cost. But Tippu Tip's local alliances were increasingly replaced by his use of proxy rulers from his own extended family as the nineteenth century wore on. Tippu Tip preferred to have his family rather than local big men in important roles given the vast sums of money that were at stake in his voyages.

The promotion of Tippu Tip's family within his trading sphere was made possible by the fact that caravans got considerably larger as the east African slave trade intensified. From having a only a limited retinue on his first voyage, he presided over around four thousand by the time he made his third trip into the eastern savannah.[89] By 1870, Tippu Tip's influence had spread as far south as the Bemba peoples on the Zambian border and as far north as Kasongo, in what is now the Maniema province. He had even installed himself as chief among a subset of the Songye and raised an army and conquered the town of Kasongo and its environs.[90] From his base in Kasongo, he attempted to take the largest slave market in eastern Africa, that of Nyangwe, from its leaders, Mwine Dugumbi and Munie Mohara. Having been notified that Tippu Tip and his vast army was soon to invade, these leaders quickly surrendered and Nyangwe came under Zanzibari suzerainty. Given that he had taken the largest slave market in the region, Tippu Tip went from being a slaver-journeyman to being the ruler of a significant booty-based quasi-state nominally under the control of the Sultan of Zanzibar but to all intents and purposes governed by Tippu Tip. Certainly, he wrote in his autobiography, *Maisha ya Hamed bin Muhammed el Murjebi yaani Tippu Tip*, that when he was in Kasongo his 'kinsmen were overjoyed ... and invested me with full authority for the area.'[91] It was probably at this point that he gained the nickname 'the porcupine with many quills' (*Nungu Wayula Miba* in Swahili), as he set about installing his allies as chiefs 'everywhere in the region between Lomami and Lualaba, north of the Luba kingdom of Kasongo Kalombo.'[92] For Jan Vansina, Tippu Tip's intrusion into the eastern savannah, as well as those made by the Swahili as a whole, was a vitally important historical moment because it shattered the political tradition explained at the start of this chapter.[93] Yet, while there is little doubt that Tippu Tip and his followers inspired a good deal of social tumult, Kongolo was a place in which the Swahili struggled to gain hegemony given that it was only on the fringes of the slaver's Kasongo-based booty-state.

Documents produced by the Belgian administration over fifty years after this period suggest that some of Tippu Tip's allies were chased out of the places in which they were installed in Kongolo and some were even killed.[94] Despite the constraints they were placed under, local peoples thus still had some agency in the 'tight corners' that the Zanzibari colonization imposed.[95] These tight corners emerged due to the uneven patterning of Kahambo's, the main Zanzibari proxy in Kongolo, and his lieutenant's, Lusana's, raids on the villages 'along the northern frontier of the Luba fire kingdom.'[96] In short, despite their military capability, the Zanzibari did not manage to subdue all the chiefs in Bùki's fire kingdom and beyond. They did not have the personnel to be able to subdue vast tracts of land that they considered unnecessary for the procurement of slaves and ivory. There is even evidence that negotiation with Tippu Tip was possible, and he was not necessarily simply the savage, 'oriental despot,' which British abolitionists sometimes suggested he was in their publications.[97] For example, a Songye chief of the Wangongwe villages in western Kongolo, Mulongo Lupembwe, grew tired of Swahili raids and sent 'an emissary named Kasongo to negotiate a settlement on his behalf with Tippu Tip and his representatives.'[98]

Unfortunately for Lupembwe, Kasongo made his own deal with Tippu Tip and sent his ally, Mobanga Kapya, to depose him. So, initially, it looked as if Swahili raiding in Wangongwe would continue unabated. However, Kahambo was killed by Kekenya as he fled the incoming Belgian forces. We could reasonably deduce from this episode that it was primarily Europeans, at least in conjunction with Africans, who drove Kahambo out of Wangongwe villages, and discount local, African agency. But, even if we did, Kahambo had still not managed to entirely subdue the peoples he had sought to enslave. Even if Lupembwe, the Songye chief, had been ousted, Zanzibari power was far from secure in Kongolo. And it was not just in the western and southern parts of what would become the territory of Kongolo that Zanzibari control was weak. In the east too, other communities had experienced at some measure of success against the slavers.

THE HÊMBÁ

Despite the power that the Zanzibari wielded in the areas that were administered by the Songye and the Luba-ized areas, their rule was far more limited in the eastern areas of Kongolo. These localities were predominantly inhabited by a group commonly referred to as the *Hêmbá*. They inhabited a swathe of land in southeastern Congo, with many since migrating to the cities in the south of Katanga, such as Elisabethville (Lubumbashi), from the hinterland and even beyond.[99] Like the Songye, however, the Hêmbá have not been the subject of extensive scholarly enquiry and they pose considerable problems of ethnogenesis for historians. The most important ethnographers of the Hêmbá are Pamela Blakely and Thomas Blakely. They worked extensively with the Hêmbá in the 1970s and recorded many of their traditions, particularly in relation to their funerals.[100] However, much of the history of the group before the 1970s remains ambiguous. According to François Nyet, who researched but never conducted fieldwork among the Hêmbá, they had a number of shared traits, not least their language, but an overarching cultural identity may have developed only *after* the nineteenth century.[101] Alongside this still unanswered question of the origin of identity, the main question that scholars continue to ask about the Hêmbá is: to what extent were they a separate ethnic constituency from the Luba?[102]

More than anything, the violence between these groups during and after decolonization in the 1960s probably led to the clear political and cultural distinctions between them that we see today.[103] However, Edmond Verhulpen suggested that the Hêmbá were a 'luba-ized' group, even suggesting that they were known as the matrilineal version of their patrilineal Luba 'cousins' before the colonial period began.[104] Viewed in this light, the Hêmbá were a disarticulated subset of the Luba. Irmgard César-Göehring later elaborated on Verhulpen's definition by suggesting that the term Luba-Hemba (Hêmbá) should be used to denote that the Hêmbá were the eastern Luba with the term 'Hêmbá' itself probably meaning 'east' as in 'people of the east.' Writing before Edmond Verhulpen and César-Göehring, Pierre Colle, in 1913, made a distinction between Hêmbá groups, suggesting that there were Luba-Hêmbá groups but that there were 'pure' Hêmbá ones, as it were, too.[105]

Viewed from Colle's perspective, the Hêmbá may not have been simply a subset of the Luba after all, but instead a distinct group in their own right that simply took on certain symbolic aspects of Luba kingship as they encountered Luba conquerors, such as Bùki Kansimba. Put simply, the Luba-Hêmbá were constituted of those Hêmbá groups who submitted themselves to the Luba and have themselves articulated their desire to be considered as Luba in addition to Hêmbá.

The Luba-Hêmbá were mostly matrilineal but, in contrast, individual 'pure' Hêmbá groups practiced matrilineal descent while others practiced double unilineal descent. Even despite this distinction, there is still considerable ambiguity built into almost any definition of how a 'pure' Hêmbá person would have described their ethnicity in the late nineteenth century. Much of this confusion relates not only to the specifics of a lineage organization but also to whether or not someone actually wants to be referred to as a member of the Hêmbá ethnic constituency.

Like the material evidence, the documentary evidence that exists suggests that the Luba and Hêmbá became or always were very closely linked. Belgian officials working in Kongolo referred to some polities in Kongolo as being populated by Luba-Hêmbá and, at other times, those self-same polities were referred to as belonging purely to the Hêmbá. Many of those I spoke with in what are now considered the Hêmbá chieftainships *claim* Hêmbá identity but in fact practice customs François Nyet associated with Luba kingship, not least in having their own chapters of the *Bumbudyè* dance society.[106] Nonetheless, it is very hard to find documentary evidence suggesting that a widespread Hêmbá identity existed, at least as we now know it, before the onset of colonial rule. Rather than a word used by a group of people who migrated together, *en masse*, Hêmbá was a word outsiders used to describe a range of different migratory groups that they themselves adopted only later on.

All the evidence, material, oral and written, suggests that local identities were far more important when migrants, probably from Tanzania originally and thereafter the Kivus and Kabambare (or both at different migratory stages), began to establish communities in Kongolo. Gerard Jacques, a territorial official who worked in Kongolo in the period after the Second World War, believed that the Hêmbá came from a region called *Luamba ya Lulindi* near what is now the town of Kabambare.[107] Nonetheless, it was only as they encountered pre-existing communities in Kongolo and elsewhere that they began to be known by them as the 'peoples of the east' and adopted that name themselves. Some of these migrants took on aspects of the Luba culture, and so became known as Luba-Hêmbá, but others did not and so became known as 'pure' Hêmbá. Although I have drawn a fairly clear distinction between the Hêmbá and the Luba, it bears repeating that there were important cultural exchanges these peoples who claimed these identities in the nineteenth century.

The migration of the Hêmbá groups from their previous abodes in the east was not wholly due to transhumance, as previous generations of scholars believed.[108] Instead, the initial Hêmbá migrations were a series of expansionist projects, executed with warriors at the helm and taking several decades to complete. We do not know when exactly these migrations took place although they likely began after 1600.[109] One of the most populous clans that currently exist among the Bena Nyembo group, the Samba, trace their origins back to the seventeenth century and this might provide us with a useful historical yardstick.[110] However, we must be very careful about the Samba narrative that Nyet uses because, as he himself admitted, the testimony he used in this case was obtained amidst a vigorous dispute among the various Nyembo clans for power in the chieftainship. Nonetheless, if we do take the Samba testimony at face value, we can assume they had control of the peoples who called themselves the Nyembo in the eighteenth century and so their migrations must have occurred in around the seventeenth century. The group now known as the Hêmbá migrated out of a densely populated area in the northeast of the Congo to a comparably less populated one in Tanganyika to amass greater social and economic capital. As such, the anthropologist César-Göehring was correct to write that the term 'Hêmbá' was initially a way of saying 'the peoples of the east' and was used by the Luba to describe the migratory groups as they settled.

The Nyembo, or for that matter any political affiliation among the Hêmbá, corresponded to Jan Vansina's model of the district, in that a variety of clans formed crisscrossing bilateral allegiances with each other.[111] In the case of the Nyembo, the two major allies were the Samba, a matrilineal clan, and the Baga Mbele, a patrilineal one.[112] The fact that there were two major allied clans that constituted the Bena Nyembo, one of the most important Hêmbá *collectivities*, a colonial term for Jan Vansina's concept of the 'district,' was far from unusual. The Hêmbá have nearly always practiced double unilineal descent. This is to say that a Hêmbá could be a member of both a patrilineage, known as *kitofu*, and a matrilineage, known as a *kilongo*. A family or household chief ruled over both the kitofu and kilongo. A son transmitted his kitofu lineage to his descendants, just as a daughter transmitted her kilongo to hers.[113] The head of the kitofu branch would typically be the brother or eldest son of the lineage patriarch whereas in the case of the kilongo the brother or eldest son of the sister would become the head. The example of the Bena Nyembo, or 'people of' Nyembo, is perhaps the simplest, as there was only one major example of a kitofu and kilongo. In the case of a number of other Hêmbá groups, there were multiple examples of each.

Individual clan histories suggest that we should be doubly skeptical of the idea that an overarching Hêmbá identity took root as the migrations from the east took place and immediately afterwards. Likewise, the Hêmbá encounters with the Luba were probably more varied than either Pierre Colle or Edmond Verhulpen's models suggest, with different Hêmbá clan alliances forming links to Luba groups that exhibited varied extents of cohesion. But the narrative that stands out from the literature, as well as the oral and written evidence, is that the Hêmbá were *not* a subset of the Luba initially but only *became* so as a range of disparate migratory groups entered a series of Luba fiefdoms. Some Hêmbá clans and districts took on some of the rituals associated with Luba kingship to demonstrate their own political power but the degree of adoption, or 'Luba-ization,' varied widely. A member of the *Bazila Nioka* ('people of the star' in Hêmbá) clan, Mukamba Kizimba, suggested that it actually fought an unsuccessful war against Bùki Kansimba in the nineteenth century.[114] Conversely, the Bena Nyembo fought successfully against Bùki Kansimba's interventions. Bùki chose Kibamba Muyumba to be his proxy among the Bena Nyembo but the incumbent chief, Katete, eventually defeated him.[115]

As much as Hêmbá clans struggled to negotiate Bùki's incursions, like all groups in Kongolo in the late nineteenth century, they also had to deal with the Zanzibari ones too. However, the Hêmbá were among the last group of peoples in Kongolo to experience Zanzibari raids. As Thomas Reefe suggests, it was the Songye groups who initially experienced Zanzibari violence before they later spread to the Hêmbá polities in the east of Kongolo.[116] The Zanzibari incursions were mostly carried out by someone called Abedi, who was probably Abed ben Salum el-Khaduri and nicknamed 'Tanganyika.' He came from Nyangwe in around the 1860s and maintained connections with his fellow Zanzibari there until 1885, when 'he was forced to return to Zanzibar to settle accounts with his Indian creditors.'[117] From his base in Sola, Abedi tried to intervene in local succession disputes with varying degrees of success. Sola later became the headquarters of the chieftainship of Bena Nkuvu in eastern Kongolo in part as a result of Abedi's exploits.

While Abedi must have been somewhat successful in implanting Zanzibari culture among the Bena Nkuvu, the fact that he had to leave Sola by the mid-1880s must have compromised Zanzibari hegemony over the Hêmbá therein. Admittedly, Abedi caused a number of refugees to flee Sola and Kongolo at large. For example, a Hêmbá clan in what is now the Bayazi chieftainship known as the *Bazila Simba* ('those would not eat a lion') fled from the Swahili in the 1890s, and so ended up scattered across Kongolo as a whole with some even crossing the border into Maniema. But when I visited the Hêmbá chieftainship of Bena Nyembo in 2015, the peoples I spoke to recalled that their ancestors had actually defeated the Zanzibari in their attempts to conquer the area in the late nineteenth century.

Whether or not local legend in Bena Nyembo is historically accurate, what is clear is that the lineage mode of governance among the Hêmbá survived the Zanzibari raids. The existence of districts among the Hêmbá is a telling sign that the equatorial tradition that Jan Vansina described was not broken by the Zanzibari. It is likely, also, that the Zanzibari proxies or *sultanis* needed a long time to shore up their legitimacy given that the very word 'sultani' could have been a word used to mock those installed by Zanzibari slavers as much as one that denoted respect. All this is not to say that the impact of the Zanzibari era should be ignored, though. That Swahili was the language Catholic missionaries later chose to educate the Hêmbá in is a telling sign of Zanzibari power among this group(s). Likewise, the fact that few chiefs in eastern Kongolo can recall their families' history before the Zanzibaris arrived is another important indication of the impact they had on the area. Moreover, many Hêmbá were taken as slaves or fled during the Zanzibari era. But, rather than demolishing the equatorial tradition, Zanizbari slavers formed a cultural layer atop pre-existing lineage systems of governance rather than re-configuring them in full. Even the most autocratic sultani had to deal with councils of notables, as per Vansina's depiction of the tradition, much as they had to work with clans and districts—and colonial officials would try to co-opt exactly these institutions into their administrative nexus later on.

CONCLUSION

Of all the groups that converged on Kongolo in the nineteenth century, the Zanzibari were by far the most brutal, with their occupation easily the most traumatic for the autochthonous peoples concerned. The history of Zanzibari slavery and slaving in Kongolo, much as elsewhere in eastern Congo, would have a tremendous impact on the historical trajectory of the peoples there and not least on the Catholic missionaries who would work in the region during and after the Zanzibari occupation. The Church would define itself against much of the core tenants of the Zanzibaris not least their slaving, polygamy and Islamic leanings. And some of the first congregants of the Catholic out-stations would be ransomed slaves, for example. Through its emphasis on monogamous marriage, the Church would also attack polygamy later on. But the Zanzibari occupation would not just create the discursive space into which the Church could insert itself, it also created a vacuum of authority and legitimacy that the Church could fill at the expense of the local administration and its concept of chieftainship.

Aside from the Church, the uneven patterning and duration of Zanzibari occupation that resulted from outside connections and economic imperatives meant that when they arrived in Kongolo, Belgian administrators would not simply see a group of sultanis straightforwardly ruling centralized polities with varying degrees of control. Although they found a number of hierarchical arrangements in place, they encountered a range of different political institutions with considerable cultural cross-overs between them. Choosing which sets of elites to patronize and which to disinherit would therefore not be as easy as it might first appear. It may have seemed obvious to enfranchise the sultani given their pre-existing powers but they were by no means revered as legitimate potentates as the following chapters will go on to demonstrate. Many Belgian officials would eventually come to know the complexities of the histories of the polities they sought to co-opt but they would still try, often in vein, to re-imagine them. They wanted to expunge the important elements of contest and negotiation that emanated in turn, first, from the violent way in which the sultanis gained power and, secondly, from the gaps in the Zanzibari conquest and the pre-existing cultures that therefore remained. As a result, the Belgian idea of chieftainship as centring on a collection of big men was unworkable in several cases. The Church, therefore, could later insert itself into the vacuum of political authority that became the lived reality of what chieftainship meant for many Congolese people in Kongolo during the early twentieth century.

Notes

1. Académie Royale des Sciences d'Outre-Mer, *Livre Blanc: Apport Scientifique de la Belgique au Développement de l'Afrique Centrale, Volume 3* (Bruxelles: Académie Royale des Sciences d'Outre-Mer, 1963), p. 1010; Smith Hempstone, *Rebels, Mercenaries, and Dividends: The Katanga Story* (New York: Praeger, 1962), p. 32.

2. Jan Vansina, *Paths in the Rainforests: Toward a History of Political Tradition in Equatorial Africa* (Madison: Wisconsin University Press, 1990), p. 83.
3. Anatoly M. Khazanov and Gunther Schlee (eds), *Who Owns the Stock? Collective and Multiple Property Rights in Animals* (New York: Berghahn Books, 2012).
4. Vansina, *Paths in the Rainforests*.
5. Ibid., p. 240.
6. Ibid., pp. 74–77.
7. Ibid., p. 75.
8. Ibid.
9. Ibid.
10. Jan Vansina, 'Population Movements and Emergence of New Socio-Political Forms in Africa,' in B. A. Ogot (ed.), *General History of Africa, Volume 5: Africa from the Sixteenth to the Eighteenth Century* (London: Heinemann, 1992), p. 50.
11. Vansina, *Paths in the Rainforests*, p. 81.
12. John Iliffe, *Honour in African History* (Cambridge: Cambridge University Press, 2005), p. 67.
13. Vansina, *Paths in the Rainforests*, p. 81.
14. Ibid., p. 82.
15. Ibid.
16. Richard J. Reid, *Warfare in African History* (Cambridge: Cambridge University Press, 2012), p. 41.
17. Jane I. Guyer, 'Traditions of Invention in Equatorial Africa,' *African Studies Review*, 39, 3 (1996), pp. 1–28.
18. Isidore Ndaywel è Nziem, *Histoire Général du Congo: De l'Héritage Ancien á la République Démocratique* (Préface de Théophile Obenga, Postface de Pierre Salmon) (Bruxelles: De Boeck & Larcier, 1998), p. 64.
19. Vansina, *Paths in the Rainforests*; Pierre de Maret, 'The Power of Symbols and the Symbols of Power through Time: Probing the Luba Past,' in Susan Keech McIntosh (ed.), *Beyond Chiefdoms: Pathways to Complexity in Africa* (Cambridge, 2005), p. 161; Edmond Verhulpen, *Baluba et Balubaïses du Katanga* (Anvers: L'Avenir Belge, 1936).
20. Pierre de Maret, 'The Power of Symbols and the Symbols of Power Through Time: Probing the Luba Past,' in Susan Keech McIntosh (ed.), *Beyond Chiefdoms: Pathways to Complexity in Africa* (Cambridge, 2005), p. 161; Mary Nooter Roberts and Allen F. Roberts, *Memory: Luba Art and the Making of History* (Washington, DC: National Museum of Art (US), 1996), p. 50.
21. Ann Wilson, 'Long Distance Trade and the Luba Lomami Empire,' *The Journal of African History*, 13, 4 (1972), pp. 575–589.
22. I am grateful to Dunja Hersak for this insight.

23. Mary Nooter Roberts and Allen F. Roberts, 'Memory: Luba Art and the Making of History,' *African Arts*, 29, 1 (1996), pp. 25–26.

24. Jan Vansina, *Kingdoms of the Savannah* (Madison: University of Wisconsin Press, 1966), p. 72; Sean Stilwell, *Slavery and Slaving in African History* (Cambridge: Cambridge University Press, 2015), p. 159.

25. E. Van Avermaet en Collaboration avec Benoît Mbuyà, *Dictionnaire Kiluba-Français* (Tervuren: Annales du Musée Royal du Congo Belge, Sciences de l'Homme Linguistique, Volume 7), p. 360.

26. Vansina, *Kingdoms of the Savannah*, p. 73. At times, Belgian colonial administrators in the twentieth century referred to the kilo-lo as *bilolo* and this term is still occasionally used in the relevant anthropological and historical literature, one example comes from: Archives Africaines, Ministère des Affairs Étrangèrs, Bruxelles (AAB), Affairs Indigène et du Main-D'œuvre (AIMO), Rapport sur l'Administration Général (RAG), Seconde Trimestre, (1920), p. 9. 'Bilolo' are not to be confused with the *bulolo*, which was a term for dignitary in Kiluba, see: E. Van Avermaet et Benoît Mbuyà, *Dictionnaire Kiluba-Français*, p. 360.

27. Vansina, *Kingdoms of the Savannah*, p. 73.

28. E. Van Avermaet et Benoît Mbuyà, *Dictionnaire Kiluba-Français*, p. 368.

29. Vansina, *Kingdoms of the Savannah*, p. 74.

30. Alisa LaGamma, *Genesis: Ideas of Origin in African Sculpture* (New York: Metropolitan Museum of Art, 2002), p. 43.

31. Luc de Heusch, *The Drunken King or the Origin of the State, Translated and Annotated by Roy Willis* (Bloomington: Indiana University Press, 1982).

32. Thomas Q. Reefe, *The Rainbow and the Kings: A History of the Luba Empire to 1891* (Berkeley: University of California Press, 1981), pp. 52–53. Thomas Reefe's model of a centralized Luba empire has been echoed in later works, such as Stilwell, *Slavery and Slaving in African History*, p. 159. The argument that the myth has been used too uncritically has been made by David Gordon, see: David M. Gordon, '(Dis)Embodying Sovereignty: Divine Kingship in Central African Historiography,' *The Journal of African History*, 57, 1 (2016), p. 60.

33. de Maret, 'The Power of Symbols and the Symbols of Power Through Time,' p. 161. Mary Nooter Roberts and Allen Roberts have even recently written that it is: 'no longer fully possible to recover a positivists 'true' picture of the Luba past,' see: Roberts and Roberts, 'Memory: Luba Art and the Making of History,' p. 26.

34. Ann Wilson cites these references: David Livingstone, *The Last Journals of David Livingstone, Volume 1* (London: John Murray, 1874); Verney Lovett Cameron, *Across Africa, Volume 2* (London: Harper & Brothers,

1873), see: Ann Wilson, 'Long Distance Trade and the Luba Lomami Empire,' p. 577.

35. Gordon, '(Dis)Embodying Sovereignty,' p. 60.

36. Reefe, *The Rainbow and the Kings.*

37. Those wishing for a more detailed rendering of the Luba genesis myth can approach a wide range of texts that have recorded it in detail, including: Reefe, *The Rainbow and the Kings*, pp. 23–40; de Heusch, *The Drunken King.*

38. Karin Barber, *The Anthropology of Texts, Persons and Publics* (Cambridge: Cambridge University Press, 2007), p. 48.

39. Vansina, *Kingdoms of the Savanna*, p. 71; Igor Kopytoff, 'Introduction,' in Igor Kopytoff (ed.), *The African Frontier: The Reproduction of Traditional African Societies* (Bloomington: Indiana University Press, 1987), pp. 3–84.

40. I take the expression 'conquest by invitation' from Cherry Leonardi, see Cherry Leonardi, *Dealing with Government in South Sudan: Histories of Chiefship, Community and the State* (Oxford: Boydell and Brewer, 2013), p. 7.

41. Vansina, *Kingdoms of the Savanna*, p. 71.

42. Reefe, *Rainbow and the Kings*, p. 81.

43. Vansina, *Kingdoms of the Savanna*, p. 71.

44. de Heusch, *The Drunken King*, pp. 8–33.

45. Vansina, *Kingdoms of the Savanna*, p. 71.

46. Ibid., p. 72.

47. Edmond Verhulpen, *Baluba et Balubaïses du Katanga* (Anvers: L'Avenir Belge, 1936).

48. Vansina, *Kingdoms of the Savanna*, p. 72.

49. Ibid.

50. Roberts and Roberts, *Memory: Luba Art and the Making of History*, p. 180; E. Van Avermaet et Benoît Mbuyà, *Dictionnaire Kiluba-Français*, pp. 70–71.

51. Jan Vansina quoted in Pierre de Marat, 'The Power of Symbols and the Symbols of Power Through Time: Probing the Luba Past,' in Susan Keech McIntosh (ed.), *Beyond Chieftdoms: Pathways to Complexity in Africa* (Cambridge: Cambridge University Press, 1999), p. 161.

52. Roberts and Roberts, 'Memory: Luba Art and the Making of History,' p. 25. Isadore Ndaywel è Nziem, 'The Political System of the Luba and Lunda: Its Emergence and Expansion,' in B. A. Ogot (ed.), *General History of Africa, Volume V: Africa from the Sixteenth to the Eighteenth Century* (London: Heinemann, 1992), p. 593.

53. Roberts and Roberts, 'Memory: Luba Art and the Making of History,' p. 57.

54. Gordon, '(Dis)Embodying Sovereignty,' p. 60.

55. Newell S. Booth Jr., 'Time and African Beliefs Revisited,' in Jacob K. Olupona and Sulayman S. Nyang (eds), *Religious Plurality in Africa: Essays in Honour of John S. Mbiti* (New York: Mouton de Gruyter, 1993), p. 88.
56. Wilson, 'Long Distance Trade and the Luba Lomami Empire,' p. 577.
57. Ibid.
58. Ibid. Not all scholars agree on the dates of Ngombe's reign, with some putting them earlier, 1795–1805, but Wilson's tally with other documents pertaining to the history of Kongolo so I have adopted hers.
59. Verhulpen, *Baluba et Balubaïsés du Katanga*, pp. 127, 350 as cited in Reefe, *The Rainbow and the Kings*, p. 230; E. Van Avermaet et Benoît Mbuyà, *Dictionnaire Kiluba-Français*, p. 89. The information about Verhulpen was from Reefe, *The Rainbow and the Kings*, p. 15.
60. Reefe, *The Rainbow and the Kings*, p. 127; Jean-Luc Vellut, 'The Congo Basin and Angola,' in J. F. Ade Ajayi (ed.), *General History of Africa, Volume 6: Africa in the Nineteenth-Century Until the 1880s* (London: Heinemann, 1989), p. 321.
61. Reefe, *The Rainbow and the Kings*, p. 131.
62. Alan P. Merriam suggests that there have been a number of different ways of spelling the Songye, including Basonge, Ba-Songwe, Bassonie and Bassongo, see: Alan P. Merriam, *An African World: The Basongye Village of Lupupa Ngye* (Bloomington: Indiana University Press, 1974), p. xi. However, this book will use the form that is most prevalent in the recent literature, 'Songye' for the sake of convenience.
63. Thomas Turner, '"Batetela," "Baluba," "Basongye": Ethnogenesis in Zaire' ("Batetela," "Baluba," "Basongye": l'ethnogenèse au Zaïre). *Cahiers d'Études Africaines* 33 (1993), p. 587.
64. Turner, '"Batetela," "Baluba," "Basongye",' p. 607.
65. Ibid.
66. Dunja Hersak, 'On the Concept of Prototype in Songye Masquarades,' *African Art*, 45, 2 (2012), p. 12.
67. Hersak, 'On the Concept of Prototype in Songye Masquarades,' p. 12; Turner, '"Batetela," "Baluba," "Basongye",' p. 606.
68. Merriam, *An African World*, p. 4.
69. Nyet, *The Formidable Statuary of Central Africa*, p. 21.
70. Ibid.
71. David P. Henige, 'Oral Tradition and Chronology,' *The Journal of African History*, 12, 3 (1971), p. 384; Hersak, 'On the Concept of Prototype in Songye Masquarades,' p. 13.
72. Douglas Johnson, 'Criminal Secrecy: The Case of the Zande "Secret Societies",' *Past and Present*, 130 (1991), pp. 170–200.
73. Vansina, *Paths in the Rainforests*, p. 130.

74. Merriam, *An African World*, p. xvii.
75. Reefe, *The Rainbow and the Kings*, p. 131.
76. Luc De Heusch, 'What Shall We Do with the Drunken King?' *Africa: Journal of the International African Institute*, 45 (1975), pp. 363–372.
77. Reefe, *The Rainbow and the Kings*, p. 132. I went to this island in 2015 as part of my fieldwork and found out that it is worshipped by other ethnic groups in Kongolo also.
78. Pierre Gossiaux, 'Les Maîtres de Buli: Esthétique et Ethno-Histoire (Avec Deux Inédits),' *Art et Exotisme*, 7 (1990), pp. 38–49.
79. Reefe, *The Rainbow and the Kings*, p. 145. Jan Vansina disagrees with this 1870 figure and suggests 1850 instead, see: Vansina, *Kingdoms of the Savannah* (Madison: University of Wisconsin Press, 1966), p. 157. Ilunga Kabale is also known as Ilunga Kalala by some scholars, see: Wilson, 'Long Distance Trade and the Luba Lomami Empire,' p. 577.
80. Many ethnic groups in the pre-colonial Congo had dynastic titles, see: Allen F. Roberts, *A Dance of Assassins: Performing Early Colonial Hegemony in the Congo* (Bloomington: Indiana University Press, 2013), p. 202.
81. Interview with Alexandre Bùki, Kongolo town centre, June 2015.
82. Vansina, *Kingdoms of the Savanna*, p. 235.
83. David Northrup, 'Slavery and Forced Labour in the Eastern Congo, 1850–1910,' in Henri Médard and Shane Doyle (eds), *Slavery in the Great Lakes Region of East Africa* (Oxford: James Currey, 2007), p. 111.
84. The Swahili caravans have featured in a number of works on east Africa, notably: Steven M. Feierman, *Peasant Intellectuals: Anthropology and History in Tanzania* (Madison: University of Wisconsin Press, 1990), p. 113; Jonathan Glassman, *Feasts and Riot: Revelry and Rebellion on the Swahili Coast, 1856–1888* (Oxford: James Curry, 1995).
85. Melvin E. Page, 'The Manyema Hordes of Tippu Tip: A Case Study in Social Stratification and the Slave Trade in Eastern Africa,' *International Journal of African Historical Studies*, 7, 1 (1974), p. 71.
86. See Jan-Georg Deutsch, *Emancipation Without Abolition in German East Africa, c.1884–1914* (Oxford: James Currey, 2006), p. 21.
87. Vansina, *Kingdoms of the Savanna*, pp. 235–236.
88. Ibid., p. 236.
89. Ibid.
90. Tippu Tip made himself chief based on a fictive kinship tie with one of Kasongo Lushi's sisters, Lushi being a Luba headman during the reign of either Kumwimbe Ngombe or Ilunga Kabale, see: Reefe, *Rainbow and the Kings*, p. 166.
91. Tippu Tip (Translated by W. H. Whiteley), *Maisha ya Hammed bin Muhammed el Murjebi yaani Tippu Tip kwa Maneno yake Mwenyewe*, Supplement to the East African Swahili Committee Journals, 28, 2 (1958), p. 77.

92. Reefe, *Rainbow and the Kings*, p. 180; Vansina, *Kingdoms of the Savanna*, p. 238.
93. Vansina, *Paths in the Rainforests*, pp. 240–242.
94. Centre de Recherche et du Documentation sur l'Afrique Centrale, Lubumbashi (CERDAC), Bena Lubunda, Chefferie Indigènes, Sans Numéro, Territoire de Kongolo, P. V. Numéro 70, 'Histoire et Origine des Bena Kayaye: Eléments recueillis aux Réunions des 10–11–13, 14–15–16, juillet 1931 du Grand Conseil des Notables des Basonge de Bena Kayaye,' p. 6.
95. John Lonsdale, 'Agency in Tight Corners: Narrative and Initiative in African History,' *Journal of African Cultural Studies*, 13, 1 (2000), pp. 5–16.
96. Reefe, *Rainbow and the Kings*, p. 168.
97. See for example MacGregor Laird, 'Remedies for the Slave Trade,' *Wilson Anti-Slavery Collection*, p. 1842.
98. Reefe, *Rainbow and the Kings*, p. 168.
99. François Nyet, *La Grande Statuaire Hemba du Zaïre* (Louvain-La-Neuve: Institut Supérieur d'Archéoligie et d'Histoire de l'Art, 1977), p. 18.
100. Pamela Blakely and Thomas Blakely, 'Ancestors, "Witchcraft," & Foregrounding the Poetic: Men's Oratory & Women's Song-Dance in Hêmbá Funerary Performance,' in Thomas Blakely, Walter Van Beek, and Dennis Thomson (eds), *Religion in Africa: Experience & Expression* (London: James Currey, 1994).
101. Nyet, *La Grande Statuaire Hemba du Zaïre*, p. 18.
102. Verhulpen, *Baluba et Balubaïsés du Katanga*.
103. Donatien Dibwe Dia Mwembu, 'L'Epuration Ethnique au Katanga et L'Ethique du Redressement des Torts du Passé,' *Canadian Journal of African Studies/Revue Canadienne des Etudes Africaines*, 33, 2/3 (1999), p. 488.
104. Verhulpen, *Baluba et Balubaïsés du Katanga*.
105. Pierre Colle (avec une Préface de Cyrille van Overbergh), *Les Baluba* (Bruxelles: Institut International de Bibliographie, 1913), p. 3.
106. E. Van Avermaet et Benoît Mbuyà, *Dictionnaire Kiluba-Français*, p. 86.
107. Gérard Jacques, *Lualaba: Histoires de l'Afrique Profonde* (Paris: Racine, 1995), p. 64.
108. Nyet, *La Grande Statuaire Hemba du Zaïre*, p. 18.
109. Tshilemalema Mukenge, *Customs and Culture of the Congo* (Washington, DC: Greenwood Publishing Group, 2002), p. 16.
110. Nyet, *La Grande Statuaire Hemba du Zaïre*, p. 26. Unfortunately, the meaning of the proper noun 'Nyembo' has now been lost, see: E. Van Avermaet et Benoît Mbuyà, *Dictionnaire Kiluba-Français*, p. 129.

111. Vansina, *Paths in the Rainforests*, p. 81.
112. Nyet, *La Grande Statuaire Hemba du Zaïre*, p. 26.
113. Ibid., p. 25.
114. Ibid., p. 30.
115. Ibid., p. 26.
116. Reefe, *Rainbow and the Kings*, p. 168.
117. Ibid.

BIBLIOGRAPHY

Académie Royale des Sciences d'Outre-Mer, *Livre Blanc: Apport Scientifique de la Belgique au Développement de l'Afrique Centrale, Volume 3* (Bruxelles: Académie Royale des Sciences d'Outre-Mer, 1963).

Avermaet, E. Van, en Collaboration avec Mbuyà, Benoît, *Dictionnaire Kiluba-Français* (Tervuren: Annales du Musée Royal du Congo Belge, Sciences de l'Homme Linguistique, Volume 7).

Barber, Karin, *The Anthropology of Texts, Persons and Publics* (Cambridge: Cambridge University Press, 2007).

Blakely, Pamela, and Blakely, Thomas, 'Ancestors, "Witchcraft," & Foregrounding the Poetic: Men's Oratory & Women's Song-Dance in Hêmbá Funerary Performance,' in Thomas Blakely, Walter Van Beek and Dennis Thomson (eds), *Religion in Africa: Experience & Expression* (London: James Currey, 1994), pp. 399–442.

Booth Jr., Newell S., 'Time and African Beliefs Revisited,' in Jacob K. Olupona and Sulayman S. Nyang (eds), *Religious Plurality in Africa: Essays in Honour of John S. Mbiti* (New York: Mouton de Gruyter, 1993), pp. 83–94.

Cameron, Verney Lovett, *Across Africa, Volume 2* (London: Harper & Brothers, 1873).

Colle, Pierre, (avec une Préface de Cyrille van Overbergh), *Les Baluba* (Bruxelles: Institut International de Bibliographie, 1913).

Deutsch, Jan-Georg, *Emancipation Without Abolition in German East Africa, c.1884–1914* (Oxford: James Currey, 2006).

Feierman, Steven M., *Peasant Intellectuals: Anthropology and History in Tanzania* (Madison: University of Wisconsin Press, 1990).

Glassman, Jonathon, *Feasts and Riot: Revelry and Rebellion on the Swahili Coast, 1856–1888* (Oxford: James Curry, 1995).

Gordon, David M., '(Dis)Embodying Sovereignty: Divine Kingship in Central African Historiography,' *The Journal of African History*, 57, 1 (2016), pp. 47–67.

Gossiaux, Pierre, 'Les Maîtres de Buli: Esthétique et Ethno-Histoire (Avec Deux Inédits),' *Art et Exotisme*, 7 (1990), pp. 38–49.

Guyer, Jane I., 'Traditions of Invention in Equatorial Africa,' *African Studies Review*, 39, 3 (1996), pp. 1–28.

Hempstone, Smith, *Rebels, Mercenaries, and Dividends: The Katanga Story* (New York: Praeger, 1962).

Henige, David P., 'Oral Tradition and Chronology,' *The Journal of African History*, 12, 3 (1971), pp. 371–389.

Hersak, Dunja, 'On the Concept of Prototype in Songye Masquarades,' *African Art*, 45, 2 (2012), pp. 12–23.

Heusch, Luc de, 'What Shall We Do with the Drunken King?' *Africa: Journal of the International African Institute*, 45 (1975), pp. 363–372.

Heusch, Luc de, *The Drunken King or the Origin of the State, Translated and Annotated by Roy Willis* (Bloomington: Indiana University Press, 1982).

Iliffe, John, *Honour in African History* (Cambridge: Cambridge University Press, 2005).

Jacques, Gérard, *Lualaba: Histoires de l'Afrique Profonde* (Paris: Racine, 1995).

Johnson, Douglas, 'Criminal Secrecy: The Case of the Zande "Secret Societies",' *Past and Present*, 130 (1991), pp. 170–200.

Khazanov, Anatoly M., and Schlee, Gunther (eds), *Who Owns the Stock? Collective and Multiple Property Rights in Animals* (New York: Berghahn Books, 2012).

Kopytoff, Igor, 'Introduction,' in Igor Kopytoff (ed.), *The African Frontier: The Reproduction of Traditional African Societies* (Bloomington: Indiana University Press, 1987), pp. 3–84.

LaGamma, Alisa, *Genesis: Ideas of Origin in African Sculpture* (New York: Metropolitan Museum of Art, 2002).

Laird, MacGregor, 'Remedies for the Slave Trade,' *Wilson Anti-Slavery Collection*, 1842.

Leonardi, Cherry, *Dealing with Government in South Sudan: Histories of Chiefship, Community and the State* (Oxford: Boydell and Brewer, 2013).

Livingstone, David, *The Last Journals of David Livingstone, Volume 1* (London: John Murray, 1874).

Lonsdale, John, 'Agency in Tight Corners: Narrative and Initiative in African History,' *Journal of African Cultural Studies*, 13, 1 (2000), pp. 5–16.

Maret, Pierre de, 'The Power of Symbols and the Symbols of Power Through Time: Probing the Luba Past,' in Susan McIntosh, Keech (ed.), *Beyond Chiefdoms: Pathways to Complexity in Africa* (Cambridge: Cambridge University Press, 2005), pp. 151–165.

Merriam, Alan P., *An African World: The Basongye Village of Lupupa Ngye* (Bloomington: Indiana University Press, 1974).

Mukenge, Tshilemalema, *Customs and Culture of the Congo* (Washington, DC: Greenwood Publishing Group, 2002).

Mwembu, Donatien Dibwe Dia, 'L'Epuration Ethnique au Katanga et L'Ethique du Redressement des Torts du Passé,' *Canadian Journal of African Studies/Revue Canadienne des Etudes Africaines*, 33, 2/3 (1999), pp. 483–499.

Ndaywel è Nziem, Isidore, 'The Political System of the Luba and Lunda: Its Emergence and Expansion,' in B. A. Ogot (ed.), *General History of Africa, Volume V: Africa from the Sixteenth to the Eighteenth Century* (London: Heinemann, 1992), pp. 588–607.

Ndaywel è Nziem, Isidore, *Histoire Général du Congo: De l'Héritage Ancien á la République Démocratique* (Préface de Obenga, Théophile, Postface de Pierre Salmon) (Bruxelles: De Boeck & Larcier, 1998).

Northrup, David, 'Slavery and Forced Labour in the Eastern Congo, 1850–1910,' in Henri Médard and Shane Doyle (eds), *Slavery in the Great Lakes Region of East Africa* (Oxford: James Currey, 2007), pp. 111–123.

Nyet, François, *La Grande Statuaire Hemba du Zaïre* (Louvain-La-Neuve: Institut Supérieur d'Archéoligie et d'Histoire de l'Art, 1977).

Page, Melvin E., 'The Manyema Hordes of Tippu Tip: A Case Study in Social Stratification and the Slave Trade in Eastern Africa,' *International Journal of African Historical Studies*, 7, 1 (1974), pp. 69–84.

Reefe, Thomas Q., *The Rainbow and the Kings: A History of the Luba Empire to 1891* (Berkeley: University of California Press, 1981).

Reid, Richard J., *Warfare in African History* (Cambridge: Cambridge University Press, 2012).

Roberts, Allen F., *A Dance of Assassins: Performing Early Colonial Hegemony in the Congo* (Bloomington: Indiana University Press, 2013).

Roberts, Mary Nooter, and Roberts, Allen F., *Memory: Luba Art and the Making of History* (Washington, DC: National Museum of Art (US), 1996).

Stilwell, Sean, *Slavery and Slaving in African History* (Cambridge: Cambridge University Press, 2015).

Tip, Tippu (Translated by W. H. Whiteley), *Maisha ya Hammed bin Muhammed el Murjebi yaani Tippu Tip kwa Maneno yake Mwenyewe*, Supplement to the East African Swahili Committee Journals, 28, 2 (1958).

Turner, Thomas, '"Batetela," "Baluba," "Basongye": Ethnogenesis in Zaire' ("Batetela," "Baluba," "Basongye": l'ethnogenèse au Zaïre). *Cahiers d'Études Africaines* 33 (1993), pp. 587–612.

Vansina, Jan, *Kingdoms of the Savannah* (Madison: University of Wisconsin Press, 1966).

Vansina, Jan, *Paths in the Rainforests: Toward a History of Political Tradition in Equatorial Africa* (Madison: Wisconsin University Press, 1990).

Vansina, Jan, 'Population Movements and Emergence of New Socio-Political Forms in Africa,' in B. A. Ogot (ed.), *General History of Africa, Volume 5: Africa from the Sixteenth to the Eighteenth Century* (London: Heinemann, 1992), pp. 25–38.

Verhulpen, Edmond, *Baluba et Balubaïses du Katanga* (Anvers: L'Avenir Belge, 1936).

Vellut, Jean-Luc, 'The Congo Basin and Angola,' in J. F. Ade Ajayi (ed.), *General History of Africa, Volume 6: Africa in the Nineteenth-Century Until the 1880s* (London: Heinemann, 1989), pp. 112–128.

Wilson, Ann, 'Long Distance Trade and the Luba Lomami Empire,' *The Journal of African History*, 13, 4 (1972), pp. 575–589.

CHAPTER 3

The Halting Development of Catholic Power in Kongolo, 1891–1917

A cette époque, l'occupation du pays n'était guère que nominal.
Victor Roelens, *Notre Vieux Congo* (1917)[1]

The turn of the century saw the consolidation of Belgian colonial rule over much of central Africa. Historians have sometimes associated turn-of-the-century Western imperialism in general with significant changes in the history of the African hinterland and this assumption both has influenced and been influenced by much of the recent historiography of the Congo.[2] The early manifestation of Belgian rule in Central Africa, the Congo Free State (CFS), for example, became so (in)famous for the atrocities it perpetuated that King Leopold II, the Belgian monarch, was forced to transfer what was effectively his own fiefdom to his parliament, meaning that the CFS would become known as the Belgian Congo by 1908. Yet, this chapter departs from other studies of Belgian rule by not making the 'red rubber' atrocities central to its story.[3] Despite its fecundity, Kongolo was peripheral to the political economy of the CFS and, initially at least, to its erstwhile successor, the Belgian Congo.

The original version of the book was revised: Belated corrections have been incorporated. The correction to the book is available at https://doi.org/10.1007/978-3-030-17380-7_9

© The Author(s) 2019
R. A. Loffman, *Church, State and Colonialism in Southeastern Congo, 1890–1962*, Cambridge Imperial and Post-Colonial Studies Series, https://doi.org/10.1007/978-3-030-17380-7_3

Belgian colonial and concession infrastructure did not extend much further into Kongolo's hinterland than its modest railway junction, which the Great Lakes Rail Company (CFL) finally completed in 1909. Victor Roelens put it best when he suggested that the colonial occupation of the region was 'little more than nominal.'[4] Instead of through Belgian territorial agents, Africans living in Kongolo experienced European occupation chiefly through a network of Catholic out-stations. Unlike many other territories in Katanga, Kongolo provided the institutional space for the Church to expand its network of out-stations. This chapter explains how the Church gained a powerful yet uneven presence in the Kongolo, first, by exploring the origins of the Catholic 'republic' inasmuch as it manifested itself in Kongolo, afterwards, by charting the slow and uneven expansion of the Belgian administration in the territory.

THE WHITE FATHERS' UNSTABLE FOOTHOLD IN SOLA

The idea of a hierarchical, state-like and almost militant European-run Catholicism developing in Central Africa might strike a contemporary reader as being rather anomalous given that most missionaries arrived in Africa without such a presence in the first instance.[5] A large part of the reason why the Church developed in the way it did in southeastern Congo is to be found in its origins in the region, which were deeply rooted in the colonial conquests undertaken at the end of the nineteenth century. The Church both shaped and was shaped by a number of prevailing militaristic currents, not least the hostility of Zanzibari slave raiders together with the ongoing colonial violence triggered by the emergence of the Free State. The Church dealt with this endemic violence, as well as the environmental hazards such as Sleeping Sickness, by adopting an authoritarian and militaristic character in the first decades of its time in Tanganyika. Where it could, it engaged in the process of forming its own state-like infrastructure. And, where it could not, it played on its connections to powerful statesmen such as Leopold II of Belgium. Yet as much as Roelens, in particular, has been identified as a particularly influential missionary, his and his missionaries' comportment was not entirely unique. Rather, the state-like and militant character of the Church in the early twentieth century was broadly in keeping with the rule rather than being the exception to it during the period of Catholic penetration of the eastern savannah. And so Roelens' approach to his work was very much in line with that of his peers rather than anything out of the ordinary.

Roelens' approach to the mission encounter was heavily influenced by that of his mission Society, the White Fathers, even if he, in the historian David Gordon's words, 'toned down some of [their] culturally relativistic doctrines.'[6] He was one of the first White Fathers to go to the Congo when he went in 1891 given that their involvement in Africa began not in Central Africa but in North Africa. The White Fathers were established in Algiers in 1867 by Charles Martial Lavigerie, who was later elevated to the position of cardinal in 1882, and Roelens would sometimes be called the 'Flemish Lavigerie' both after the Cardinal and his own authoritarian attitude.[7] Lavigerie had wanted to convert Muslims living in the Maghreb but his Society had little success in this endeavour and so he soon turned his attention to the south of the continent.[8] One of the only lasting reminders of the White Fathers' encounters in North Africa were the distinctive white cassocks they wore so as to fit into their surroundings after which they were named.[9] They retained these robes even as many left the Maghreb and soon became noted for them hence their appellation. Despite the magnificence of their headquarters in Algeria, and latterly in Rome, the White Fathers rarely lived in such splendour in their respective mission fields. Much like the Spiritans, who we will meet later on, Lavigerie wanted his missionaries to live on the lands upon which they constructed their missions.[10] This reliance on the land and the societies they encountered, alongside their own professional curiosity, meant that many White Fathers became ethnographers in their own right and published in a range of in-house journals.[11]

Lavigerie insisted that his missionaries engage in the serious study of local languages. After only six months in the mission field, a White Father was theoretically forbidden to communicate in any other language around the out-station.[12] Roelens echoed Lavigerie's stress on learning local languages. Jean Vandermeiren, who would go on to play an important part in the White Fathers' work in Kongolo, produced a French-Kiluba-Hêmbá dictionary in 1913, for example.[13] Although Lavigerie's 'gradualist' model of conversion had failed in North Africa, one which allowed for his missionaries to work with local traditions rather than seeking to eviscerate them, he demonstrably clung to it in the Congolese context. Rather than trying to work against local traditions, therefore, Lavigerie refused to buy into the imperial 'civilizing mission.'[14] However, as the historian Viera Pawlivoka-Vilhanova reminds us, 'no compromise would be tolerated as far as Christian conversion was concerned.'[15] Indeed, Lavigerie envisaged a Christian kingdom, one even recognized as a state by what might today be termed 'the international community,' which would consist entirely of subjects who would know only a pristine Catholic culture. Such a culture would be unpolluted by the temptations of waged labour and the currents of Marxist thought that Lavigerie and Roelens associated with an industrializing Europe.[16] Moreover, occasionally the insistence on a pure Christian polity led Roelens and his followers in Kongolo, such as Auguste Van Acker, into conflict with local expressive cultures. As Gordon, following Valentine Mudimbe, has suggested, therefore, Roelens was 'a paradigm of colonizing Christianity.'[17]

Life was tough for many of the first White Fathers in East and Central Africa and many did not survive for long in the eastern savannah in the pursuit of Lavigerie's and later Roelens' theocracy. Given the arduous nature of the journey from North to East Africa, the White Fathers made considerable progress in their early years. The first contingent of White Fathers charged with realizing Lavigerie's 'kingdom' left Marseilles for Africa on 22 April 1878 and had already reached the Tanzanian port of Ujiji by 22 January 1879.[18] Initially, Lavigerie wanted these missionaries to identify an African head of his Christian 'kingdom' and, in July, it looked like they were close when they approached King Rumoke of Burundi who had offered them sanctuary and authorized the opening of a mission.[19] However, Rumoke was not prepared to be the African king Lavigerie had hoped for given it would involve his leaving his home. Given that no African monarch would protect his missionaries, Lavigerie asked the Knights of Malta to help but they also refused. So, the Cardinal turned to Leopold-Louis Joubert, a former Papal Zouave, to realize his plans. Together with Joubert, the first White Fathers opened an out-station on the shores of Lake Tanganyika on 25 November.[20]

With Joubert leading the militaristic side of the early mission encounter, Lavigerie nominated Roelens, born in Ardooie, Flanders, to act in his stead in 1892. Given that Leopold II feared the encroachment of non-Belgian missionaries, as he suspected that they could be a fifth column for his imperial rivals, Lavigerie made an inspired choice in appointing Roelens.[21] By 1893, Roelens had already established a mission in Baudouinville.[22] And Lavigerie eventually made him the Titular Vicar of Girba and Vicar Apostolic of Upper Katanga in 1895.[23] Lavigerie's nomination and later promotion of Roelens as leader of the White Fathers in southeastern Congo meant that, unlike their Spiritan counterparts, the Society never had to leave the Congo Free State. Rather than being exiled, Leopold II granted the White Fathers giant swathes of land in the Congo that became the Vicariate of Upper Congo (*Haut Congo*).

Fig. 3.1 Victor Roelens (centre left), Auguste-Léopold Huys (centre right) and Stefano Kaoze (centre, second row) in 1931 (Royal Museum of Central Africa, AP.0.2.10246, Photo 1)

It cannot be an accident, either, that many of those appointed to work with Roelens in the twentieth century, such as Auguste Van Acker and Joseph Vandermeiren, were also from Flanders.[24] Moreover, Roelens' coadjutor, Auguste-Léopold Huys, was also from there too (see Fig. 3.1).

As Bambi Ceuppens suggests, many of the Catholic missionaries working the Congo as a whole were from West Flanders with Roelens being an interesting exception having been born in Ardooie in East Flanders.[25] Flemish staff were near indispensable in reassuring Leopold II that there would be as little Francophone presence as possible in the White Fathers' vicariates in eastern Congo.

Lavigerie's close relationship with Leopold II had many positive outcomes in the short term. First, it meant that he was eventually granted the rights to Emile Storms' bases, particularly that in Baudouinville (now Kirungu) on Lake Tanganyika, as a nucleus from which he could set about building his Christian 'kingdom.'[26] Storms was apoplectic at having to cede these bases but there was little he could do in the face of monarchial pressure. What is more, these two stations would be joined by another three that were founded by Isaac Moinet in 1885 with the missionary seeing himself very much as the 'Acting King of Mpala.'[27] At the end of 1886, 'the area to the West of Lake Tanganyika was established for [the White Fathers] as the Apostolic Vicarage of Upper Congo.'[28] And Roelens ruled a triangle of land between the towns of Baudouinville, Mapala and Lusaka with precious little reference to King Leopold's Free State—which was still very much in an embryonic state in eastern Congo.[29] Contrary to Free State law, adultery would be punished with whipping and even imprisonment, for example. Despite the fact that many of the early Free State forts had been ceded to the White Fathers, though, the fact that Leopold's state had been recognized by international law meant that Lavigerie's own 'kingdom' on the shores of Lake Tanganyika would not in fact be recognized as a separate state.[30] That said, the White Fathers' mission in the Congo looked increasingly *like* a state and not only because it had a standing army.

After Storms' stations were ceded to the White Fathers, Joubert very much saw himself as Emile Storms' successor. Acting at a distance from but in reality on behalf of Roelens as well as Lavigerie, Joubert had a number of pastoral powers once Lavigerie had installed him as the de facto 'King of Mpala'—even if these were challenged by a range of actors including Zanzibari slavers.[31] To counter any threats to his authority, Joubert raised an army of loyalists who were looked upon favourably by the administration even decades afterwards.[32]

As Joubert's army suggests, the early mission encounters in Tanganyika, and by extension Kongolo, took place within a distinctly militaristic and masculine culture. Lavigerie's 'kingdom' would be built in the first instance by men. Although the White Fathers would eventually be joined in their endevours by nine White Sisters, who reached the Congo in 1895, they would not get as far as Kongolo.[33] In fact, the nuns most directly involved in the mission encounters in Kongolo would be the Sisters of the Immaculate Heart of Mary (*Soeurs du Coeur Immaculé de Marie*), who were associated with the Spiritan fathers. Yet Emilio Callewaert, from the Spiritans, would only create this order after the First World War. And the White Fathers mission in what is now northern Tanganyika was also to be named after a male saint—one of the patron saints of Bruges; Saint Donatien. So, the mission as a whole was known as *Bruges-Saint-Donat.*

The preponderance of men, and the relative absence of women in the out-stations, reflected the frontier nature of the White Fathers' early expansion into Kongolo. The White Fathers' mission in the territory did not emanate from a steady expansion of their Baudouinville complexes. Rather, their mission further inland was founded more in a pioneering, almost speculative, manner. Indeed, the White Fathers first entered Kongolo from the north, from the Zanzibari stronghold of Maniema. This was not surprising as they had first established bases in and around Tippu Tip's *bomas* or 'forts'—and there were plenty of them in this region—after they had established out-stations in Baudouinville. Consequently, the out-station that first housed the Bruges-Saint-Donat mission was initially situated in a place the White Fathers called 'Old Kasongo' (known locally as *Tongoni*) situated roughly in the centre of what is now the province of Maniema. Kasongo was one of Tippu Tip's bases and so it is likely that the White Fathers redeemed slaves during their time there.[34] Being over 350 kilometres from Lake Tanganyika, Bruges-Saint-Donat was on the periphery not only of the White Fathers' mission complexes that were developing in Baudouinville and Mpala but also of any tangible state infrastructure. Indeed, their Bruges-Saint-Donat out-station was one of the first to be built so far away from the encroaching colonial state with the administration stating clearly that they did so at their own risk. The first White Fathers in the eastern Congolese hinterland thus had to deal on their own with all the vulnerabilities that accompanied their geographical isolation from the rest of their co-religionists and the harsh conditions in southeastern Congo.

Eventually, the fact there was little state infrastructure presented them with numerous opportunities to expand but that was not how Victor Roelens initially saw it. His mission in the riverine parts of eastern Congo seemed beset by setbacks related to the upheavals associated with the Zanzibari slavers.[35] Tippu Tip, along with a large group of his dependents, had established a substantive settlement in Kasongo in the 1860s and, subsequently, he and his followers had created plantations around the settlement to feed those within it.[36] The White Fathers had got to Kasongo in 1903 with the aim of converting the Zanzibaris based there and, also, to stop what was left of the East African slave trade.[37] Yet, they did not manage to spend much time in Tongoni before many fell ill with the Sleeping Sickness virus. The proliferation of this deadly disease forced Roelens to look for alternative locations for an out-station.[38] Eventually, he asked another White Father, Auguste Van Acker, to journey down from Kasongo to see if the south provided more habitable conditions than the north (see Fig. 3.2).

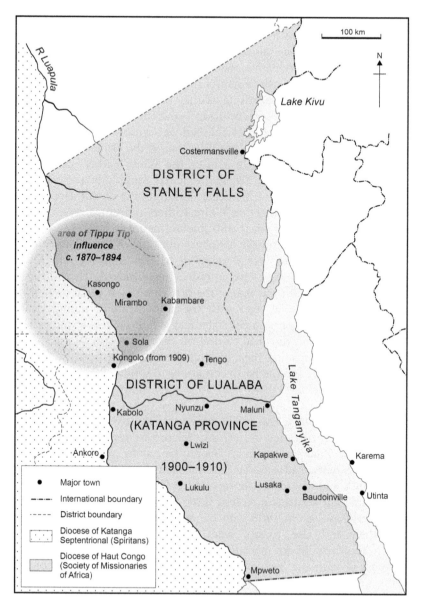

Fig. 3.2 Administrative, trader and mission boundaries in Southeastern Congo, 1885–1910

Van Acker left Tongoni and arrived in a settlement called Sola, named after its chief, in what is now the chieftainship of Bena Nkuvu in 1909 (see Fig. 3.2). The town was inhabited by peoples now understood to be from the Hêmbá ethnic group. When he arrived in Sola, though, it is unlikely that many—if any—of the local population there would have understood themselves to have been part of any overarching Hêmbá identity. Instead, they would have understood themselves to have been simply part of the Bena Nkuvu district, or 'peoples of the turtle,' which was their food taboo.[39] This supposition is supported by the White Fathers' mission diaries, which constantly referred to the peoples Van Acker encountered in these early years as the 'Bena Nkuvu' and so that is how they will be referred to in this chapter. On his early trips to the lands occupied by the Bena Nkuvu, Van Acker 'found no marks' on their skin so he reported to his superiors that Sola could be an appropriate place for the White Fathers to establish an out-station.[40] It proved such a successful place to resettle the Bruges-Saint-Donat mission, in fact, that Old Kasongo was abandoned altogether with the whole mission moving to Sola in 1909. And Van Acker soon took over as the superior of the out-station—a position he would hold until 1921.[41] In their diaries, the White Fathers recorded that they brought their followers from what they called the 'Bango Bango' ethnic group with them from Kasongo when they journeyed south.[42]

For some months, even a year, after the arrival in Sola, the Bango Bango were the only members of the White Fathers' congregation. So, penning his diary entry one night, exasperated, Van Acker commented that the Bena Nkuvu converted at the same pace of tortoises, their food taboo.[43] His comment betrayed a good deal of frustration at the difficulties the White Fathers were having in their new location. Multiple factors had conspired to undermine the conversion rates, with one of the most important being the local political economy. Van Acker and his colleagues found a thriving food production ethos among the Hêmbá groups they encountered when they first arrived in Sola. And, ironically, the local harvesting of corn was important in ensuring a ready supply of food for the missionaries. Yet what nourished the White Fathers ended up impeding their progress. The strength of the corn economy meant that very few of the Bena Nkuvu were prepared to sacrifice a day in the fields for a Sunday service and/or any of the attendant classes. Far from diminishing with the emergence of colonial capitalism, the mission presence actually galvanized the local Hêmbá economy by giving it a ready market in the form of the missionaries. At around the same time, the coming of the CFL railway meant that many Bena Nkuvu tried to sell their corn to the railway workers in and around Kongolo's town centre. The White Fathers constantly complained that their Sunday masses were sparsely attended and the grain economy featured heavily in their explanations as to why.

Aside from the economy, another field of contention between the White Fathers and the Bena Nkuvu in the first years of the mission encounter was the power to heal. Bena Nkuvu elders had long since formed a closed association known as the Bamangimba (*Bagabo*) to offer remedies to those who were ill.[44] Given that the elders had already convened a group to deal with illnesses, the local Bena Nkuvu did not go to them for healing. In the beginning, Acker even reported in the superior's diary that the Bena Nkuvu would 'never take white medicine.'[45] Yet the power to heal was crucial to many missions as it demonstrated their utility to the local population in the face of mistrust and so Van Acker was keen to break the power of the Bagabo.[46] He was less concerned with healing as a 'technique of civilization,' though he was probably more concerned with it than he would have liked to admit, and more as a means of establishing the legitimacy of the mission in the eyes of the local population.[47] Acker began his struggle by asking those who had converted to Christianity to surrender their badges and their medicine, which they referred to as their *dawa*.[48] The surrendering of the badges, which was sometimes accompanied by the burning of insignia, as well as their medicine angered many members of the Nkuvu gerontocracy who saw it as an affront to their own social and political powers. While Acker and his colleagues, such as Gustave Motte, would create a pharmacy as soon as they were able, it would therefore take a number of years for this facility to become popular with the Bena Nkuvu.

Given that the mass conversion of the Hêmbá looked some way off, the White Fathers expanded their repertoire of techniques to try to increase their number beyond their original selection of Bango Bango and Bena Nkuvu stalwarts. One of their first ideas to gather followers involved Van Acker and his colleagues, such as Gustave Motte, collecting as much meat as they could and then going on what they described as 'great walks' in which they would hand the aforementioned meat out to those who trailed them. Although the mission records do not explain from where this meat was procured or, indeed, what exactly this meat was, the walks proved popular among the Bena Nkuvu. However, the

White Fathers worried that those who followed them were only doing so in the hope of gaining food rather than to listen to their message. So, in addition to these 'great walks,' the White Fathers hosted football matches after Van Acker found a football in one of the mission 'hangars,' with these hangers being constituted only of a thatched roof supported by wooden poles. The idea in this instance was to hold a football match and invite as many people as possible to play in it. Afterwards, a bell would ring and the White Fathers would encourage the assembled teams to pray. The mission diaries suggested that 'no one dared refuse' to do so after the matches and so this was a somewhat effective evangelization tool.[49]

Yet the same sort of criticisms that could be levelled at 'great walks' could equally be raised in the context of the football matches—namely that Africans simply enjoyed playing football and were far less serious about converting. The effectiveness of the football games and the 'great walks' would also have been impeded by the fact that the messages that were conveyed to those Bena Nkuvu who followed the White Fathers were not entirely clear. While Auguste Van Acker had learned a lot about the languages spoken in and around Albertville (Kalemie), not least Swahili, he had not yet learned Hêmbá or the version of the language that was spoken by the Bena Nkuvu.[50] It would only be when Jean Vandermeiren had published his French/Hêmbá dictionary that the White Fathers' knowledge of Hêmbá would grow and as the language could be the taught to missionaries who were new to the field. So, proselytization in the missionaries' pre-War encounters with the Hêmbá was predominantly in Swahili, which both Van Acker and Vandermeiren would have learnt while in Tongoni. Although Swahili would have conveyed the necessary parts of their message, the White Fathers' ability to preach using local idioms would have been limited and they would have had to have worked with their Bango Bango and a small smattering of Bena Nkuvu converts as intermediaries.

Given that many of the Bena Nkuvu were initially more interested in food and football than in the Catholic faith, the White Fathers began to pursue what Thomas Turner has described as a 'Constantine strategy.'[51] In other words, they attempted to convert local leaders in the hope that they would subsequently convert their followers in much the same way that their Jesuit counterparts did in other parts of the world. This was a strategy that many White Fathers had been reluctant to resort to because it involved converting *individuals* and not the community as a whole, hence their initial preference for 'great walks' and football matches. The universalizing Catholicism Roelens had wanted would not necessarily result from the conversation of chiefs—many of which were sultani who had been installed by the Zanzibari. In any case, the chiefs of the Bena Nkuvu proved largely indifferent to the gospel. When they did recognize the Christian God, they saw him as simply one of many deities that could be worshipped alongside their ancestors and not necessarily one that took their place.[52] It appears that what the Hêmbá scholar, Ntole Kazadi, called the 'cult of the spirits' remained prevalent among the group until the very end of the colonial period and even beyond in some cases.[53]

Chiefs did sometimes convert when the presence of the colonial political economy became more pronounced in the lead up to and during the First World War. Mutindi, one of the first chiefs to rule the Bena Nkuvu in the early colonial period, converted after having been imprisoned by the Belgian regime with his predecessor never having done the same.[54] Mutindi's inclination towards Christianity might have arisen simply because by the time the Belgian administration did graft out more of a presence in the hinterland, chiefs had had more exposure to the gospel. Likewise, chiefs may have converted as missionaries began to feel more secure in their surroundings and subsequently became more securely established there. But it is more likely that chiefs like Mutindi saw missionaries as important mediators between them and the colonial administration. His stretch in prison might have persuaded him of the need to ally himself with missionaries to best advise him on how to avoid incarceration in future. Whatever Mutindi's predilections and motivations, the White Fathers developed a difficult relationship with the institution of chieftainship throughout their time in Sola. Though at times attentive to the vulnerabilities chiefs experienced, Van Acker often lamented the materialistic desires of many chiefs together with what they perceived to have been their rather instrumental use of Christianity.

As the conversion of chiefs looked some way off, and mass conversion even more so, the closed-chapel (*ferme-chapelle*) complex became the most important means for the White Fathers to convert the Bena Nkuvu. Closed chapels usually consisted of a chapel surrounded by thatched dwellings for the African catechists who attended it.[55] They would later face opposition from metropolitan Belgian socialists but the system nonetheless remained in place nearly until the end of the colonial period.[56] The White Fathers had begun to construct a closed chapel in Sola before the First World War but it would not take shape until after the ending of international hostilities. The closed-chapel complex aimed to cut children off from the Equatorial tradition with the aim of surrounding them with exactly the kind of pristine Catholic culture Lavigerie had always planned for his Christian 'kingdom.' Yet the War considerably hampered the White Fathers' efforts to proselytize—much as it did their Spiritan counterparts.[57] The exigencies of colonial wartime recruitment bore down heavily on the emergent Christian communities and deprived them of potential converts. Likewise, getting supplies to the Sola outstation was not easy during wartime with many Fathers surviving only on a skeletal diet. Procuring supplies was impeded by the conflicts between the allied and the German forces on Lake Tanganyika meaning that shipping across Lake Tanganyika was disrupted as German ports in the Tanganyika colony blockaded Belgian colonies. Likewise, building work had to cease as the White Fathers concentrated on their survival above everything else.

In addition to their lack of resources, conversion was also considerably set back after Mutinidi's authority was catastrophically undermined given that he could not stop the night-time raids in which colonial officials kidnapped male members of the Bena Nkuvu. If the White Fathers had converted the chief in the belief that his followers would do so afterwards then this plan temporarily collapsed along with the chief's respectability. Secondly, the White Fathers' efforts to portray themselves as a benign and even protective force in the hinterland was also undermined by the nightly raids—even if there was not much they could ever have done to stop them. The White Fathers were reluctant to critique the administration for fear of being asked to leave the area or even the Congo. The War thus left a painful legacy in Sola. Unsurprisingly, the White Fathers commented that the Bena Nkuvu were 'rebellious' afterwards.[58] That so many Hêmbá had been kidnapped by colonial officials as they slept only increased their kinfolks' resentment towards the newly ensconced Belgian colonial regime. And the White Fathers found themselves bearing the brunt of this hostility, as it was they who wanted to preach in the hinterland. The administration simply had not got the resources to establish permanent bases in the lands occupied by the Bena Nkuvu. However, after the War, Belgian functionaries hanged those Africans who they believed had committed crimes near to the mission outstation in Sola. These macabre public spectacles meant that locals increasingly identified the missionaries with the colonial residency, which again set back their efforts to expand their local following.

Yet the White Fathers were optimistic in some respects not least in that they saw the slow but steady expansion of the state administration into their affairs as helpful in the sense that it began to punish those who spoke out against the mission.[59] Not only that, but state agents burned surrounding villages that threatened to evade tax collections forcing many Congolese people into grander agglomerations that the missionaries could more easily reach.[60] Far from sympathizing with the plight of the Congolese whose villages had been burned, the missionaries feared the administration's lack of resources might impede them from continuing this work.[61] One of the large villages that resulted from this state programme of expansion was near Sola and so Van Acker supported it to a large degree.[62] The burning of villages notwithstanding, the local people and in particular the local children seemed to be more open to talking with the missionaries. Van Acker suggested in his annual report that the 'children did not hide from us anymore.'[63] From having been apart from the state for a number of years, therefore, the Church welcomed its involvement inasmuch as it saw it as cowering the local people into respecting the European presence. But the iron fist the state showed during the First World War, particularly in terms of its forced recruitment, would not be easily forgotten by the local Bena Nkuvu population.

African Agency and the Patterning
of the Spiritan Advance

While Victor Roelens' White Fathers worked in Sola, on the right bank of the Lualaba River, the Holy Ghost Fathers (HGF), more commonly known as the Spiritans would eventually work on the left bank (see Fig. 3.2). The Spiritans, like the White Fathers, had already spent a long time in Africa before they ever set foot in Kongolo. Founded in 1703, their aim was to educate priests from poor backgrounds. The Society originated in Brittany, in northwestern France, but it steadily built seminaries elsewhere in the country. They initially faced some opposition from the Jansenist movement, which saw them as a threat because they were expanding into areas in which they had traditionally enjoyed a strong presence.[64] Moreover, they needed quite a bit of time to become established, especially after their tussles with the Jansenists, and so their early members had to wait several decades before they could participate in any missionary activities.[65] And before the 1750s, any cleric seeking missionary work first had to first pass through the

Vatican's Foreign Missionary Society to be appointed to the relevant overseas diocese. However, following a series of representations made by a Spiritan called Father Dosquet, they found themselves in a position to be able to send missionaries directly to Quebec without having to go through the Vatican bureaucracy first.

The Spiritans first landed in Africa in 1778. In the first instance, they were concentrated in West Africa and specifically Senegal.[66] And it was only in the mid-nineteenth century, under the stewardship of a Jewish convert called Francis Libermann, sometimes considered the 'second' founder of the Spiritans, that the Society began to expand its presence in Africa. Libermann's approach to mission work foreshadowed Lavigerie's in many respects not least in his urging his missionaries to 'become black with the blacks.'[67] In making this statement, Libermann was, much like Lavigerie later on, extolling an approach whereby local cultures would be taken into account in the mission encounter and, furthermore, that the Spiritans would learn local languages. More than this, however, Libermann was suggesting that his missionaries develop close relationships with their respective congregations in such a manner that they could operate in a self-sustaining way. Libermann's wishes would be put to the test in 1842, when the Spiritans created their first mission field in Africa with the inauguration of the 'Vicariate of the Two Guineas' that extended along much of Africa's western coastline. Much like the White Fathers, they were reliant on their localities for survival as opposed to their European headquarters. So, Spiritan out-stations nearly always grew crops.

Alongside the economic necessities they dealt with in the early phase of their African mission work, the Spiritans placed a heavy emphasis on education. Writing in the 1878 edition of the Society's constitution, Francis Libermann urged his missionaries 'to pay special attention to the children of chiefs and other leading personalities of the land so that later on their influence might be put to use for the benefit of the people.'[68] Correspondingly, the Spiritans in Kongolo were strongly influenced by the ways in which their Society generally structured their educational activities. Initially, they established bush schools whose purpose was to teach 'the first elements of religion, reading, writing and arithmetic,' with all these subjects being taught initially in a local language and most probably Swahili in the context of Kongolo.[69] It was only until after the Second World War that the Society generally invested in secondary education facilities. Spiritan schools were usually modest. In addition to their humble architecture, the bush schools relied on catechists or lay preachers giving up their time to teach new students when a number of better-paid jobs steadily became available. This in turn made the schools vulnerable to periods of economic growth in which their teachers could be lured away from the out-stations by high-paying jobs associated either with the CFL or even the UMHK.

Because the vast majority of those educated in Spiritan schools were so young, the Society began primarily as a children's movement. Like the White Fathers, many Spiritan missionaries believed that Congolese adults were beyond saving as they were simply too attached to their old ways of life to convert.[70] Children, however, were thought to have been far more open to the gospel.[71] Given the proliferation of the East African slave trade, the Spiritans ransomed captives at first, with many of the people they bought being children.[72] The Spiritan historian Henry Koren claims that this process of ransoming slaves was 'heartbreaking ... but seemed to them the only way to make a beginning.'[73] Koren never elaborated on why ransoming slaves was 'the only way' to build a congregation, though expediency must have played a large part in whatever thinking lay behind this policy. After prolonged reflection, the idea of ransoming slaves made the Spiritans too uncomfortable and so they abandoned this practice wherever they could.[74] The Society decided that by ransoming slaves they were indirectly contributing to the East African Slave Trade because they gave the Swahili slavers another market outside of their traditional coastal clientele. It is telling, also, that many of the porters who the Spiritans used to transport their goods to Kongolo in the first instance were from Kasongo—one of Tippu Tip's bases.[75]

Philippe-Prosper Auguard, who became the Vicar Apostolic of French Upper Congo, suggested that slaves were no longer being traded in the Lower Congo by the late 1880s.[76] Auguard's time-frame seems like an underestimation, though, given that the Spiritans only began their explorations of a possible foothold in the CFS in 1874. Likewise, it was only in 1880 that the Spiritans founded their first headquarters in Boma, which became the capital of the Congo Free State in 1885. So, according to Auguard, the Society only ransomed slaves for a maximum of six years, which seems unlikely.[77] Whatever the truth of the Spiritans' relationship with the East African Slave Trade was, though, ransomed slaves were important members of the early congregations because they could translate key Christian concepts into local vernaculars and Swahili in particular. Much as Adrian Hastings has observed for Africa as a whole, the Spiritan advance in the Congolese hinterland was a 'black advance or it was nothing.'[78]

One of the most important local Spiritan lay catechists in Kongolo's early history was a man called Bernard Kakese.[79] Kakese's biography was evidently a matter of great interest for the first generation of Spiritan missionaries to reach Kongolo, as he was held up by them as an exemplary catechist. Unfortunately, however, their interest in him did not extend to them publishing an authoritative biography about his life nor to quoting him directly in their in-house publications. Short of their own investigations and his own words, European missionaries relied largely on hearsay about Kakese's history. One of the catechists from around the place where he made his name, Lubunda in northern Kongolo, apparently 'certified' that he came from as far away as Stanleyville (now Kisangani).[80] In language that is strongly indicative of ransoming, this same Spiritan source went on to claim that Kakese was 'given' to the Spiritan chaplain, Emilio Callewaert, by the 'Sacred Heart' or Scheutist missionaries who had already acquired a base in the city.[81] That the Scheutists had reached the bend in the Congo River before the Spiritans was not an accident and owes something to the age of nationalism in which both sets of missionaries had been working.[82]

Initially, Leopold II believed that Philippe-Prosper Auguard had collaborated too closely with the French-backed explorer Pietro Paolo Savorgnan di Brazzà, who went on to found the French Congo in 1903.[83] Naturally, Auguard never had a meaningful choice of whether or not to collaborate with whichever colonial power was in nominal authority in any given territory because his superiors enjoined all members of his Society to 'render unto Caesar.' In other words, missionaries were generally told to work with whichever authority held sway over the territory they sought to preach in. In any case, unlike the White Fathers, the Spiritans were cast out of the Free State by 1886. As the introduction suggested, Leopold II preferred to have Belgian nationals staffing mission enclaves in his Free State and as such felt he had found a ready replacement for the Spiritans in the form of the Scheut Fathers.[84] However, as they were only established in 1862, they did not have the capacity to staff missions across the entire CFS by the time the Spiritans were ordered to leave. It took Leopold II almost until his death to acknowledge the deficiencies of his nationalist mission strategy. But eventually, given the resource limitations the Scheut Fathers experienced, the Spiritans were allowed back into the Congo by 1907.

Bernard Kakese became one of the first Africans to join the Spiritans after they returned to the Congo. Thereafter, he gave over twenty-five years of service to them with his brethren giving him much credit for his role in 'pioneering the evangelization of the bush.'[85] Like his co-religionists, Kakese followed the Congo River south of Stanleyville to Kindu, a town to the north of Kongolo. Afterwards, the Society made their way south with the help of an ever-expanding network of railway stations and labour camps being built by Baron Empain's Great Lakes Railway Company (*Compagnie du Chemin de Fer du Congo Supérieur aux Grands Lacs Africains*) (CFL) (see Fig. 3.3). Fathers Villetaz and Brangers were the first European Spiritans to arrive in Kongolo, with Villetaz directing Kakese to two mission sites; namely Lusuma-Malila and, secondly, Lubunda. However important Kakese was, Villetaz saw him very much as a subordinate rather than an equal in a relationship that would be characteristic, regrettably, of many of the early and even late colonial mission encounters to some extent.

Because some of the first Spiritans to arrive there, Villetaz and Brangers, believed that the marshy lands of Lubunda were dangerous to their health, they sent Kakese into communities there to convert other Africans in their stead.[86] It was only later on, when they discovered that the environment was safe for them, that Villetaz and Brangers, among others, helped to construct educational and other facilities in Lubunda. Thereafter, they sought to find the means to help Kakese go to school and further his studies as well as sending him into potentially inhospitable terrain. Soon, exactly as Villetaz and Brangers had hoped, Kakese went on to play a vital role in converting a number of local Africans in Lubunda and in making the *Braine L'Alleud* out-station in Lubunda, named after the eponymous Walloon municipality, a success. Yet, unlike many of their early converts, Kakese was not a child and was even married *before* he arrived in Kongolo. Many Spiritans believed that his marriage was an obstacle to his ambition to enroll in the seminary and become a priest. Yet Kakese said in 1918 that he 'considered [his wife] dead.'[87] Whether Kakese's wife was really dead, or was dead to him as a sign of his previous life, is unclear. Nevertheless, he argued that his former marriage should not disbar him from ordination. At the same time, he was determined that his age should not prevent him from learning what he needed to in order to become a priest.

While Kakese never realized his dream of becoming a priest, the overall success of the Spiritans in Lubunda in the long term is beyond dispute. At the same time that Kakese was drawing in African followers, Emilio Callewaert, the Apostolic Vicar, constructed a number of

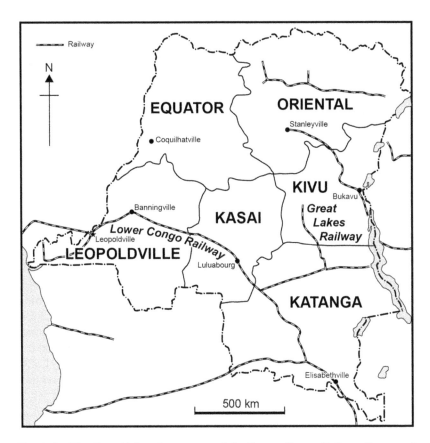

Fig. 3.3 The Great Lakes Company and the Lower Congo Railway Company's lines in the Congo

facilities in and around the places in which his catechist worked. Like many missionaries who arrived in the Congo at the time, he was concerned that as colonial concessions spread their interests further into the interior, Africans' outlooks would become more secular. So, Callewaert, along with catechists such as Kakese, worked tirelessly to prevent the proletarianisation of the African workforce in Kongolo. He founded out-stations in several places in addition to Lubunda, which included ones in Kindu, Kongolo and Nkulu.[88] But it was Lubunda that became central to Callewaert's ambition of creating a pure Christian community in the Congolese bush. It eventually rose to become one of the most important mission centres in the whole of the Tanganyika district and even Katanga at large. In many respects, Lubunda was to the Spiritans what Baudoinville and Mpala, on the shores of Lake Tanganyika, were to the White Fathers.

Lubunda exemplified the *école-chapelle* (school-chapel) system, the purpose of which mirrored the *ferme-chapelle* system used by the White Fathers yet, as its name suggests, it contained a school as well as a chapel.[89] The school-chapel system was first developed by the Jesuit mission order at the turn of the century and later copied by most other Catholic missionaries working in the Congo.[90] Although the White Fathers' *ferme-chapelle* system in Sola evolved into an *école-chapelle* system once a school was built, the Spiritans excelled in the number of schools they established in Kongolo. The school-chapel system was a means of training catechists and African teachers as well as the sons of chiefs yet it was not a seminary to train priests—these would follow shortly afterwards. While Lubunda initially only consisted of a school-chapel complex, the missionaries there eventually built a teacher-training college meaning that catechists from across the region, not least Kakese, were sent there to learn the basics of the faith. As opposed to central Kongolo, where the Spiritans also had a presence, Lubunda boasted a large number of potential converts if one looks simply at the in-house mission statistics. In February 1914 alone, Spiritan documents suggest that 2000 students of the catechism were registered with the Lubunda fathers.[91] Some of the grandeur of the Lubunda enclave is captured in a photo taken of the interior of its church in 1926 as shown in Fig. 3.4.

Despite the zeal with which Callewaert and his colleagues went about their evangelism, the Spiritan success in Lubunda was not immediately replicated elsewhere in Kongolo, in the *St-Coeur de Marie de Kongolo* mission. As well as converting the African workers in the CFL junction near to Kongolo, the Society had wanted to proselytize among the peoples of southern Kongolo. However, Callewaert and his followers could not settle there, as the Spiritan ethnographer, Father Conrad, believed that the Luba who inhabited the region were simply 'too turbulent.'[92] Given that we do not know very much about Kekenya and his progeny's rule before the arrival of the Belgian regime, we cannot be sure what Conrad was seeing as he entered Kongolo. Some Luba in Kongolo may have joined an uprising that took place under Kasongo Nyembo following Belgian demands for tax from the residents based further to

Fig. 3.4 Interior of the church at Lubunda, Kongolo, 1926 (Royal Museum of Central Africa, Tervuren, AP.0.2.12875-2, Photo 1)

the south of the territory. The Belgian regime would only succeed in crushing Nyembo's revolt by 1917 and so its chronology matches roughly that of Conrad's writing.[93] Likewise, the colonial administration did not begin to effectively tax Africans in Kongolo until the end of the First World War, which potentially demonstrated that they were afraid of exacerbating the 'turbulence' there.[94]

In the same letter that he explained that he did not want to evangelize in southern Kongolo, Conrad characterized the Luba as 'warriors.' Conrad's description was interesting given that many scholars translate the word 'Luba' as 'warrior' in English. However, the epicentre of the Luba revolt was not in Kongolo and as the Luba in the territory because they were not yet taxed there and so they would have had little incentive to join Nyembo's revolt. Instead, the Luba were witnessing violent competitions for power between the sultani and the leaders who they had ousted after the Swahili incursions. Given that there was evidently so much social tumult in southern Kongolo, Conrad did not expect to be able to evangelize there for some time. And so the Spiritans concentrated on their work in Lubunda and in the town centre. The fact that the Spiritans, as well as the White Fathers, did not establish out-stations in the Luba regions in southern Kongolo meant that Protestants would have a chance to work there later on. But a Protestant presence would not emerge until the early interwar period and both sets of Catholic missionaries had enough to get on with in their own respective mission fields.

Once established in Kongolo's town centre, the Spiritans encountered a group that colonial officials later described as the 'Yashi' as well as the Lingalaphone labourers living in the CFL work-camp who had been recruited from the West of the colony. Colonial officials and some missionaries originally believed that the Bayazi were in fact a predominantly Songye group, and hence called them the Ya<u>shi</u>, reflecting standard Songye naming conventions. However, given that they were a grouping that comprised a Hêmbá clan called the *Bazila Simba* (those who do not eat lions), the Baya<u>zi</u> [my underline] were not in fact a Songye subset. The Bayazi organized their societies on a lineage model, much as the Luba did, and so they frequently practiced ancestor worship. Ancestors were often venerated on mounds so as to emphasize the transcendence of the dead over the world of the living and the Bayazi followed this convention. They held one mound in particular, which they called *Lumpibwe* near to what is now the suburb of Misalwe, to be so sacred that they prohibited the Spiritan fathers from building on it. The fact that the Spiritans could not use this particular mound in the centre of Kongolo hurt their morale, as they had originally hoped to build 'a church that would reach the sky' on the site.[95]

What Adeline Masquelier would describe as the 'spiritual geography' of the Bayazi profoundly influenced the early patterning of Christian presence in Kongolo.[96] As they could not build on the mound that they had hoped to have done, the Spiritans could only build a 'provisional' chapel and a house before King Albert 1 of Belgium arrived there on a state visit on 13 June 1909. The 'provisional' chapel was very much that, as it was made mostly from straw and so needed replacing almost as soon as the Belgian monarch had seen it. As well as local cosmologies influencing the mission encounter, African labour was also vital.

When it was finally completed, the Spiritans' permanent residence was constructed not by the Europeans, for example, but by the African members of the Society. Spiritan archives do not give many details about the process by which they recruited African porters or labourers. Given that slavery still existed in Kongolo in the early 1900s, it might have been that the Spiritans simply redeemed slaves from a local big man but this is far from certain. What is sure is that by the end of 1911, despite having recruited Africans from outlying villages, no stable church had been erected and the Spiritan infrastructure in the town centre looked fragile. Far from being a spiritual Bula Matari, therefore, the Church looked nearly as fragile as its secular European counterparts.

The outbreak of the First World War only accentuated the difficulties the Spiritan missionaries already faced. As opposed to their very early history in Kongolo, whereby they could recruit Africans to help build mission facilities, Father Villetaz and a religious brother could not find enough workers to continue proselytizing.[97] Likewise, the outbreak of international hostilities caused acute food shortages as the Germans blockaded the Belgian Congo given that it formed part of the alliance they were fighting. The Fathers in Kongolo's town centre complained that at the end of 1914, there was no milk, coffee, sugar, bread or wine. The situation worsened when a recession struck in 1915, which served to catalyze these resource shortages. The difficulties posed by the War meant that they had to postpone their ambitious plans to build more out-stations until 1918. Yet, they were well established in Lubunda even if their presence in the town centre looked fragile. Catechists, such as Bernard Kakese, were taking the gospel message ever further into Kongolo's hinterland. And so what Jean and John Comaroff described as the 'long conversation' between European missionaries and Africans, in this case the Spiritans and African societies in Kongolo, had begun.[98]

Kongolo as Peripheral to the Belgian Administration

While the Spiritan and White Fathers' long conversation with African societies was beginning, as the missionaries' reports suggest, Belgian colonial power was not very influential in Kongolo until the First World War. Although the infrastructure the missionaries had established was insecure, and they had had only halting success in converting local peoples, their built infrastructure was far more developed than that of the state in the proto-colonial and early colonial periods. There were a number of reasons why the Church established a more substantial presence than the state in Tanganyika but first and foremost among them was that it was there to claim souls and not to make a financial profit and so it was undeterred by the lack of mineral resources in the region in the first instance. Conversely, profit was absolutely essential in the mind of Leopold II, whose role was crucial in establishing Belgian rule in Africa. The Belgian King had always been dissatisfied with the model of constitutional monarchy that proliferated in many European states since the continent's 'age of revolutions.'[99] He was afraid in particular of depending wholly on the Belgian parliament for his purse and so the King had long dreamt of acquiring a colony that would give him a consistent and a private source of funds. The ways in which he acquired the Congo in a bid to gain an independent stream of revenue are by now very well-known and so this chapter will focus instead on explaining the uneven projection of Belgian power across Central Africa during the *fin-de-siècle*.[100]

For readers unfamiliar with Leopold's acquisition of the Congo, however, some brief words are in order. Leopold II had scoured the globe for some time to find suitable colonies before he set his sights on the Congo.[101] And, as he was to discover, no European state, save for Portugal, had made any large-scale incursions into the Congo River Basin by the 1870s.[102] Luckily for Leopold II, Portugal had rarely if ever publically articulated a formal desire to annex the *whole* of the Congo. Rather, Portugal assumed that it would have trading rights in the Congo Basin because of its long-standing Angolan colony. This assumption on the part of Portugal gave Leopold an opportunity to annex that Congo. So, he sought out and patronized Henry Stanley so he could use his knowledge of and presence in the Congo Basin to help erect tangible signs of his de facto sovereignty there.[103] The work of the Welsh-born journalist-cum-explorer, Henry Stanley, was among the first major reasons he began to consider a colony in Central Africa at all.[104] Using the host of out-stations that Stanley had built, as well as treaties the explorer had signed with those he believed to have been Congolese chiefs, Leopold II claimed *de jure* sovereignty of most of the Congo Basin at the Berlin Conference in 1885.[105] Stanley's work meant that despite Portugal's presence in parts of the Congo, Leopold managed to secure the rights to this enormous territory.

After the Berlin agreement, the occupation of the Congo by forces acting on the King's behalf accelerated. Rather than a well-ordered series of campaigns, though, the Belgian conquest(s) was a chaotic and haphazard affair. The subordination of the Congolese people to Leopold II's emergent state had not even been completed by the time the King died in 1909.[106] What is more, generals, notably Francis Dhanis, sought their own glory and greater social status in Belgium and did so by launching conquests in a corner of the globe that ironically few Belgians had even heard of before the onset of their King's imperial adventure and so they operated with minumum accountability.[107] One of the most difficult jobs for any historian examining the so-called 'Belgo-Arab' wars of colonial conquest in the late 1880s and early 1890s is distinguishing any historical truths from the *post facto* narratives. Such stories tried to make a range of overlapping and often incoherent conflicts appear ordered and respectable.[108] Contrary to official stories, though, it was not always clear to the Belgians' who they were supposed to be fighting and when they should have been fighting them. The confusion about who was fighting whom only added to the general atmosphere of chaos and violence that generally accompanies war.[109]

For a long time, Leopold II's apologists had argued that his gendarmerie, collectively known as the *Force Publique*, was created in 1886 specifically to bring an end to the infamous Swahili slave trade.[110] The Belgian Anti-Slavery Society, created in 1890, believed this and had lobbied successfully for the Zanzibari to be forcibly removed from their stations in eastern Congo. Indeed, one of the main reasons why other states granted Leopold II the Free State in the first place was in part to further his supposed struggle against slavery.[111] Given this abolitionist crusade, the Belgian wars of conquest against those who resisted their early encroachments, such as the Luba peoples living to the south of Kongolo, soon began to involve conflicts with some of the Swahili too.[112] In other words, the Belgians fought the Swahili in particular but also other groups of Africans such as the Luba. Yet, the Force Publique did not necessarily fight all these peoples at the same time. A consensus has emerged among historians that there was in fact no monolithic fight that pitted *all* the Belgians against *all* the Swahili *all* of the time.[113] Indeed, someone who embodied this very ambiguity was Tippu Tip, the premier slave trader in the eastern savannah, who featured strongly in the last chapter. Rather than being targeted by the Force Publique, he was actually made the governor of Stanleyville, a large swathe of territory in eastern Congo named after the eponymous explorer, in 1887.[114] Likewise, many of the sultanis that Tippu Tip promoted were in fact retained by the incoming regime; be it as CFS-backed chiefs or as recruits to the Force Publique.

The wars of conquest that resulted from Leopold II's attempts to realize his authority over peoples living in the Congo Basin were so spatially and temporarily contingent it is unfortunately unlikely we will ever be able to map them out in their entirely.[115] Despite the limitations of the sources pertaining to the 1890s, we do know some important ways in which this war effected Tanganyika. First, by 1895, the Force Publique had expelled many of the major Zanzibari leaders, most notably Rumaliza, from Tanganyika or at least the Mpala-Lusaka-Baudouinville triangle that Roelens ruled with nearly no interference from any other European authority.[116] We also know that Kongolo and its environs were first annexed by troops acting on behalf of Leopold II's International African Association. Formed in 1876, it was supposed to further humanitarian motives, not least Leopold II's much vaunted anti-slavery cause. In reality, the AIA was a front organization for the King's imperial ambitions.[117] As opposed to targeting slavers specifically, it engaged far more in outright conquest regardless of whether or not those who stood in its way were actually slavers. Again, we need to be careful to ask if the brutality of those Africans who opposed the AIA has been exaggerated to support the Association's claims to legitimacy.[118]

Whatever the truth of its own account of its history, we know that AIA ran five expeditions to Tanganyika from the late 1870s to the early 1880s. Its most common passage there was to pass through what is now Tanzania and, thereafter, to cross Lake Tanganyika. This was exactly the route that Emile Storms, one of the first Belgian conquerors to go there, had used.[119] He left the coastal Tanzanian town of Bagamoyo on 9 June 1882 and, on 27 September that year, arrived at Mpala, on the Congolese side of Lake Tanganyika. He played a vital role in the production of early Belgian hegemony there, building a fortification, or *boma* in Swahili, and projecting his authority from this settlement.[120] He was one of the first members of the Association to petition a selection of Congolese chiefs to accept the authority of the AIA over their lands.

While some of the Association's annexation of Tanganyika involved signing treaties with local big men, it was based far more straightforwardly on violence. Having arrived in Mpala, Emile Storms led a punitive expedition against Lusinga, a powerful African warlord who lived in the settlement's environs.[121] After defeating him, Storms carried Lusinga's embalmed head back to Mpala as a trophy. By the time it had ended, the battle for sovereignty in Mpala and its hinterland had cost the lives of around fifty Africans and many, many more had been captured. It bears repeating that Storms would end up surrendering Mpala to the White Fathers in 1885 as a result of them recognizing the suzerainty of the Free State. But until the Berlin Conference, Mpala was a powerful staging post for the Free State forces to use to make their way further into the interior.

Jerome Becker was the man tasked with leading a mission to link a selection of bomas taken from the defeated Swahili on the shores of Lake Tanganyika with those he would build or conquer from his African rivals further inland. Becker's ambition was to get as far as the slave market in Nyangwe, in what is now the province of Maniema, just to the north of Kongolo. He was joined by three deputy lieutenants; Francis Dhanis, Adolphe Durutte and Jules Dubois. Exemplifying the disorder that characterized the Leopoldian conquests, the Becker mission was put back almost a year when its leader fell seriously ill. Subsequently, Becker delayed ceding command of the mission to his deputy, Adolphe Durutte, until 15 May 1885. Even then, Durutte had to turn back from his mission after only a week. In the end, of the twenty-five men the AIA had sent to Nyangwe, only nine made it back alive. Despite the fact that Durutte's mission must therefore be considered a failure, the existence of a 'Mount Dhanis' in eastern Kongolo, in what is now the chieftainship of Bena Nyembo, suggests that Dhanis might have actually reached the territory on this mission.[122] If he did not in fact pass through Kongolo in 1885, then he may well have done so the following year, when he got as far as Basoko, a settlement just outside Stanleyville (Kisangani).

While we have very little evidence to suggest that European power intruded into Kongolo in the 1880s, there were some relevant Belgian administrative developments there in the early 1890s. The man initially most connected to the early Free State expansion in Tanganyika was Alexandre Delcommune.[123] He took charge of the *Compagnie Congolaise pour le Commerce et l'Industrie* (Congolese Company for Trade and Industry) (CCCI) mission to Katanga, also known as the Bia-Franqui expedition, from 1890 to 1893.[124] Unlike those of the International African Association, Delcommune began his own journey into the interior of the Congo from the West. Rather than arriving via Lake Tanganyika, then, he travelled by way of the Lualaba River. He passed through Tanganyika in his search for gold and, also, to find a potentially favourable place for settlers. Yet in his later writings, he suggested that he did not spend much time there and so he may not have even stopped in Kongolo.[125] Rather than gold, which was found in very small quantities in the centre of Katanga, or even copper, which was found to the south of Baudouinville, tin was the mineral most common in Tanganyika. And Delcommune did not exhibit much interest in its ore.[126]

To further his claim to resources elsewhere, Delcommune created the Katanga Company (CK) in 1891, whose land claims included what is now the territory of Kongolo. While the CK was chiefly organized to counter the British industrialist Cecil Rhodes' claim to the mineral-rich lands in the south, we must presume Delcommune believed that there might have been minerals in Kongolo as well. In 1900, the CK merged with the British-led Tanganyika Concessions Limited Company to create the sprawling CSK concession corporation.[127] Like it did with its predecessor, the CK, the Free State granted the CSK a large amount of internal autonomy that included the ability to tax in kind by 1903.[128] It was under the aegis of the CSK that some of the first rudiments of the colonial administration appeared in Kongolo. Despite its large levels of autonomy from the central administration based in Boma, the CSK followed normal Free State procedure in terms of dividing up the lands it occupied into zones, the largest unit after that of the province, which were in turn divided into sectors (*secteurs*), which were themselves then partitioned into postes.[129]

The CK created the sector of Lualaba-Kasaï appeared in the CFS in 1894. Its headquarters were in Lusambo and it comprised a large part of southeastern Congo.[130] By 1908, Lualaba-Kasaï had ten posts, which were broadly equivalent to their successors, the 'territories' (*territoires*). The language used by the CFS annual to describe the administrative divisions within this sector is telling. The word 'post' suggests a hastily constructed settlement and evokes a prevailing mood of warfare and unrest. That a major centre of Lualaba-Kasaï, Kiambi, was described as the 'seat of the council of war' provides further evidence that the district was far from 'pacified' before the CSK turned it over to Boma, the Free State capital.[131] Likewise, the rudimentary facilities available in the 'posts' as a whole suggests that the CSK administration was still at an embryonic stage of development by the time Leopold II gave up his claims to the Congo Basin.

The bureaucratic process of transferring the Free State to the Belgian parliament after the 'red rubber' atrocities was finally completed in 1908.[132] By 9 September, 'all executive and legislative decisions made in the king's name had to be countersigned by [a] newly appointed minister of [the] colonies, who was both a parliamentarian and a member of the cabinet.'[133] The CSK remained in charge of southeastern Congo, but leading administrators were making every effort to integrate the Committee's administration into what became known as the Belgian Congo (1908–1960). By 1910, they had succeeded.[134] Katanga retained its own Vice Governor-General until 1933 and they reported to the

Governor-General responsible for the colony as a whole as well as being able to manage the province with a large degree of autonomy.[135] Along with incorporating Katanga, Belgian officials made prolonged efforts to turn the military power of the CFS into a colonial government. Most of the differences between the Belgian Congo and the CFS were rhetorical rather than actual, though, at least in the years before the First World War. The old CSK administrative divisions were rebranded, for example 'postes' became *territoires* (territories) and the sectors were rebranded as 'districts,' but this never resulted in a greater Belgian presence in northern Katanga.[136] Altogether, the history of colonial Kongolo in the nineteenth and early twentieth century remained one of marginality and distance from the major centres of capital accumulation and colonial labour recruitment.

COLONIAL REIMAGININGS OF CHIEFTAINSHIP IN EARLY COLONIAL KONGOLO

After 1910, Kongolo fell under the aegis of the district of Tanganika-Möero, which, as territories as a whole were administratively formalized in 1912, hosted Kabalo, Nyunzu, Albertville and Manono as well.[137] The institution of chieftainship, the lowest yet most fundamental division of the colonial administrative hierarchy, operated below the level of the territory, was carried over from the Free State to take its place in the government of the Belgian Congo. However, Leopold II's successor, Albert I, issued new decrees that sought to instruct Belgian agents more precisely as to their operation.[138] The sphere of chieftainship would be where the Belgian conquerors would attempt to convert their military authority into civic government yet their efforts to do so could at best be described as only fleetingly successful in the context of Kongolo. The Church managed to challenge the colonial construction of chieftainship almost at will in the early colonial period. As it would be the crucible in which so many contests for power between the Church and the Belgian administration would play out, it is worth outlining the history of colonial chieftainship in the Belgian Congo in detail.

The colonial version of chieftainship in the Congo had its roots in a Decree that Leopold II passed on 6 October 1891, which appropriated 'vacant lands' for the crown and 'required that at the certification and investiture of each African chief a list would be made of the prestations in [goods, labour services (corvées) and labourers to be furnished.'[139]

The main idea behind the construction of colonial chieftainship was to co-opt African elites into the Free State administration or, in the case of Kongolo, that of the CK and, later, the CSK. African elites, in turn, were meant to subordinate their followers into a peasant class from which agricultural products and labourers could be extracted.[140] Belgian agents in much of eastern Congo did not pay much attention to delineating chieftainships in the 1890s, partly because the invading Force Publique had not yet completed its conquest of the region and/or put down all rebellions there.[141] As the 'red rubber' atrocities came to the world's attention, though, the Free State reformed the basis of chieftainship so as to rehabilitate its reputation. From their previously 'direct' mode of administration, borrowed from largely the French colonies, the Free State opted for a much more indirect approach drawn more from the British model that privileged the power of pre-existing elites.

In 1903, the Leopold II issued a Decree that instructed all Free State officials to base their administration of chieftainship on 'pre-existing traditions,' which had a direct bearing on Kongolo. Writing their reports later on, CSK officials suggested that a prominent member of the Bùki family was given a chief's medal to demonstrate that he was a Free State ally at some point before the end of Leopold's rule.[142] The family history of this Bùki is unclear, however. As the last chapter suggested, Edmund Verhulpen suggested that the first Bùki was Kumwimbe Ngombe's son, even though two colonial sources suggest that he was in fact 'the son of Ilunga Sungu.'[143] Whatever the truth of the first Bùki's parentage, his son, Kekenya, inherited the throne after him and he ruled until around 1870. So, we can surmise that the Bùki the colonial regime encountered first was either one of Kekenya's grandsons or, in fact, one of Kekenya's own sons. Even considering that the 'colonial' Bùki eventually died in 1947, and allowing for the fact that he had to have been born before 1870, it is very possible that the Bùki installed by the Free State was indeed Kekenya's eldest son. So, I will presume that the Bùki who the colonial regime installed was one of Kekenya's sons.[144]

After his enthronement, Kekenya's son, hereafter simply referred to as 'Bùki,' ruled a number of subjects who had not all accepted Luba sovereignty. Unfortunately, the lack of CSK sources pertaining to this decision means that we can only speculate as to why the Committee invested Bùki with the powers it did. He was probably installed more as a result of expediency, though, than in accordance with any particular overriding political principle. He was someone who CSK officials must have felt had at least some control of the lands just under the fifth parallel, Father Conrad's reservations notwithstanding, and so they were content to ally themselves with him. Conversely, it is not hard to see why Bùki would have accepted his role as a CK/CSK ally because, as Lewis Gann and Peter Duignan have suggested, 'indigenous chiefs benefitted from collaboration with the Belgians [as] the Belgians backed their supporters against domestic rivals.'[145] And, as someone ruling peoples who had not all accepted Luba suzerainty, acquiring colonial support was vital to maintain Bùki's power. As he had been installed there, it was not a surprise that Bùki's domains would have been named 'Kongolo' after one of the mythical founders of the Luba monarchy.

Bùki's chieftainship was one of the only ones in Kongolo to be delineated during the Free State/CSK era. Indeed, the lack of 'pre-existing traditions' mapped out by CFS/CSK officials after 1903 prompted Leopold II to issue yet another Decree pertaining to rural government in the Congo in 1906. More than any other, the 1906 Decree made it clear that chieftainships based on pre-existing series of elites had to be identified and sooner rather than later. While elsewhere in the Free State, administrators paid heed to it, most chieftainships in Kongolo were still not identified until after the CSK territories were handed over to the Belgian Congo in 1910. And so, for a long time, Bùki remained one of the only colonial chiefs in Kongolo. Yet, along with the installation of the CFL junction, Bùki's enthronement meant that Kongolo was drawn far more meaningfully into the colonial administration. In 1911, Van Walleghem, chief of staff at a poste outside Kongolo, called Mbuli, founded a new administrative bureau in Kongolo itself. To project colonial power further into the hinterland, and to find more African political brokers to help achieve this, he went first to Bùki's domains. There, he was shocked to see a Luba chieftain ruling peoples who did not all share a Luba heritage. So, he withdrew a medal that Bùki must have been given not long before Van Walleghem arrived. Van Walleghem also suggested that Bùki must have been a *mungeni*, or foreigner in Luba, and was therefore an illegitimate ruler.

Van Walleghem's version of Luba history was not so far at odds with the prevailing realities, particularly given that Bùki's heritage related back to a fire king in the form of Bùki Kansimba. While Van Walleghem had arrived at a similar conclusion to that of many subsequent historians, he did not see the Luba culture as a contested model of sovereignty. Rather, he saw it more as a 'social fact,' a near biological kinship identity that determined the model of sovereignty to which its adherents were bound in perpetuity. According to Van Walleghem, the only resolution to the problem of political authority in southern Kongolo was to reinstall Bùki's vassals, or *bilolo*, to their rightful positions of power and that they had enjoyed prior to the CK's arrival. In so doing, he carefully followed the strictures of both the 1903 and 1906 Decrees. As one can imagine with so many big men being installed, though, the structure of colonial government in rural Congo quickly became unwieldy.

In 1914, the District Commissioner (DC) of Tanganika-Möero wrote to the Vice Governor-General of Katanga, Johan Maximillian Kesler, to complain that the Luba had 'numerous conglomerations' that had developed with many vying to be recognized by the colonial state as sovereign.[146] Despite this information, the devolved version of Belgian chieftainship would only be revised after the First World War when the colonial conquests were completed. Whether or not Bùki ruled people who did not recognize the sanctity of Luba kingship, the salient point was that colonial officials had begun their efforts to collaborate with him in order to establish a hierarchical Luba monarchy in southern Kongolo. Afterwards, Belgian officials, such as Van Walleghem, planned to use what they saw as this 'traditional' African polity to help them to enforce their orders. Although he may have questioned the extent of Bùki's sovereignty over non-Luba peoples, Van Walleghem and his successors never debated the authoritarian nature of Luba kingship despite this interpretation being deeply unhistorical.

Having installed Bùki in southern Kongolo, Belgian officials then went to find other African potentates who they could co-opt into their administration. In so doing, they aimed to project their colonial power further into the hinterland. Jean Baptiste Coussement, who took over as head of the territorial service in Kongolo from Van Walleghem in 1913, worked to extend the reach of the colonial administration. However, rather than working extensively with the Luba, his main contacts involved a Songye group known as the Bena Kalonda, in western Kongolo. The Bena Kalonda had installed themselves on land that was, in Jean Coussement's words, 'rich in food supplies and livestock.' For a Belgian official living on the edges of the European trading networks at the time, to find a local place rich in food supplies must have been very heartening.

Coussement's understanding of Songye polities contrasted with Van Walleghem's view of the Luba. Rather than seeing an outsider monarch vying for power with his respective bilolo, he suggested that a tradition of rotating chieftainship existed among the Bena Kalonda. In this context, rotating chieftainship consisted of the head of one of series of noble lineages controlling the chieftainship at one time with another lineage controlling it afterwards. The process of rotation between noble lineages was supposedly governed by councils of notables. In practice, though, rotating chieftainship was usually put in place to mediate lineage disputes. Ironically, Coussement claimed it had actually inspired succession disputes among the Bena Kalonda and so he aimed to stop them practicing rotating chieftainship.[147] So, in a letter to his superiors, he wrote that rotating chieftainship was simply a corrupt bargain between rural elites that would not be missed by colonial subjects were it to end. Yet, there is more than a little room to be sceptical of Coussement's reasoning for closing down the Bena Kalonda's system rotating chieftainship.

Coussement saw rotating chieftainship as an impediment to the kind of autocratic government that could enforce unpopular colonial orders. For example, if notables decided that a chief should be elected who was less amiable to the colonial occupation than an alternative candidate then this could pose a problem for the Belgian administration. Rather than base Bena Kalonda's chieftainship on a quasi-electoral basis, therefore, Coussement decided to use another Songye institution to promote colonial chieftainship instead: the *Sultani Ya Miti* (Tree Sultans). The Tree Sultans were lineage heads who had survived the Swahili onslaught in the late nineteenth century and occupied a series of sacred groves, or *hatas*, in Songye villages.[148] Given that the Swahili installed sultanis as leaders in Songye villages as their proxies, the Sultani Ya Miti were supposedly looked upon as more authentic leaders even if their secular powers had been severely constrained by their Swahili-installed competitors. Mwana Goy, for example, had been chased out of Bena Kalonda at the behest of Tippu Tip's proxy, Mohamedi Lusana. However, by installing a Sultani Ya Miti as chief, Coussement planned to harness the legitimacy the Tree Sultans enjoyed to help him to establish a viable colonial version of chieftainship among the Bena Kalonda. So, in 1913, Coussement enthroned Yakitenge as the first colonial chief of the group. He chose Yakitenge in part because the latter was installed by rotation *as well as* being a Sultani Ya Miti. In the short term, then, not much changed aside from the fact that the principle of installing Sultani Ya Miti had been established over and above that of rotating chieftainship.

The history of Coussement and Van Walleghem's encounters with African polities in Kongolo illustrates the extent to which colonial agents sought to ally themselves with a disinherited rural aristocracy that was capable of enacting European orders in some cases. The strength of their African allies was especially important before the First World War, when the colonial conquests were not yet completed.[149] Colonial officials worked carefully to ensure that the elites they chose to deal with, as well as the discourses that sustained them, were popular with as many of their noble subjects as possible. To shore up their allies' rule, in every instance, be it the installation of a Sultani Ya Miti or a Luba Mulopwe, the Belgian administration tried to infuse local African traditions with a distinctively hierarchical character. In so doing, they aimed to close down the precious few discursive mechanisms for civic debate that remained after the ravages of Zanzibari colonization. Before the Swahili and Belgian occupations, leadership among local groups in Kongolo tended to be based on what John Iliffe described as 'civil distinction, the management of a household, and virtuous character.'[150] Afterwards, though, it was more dependent on the extent to which one collaborated with the colonial administration. At the same time, African leaders were naturally keen to promote their traditional credentials to their subjects as opposed to their colonial connections.

The popularity and power of African colonial allies was based at least in part on a series of Belgian interpretations of local Congolese political institutions that did not coincide with those of their subjects, however. For example, it would not have been obvious to most Africans that the Sultani Ya Miti had the right to levy taxes, because their role had become far more spiritual than secular. So, unsurprisingly, Songye subjects were very hostile to the Sultani Ya Miti once hut taxes began to be enforced later on. Likewise, Luba subjects did not regard their fire kings as people who extracted tribute but rather as cultural emissaries whose job it was to teach 'kingly manners' and not to behave like common despots.[151] Overall, these intrusions did not amount to an *invention* of tradition(s) but rather, as Terence Ranger's auto-critique of his own 'invention of tradition' thesis suggested, it was a *reimagining* of them or at least a halting reimagining of them.[152] Belgian officials, such as Engels, were adamant that African polities should be constituted according to what he called 'pre-existing customs.'[153] Yet it was obvious to everyone concerned that many important facets of these 'customs' had been altered.

The Hêmbá lineages on the right bank of the Lualaba River provided very few political institutions that were as obviously open to the infusion of colonial authoritarianism as that of the Balopwè, for example, especially given their often highly decentralized precolonial polities. Yet Alisa LaGamma's work, following that of Ngasha Mulumbati, argues that Hêmbá lineages could also have offered Belgian officials at least some institutions that could be moulded into hierarchical ones and not least in the case of Hêmbá chieftainship itself.[154] For example, 'only the direct descendants of the founding ancestor were eligible to succeed to power' in most Hêmbá lineages.[155] When a chief died, 'the eldest among his brothers and cousins became his successor.'[156] Again, misunderstandings were rife given that a Hêmbá chiefs' role was actually meant to be far more that of a problem solver, as well as that of a guardian of the community, than of a despot.[157] Given the discrepancy between the colonial interpretation of Hêmbá chieftainship and the precolonial, pre-Zanzibari realities of it, it is unsurprising that the imposition of Belgian power on the right bank provoked serious conflicts throughout the period of Belgian rule and even beyond it.

The difficulties associated with the infusion of colonial authoritarianism into pre-existing modalities of chieftainship were aptly illustrated by events in the Hêmbá chieftainship of Bena Mambwe. Like most others, the substance of Mambwe's social constitution mirrored that of a 'district' defined as per the tradition outlined in the first chapter. In other words, it was a loose alliance between houses, although in colonial and postcolonial parlance districts were known as 'collectivities' and/or 'chieftainships.'[158] The pressures of enforcing colonial directives catalyzed rivalries between houses that exploded during the reign of Ngombe Beya Mayanga. Mayanga was the first chief of the Mambwe collectivity to be officially recognized by the Belgian colonial state.[159] The administration enthroned him in 1906, in line with Leopold's Decree.[160] The Belgians installed Mayanga because they argued that his supremacy over those presumed to be his subjects was far more complete than those of his peers from other clans, with clans again being defined, again, as per the Equatorial African tradition as the alliance of extended families.[161]

What evidence there was of Mayanga's supremacy was unclear, though. According to colonial documents, villagers often said he suffered from a 'superiority complex' with these same documents also reporting that he relentlessly pursued his ambition of total dominance of Bena Mambwe.[162] Again, Belgian agents may have deliberately exaggerated Mayanga's 'superiority complex' so as to blame him for having to enforce their own unpopular orders. Yet, although Mayanga had succeeded in curtailing a modicum of factional infighting, and had established the predominance of his own Bazila Koni clan, his regular recruitment of porters for the Force Publique during World War One made him extremely unpopular.[163] In the end, the long-serving chief was killed during one of his wartime porter conscription campaigns in Zola, a village controlled by the Bazila Koni clan's rivals, the Bazila Nyoka.[164] The colonial regime was shocked by Mayanga's assassination. Later, in 1920, the assistant District Commissioner, Tytgat, opened an inquiry into the causes of his death.[165] Yet, the study itself did little to alleviate the unstable political situation in Bena Mambwe that the attempted colonial imposition of rural despotism had fermented.[166]

Even with occasional African support, the self-styled 'Bula Matari' ('Breaker of Rocks') administration struggled to entrench its rule anywhere in Kongolo's hinterland. Instead, it would be truer to say that a series of pre-existing African elites had gained a new set of European allies. As they wrestled to infuse them with—or reinforce—authoritarian elements within pre-existing political traditions, colonial officials had very few resources at their disposal. From the photographic evidence that remains from the *Service Photographique*, a colonial propaganda outlet, we know that there was a tax office as well as a territorial bureau in Kongolo by 1913 (see Fig. 3.5).[167]

Other sources suggest that there was a prison around that time as well.[168] But there were precious few other resources or infrastructure that the administration could mobilise to reimagine African political institutions in the territory. As Mayanga's assassination underlined, the War put tremendous pressure on the already skeletal Belgian administration. Apart from compromising its ability to act effectively to protect its African allies, it meant that the administration recruited a significant number of soldiers from southeastern Congo as a whole. And this wartime recruitment considerably depopulated the territory at just the moment when colonial officials were hoping to explore its potential to act as a labour reserve for the *Haut Katanga Industriel* (HKI) complexes in the south.[169] Because colonial chieftainship was imposed on African societies in Kongolo in part to recruit labourers, it is important to outline how this recruitment was organized.

In 1911, the administration created the Katangese Labour Exchange or the *Bourse du Travail du Katanga* (BTK).[170] The BTK was a parastatal organization that had a monopoly on worker recruitment for the whole of Katanga and its constituent concession companies.[171] Rather than a normal

Fig. 3.5 The tax office in Kongolo, 1913 (Royal Museum of Central Africa, AP.0.0.29990, Photo 1)

'bottom-up' labour exchange that functioned as a mutual aid society, as was the case with most European versions at the time, the BTK was very much a state-driven institution. It had a hard task given that some areas of southeastern Congo were sparsely populated.[172] So, those officials charged with working for the BTK surveyed regions, such as Kongolo, in their per-petual hunt for labour and mostly for the HKI complexes. In 1913, a BTK official called Gravwets, prospected Kongolo and suggested that it could 'provide [the BTK] with labour, especially as local needs are limited.'[173] In fact, local needs were not limited at all if you were an African looking to build a social following and work the land. But Gravwets was, of course, referring to the needs as defined by the colonial state. As such, his words support the claim that the widespread use of forced agricultural labour had not as yet been introduced. So, there were no 'obligatory cultures,' as they were known in colonial parlance, in Kongolo before the First World War. That the expansion of colonial agriculture was stalled in Kongolo was unsurprising given how unstable chieftainship was.

In sum, by the end of the First World War, the consolidation of Belgian rule in Kongolo had barely begun. From a clutch of buildings in Kongolo's town centre, mostly concentrated around the CFL rail junction, Belgian officials tried to forcibly recruit as many African men as it could to HKI and to the *Force Publique* during the War. They did this either through a network of chiefs with whom they had allied themselves or by dint of their own efforts. To some Africans in the territory, then, the Belgian administration felt like a powerful force because it had succeeded in kidnapping or recruiting them. Likewise, Bùki had found that the territorial service could control his political trajectory almost at will. But, there were very serious limits to the Belgian administration's power and particularly with regard to the hinterland. Although Belgian officials had allied themselves with Bùki, as well as having made progress in reinforcing and/or creating a more authoritarian Hêmbá version of chieftainship, more work needed to be done. The Belgians had not succeeded in securing their system of decentralized despotism, as Mahmood Mamdani would characterize it, in the hinterland.[174] The new, dictatorial modalities of local African political thought were not consistently respected by colonial subjects—as Mayanga's story graphically illustrates.[175] To add insult to injury, the continual shortage of Belgian personnel meant that their capacity to intervene in local politics to support their chiefly allies was considerably undermined. The War had heaped yet more pressure on the already pressured administration by catalyzing African hostility towards it as well as setting back its efforts to regulate and reorder political life outside the confines of the CFL junction. The profound weaknesses in secular Belgian coverage of Kongolo meant that significant gaps emerged in European coverage of Kongolo into which the Church could productively insert itself even if did not do so in the southern parts of the territory until after the Second World War.

CONCLUSION

For all the hostility their association with Belgian agents aroused, Catholic missionaries were still the most powerful group of European incomers in Kongolo during the *fin-de-siècle*. They built congregations of varying degrees of significance in the gaps left by the Belgian administration as it focused on mining sites elsewhere in Katanga. Just like their colonial counterparts, though, the power that the Church enjoyed was still contingent and subject to constraints imposed on it by local leaders—who were especially important on the mission frontier. That the Church was not all-powerful meant that it never attained a hegemonic position in Kongolo by the beginning of the twentieth century. Victor Roelens might have declared that Tanganyika was a 'republic' with himself as its president, but this polity, especially as far as Sola and its environs were concerned, was far more spiritually plural than he would have liked.[176] And instead of African societies adapting themselves to Christian practices and beliefs, missionaries often had to tailor their approach to conversion to the intricacies of the social world of African society in Kongolo instead. The Spiritans had arguably experienced more success in Kongolo than the White Fathers. Their Lubunda complex was a stark statement of intent by a group of missionaries who were keen on preventing the extension of secularism across the CFL's ever-expanding network. Lubunda's baptismal rates, for example, were very high even before (and during) the First World War if mission statistics are to be believed. In short, it was clear that a Catholic culture of sorts was beginning put down roots in Kongolo even if it was more fragile than the literature has so far suggested.[177]

Although the Lubunda and Sola out-stations might appear to be two distinct regional poles, they would combine later in that converts from among the Hêmbá and Bango Bango groups would be trained in Lubunda if they could not gain places in the Sola primary school. By the end of the First World War, the school at the Sola out-station had become far more popular and so parents encountered ever more competition in order to send their offspring there. Consequently, the White Fathers were a major exploratory branch of the Catholic edifice in Kongolo. Whereas Songye, Kusu and Luba students attended the primary and teacher-training schools at Lubunda, many of those who would become sympathetic to colonial capitalism later on came from eastern Kongolo. Although the White Fathers initially struggled for converts, they would eventually draw many into their Sola out-station as the following chapters will show. Conversely, because Father Conrad had found the Luba areas 'too turbulent' to establish bases in the early twentieth century, there would be no Catholic presence in southern Kongolo until 1955.[178] By extension, the lack of Catholic presence among the Luba meant that, at least as far as Kongolo was concerned, this group became more distanced from the state given they had to commute to gain access to the social mobility that mission schooling offered. That the Luba or Songye had to travel to engage with Catholicism, either north to Lubunda or across the River to Sola, meant that comparatively fewer of them would become literate and numerate when considered alongside their Báhêmbá and Bango Bango cousins. Rather, it tended to be largely the pre-colonial Luba title-holders and their progeny that rose to prominence in Catholic out-stations in Kongolo later on. Even given access to mission education, though, it might appear counter-intuitive that any rural Congolese people, Luba or otherwise, would come to regard Euro-centric capitalism with anything other than contempt.

Despite the hostility that its wartime recruitment had aroused in the territory, there was no great rebellion against the colonial administration in Kongolo of the scale of those that took place in other parts of southeastern Congo.[179] Rather, the regime was reduced to recruiting African soldiers into the Force Publique when and where it could do so. The bitty narrative of early Belgian intrusions into Kongolo's political scene given in the opening section of this chapter has served, I hope to underline the fact that there was a distinct lack of sustained colonial presence in the territory until the end of the War. The hanging of Africans outside the Sola mission station might be evidence, perhaps, of a very rudimentary and frontier-style justice system. And it is true that some chiefs had been endorsed by Belgian functionaries before War, notably Bùki and some of his Songye neighbours. However, overall, most of Kongolo was not partitioned into the ethnic enclaves that the Decrees of 1903 and 1906 had urged colonial officials to do. As a result, rather than an all-powerful 'Bula Matari' force, this chapter has cast Belgian administrators more as 'incomers.'

As Aldwin Roes has suggested, the 'European network was but one of several expansionist movements encroaching on the Congo basin.'[180] Like the African immigrant groups that arrived there before them, they were, first, foreign to Kongolo and, secondly, they also jostled for power armed only with few resources. Thirdly, the Belgian incomers attempted to reach out to powerful allies where they could to sustain and project their power into the hinterland. And in their search for allies, Belgian agents distorted but crucially did not dissolve pre-existing political institutions as they attempted to imbue them with autocratic power and colonial violence. In fact, the fissiparous nature of local authority dovetailed with the equally fragmented and competing colonial and missionary authorities. After the War, Belgian agents tried to extend their African allies' powers and make their re-imagining of local variants of the tradition more of a reality in Kongolo's hinterland. Yet these efforts would mostly fail and allow even more space for the Catholic Church to expand into.

NOTES

1. Victor Roelens (ed. N. Antoine), *Notre Vieux Congo 1891–1917, Souvenirs du Premier Evêque du Congo Belge* (Namur: Editions Grands Lacs, 1948), p. 164.
2. For a general, British appraisal of early colonial imperialism in Tropical Africa, see for example, P. J. Cain and A. G. Hopkins, *British Imperialism: 1688–2000, Second Edition* (London: Routledge, 2002), pp. 565–592.
3. Rose-Hunt, *A Nervous State: Violence, Remedies and Reverie in Colonial Congo* (Durham: Duke University Press, 2016).
4. Roelens, *Notre Vieux Congo 1891–1917*, p. 164.
5. Mika Vähäkangas, *In Search of the Foundations for African Catholicism: Charles Nyamiti's Theological Methodology* (Leiden: Brill, 1999); Adrian Hastings, *African Catholicism: Essays in Discovery* (London: SCM Press, 1989); and Phyllis Martin, *Catholic Women of Congo-Brazzaville: Mothers and Sisters in Troubled Times* (Bloomington: Indiana University Press, 2009).
6. David M. Gordon, 'Slavery and Redemption in the Catholic Missions of Upper Congo, 1878–1909,' *Slavery and Abolition: A Journal of Slave and Post-slave Studies*, 38, 3 (2017), p. 585.
7. Jean-Claude Ceiller, *Histoire des Missionnaires d'Afrique (Pères blancs): de la Fondation par Mgr Lavigerie à la Mort du Fondateur (1868–1892)* (Paris: Karthala, 2008), p. 280; Gordon, 'Slavery and Redemption in the Catholic Missions of Upper Congo, 1878–1909,' p. 585.
8. Aylward Shorter, *Les Pères Blancs au Temps de la Conquête Coloniale: Histoire des Missionnaires d'Afrique 1892–1914* (Paris: Karthala, 2011), p. 190.
9. Karen E. Fields, 'Christian Missionaries as Anticolonial Militants,' *Theory and Society*, 11, 1 (1982), pp. 95–108.
10. Loffman, 'On the Fringes of a Christian Kingdom,' p. 5.
11. Jean-Pierre Chrétien, *The Great Lakes of Africa: Two Thousand Years of History, Translated by Scott Straus* (New York: Zone Books, 2003), p. 35.
12. Viera Pawlikova-Vilhanova, 'The Role of Early "Missionaries of Africa" or "White Fathers" in the Study and Development of African Languages,' *Asian and African Studies*, 20, 2 (2011), pp. 274–275.
13. Jean Vandermeiren, *Vocabulaire Kiluba-Hemba-Français/Français-Kiluba-Hemba* (Bruxelles: Ministère des Colonies, 1913).
14. Pawlikova-Vilhanova, 'The Role of Early "Missionaries of Africa",' pp. 273–274.
15. Ibid., p. 274.
16. Valentine Yves Mudimbe, *The Idea of Africa* (Bloomington: Indiana University Press, 1994), p. 106; Allen F. Roberts, 'History, Ethnicity

and Change in the "Christian Kingdom" of Southeastern Zaire,' in Leroy Vail (ed.), *The Creation of Tribalism in Southern Africa* (Berkeley: University of California Press, 1991), p. 197; and Gann and Duignan, *The Rulers of Belgian Africa, 1884–1914*, p. 26.

17. Gordon, 'Slavery and Redemption in the Catholic Missions of Upper Congo, 1878–1909,' p. 585.
18. Mudimbe, *The Idea of Africa*, p. 106.
19. Ibid.
20. Ibid.
21. Ibid.
22. Gordon, 'Slavery and Redemption in the Catholic Missions of Upper Congo, 1878–1909,' p. 585.
23. Sundkler and Steed, *A History of the Church in Africa*, p. 603.
24. Archives Générales des Missionnaires de l'Afrique, Rome (AGM), Petit Écho des Missions d'Afrique, Supplément: Notices Nécrologique, Rapport numéro: 33, 'Le Père Auguste Van Acker,' p. 48; AGM, Petit Écho des Missions d'Afrique, Supplément: Notices Nécrologique, XXVᵉ Année, N° c. 270, 1937, 'Le Père Joseph Vandermeiren,' p. 81.
25. Bambi Ceuppens, *Congo Made in Flanders? Koloniale Vlaamse Visies Op 'Blank' en 'Zwart' in Belgisch Congo* (Gent: Academia Press, 2003), p. 54.
26. Roberts, 'History, Ethnicity and Change,' p. 197.
27. Ibid.
28. A. M. Delathuy, *Missie en Staat in Oud-Kongo, 1880–1918: Witte Paters, Scheutisten en Jezuïeten* (Bercham: EPO, 1992), p. 11.
29. Ibid., p. 12.
30. Roberts, 'History, Ethnicity and Change,' p. 197.
31. Ibid.
32. Ibid., p. 198.
33. Archivi della Congregazione per l'Evangelizzazione dei Popoli, Rome (CEP), 'Victor Roelens to Mieczysław Halka-Ledóchowski, Baudounville, 22 dicembre 1898,' Fondo 142, NS. 145, p. 152.
34. Sean Stilwell, *Slavery and Slaving in African History* (Cambridge: Cambridge University Press, 2015), pp. 107–108.
35. Roelens, *Notre Vieux Congo*, pp. 162–165.
36. Stilwell, *Slavery and Slaving in African History*, p. 108.
37. Jean Stengers, 'King Leopold's Congo,' in Roland Oliver and G. N. Sanderson (eds), *The Cambridge History of Africa, Volume 6 from c. 1870–1905* (Cambridge: Cambridge University Press, 1985), p. 346.
38. Roelens, *Notre Vieux Congo*, p. 164.
39. Loffman, 'On the Fringes of a Christian Kingdom,' p. 8.
40. Loffman, 'In the Shadow of the Tree Sultans,' p. 543.

41. AGM, Société des Missionnaires de l'Afrique, Rome (Pères Blancs), *Petit Écho des Missions d'Afrique* (P.B.), Supplément: Notices Nécrologique, Rapport numéro: 33, 'Le Père Auguste Van Acker,' p. 48.
42. Loffman, 'In the Shadow of the Tree Sultans,' p. 548. Interestingly, the mother of the current President of the DRC, Joseph Kabila, was a member of the Bango Bango group.
43. Loffman, 'In the Shadow of the Tree Sultans,' p. 548.
44. Ibid., p. 545.
45. Ibid.
46. Ibid.
47. Jean Comaroff, 'The Diseased Heart of Africa: Medicine, Colonialism and the Black Body,' in Shirley Lindenbaum and Margaret M. Lock (eds), *Knowledge, Power, and Practice: The Anthropology of Medicine and Everyday Life* (Berkeley: University of California Press, 1993), p. 315.
48. Loffman, 'In the Shadow of the Tree Sultans,' p. 548.
49. Ibid., p. 544.
50. Hêmbá varies ever so slightly across different chieftainships in Kongolo.
51. Thomas Turner, *The Congo Wars: Conflict, Myth and Reality* (London: Zed Books, 2007), p. 57.
52. Valérien Milingo, 'Droits Fonciers et Redevances Coutumières Hemba (Zaïre),' *Droit et Cultures Nanterre*, 3 (1982), pp. 61–83; Valérien Milingo, *La Société Hemba (Zaire) et son Rapport á la Terre*, Mémoire Sous la Direction de Eric de Dempierre (Paris: université de Paris 10, 1977).
53. Ntole Kazadi, 'Meprises et Admires: L'Ambivalence des Relations Entre les Bacwa (Pygmees) et les Bahemba (Bantu),' *Africa*, 51, 4 (1981), pp. 836–847.
54. Loffman, 'In the Shadow of the Tree Sultans,' p. 545.
55. René Lemarchand, *Political Awakening in the Belgian Congo* (Berkeley: University of California Press, 1964), p. 124.
56. Ibid.
57. Aylward Shorter, *African Recruits and Mission Conscripts: The White Fathers and the Great War* (Rome: Missionaries of Africa, 2007).
58. Loffman, 'In the Shadow of the Tree Sultans,' p. 539.
59. AGM, *Rapports Annuels: Treizième Année (1917–1918)* (Alger: Imprimerie des Missionnaires de l'Afrique, 1918), p. 405.
60. Ibid.
61. Ibid.
62. Ibid.
63. Ibid.
64. Henry J. Koren, *To the Ends of the Earth: A General History of the Congregation of the Holy Ghost* (Pittsburgh: Duquesne University Press, 1983), p. 34.

65. Koren, *To the Ends of the Earth*, pp. 20–40.
66. Ibid., p. 432.
67. Reuben Loffman, 'Same Memory, Different Memorials: The Holy Ghost Fathers (Spiritans), Martyrdom and the Kongolo Massacre,' *Social Sciences and Missions*, 31 (2018), p. 222.
68. Quoted from Koren, *To the Ends of the Earth*, p. 437.
69. Koren, *To the Ends of the Earth*, p. 437.
70. Bengt Sundkler and Christopher Steed, *The History of the Church in Africa* (Cambridge: Cambridge University Press, 2000), p. 265.
71. Sundkler and Steed, *The History of the Church in Africa*, p. 265.
72. Koren, *To the Ends of the Earth*, p. 451.
73. Ibid.
74. Ibid.
75. Archives du Saint-Esprit, Chevilly-Larue, Val de Marne (CSSp), *Bulletin Officiel*, 'Congo Belge: Fondation d'Une Nouvelle Station: Kongolo,' Numéro 270, Aout 1909, p. 219.
76. Jelmer Vos, 'Without the Slave Trade, No Recruitment: From Slave Trading to "Migrant Recruitment" in the Lower Congo, 1830–1890,' in Benjamin N. Lawrance and Richard Roberts (eds), *Trafficking in Slavery's Wake: Law and the Experience of Women and Children in Africa* (Athens, OH: Ohio University Press, 2012), p. 59.
77. Koren, *To the Ends of the Earth*, p. 544.
78. Adrian Hastings, *The Church in Africa, 1450–1950* (Oxford: Oxford University Press, 1995), p. 438.
79. P. Coulon, *Le Catholicisme et la Vapeur au Centre de l'Afrique par Philip Auguard* (Paris: Maison Mère, 1894).
80. P. Coulon, *Le Catholicisme et la Vapeur au Centre de l'Afrique par Philip Auguard*.
81. Ibid.
82. Eric Hobsbawm, *Age of Empire, 1875–1914* (London: Hachette, 2010).
83. Koren, *To the Ends of the Earth*, p. 259.
84. M. Storme, *Het Onstaan van de Kasai-Missie* (Bruxelles: Académie Royale des Sciences d'Outre-Mer, 1961).
85. P. Coulon, *Le Catholicisme et la Vapeur au Centre de l'Afrique par Philip Auguard*.
86. Ibid.
87. Ibid.
88. Loffman, 'In the Shadow of the Tree Sultans,' p. 541.
89. The closed-chapel system has been the subject of an extensive literature, see: Wyatt MacGaffey, 'Education, Religion, and Social Structure in Zaïre,' *Anthropology & Education Quarterly*, 13, 3 (1982), pp. 238–250; Ciparisse, Gérard, 'Les Structures Traditionnelles de la Société Mpangu

Face à L'Introduction D'une Méthode Occidentale de Développement: Les Fermes-Chapelles du Bas-Congo (1895–1911). II: Annexes,' *Bulletin de l'Institut Historique Belge de Rome Roma*, 51 (1981), pp. 401–684.

90. Anne-Sophie Gijs, 'Émile Van Hencxthoven, un jésuite entre Congo et Congolais… Conflits de conscience et d'intérêts autour du supérieur de la mission du Kwango dans l'État indépendant du Congo (1893–1908),' *Revue d'Histoire Ecclésiastique*, 105, 3–4 (2010), pp. 652–688.

91. Loffman, 'In the Shadow of the Tree Sultans,' p. 542.

92. Ibid., p. 541.

93. John Higginson, *A Working Class in the Making: Belgian Colonial Labor Policy, Private Enterprise and the African Mineworker, 1907–1951* (Madison: University of Wisconsin Press, 1989), p. 20.

94. Rose-Hunt, *A Colonial Lexicon*, p. 56.

95. Loffman, 'In the Shadow of the Tree Sultans,' p. 541.

96. Adeline Masquelier, *Women and Islamic Revival in a West African Town* (Bloomington: Indiana University Press, 2009), p. 157.

97. Loffman, 'In the Shadow of the Tree Sultans,' p. 542.

98. Comaroff and Comaroff, *Of Revelation and Revolution, Volume 2*, p. 63.

99. Eric Hobsbawm, *The Age of Revolution: Europe 1789–1848* (London: Wiedenfield and Nicolson, 1962).

100. The history of Leopold's annexation of the Congo has been most famously explained in Hochschild, *King Leopold's Ghost*. An edited collection appeared recently that also documented Leopold's role in the founding of the Congo in more detail, though, see: Vincent Dujardin, Valérie Rosoux and Tanguy de Wilde, *Léopold II: Entre Génie et Gène: Politique Étrangère et Colonisation* (Paris: Éditions Racine, 2009). See also: Auguste Roeykens, *Le Dessein Africaine de Léopold II: Nouvelles Recherches sur sa Genèse et sa Nature (1875–1876)* (Bruxelles: Académie Royal des Sciences Coloniales, 1955). Leopold II has been the subject of a number of biographical works, including: Emmerson, *Leopold II of the Belgians* and Neal Ascherson, *The King Incorporated: Leopold the Second and the Congo* (London: Granta Books, 1963).

101. What is less well-known was that Leopold II also gained a concession in Tianjin, in China, in 1902, but this was far less significant in historical terms than his Congo adventure.

102. Miguel Bandeira Jerónimo, *The 'Civilising Mission' of Portuguese Colonialism, 1870–1930* (London: Palgrave Macmillan, 2015), p. 13.

103. Henry Morton Stanley, *The Congo and the Founding of Its Free State: A Story of Work and Exploration, 2 Volumes* (London: Sampson Low, Marston, Searle and Riyington, 1885).

104. Henry Morton Stanley, *How I Found Livingstone: Travels, Adventures and Discoveries in Central Africa Including Four Month's Residence with Dr. Livingstone* (London, 1872).

105. These treaties have been the subject of some debate. Tim Jeal argues that they were fair and did not amount to land stealing, see: Tim Jeal, *Stanley: The Impossible Life of Africa's Greatest Explorer* (New Haven: Yale University Press, 2007), p. 283. However, Georges Nzongola-Ntalaja suggests Stanley was duplicitous, see: Nzongola-Ntalaja, *The Congo: From Leopold to Kabila*, p. 16.

106. The propaganda propounded by Belgian elites to convince their subjects to applaud the country's adventures in Africa are the subject of a book by Matthew Stannard, see: Stannard, *Selling the Congo*. For a more in-depth survey of long-lasting resistance to the Free State and the Belgian Congo, see: Jean-Luc Vellut, 'Rural Poverty in Western Shaba, c. 1890–1930,' in Robin H. Palmer and Neil Parsons (eds), *The Roots of Poverty in Central and Southern Africa* (Berkeley: University of California Press, 1977), p. 298.

107. Martin Ewans, *European Atrocity, African Catastrophe: Leopold II, the Congo Free State and Its Aftermath* (London: Psychology Press, 2002), p. 140.

108. See for example the work of Free State apologists such as: Henry Wellington Wack, *The Story of the Congo Free State: Social, Political and Economic Aspects of the Belgian System of Government in Central Africa* (New York: G. P. Putnam's Sons, 1905), pp. 177–196.

109. One such official narrative is by Sidney Langford Hinde, who was one of the most important commanders of Free State forces at this time, see: Sidney Langford Hinde, *The Fall of the Congo Arabs* (London: Methuen and Company, 1897).

110. Lewis H. Gann and Peter Duignan, *The Rulers of Belgian Africa, 1884–1914* (Princeton: Princeton University Press, 1979), p. 65.

111. An interesting contemporary, legal viewpoint on this is: Jesse S. Reeves, 'The Origin of the Congo Free State: Considered from the Standpoint of International Law,' *The American Journal of International Law*, 3, 1 (1909), pp. 99–118.

112. Bogumil Jewsiewicki, 'Belgian Africa,' in Andrew Roberts (ed.), *The Cambridge History of Africa, Volume 7: 1905–1940* (Cambridge: Cambridge University Press, 1986), p. 471.

113. Rose-Hunt, *A Colonial Lexicon: Of Birth Ritual, Medicalization, and Mobility in Colonial Congo* (Durham: Duke University Press, 1999).

114. Iain R. Smith, *The Emin Pasha Relief Expedition, 1886–1890* (Oxford: Clarendon, 1972).

115. Some maps were provided by P. Ceulemans but these were highly impressionistic, see: P. Ceulemans, *La Question Arabe et la Congo (1883–1892)* (Bruxelles, 1959).

116. Delathuy, *Missie en Staat*, p. 12.

117. Kevin C. Dunn, *Imagining the Congo: The International Relations of Identity* (London: Palgrave Macmillan, 2003), p. 21. As Dunn suggests, the AIA became the International Association of the Congo (IAC) in 1879.

118. M'Siri, the Yeke ruler, was a very famous case of an African warlord made to look more brutal the more colonialism penetrated into southeastern Congo, see: Hugues Legros, Chasseurs d'Ivoire. Une Histoire du Royaume Yeke du Shaba (Zaïre) (Bruxelles: Éditions de l'Université de Bruxelles, 1996).

119. Emile Storms has been the subject of a book by Allen F. Roberts, *A Dance of Assassins: Performing Early Colonial Hegemony in the Congo* (Bloomington: Indiana University Press, 2016).

120. Roberts, *A Dance of Assassins*.

121. Jean Omasombo et al., *Tanganyika*, p. 142.

122. Lewis Gann and Peter Duignan suggest that Dhanis did reach Kasongo, to the north of Kongolo, but do not give a date for this, see: Gann and Duignan, *The Rulers of Belgian Africa, 1884–1914*, p. 73.

123. Alexander Delcommune, *Vingt Années de Vie Africaine, Récits de Voyages, D'Adventures et D'Exploration au Congo Belge 1874–1893*, 2 *Volumes* (Ferdinand Larcien: Brussels, 1922).

124. R. J. Cornet, *Katanga: Le Katanga Avant Les Belges et L'Éxpedition Bia-Franqui-Cornet* (L. Cuypers: Brussels, 1946); Jacques Depelchin, *From the Congo Free State to Zaire: Towards a Demystification of Economic and Political History* (London: African Books Collective, 1992), p. 148.

125. Delcommune, *Vingt Années de Vie Africaine*.

126. Bandeja Yamba, 'Industrialisation, Travail et Collectivités Rurales au Shaba (Ex-Katanga), 1900–1960,' *African Economic History*, 19 (1990–1991), p. 56.

127. Bernard Waites, *South Asia and Africa After Independence: Post-colonialism in Historical Perspective* (London: Palgrave Macmillan, 2012), p. 234.

128. Jean-Luc Vellut, 'Rural Poverty in Western Shaba, c. 1890–1930,' p. 299.

129. Jean-Luc Vellut, *Guide de l'Étudiant en Histoire du Zaïre* (Kinshasa: Centre de Recherches Pédagogiques, 1974), p. 116; René Lemarchand, *Political Awakening in the Belgian Congo* (Berkeley: University of California Press, 1964), p. 62; and Ndaywel é Nziem, *Histoire Générale du Congo*, p. 321.

130. Archives Africaine, Ministère des Affaires Etrangères, Bruxelles (AAB), 'Divisions et Subdivisions Territoriaux,' 1908.

131. Victor Roelens also described Kiambi as a 'military post' in his memoire *Notre Vieux Congo*, see: Victor Roelens, *Notre Vieux Congo 1891–1917*, p. 65.

132. For more in-depth coverage of the handover process, see: Guy Vanthemsche, *Belgium and the Congo, 1885–1980* (Cambridge: Cambridge University Press, 2012), pp. 41–42;Gann and Duignan, *The Rulers of Belgian Africa, 1884–1914*, p. 150.

133. Gann and Duignan, *The Rulers of Belgian Africa*, p. 158.

134. Ibid., p. 200.

135. Ibid., p. 161.

136. Many authors have made this point including: Julia Seibert, '"Travail Libre ou Travail Forcé"—Die "Arbeiterfrage" im Belgischen Kongo 1908–1930,' *Journal of Modern European History*, 7, 1 (2009), pp. 95–110.

137. Kabalo was a Luba word meaning 'place where local people who were recruited were directed,' see: E. Van Avermaet et Benoît Mbuyà, *Dictionnaire Kiluba-Français*, p. 45.

138. The Belgian monarch could issue decrees (décrets) without parliamentary countersignature being required, see: Gann and Duignan, *The Rulers of Belgian Africa, 1884–1914*, p. 162.

139. David Northrup, *Beyond the Bend in the River: African Labour in Eastern Zaire, 1865–1940* (Athens, OH: Ohio University Press, 1988), p. 37.

140. Osumaka Likaka, 'Rural Protest: The Mbole Against Belgian Rule, 1897–1959,' *International Journal of African Historical Studies*, 27, 3 (1994), p. 594.

141. Nzongola-Ntalaja, *The Congo: From Leopold to Kabila*, p. 42.

142. Hein Vanhee, 'Les Chefs Médailles,' in Jean-Luc Vellut, Sabine Cornelis, Danielle De Lame, Gauthiers Villers, Zana Etambala, Johan Lagae and Philippe Maréchal (eds), *La Mémoire du Congo: le Temps Colonial* (Tervuren, Musée royal de l'Afrique centrale: Gand, Éditions Snoeck, 2005), pp. 79–82.

143. These sources are detailed in Reefe, *The Rainbow and the Kings*, pp. 229–230. These sources are (1) A. van Malderen, 'Historique des Bena Kwizimu,' (2 August 1921) and (2), Maemans, 'Chefferie Bùki: Histoire Succinct (November, 1924)' and (3), Verhulpen, *Baluba et Balubaïsés du Katanga*, pp. 127, 350. Lists of Luba sovereigns have been usefully outlined by a number of scholars, for example: Ndaywel é Nziem, *Histoire Générale du Congo*, p. 141.

144. There is a document that says Mulopwe Ngoy (Bùki) was the 'little son' of Bùki and this might mean he was young enough to be Kekenya's son, see: ABB, Affaires Indigène et du Main-d'Oeuvre (AIMO), 1735, Rapport Annuel de l'Administration Général (RAG), (2 March 1925), p. 10.

145. Gann and Duignan, *The Rulers of Belgian Africa, 1884–1914*, p. 113.

146. Reuben Loffman, 'In the Shadow of the Tree Sultans: African Elites and the Shaping of Early Colonial Politics on the Katangan Frontier,' *Journal of Eastern African Studies*, 5, 3 (2011), p. 539.
147. Loffman, 'In the Shadow of the Tree Sultans,' p. 538.
148. Sacred groves are the subject of an edited collection, see: Michael J. Sheridan and Celia Nyamwenu (eds), *African Sacred Groves: Ecological Dynamics and Social Change* (Oxford: James Currey, 2008).
149. Ndaywel é Nziem, *Histoire Générale du Congo*, p. 372.
150. Iliffe, *Honour in African History*, p. 67.
151. de Heusch, 'What Shall We Do with a Drunken King?' pp. 363–372.
152. Terence O. Ranger, 'The Invention of Tradition Revisited: The African Case,' in Terence O. Ranger and Olufemi Vaughan (eds), *Legitimacy and the State in Twentieth-Century Africa: Essays in Honour of A. H. M. Kirke-Greene* (Oxford: James Curry, 1993), pp. 62–111.
153. AAB, AIMO, 1773, Basankusu, 11 Juin 1915, Numéro 592, p. 5.
154. LaGamma, *Heroic Africans*, pp. 226–227.
155. Ibid., p. 226.
156. Ibid.
157. Ibid., p. 227.
158. Vansina, *Paths in the Rainforests*, p. 82.
159. AAB, AIMO 1735, Rapport de l'Administration Général (RAG): Premier Semestre, 1924, p. 11; AAB, AIMO 1735, RAG: Deuxième Semestre, 1920, p. 3; Archives Générales de la Société Général des Missionnaires, Rome (AGMR), diaries, 25 May 1919, Sola: Bruges St. Donat (1904–1925), p. 93; and Michel Lwamba Bilonda, *Biographie Historique du Congo: Collection Documents et Travaux*, XX (Lubumbashi: CERDAC, 2000), p. 42.
160. Bilonda, *Biographie Historique du Congo*, p. 45.
161. Vansina, *Paths in the Rainforests*, p. 82.
162. Bilonda, *Biographie Historique du Congo*, p. 44.
163. Ngombe had largely succeeded in asserting the primacy of the Bazila Koni faction over the Bena Matembe and Nyoka, see: Bilonda, *Biographie Historique*, pp. 44–45; AGMR, diary, 25 May 1919, Sola: Bruges St. Donat (1904–1925), p. 93.
164. Interview with Muganza Walunga Augustin, Makutano, Bena Mambwe, 15 April 2009.
165. AAB, AIMO 1735, RAG: Deuxième Semestre, 1924, p. 11.
166. Mahmood Mamdani, *Citizen and Subject: Contemporary Africa and the Legacy of Late Colonialism* (Princeton: Princeton University Press, 1996).
167. The UN now uses the headquarters building but I could not find a trace of the original accountancy building during my fieldwork.
168. Loffman, 'In the Shadow of the Tree Sultans,' p. 545.

169. Allen F. Roberts, 'History, Ethnicity and Change in the "Christian Kingdom" of Southeastern Zaire,' in Leroy Vail (ed.), *The Creation of Tribalism in Southern Africa* (Berkeley: University of California Press, 1991), p. 200.
170. L. H. Gann and Peter Duignan, *Colonialism in Africa, 1870–1960* (Cambridge: Cambridge University Press, 1975), p. 415.
171. Johannes Fabian, Kalundi Mango and Walter Schicho (eds), *History from Below: The Vocabulary of Elisabethville by André Yav: Texts, Translation and Interpretive Essay* (Amsterdam: John Benjamins Publishing, 1990), p. 136.
172. Gann and Duignan, *Colonialism in Africa, 1870–1960*, p. 415.
173. AAB, Main-d'œuvre Indigène (MOI), 3553, Gravwets, Rapport Général sur mon Voyage D'Inspection, p. 4.
174. Mahmood Mamdani, *Citizen and Subject: Contemporary Africa and the Legacy of Late Colonialism* (Princeton: Princeton University Press, 1996).
175. Mamdani, *Citizen and Subject*, pp. 37–61.
176. Comaroff and Comaroff, *Of Revelation and Revolution*, p. 63.
177. David Northrup, 'A Church in Search of a State: Catholic Missionaries in Eastern Zaïre, 1879–1930,' *Journal of Church and State*, 30, 2 (1988), pp. 309–319.
178. Loffman, 'In the Shadow of the Tree Sultans,' p. 541.
179. There were several examples of rebellions in the late CFS period including those of the Force Publique in Luluabourg (1895), Lusambo (1898) and Ituri (1897) and those led by African aristocrats among the Mbudja and the Zande from 1895 to 1904, see: Ndaywel è Nziem, *Histoire Général du Congo*, pp. 304–305. For rebellions in the CFS and early Belgian Congo, see also: Gann and Duignan, *The Rulers of Belgian Africa, 1884–1914*, pp. 114–115.
180. Aldwin Roes, 'Towards a History of Mass Violence in the Etat Indépendent du Congo, 1885–1908,' *South African Historical Journal*, 62, 4 (2010), p. 637.

BIBLIOGRAPHY

Bilonda, Michel Lwamba, *Biographie Historique du Congo: Collection Documents et Travaux*, XX (Lubumbashi: CERDAC, 2000).
Cain, P. J., and Hopkins, A. G., *British Imperialism: 1688–2000, Second Edition* (London: Routledge, 2002).
Ceiller, Jean-Claude, Histoire des Missionnaires d'Afrique (Pères blancs)*: de la Fondation par Mgr Lavigerie à la Mort du Fondateur (1868–1892)* (Paris: Karthala, 2008).
Ceulemans, P., *La Question Arabe et la Congo (1883–1892)* (Bruxelles, 1959).

Ceuppens, Bambi, *Congo Made in Flanders? Koloniale Vlaamse Visies Op 'Blank' en 'Zwart' in Belgisch Congo* (Gent: Academia Press, 2003).

Chrétien, Jean-Pierre, *The Great Lakes of Africa: Two Thousand Years of History,* Translated by Scott Straus (New York: Zone Books, 2003).

Ciparisse, Gérard, 'Les Structures Traditionnelles de la Société Mpangu Face à L'Introduction D'une Méthode Occidentale de Développement: Les Fermes-Chapelles du Bas-Congo (1895–1911). II: Annexes,' *Bulletin de l'Institut Historique Belge de Rome Roma,* 51 (1981), pp. 401–684.

Comaroff, Jean, 'The Diseased Heart of Africa: Medicine, Colonialism and the Black Body,' in Shirley Lindenbaum and Margaret M. Lock (eds), *Knowledge, Power, and Practice: The Anthropology of Medicine and Everyday Life* (Berkeley: University of California Press, 1993), pp. 305–329.

Comaroff, Jean, and Comaroff, John, *Of Revelation and Revolution, Volume 2: The Dialectics of Modernity on a South African Frontier* (Chicago: University of Chicago Press, 1997).

Cornet, R. J., *Katanga: Le Katanga Avant Les Belges et L'Éxpedition Bia-Franqui-Cornet* (L. Cuypers: Brussels, 1946).

Coulon, P., *Le Catholicisme et la Vapeur au Centre de l'Afrique par Philip Auguard* (Paris: Maison Mère, 1894).

Delathuy, A. M., *Missie en Staat in Oud-Kongo, 1880–1918: Witte Paters, Scheutisten en Jezuïeten* (Bercham: EPO, 1992).

Delcommune, Alexander, *Vingt Années de Vie Africaine, Récits de Voyages, D'Adventures et D'Exploration au Congo Belge 1874–1893, 2 Volumes* (Ferdinand Larcien: Brussels, 1922).

Depelchin, Jacques, *From the Congo Free State to Zaire: Towards a Demystification of Economic and Political History* (London: African Books Collective, 1992).

Dujardin, Vincent, Rosoux, Valérie, and Wilde, Tanguy de, *Léopold II: Entre Génie et Gêne: Politique Étrangère et Colonisation* (Paris: Éditions Racine, 2009).

Dunn, Kevin C., *Imagining the Congo: The International Relations of Identity* (London: Palgrave Macmillan, 2003).

Emmerson, Barbara, *Leopold II of the Belgians* and Neal Ascherson, *The King Incorporated: Leopold the Second and the Congo* (London: Granta Books, 1963).

Ewans, Martin, *European Atrocity, African Catastrophe: Leopold II, the Congo Free State and Its Aftermath* (London: Psychology Press, 2002).

Fabian, Johannes, Mango, Kalundi, and Schicho, Walter (eds), *History from Below: The Vocabulary of Elisabethville by André Yav: Texts, Translation and Interpretive Essay* (Amsterdam: John Benjamins Publishing, 1990).

Fields, Karen E., 'Christian Missionaries as Anticolonial Militants,' *Theory and Society,* 11, 1 (1982), pp. 95–108.

Gann, L. H., and Duignan, Peter, *Colonialism in Africa, 1870–1960* (Cambridge: Cambridge University Press, 1975).

Gann, L. H., and Duignan, Peter, *The Rulers of Belgian Africa, 1884–1914* (Princeton: Princeton University Press, 1979).

Garvey, Brian, *Bembaland Church: Religious and Social Change in South Central Africa, 1891–1964* (Leiden: Brill, 1994).

Gijs, Anne-Sophie, 'Émile Van Hencxthoven, un jésuite entre Congo et Congolais… Conflits de conscience et d'intérêts autour du supérieur de la mission du Kwango dans l'État indépendant du Congo (1893–1908),' *Revue d'Histoire Ecclésiastique*, 105, 3–4 (2010), pp. 652–688.

Gordon, David M., 'Slavery and Redemption in the Catholic Missions of Upper Congo, 1878–1909,' *Slavery and Abolition: A Journal of Slave and Post-slave Studies*, 38, 3 (2017), pp. 577–600.

Hastings, Adrian, *African Catholicism: Essays in Discovery* (London: SCM Press, 1989).

Hastings, Adrian, *The Church in Africa, 1450–1950* (Oxford: Oxford University Press, 1995).

Headrick, Daniel, *The Tools of Empire: Technology and European Imperialism in the Nineteenth-Century* (Oxford: Oxford University Press, 1981).

Heusch, Luc de, 'What Shall We Do with the Drunken King?' *Africa: Journal of the International African Institute*, 45 (1975), pp. 363–372.

Hinde, Sidney Langford, *The Fall of the Congo Arabs* (London: Methuen and Company, 1897).

Hobsbawm, Eric, *The Age of Revolution: Europe 1789–1848* (London: Wiedenfield and Nicolson, 1962).

Hobsbawm, Eric, *Age of Empire, 1875–1914* (London: Hachette, 2010).

Iliffe, John, *Honour in African History* (Cambridge: Cambridge University Press, 1995).

Jeal, Tim, *Stanley: The Impossible Life of Africa's Greatest Explorer* (New Haven: Yale University Press, 2007).

Jenkins, Philip, *The Next Christendom: The Coming of Global Christianity, Third Edition* (Oxford: Oxford University Press, 2011).

Jerónimo, Miguel Bandeira, *The 'Civilising Mission' of Portuguese Colonialism, 1870–1930* (London: Palgrave Macmillan, 2015).

Jewsiewicki, Bogumil, 'Unequal Development: Capitalism and the Katanga Economy, 1919–1940,' in Robin H. Palmer and Neil Parsons (eds), *The Roots of Poverty in Central and Southern Africa* (Berkeley: University of California Press, 1977), pp. 317–344.

Jewsiewicki, Bogumil, 'Belgian Africa,' in Andrew Roberts (ed.), *The Cambridge History of Africa, Volume 7: 1905–1940* (Cambridge: Cambridge University Press, 1986), pp. 460–493.

Kazadi, Ntole, 'Meprises et Admires: L'Ambivalence des Relations Entre les Bacwa (Pygmees) et les Bahemba (Bantu),' *Africa*, 51, 4 (1981), pp. 836–847.

Koren, Henry J., *To the Ends of the Earth: A General History of the Congregation of the Holy Ghost* (Pittsburgh: Duquesne University Press, 1983).

LaGamma, Alison, *Heroic Africans: Legendary Leaders, Iconic Sculptures* (New Haven: Yale University Press, 2011).

Legros, Hugues, *Chasseurs d'Ivoire: Une Histoire du Royaume Yeke du Shaba (Zaïre)* (Bruxelles: Éditions de l'Université de Bruxelles, 1996).

Lemarchand, René, *Political Awakening in the Belgian Congo* (Berkeley: University of California Press, 1964).

Likaka, Osumaka, 'Rural Protest: The Mbole against Belgian Rule, 1897–1959,' *International Journal of African Historical Studies*, 27, 3 (1994), pp. 589–617.

Loffman, Reuben, 'In the Shadow of the Tree Sultans: African Elites and the Shaping of Early Colonial Politics on the Katangan Frontier,' *Journal of Eastern African Studies*, 5, 3 (2011), pp. 535–552.

Loffman, Reuben, 'On the Fringes of a Christian Kingdom: The White Fathers, Colonial Rule, and the Báhêmbá in Sola, Northern Katanga, 1909–1960,' *Journal of Religion in Africa*, 45 (2016), pp. 279–306.

Loffman, Reuben, 'Same Memory, Different Memorials: The Holy Ghost Fathers (Spiritans), Martyrdom and the Kongolo Massacre,' *Social Sciences and Missions*, 31 (2018), pp. 217–250.

MacGaffey, Wyatt, 'Education, Religion, and Social Structure in Zaïre,' *Anthropology & Education Quarterly*, 13, 3 (1982), pp. 238–250.

Mamdani, Mahmood, *Citizen and Subject: Contemporary Africa and the Legacy of Late Colonialism* (Princeton: Princeton University Press, 1996).

Markowitz, Marvin D., *Cross and Sword: The Political Role of Missionaries in the Belgian Congo, 1908–1960* (Stanford: Hoover Institution, 1973).

Marre, Francis, *Jules Renkin et la Conquête Africaine* (Bruxelles: G. van Oest, 1917).

Martin, Phyllis, *Catholic Women of Congo-Brazzaville: Mothers and Sisters in Troubled Times* (Bloomington: Indiana University Press, 2009).

Milingo, Valérien, *La Société Hemba (Zaire) et son Rapport á la Terre*, Mémoire Sous la Direction de Eric de Dempierre (Paris: université de Paris 10, 1977).

Milingo, Valérien, 'Droits Fonciers et Redevances Coutumières Hemba (Zaïre),' *Droit et Cultures Nanterre*, 3 (1982), pp. 61–83.

Mudimbe, Valentine Yves, *The Idea of Africa* (Bloomington: Indiana University Press, 1994).

Ndaywel è Nziem, Isidore, *Histoire Général du Congo: De l'Héritage Ancien á la République Démocratique* (Préface de Théophile Obenga, Postface de Pierre Salmon) (Bruxelles: De Boeck & Larcier, 1998).

Northrup, David, 'A Church in Search of a State: Catholic Missionaries in Eastern Zaïre, 1879–1930,' *Journal of Church and State*, 30, 2 (1988a), pp. 309–319.

Northrup, David, *Beyond the Bend in the River: African Labour in Eastern Zaire, 1865–1940* (Athens, OH: Ohio University Press, 1988b).

Nzongola-Ntalaja, Georges, *The Congo: From Leopold to Kabila: A Peoples' History* (London: Zed Books, 2002).

Omasombo, Jean, Kasyulwe, Désiré Kisonga, Léonard, Guillaume, Zana, Mathieu, Simons, Edwine, Krawczyk, Joris, and Laghmouch, Mohammed, *République Démocratique du Congo: Tanganyika: Espace Fécondé par le Lac et le Rail* (Tervuren: Musée Royale de l'Afrique Centrale, 2014).

Pawlikova-Vilhanova, Viera, 'The Role of Early "Missionaries of Africa" or "White Fathers" in the Study and Development of African Languages,' *Asian and African Studies*, 20, 2 (2011), pp. 267–288.

Ranger, Terence O., 'The Invention of Tradition Revisited: The African Case,' in Terence O. Ranger and Olufemi Vaughan (eds), *Legitimacy and the State in Twentieth-Century Africa: Essays in Honour of A. H. M. Kirke-Greene* (Oxford: James Curry, 1993), pp. 62–111.

Reefe, Thomas Q., *The Rainbow and the Kings: A History of the Luba Empire to 1891* (Berkeley: University of California Press, 1982).

Reeves, Jesse S., 'The Origin of the Congo Free State: Considered from the Standpoint of International Law,' *The American Journal of International Law*, 3, 1 (1909), pp. 99–118.

Roberts, Allen F., 'History, Ethnicity and Change in the "Christian Kingdom" of Southeastern Zaire,' in Leroy Vail (ed.), *The Creation of Tribalism in Southern Africa* (Berkeley: University of California Press, 1991), pp. 193–214.

Roberts, Allen F., *A Dance of Assassins: Performing Early Colonial Hegemony in the Congo* (Bloomington: Indiana University Press, 2016).

Roelens, Victor (ed. N. Antoine), *Notre Vieux Congo 1891–1917, Souvenirs du Premier Evêque du Congo Belge* (Namur: Editions Grands Lacs, 1948).

Roes, Aldwin, 'Towards a History of Mass Violence in the Etat Indépendent du Congo, 1885–1908,' *South African Historical Journal*, 62, 4 (2010), pp. 634–670.

Rose-Hunt, Nancy, *A Colonial Lexicon: Of Birth Ritual, Medicalization, and Mobility in the Congo* (Durham: Duke University Press, 1999).

Rose-Hunt, Nancy, *A Nervous State: Violence, Remedies, and Reverie in Colonial Congo* (Durham: Duke University Press, 2016).

Roeykens, Auguste, *Le Dessein Africaine de Léopold II: Nouvelles Recherches sur sa Genèse et sa Nature (1875–1876)* (Bruxelles: Académie Royal des Sciences Coloniales, 1955).

Sheridan, Michael J., and Nyamwenu, Celia (eds), *African Sacred Groves: Ecological Dynamics and Social Change* (Oxford: James Currey, 2008).

Shorter, Aylward, *African Recruits and Mission Conscripts: The White Fathers and the Great War* (Rome: Missionaries of Africa, 2007).

Shorter, Aylward, *Les Pères Blancs au Temps de la Conquête Coloniale: Histoire des Missionnaires d'Afrique 1892–1914* (Paris: Karthala, 2011).

Smith, Iain R., *The Emin Pasha Relief Expedition, 1886–1890* (Oxford: Clarendon, 1972).

Stanley, Henry Morton, *How I Found Livingstone: Travels, Adventures and Discoveries in Central Africa Including Four Month's Residence with Dr. Livingstone* (London: Sampson Low, Marston and Company Limited, 1872).

Stanley, Henry Morton, *The Congo and the Founding of Its Free State: A Story of Work and Exploration, 2 Volumes* (London: Sampson Low, Marston, Searle and Riyington, 1885).

Stannard, Matthew, *Selling the Congo: A History of Pro-Empire Propaganda and the Making of Belgian Imperialism* (Lincoln: University of Nebraska Press, 2011).

Stengers, Jean, 'King Leopold's Congo,' in Roland Oliver and G. N. Sanderson (eds), *The Cambridge History of Africa, Volume 6 from c. 1870–1905* (Cambridge: Cambridge University Press, 1985), pp. 315–358.

Stilwell, Sean, *Slavery and Slaving in African History* (Cambridge: Cambridge University Press, 2015).

Storme, M., *Het Onstaan van de Kasai-Missie* (Bruxelles: Académie Royale des Sciences d'Outre-Mer, 1961).

Sundkler, Bengt, and Steed, Christopher, *The History of the Church in Africa* (Cambridge: Cambridge University Press, 2000).

Turner, Thomas, *The Congo Wars: Conflict, Myth and Reality* (London: Zed Books, 2007).

Vähäkangas, Mika, *In Search of the Foundations for African Catholicism: Charles Nyamiti's Theological Methodology* (Leiden: Brill, 1999).

Vandermeiren, Jean, *Vocabulaire Kiluba-Hemba-Français/Français-Kiluba-Hemba* (Bruxelles: Ministère des Colonies, 1913).

Vanhee, Hein, 'Les Chefs Médailles,' in Jean-Luc Vellut, Sabine Cornelis, Danielle De Lame, Gauthiers Villers, Zana Etambala, Johan Lagae, and Philippe Maréchal (eds), *La Mémoire du Congo: le Temps Colonial* (Tervuren, Musée royal de l'Afrique centrale: Gand, Éditions Snoeck, 2005), pp. 79–82.

Vanthemsche, Guy, *Belgium and the Congo, 1885–1980* (Cambridge: Cambridge University Press, 2012).

Vellut, Jean-Luc, *Guide de l'Étudiant en Histoire du Zaïre* (Kinshasa: Centre de Recherches Pédagogiques, 1974).

Vellut, Jean-Luc, 'Rural Poverty in Western Shaba, c. 1890–1930,' in Robin H. Palmer and Neil Parsons (eds), *The Roots of Poverty in Central and Southern Africa* (Berkeley: University of California Press, 1977), pp. 294–316.

Vos, Jelmer, 'Without the Slave Trade, No Recruitment: From Slave Trading to "Migrant Recruitment" in the Lower Congo, 1830–1890,' in Benjamin N. Lawrance and Richard Roberts (eds), *Trafficking in Slavery's Wake: Law and the Experience of Women and Children in Africa* (Athens, OH: Ohio University Press, 2012), pp. 45–64.

Wack, Henry Wellington, *The Story of the Congo Free State: Social, Political and Economic Aspects of the Belgian System of Government in Central Africa* (New York: G. P. Putnam's Sons, 1905).

Waites, Bernard, *South Asia and Africa After Independence: Post-colonialism in Historical Perspective* (London: Palgrave Macmillan, 2012).

Yamba, Bandeja, 'Industrialisation, Travail et Collectivités Rurales au Shaba (Ex-Katanga), 1900–1960,' *African Economic History*, 19 (1990–1991), pp. 55–76.

CHAPTER 4

The Failure of 'Great' Chieftainships and the Consolidation of Catholic Authority, 1918–1932

In patientia vestra possidebitis animas vestras.
Luke 21:19

The last chapter explained how two sets of Catholic missionaries, namely the Spiritans and the White Fathers, exploited a lack of state coverage to establish a significant if unevenly spread presence in the territory of Kongolo. This chapter moves the story on by arguing that those missionaries consolidated their power under Louis Franck, the post-War Minister of the Colonies (1918–1924), and his successors during the interwar period. Before the War, missionaries had acquired substantial social and political influence in the hinterland. In many cases, their claims to land and followers came at the expense of that of local chiefs and sub-chiefs. After the War, Louis Franck thought that the time was right to erect a series of what he called 'great chieftainships' that were supposed to consolidate the range of settlements that had emerged from the 1903/1906 Decrees.[1] Rather than thousands of them, there would be fewer chieftainships and chiefs but chieftainships would be far larger and ruled by paramount chiefs. Franck believed that these 'great chieftainships' should

---

The original version of the book was revised: Belated corrections have been incorporated. The correction to the book is available at https://doi.org/10.1007/978-3-030-17380-7_9

119
R. A. Loffman, *Church, State and Colonialism in Southeastern Congo, 1890–1962*, Cambridge Imperial and Post-Colonial Studies Series, https://doi.org/10.1007/978-3-030-17380-7_4

be closely related—if not actually identical—to those rent asunder during the Belgian wars of conquest in the late nineteenth and early twentieth centuries. Franck's predecessor, Jules Renkin (1908–1918), had already delineated chiefs' roles more clearly than they had ever been under the Free State—but Franck wanted to push this legislation much further.[2]

Under Louis Franck's policies, there would be fewer hamlets and so African subjects would theoretically be easier for chiefs and territorial administers to tax, recruit and survey. In Belgian officials' minds, the early interwar era was thus not to be the one of the missionary, such as Victor Roelens, but that of the African chief. But given that it was on the periphery of the political economy of the Belgian Congo, and hosted very few administrators, Kongolo represented a near insurmountable challenge to the construction of the 'great chieftainships.' While scholars of imperial history have traditionally seen the interwar period as one of secular state consolidation, this rule does not hold for Kongolo.[3] As Louis Franck's scheme floundered, the Church built on the power it had already accrued in the early twentieth-century and drew ever more Africans in Kongolo into its congregations. At times, clerics were even able to impose their own law codes when they diverged from those of the Belgian administration much as they were during the proto-colonial period.

TOWARDS A STRONGER VERSION OF INDIRECT RULE?

After the First World War, Louis Franck, the new Minister of the Colonies, was determined to address the setbacks the colonial state had faced during its early years. After Decrees published in 1903, 1906 and 1910, rural Congo had been divided into a vast patchwork of chieftainships and semi-autonomous sub-chieftainships and that was when such polities had been created at all.[4] While the officials who had helped to establish them naturally believed that they were more than justified ethnographically, their sheer number undermined their chiefs' statuses within the administration.[5] There were as many as 4000 recognized chiefs by 1918 as compared with only 2200 in 1911.[6] In Kongolo alone, there were thirty-eight chieftainships, even as late as 1922.[7] Auguste Van Acker also lamented that the lack of legitimate chiefs hindered mission work given the power struggles going on both in Sola and more generally across eastern Kongolo.[8] Although destabilizing African leaders' authority had been considered an integral part of Free State policy during the era of the colonial conquests, undermining chiefs' powers did not matter much as they neared completion. Quite the reverse. In Louis Franck's view, chiefs' powers needed to be strengthened if they were ever to be made fully responsible for brokering colonial rule in the hinterland.

The post-war Depression (1918–1919), which saw Belgian functionaries strike against their superiors over pay, meant that passing on some of their duties to local chiefs and their subordinates seemed a very attractive proposition from a financial standpoint.[9] In contrast, the thought of patronizing 4000 African potentates over the long term without the Belgian taxpayer becoming heavily involved in financing this patronage was impracticable. So, the number of chiefs in the Belgian Congo would have to be reduced if their status within the colonial administration was to be sustainable.[10] In practical terms, this reduction meant that many sub-chieftainships would have to be amalgamated into each other to create a smaller number of so-called 'great chieftainships.'[11] 'Great chieftainships' would have heavily populated headquarter towns meaning that functionaries could reach local African populations more easily. After their creation, they would be ruled by a paramount chief whose position was supposed to be sanctioned—ideally—by a robust claim to pre-colonial authority. In enacting this policy, Louis Franck's thinking broadly coincided with that of the British style of indirect rule, pioneered by Frederick Lugard, in which kingdoms ruled over African territories with minimal oversight by European officials.

Unfortunately, Louis Franck never produced a Lugardian tome like *The Dual Mandate*, in which his policies were outlined, and so his policies often need to be read between the lines of administrative documents.[12] Franck's ur-text on the Congo, entitled *Congo, Land en Volk*, was more a survey of what he believed to have been the major features and challenges of governing the Belgian Congo in the early 1920s than an exposition of his vision for changing them.[13] Despite the lack of a systemic treatise explaining his version of indirect rule, Franck's subordinates in Kongolo understood that their most pressing administrative task was to create and/or resurrect 'great chieftainships' in the territory. In their territorial and district reports, many claimed to have believed as Franck did that the remnants of the feudal enclaves that had been destroyed by the colonial conquests still remained; albeit in rather diffuse forms. Put differently, they believed as Franck did that African subjects held land given to them by chiefs who expected their loyalty in return. Maurice Lippens, one of the Governors of the Belgian Congo under Franck's tenure, believed heartily in this approach. Coming from one of Belgium's most prestigious families, as well as being a major financier,

Maurice Lippens lent an air of respectability to Franck's bold experiment. Lippens had considerable colonial experience in his own right and was suitably anti-clerical for Franck's taste and, so, in many ways, was a natural choice for the Minister to promote as Governor-General of the Belgian Congo in 1921.

Like Franck, Lippens was deeply inspired by Lugard; calling his *Dual Mandate* 'a beacon of light to us all' in a speech to the Royal African Society of the UK in London.[14] Lippens might well have been playing to his hosts by lauding Lugard's work but his comments surely betray at least some evidence of his interest in the British model of indirect rule. And, although Lippens disagreed with his masters in Brussels over the construction of a narrow-gauge railway in Buta and subsequently resigned in 1923, his successor, Martin Rutten (1923–1927), continued to advocate Franck's policies.[15] Outside of the metropolitan and colonial capitals, the man most responsible for implementing Louis Franck's policies in Kongolo was Georges Van Der Kerken, a keen ethnographer and the then District Commissioner (DC) of Tanganika-Möero.[16] Like his superiors in Brussels and Boma, Van Der Kerken was convinced that his district was a place in which Franck's robust vision of indirect rule could flourish.[17] He was joined in his pursuit of Franck's policies by a string of territorial administrators of Kongolo, including Van Der Sraeten and Larmoyer.[18] Yet Kongolo's volatile history, much like that of the colony as a whole, meant that Van Der Kerken and his subordinates would not be able to dictate the intricacies of African public life to quite the extent that they had hoped.

As the third chapter suggested, the First World War had caused widespread resentment among Africans living in Kongolo exactly as it had in other parts of the Congo. The nightly kidnapping raids undertaken by Belgian functionaries had provoked widespread anguish among local people—particularly given the land-rich and people-scarce economy that existed in the Congo. The forced removal of able-bodied men, or *Hommes Adultes Valides* (HAVs), from communities was devastating given the labour that they performed for commercial as well as subsistence purposes. And, as in other areas across the colony, African hostility to the Belgian administration only increased when the former sought to tax the latter as the War was coming to a close. Colonial officials acknowledged this anger and realized they needed to placate their subjects.

First, Belgian functionaries handed out cash premiums to some African elites. Secondly, they gave those who fought in the War and who had survived the opportunity to buy land in Kongolo's town centre in a scheme called *licencies* (retirement).[19] The areas designated as part of the licencies were important because they formed the basis for some of the first Africans in Kongolo outside the CFL work camp to live in Kongolo's town centre and hence outside the areas ruled by so-called 'customary' or chiefly rule. Rural Africans now saw that there were alternatives to living under the arbitrary rule of their colonial-backed rural aristocracies and so many tried to gain access to town centre accommodation in the years following the War. African migration to the licencies, which included clandestine female as well as male migration, presented yet another challenge to the colonial construction of chieftainship in Kongolo.[20] If a chief's income and hence prestige was based on the number of people living in their chieftainship then the emigration of their subjects to the licencies systematically undermined their power.

Where they could not create licences or hand out cash premiums, Belgian functionaries simply had to work with the profound and profuse anger that they and their predecessors had inspired. If 'great chieftainships' were ever to be mapped out, therefore, then the exercise would have to be done in the midst of profound African hostility. Despite all the lingering resentment against his rule in Tanganika-Möero, and by extension Kongolo, Van der Kerken remained optimistic that the hinterland could be consolidated into the 'great chieftainships' that Louis Franck had prescribed (see Fig. 4.1 for territories within Tanganyika-Moero).

His optimism derived in a large measure from his belief that the patchwork of chieftainships that had already been mapped out before the War could be amalgamated into 'great' ones with relative ease. Likewise, the task of rebuilding pre-colonial polities would be speeded by the arrival of a new cadre of colonial officials, trained at a recently established university that Louis Franck himself had opened in Antwerp called the *Ecole Coloniale Supérieure* (Colonial College) (ECS) later known as the *Université Coloniale*.[21] Edmond Verhulpen, who wrote the influential ethnography of the Luba peoples, went to this very University. The idea was that if these colonial officials, trained in ethnography like Verhulpen, looked hard enough they would inevitably find the remanence of pre-colonial polities. This kind of thinking obviously draw heavily on a largely ahistorical conception of the African past in which chieftainships were simply social facts rather than historically constructed political institutions.

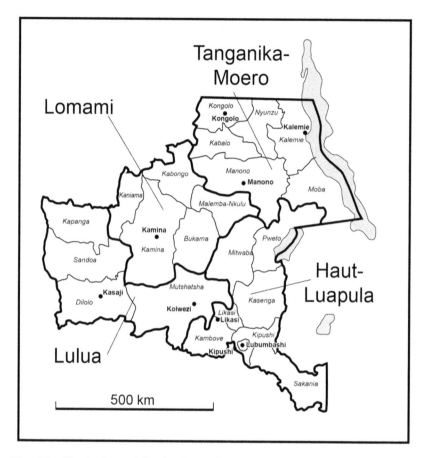

Fig. 4.1   Territories and districts in southeastern Congo

Despite all the evidence they encountered to the contrary, Belgian functionaries rarely if ever relinquished their Euro-centric way of understanding local societies in Kongolo. Colonial reports written about the district of Tanganika-Möero as a whole were laced with references to antiquity as a means of summarizing colonial administrative policy.[22] Correspondingly, and as previously noted, Belgian functionaries understood African polities to be based on a rather reductive feudal model that would have even been inaccurate even in a European context. In 1920, Van der Kerken claimed that there was 'fully fledged feudalism' in the

Tanganika-Möero district.[23] Likewise, one of his subordinates referred to the Luba sub-chiefs, the *bilolo*, simultaneously as 'dukes, counts and barons.'[24] Although Belgian officials saw Tanganika-Möero as exhibiting the rudiments of a feudal system, they also admitted that there were places in which there no obvious leaders. In these seemingly acephalous communities, Belgian functionaries supported African leaders who could amass a significant number of followers.

The Hêmbá Bayazi communities, which were grouped with Songye chieftainships in Kongolo for convenience, exemplified the fact that—whatever Louis Franck's dictates were—expediency was still a very important part of the way in which local colonial statecraft was fashioned there. Moreover, as optimistic as he had been about establishing 'great chieftainships' in Tanganika-Möero, Van der Kerken left the district having never succeeded in reshaping its polities along Franck's lines. However, his successor, Joseph Van den Boogaerde, was marginally more successful in his effort to erect 'great chieftainships' there. In part, Van den Boogaerde could think more seriously than his predecessor about building 'great' chieftainships because he was less encumbered by the immediate aftermath of the First World War. When he took over in the early 1920s, he served in a province whose economy was already beginning to show strong signs of growth; not least in terms of its all-important mineral industry. One of the main places in which Van den Boogaerde sought to make a difference in Kongolo was the Bùki chieftainship in the south of the territory. This polity and its neighbours were important because they were the largest in Kongolo. So Van den Boogaerde returned to Van Walleghem's previous studies of Bùki's lineage that he had completed in 1911, just after the CSK era, and began to revise them in line with Franck's vision.

While Van Walleghem concluded that Bùki must have been a foreigner, or *Mugeni* in Luba, Van den Boogaerde thought that he could be a legitimate ruler of a 'great chieftainship' in southern Kongolo. So, just as Van Walleghem had promoted Bùki's vassals, or *bilolo*, to positions of power, Van den Boogaerde subordinated them to Bùki. In effect, he had recreated the administrative structure of the Bùki chieftainship almost exactly as it was *before* Van Walleghem's visit in 1911. Afterwards, in 1920, he reported that Bùki was the only person capable of consolidating the plethora of sub-chieftainships in southern Kongolo. He even went as far as comparing Bùki to one of the most famous Luba chiefs, Kasongo Nyembo; suggesting that Bùki was the 'Kasongo Nyembo of the north.'[25] Given that Kasongo Nyembo's Luba rebellion had finally been defeated in 1917, Van den Boogaerde felt that it was now acceptable to compare the power Bùki had amassed under colonial rule with that of the rebellious chief.[26] He went on to describe Bùki as: 'a handsome man, young, smart ... the administration has a vested interest in seeing the re-possession of his rights ... his reinstatement is required.'[27] He added that: 'it would be perfect if Bùki could be installed in the presence of Kasongo Nyembo.'[28] Just as Terence Ranger has previously argued, colonial officials were always at pains to hit just the right symbolic note to underwrite their system of indirect rule.[29] Similarly, the administration cast itself as a custodian of local political tradition to justify their authority.

Van den Boogaerde claimed that before being submitted to Bùki's jurisdiction, the 'small groups' to be brought under his control were 'unregulated, without stable authority.'[30] His idea was to shore up colonial authority under the aegis of the Luba strongman thereby fashioning 'an extremely valuable auxiliary to the territorial administrator.' Van den Boogaerde's use of the word 'auxiliary' is important in this context, as Bùki was both ruled by and simultaneously a key part of the Belgian colonial administration. Being the supposed inheritor of Kumwimba Ngombe's fire kingdom, as explained in the second chapter, he was the very embodiment of Franck's new plans for the hinterland. But Van den Boogaerde did not want him to rule without a substantial degree of state surveillance. He was even irritated at the idea that Bùki would refract Belgian modernity through Luba cultural practices.[31] In Van den Boogaerde's mind, Bùki would be a subaltern who should obey and do nothing more.

Despite his lingering reservations about following what he took to have been Louis Franck's dictates too literally, Van den Boogaerde quickly dispatched his colleague, Tytgat, then working as a Territorial Agent (TA) to Nyunzu, Kongolo's eastern neighbour, to meet Bùki and resurrect his political power.[32] We do not know why Bùki was not in Kongolo at the time nor, unfortunately, do not have a record of Tytgat and Bùki's conversation(s). But they must have had a successful encounter because Bùki was installed shortly after it. Having sent an emissary to confirm he was happy to be reinvested, Van den Boogaerde then needed to justify both to his superiors and to those who Bùki would rule why the latter was being granted over-arching power in southern Kongolo for a second time. Van den Boogaerde did this chiefly by outlining Bùki's royal genealogy.

His dynastic history of Bùki's family began with M'Bili Kiluhwe who he claimed was 'the great Baluba ancestor.'[33] It is likely that he meant

Mbidi Kiluwe, one of the Luba founders who had initially migrated to Nkongolo's domains. According to Van den Boogaerde, Kilhuwe actually lived in the region we now know as the territory of Kongolo; though this was extremely unlikely to have been the case in reality.[34] Nevertheless, after his evidently re-imagined rendition of the early parts of the Luba genesis myth, Van den Boogaerde's version of it began to coincide with more traditional accounts. For example he suggested that after Kiluhwe's death, Kalala (Kalalé) Ilunga succeeded him in a manner that dovetails with the traditional emphasis on Ilunga's defeat of Nkongolo. Van den Boogaerde believed that Kalalé Ilunga's dynasty consisted of warlords and conquerors who 'extended their empire even among the Kazembe, in [Northern] Rhodesia ... and even into the Maniema [province].'[35] He wrote that these conquests were important because they elevated the status of Ilunga's dynasty to such a level of prestige that peoples from other groups came to pay tribute to Kalalé Ilunga 'of their own free will (the word 'prestige' is of course used not by accident but exactly in accordance with Belgian colonial rule in this sentence).'[36] By highlighting that outside groups had freely paid tribute to him, Van den Boogaerde emphasized Ilunga's legitimacy and by extension that of Bùki and of the colonial state in general.

At some point in his version of the Luba genesis myth, Van den Boogaerde had to insert Bùki into the Luba royal line that he had outlined if he was to fully justify his amalgamation of the bilolo that would be subordinated to him. He began this task by suggesting that Ilunga Sungu succeeded Kalalé Ilunga who was succeeded by Kumwimba Ngombe. He asserted that Ngombe had led 'a major expansive thrust towards the southeast [of Katanga] in 1832.'[37] He then indicated that Ngombe had two sons, one was Bùki.[38] With his brother, Ilunga Kabale (d.1870), staying put to continue the Ilunga lineage in north-central Katanga, Bùki travelled to the Kongolo region and was afterwards revered as the son of Kumwimba Ngombe. He inherited his father's honorary title of 'Mulopwe/Mulohwa' (King) as well as his uncles' 'Bùki' epithet.

Although he believed royal blood ran in Bùki's veins, Van den Boogaerde never instated him on a par with Kasongo Nyembo or with Kabongo because he felt the latter were more senior than he. Rather, Van den Boogaerde's idea was that, in the long term, Bùki would be subordinated to Nyembo and Kabongo who would both head up strong polities of their own. Nyembo or Kabongo would take over Bùki's kingdom in the event of the latter's death. In Van den Boogaerde's mind, therefore, Bùki's kingship was a stopgap measure on the way to what he hoped would become a supra-Luba polity; perhaps one of the grandest of the 'great chieftainships.' Furthermore, he hoped that Kasongo Nyembo would outlive Kabongo, as he was the 'living depositary of power, the incarnation of the spirit of the ancestors,' the true *Lisala* or king.[39] A more apt illustration of Karen Fields' conception of the colonial state as a consumer of power must be hard to find than Van den Boogaerde's description of Kasongo Nyembo as a 'living depositary of power.'[40] In short, Van den Boogaerde's localized version of a Luba kingdom in Tanganika-Möero was his translation of Franck's vision of consolidated African polities in Kongolo and relied heavily on Luba history; however misconstrued his reading of it may have been.

After Van den Boogaerde had added a number of smaller chieftainships and sub-chieftainships into Bùki's polity, the Luba headman became its paramount chief. Adding sub-chieftainships onto 'great' chieftainships, such as Bùki's, was originally thought to have been neither controversial nor cumbersome since they were supposedly simply reconstructions of what had been in place before the colonial conquests. So, after announcing that all the necessary ethnographic studies had been completed, Van den Boogaerde repeated what his predecessors had already argued: 'it will not be hard to implement indirect rule in our administration.'[41] Louis Franck himself visited the DC before he compiled his synthesis of Tanganika-Möero's ethnography and Franck's presence must have sped Van den Boogaerde's efforts. His optimistic appraisal of the ethnographic situation in Kongolo potentially stemmed more from the fact that he wanted to appear to have succeeded in carrying out his orders than from the prevailing realities of local politics at the time. He would have been well aware that his superiors, and potentially even Louis Franck, would read his appraisal of the Luba situation and so there was a tangible pressure to please them.

Van den Boogaerde was unsure about the sociopolitical structure of the Luba phenomenon over and above being able to delineate Bùki's lineage with some degree of accuracy. He also may not have even realized that Bùki was a 'fire' king (*mulopwe wa mudilo*), which is to say not someone of innate regal status but rather a person who had been granted royal insignia by a Luba king. Given his uncertainty over how Luba societies were governed, it is in one sense odd that Van den Boogaerde felt able to pronounce the ethnographic studies needed to implement Franck's vision in southern Kongolo had been completed. Aside from his need to impress his superiors, part of his confidence may have emanated from the fact that he had also access to some missionary knowledge from his base in Albertville. In a report he wrote in 1920, he quoted from a book by a 'reverend father' that must have been the one published by Pierre Colle in 1913.[42] Wherever his confidence came from, with the ethnographic work 'complete' in Van den Boogaerde's mind—all that remained to be done was to put Franck's new vision into practice and sub-ordinate the sub-chiefs who Buki was to govern to him. Yet the sub-chiefs would ensure that Bùki's installation as their superior would be a controversial and deeply fraught process.

NEO-TRADITIONALISM AND BÙKI'S 'GREAT' CHIEFTAINSHIP

Bùki was reinstalled as chief of the Kivuzimu (Bakwezimu) grouping in what became the 'Bùki' chieftainship in August 1921.[43] By 1922, he had been granted authority over four other 'groupings,' which were still called sub-chieftainships in Kongolo, namely: Mwange, Mulimi, Kalungu and Kansimba (see Fig. 4.2).[44] Much as they had relied on a reimagined version of Luba lineage history to identify Bùki, colonial officials brokered his enthronement using a neo-traditional institution known as a *shauri* in Swahili. The word 'shauri' is Swahili for a conversation. It was adopted by nineteenth-century African merchants to concurrently mean a set of 'rituals and diplomatic ceremonies ... to overcome ... mutual mistrust and to prepare the space for negotiations' between parties with

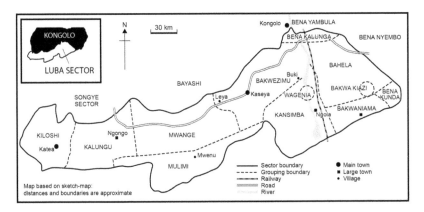

Fig. 4.2   Bùki's 'great' chieftainship in southern Kongolo

competing interests.[45] Belgian officials, keen to legitimize their rule via 'traditional' modalities after the First World War, imported the institution of the shauri into the Congo from their German counterparts. The shauri was effective because while it could masquerade as an 'authentically' local African institution, it was also an extremely malleable one. This is why one scholar described it as 'a bricolage of cultural practices of different origins.'[46] Once implanted into the repertoire of Belgian rule, it was used repeatedly throughout the early colonial period, at least in Kongolo, before more bureaucratised institutions, such as the Belgian version of a chief's council, replaced it.[47] Shauris were convened on a semi-regular basis to discuss controversial issues related to colonial government both in the Bùki chieftainship and beyond until the Depression (1929–1939).[48] As shauri meetings were not minuted, though, there are no colonial reports pertaining to what took place at the meeting that sanctioned Bùki's enthronement.

From a colonial standpoint, the shauri convened to oversee Bùki's installation succeeded in part because Raymond Leslie Buell, then research director for the US Foreign Policy Association, confirmed that Bùki's domains dramatically expanded in 1922. By 1926, Buell completed an investigation into the 'political conditions in Africa' on behalf of the Association and used the growth of Bùki's chieftainship to support his optimism vis-à-vis the Franck's new system of colonial governance.[49] In 1924, two years after having his authority extended over four new sub-chiefdoms, Buell confirmed that Bùki had had even more polities attached to his growing chieftainship. That year, a new Belgian study was commissioned into Bùki's installation that replicated Van den Boogaerde's in that it again justified Bùki's newly elevated position by rehearsing the long-standing argument that he was the heir to his ancestors' conquests.[50] By that time, Maemans had taken over as the DC of Tanganika-Möero and, much like his predecessor, he believed that Bùki was the right man to unite the disparate series of polities across southern Kongolo.[51]

Bùki's claims to power over Songye polities, such as Bena Kiloshi, were lent added credibility by the fact that Maeman's argued a number of chiefs there already paid Bùki tribute.[52] By 1925, the land under Bùki's jurisdiction had grown to become five times bigger than that which he had presided over in 1921. There were now around 4500 people subject to Bùki's writ as compared to the 900 he had previously ruled. That year, the Belgians even began to refer to his domains as a 'regional sector' instead of by their normal 'chieftainship' label because it encompassed so many different groups. Yet as sectors, or amalgamations of chieftainships governed by someone who was not drawn from local lineages, were still under development and even prohibited, Bùki's domains would be more commonly referred to as a 'great' chieftainship.

On 6 April 1926, N. Labrique, who had taken over from Maemans as DC, finally gave Bùki his chief's medal and so he became the *chef-médaillé* of a vast new 'Luba' polity in southern Kongolo.[53] Colonial district reports, both in the lead-up to Bùki's installation and afterwards, indicate that Belgian functionaries went to great lengths to legitimize and articulate the chief's revivified authority to his subjects and to his subordinates. In their annual district and territorial appraisals, functionaries referred to Bùki strictly by his regal titles, 'Mulopwe Ngoy,' rather than his familial epithet, or, of course, his ancestor's status as a 'fire king.' For example, *Ngoy* was/is a title typically given to a Luba noble and on occasion to a king, with *Mulopwe* being the title given to a Luba paramount chief and sacral king, which is, in most cases, more senior than Ngoy.[54] As the second chapter suggested, Mulopwe is a reference to the foreigner(s) in the Luba genesis myth who brought sacred kingship to the Luba after Nkongolo's tumultuous rule.[55] When they named the territory 'Kongolo,' colonial officials must not have known that Nkongolo was the antagonist of every recorded version of the Luba genesis myth. Or, alternatively, they knew that Nkongolo was the founder of the Luba peoples and overlooked the more negative aspects of his mythical life as recounted in the genesis myth. Another reason officials could have called the territory 'Kongolo' was that they named it after a Luba subset called the Kongolo peoples, who migrated north to Maniema shortly after the colonial conquests but no longer live there today.

The name of the territory notwithstanding, Bùki was enthroned with all the pomp and circumstance the colonial regime could muster. Mulopwe were generally given very ornate installations, part of which involved them being hoisted above the assembled throng by a group of their most senior followers to demonstrate their 'divine' and 'heavenly' nature.[56] Before his enthronement, Belgian functionaries had also ensured the medal that Bùki received as paramount chief was more intricate than those given to his subordinate chiefs. After a complex and lavish investiture ceremony, rich in the hybridized symbolism that accentuated colonial hierarchies under indirect rule, Bùki and his colonial allies set about reducing the autonomy that his subordinates had enjoyed before the imposition of his rule.[57]

The subordination of African leaders accustomed to exercising sovereignty independently after Walleghem's 1911 visit to Kongolo, proved controversial. Muzinga Lenge Ngombe, the then chief of the Bakwezimu, a sub-chieftainship before Louis Franck's ascension to office, was not content to be subjected to the dictates of someone he perceived to be a foreigner.[58] Disgusted by the new arrangements, he threw the medal that symbolized his diminished status at Labrique's feet. Afterwards, Labrique recovered the medal and gave it to Bùki, signifying the Luba headman's complete control of both the 'great' chieftainship and the Bakwezimu grouping. The matter did not end there, though. Oral sources suggest Ngombe mobilized his Bakwezimu allies to begin a 'tribal war' to secede from Bùki's rule. We do not know how extensive that 'war' was but later colonial reports suggest that the Bakwezimu continued to view Bùki as an illegitimate imposition for many years to come. They even formed hamlets away from the roads that held Bùki's polyglot territory together.

Unperturbed by the violence that their elevation of their new protégé caused, the Belgian administration continued to make many of the groups on the left side of the Lualaba River recommence paying tribute to Bùki.[59] But despite receiving colonial favour early on, Bùki frustrated his European overlords when it came to following orders that did not serve his own interests. He was not content to become the simple colonial mouthpiece that Van den Boogaerde had wanted him to be when he first conceived of him as a 'great' chief. Just as in Zimbabwe, colonial chiefs in the Belgian Congo were not 'merely the tools of officialdom … they had their own frustratingly unpredictable agendas.'[60] There were some other chiefs who openly confronted the administration elsewhere in the Congo at around this time, among them the Songye chief, Lumpungu II, 'who was summarily executed in 1936 for boldly writing to King Leopold II … with a request for independence.'[61] But Bùki was not anti-colonial in the same way that Lumpungu II was. Instead, he was more concerned to shore up his status within the colonial administration than to oppose it in its entirety. Bùki's vassal status irked him most during a Sleeping Sickness outbreak at the end of the 1920s.

In 1928, eighty-seven cases were reported against a general backdrop of poverty in his chieftainship.[62] But Bùki supposedly displayed a 'nonchalant' attitude to helping Belgian agents to combat the disease in his 'great' chieftainship. Again, we cannot be sure why Bùki adopted this so-called 'nonchalant' attitude to Sleeping Sickness but it is likely that participating in regrouping villages, a time-honoured colonial means of dealing with the disease, worried him as it was already deeply unpopular with villagers and, secondly, he had no control over the process. By reinforcing an unpopular demand, Bùki risked undermining his local reputation. But his colonial overlords gave him little choice but to comply. By 1929, Labrique considered disciplining Bùki as the disease spread further and officials believed that urgent action was needed.[63]

Relations between Bùki and the colonial administration worsened in 1930 after he was involved in 'an incident' in which he burned the proceeds of a hunt in a village called Kisengwa in another territory.[64] Colonial records note only that the situation was 'brought under control by prolonged cooperation between the responsible colonial agents.' As is typical of archival colonial records of this kind, we are left to guess what the details involved in the 'prolonged cooperation' mentioned in the report actually were. Nonetheless, Bùki had, in the words of a colonial official at the time, shown a penchant for 'punishing his enemies.'[65] According to a number of oral sources, he had also extorted 'extra-legal payments from the populace under [his] control.'[66] Some of my informants also claimed that he kidnapped young women, presumably in an effort to gain control of the circulation of bride-wealth and thereby reinforce his authority.[67,68]

Although even today some local people in southern Kongolo do not remember him fondly, it bears repeating that the process of amalgamating polities, promoting chiefs, and demoting nobles unaccustomed to outsiders' rule often resulted in new leaders arbitrarily enforcing their authority. In other words, Bùki was as much a product of the system that promoted him as he was that of his own beliefs. He typified the patriarchal, lineage-based leader that the historian Bogumil Jewsiewicki believes was so important in the implementation of Franck's 'indigenisation' policy in the 1920s.[69] While his actions in relation to those he considered his enemies might appear extremely—and excessively—severe they must be understood within the context of the tumultuous interwar period. As much as chiefs may have enjoyed the support of the technologically aided colonial state, they were often starkly exposed to their subjects' anger and even violence. Pre-colonial factional conflicts, many of which had arisen from the period of Zanzibari colonization explained in the second chapter, were a common source of danger.

If chiefs were believed to have been installed by Zanzibaris, for example, they were looked upon with distaste and even disgust by many in their chieftainships.[70] Likewise, the pressure to impose highly unpopular colonial orders on their subjects accentuated the hostility chiefs encountered. Headmen like Bùki, who were put in charge of those not even deemed to share in their cultural understandings of sovereignty were doubly insecure. White Father diaries contended that many chiefs in eastern Kongolo were even 'ignorant' of the 'customs' of their subjects, who took the opportunity to revolt whenever the chance arose.[71] Given the seemingly perpetual dangers they experienced, 'punishing enemies' was arguably one of the only means chiefs had of retaining their power. All the while, it made sense for colonial officials to portray chiefs as inhumane and brutal rather than acknowledge the part their own thinking and directives played in stoking rural violence in the Congo.

Given that Bùki's rule had not been consolidated in southern Kongolo by the latter half of the 1920s, he must have felt insecure in his new position. If nothing else, the less than cordial nature of his investiture alerted him to the substantive opposition he faced. Added to the hostility that he encountered from his subordinates, Bùki could not have held the colonial state and its changeable policies in particularly high esteem. Different administrators had asked for Bùki's compliance for contradictory plans over a relatively short space of time. So, he was well aware that he could not take one iteration of the administration's version of indirect rule for granted nor his place within it.

Conversely, one must also consider how Bùki's subjects felt about the changes that had taken place *vis-à-vis* their political elites. Someone growing up in the Bakwazimu grouping would have seen Bùki installed as a paramount chief, demoted to a sub-chief, and reinstalled as a paramount chief—and all in less than a generation. The violence that Bùki was said to have imposed on his subjects demonstrated both their not taking his rule as seriously as he would have liked as well as his attempts to control them in the context of the capricious colonial overlordship he experienced. While Bùki's 'great' chieftainship was the most obvious examples of the failure of the challenges the administration faced in fashioning local polities as it wished, similar stories emerged in official reports about other chieftainships across Kongolo. In fact, a report written in 1926 lamented the 'chaos' that characterized most polities in the district of Tanganika-Möero at the time.[72] The author suggested that few chiefs boasted any meaningful authority over their subjects and too little had been done to enforce their power in the face of profound opposition in some cases.

The White Fathers' diaries indicate that the chaos on the left bank was mirrored in part by insecurity on the right—although the administration had made some progress there. Many of the Hêmbá chieftainships had been mapped out by the time that Bùki's installation had been completed in the mid-1920s. Mukelenge Tambwe became the chief of the Bena Nkuvu just as Nongolola reigned over Bena Yambula by 1923.[73] There were few chieftainships that were more populous than Bena Nkuvu and Bena Mambwe though the administration also placed a great deal of importance on Bena Mambwe where the chief, Simpompo, had experienced a number of challenges to their rule. The administration believed that the Hêmbá practiced matriarchal succession and that this produced chiefly heirs who were more legitimate than the Luba monarchs on the left bank.[74] Ignoring the fact that most Hêmbá groups practiced double unilineal descent, the administration did not in fact make chieftainship work quite as smoothly as they suggested, however. The White Fathers commented at length on Tambwe's succession, saying that numerous nobles had petitioned the administration to forward their own case for chieftainship.[75]

In sum, Franck's consolidated vision of indirect rule, which hinged on the identification of chiefs who could boast some sort of loyalty from their subjects, floundered both during and after he left office in 1924. His successors may have been noted for their interest in what in colonial parlance was described as 'native affairs' but they never followed through with Franck's vision. As Michael Meeuwis has argued in the cultural and linguistic context, Louis Franck's policy of adaptationism, or a strengthened version of indirect rule, 'was never applied to its fullest consequences and implications.'[76] What progress that had been made came about as a result of the appropriation by Belgian officials of African ceremonies, such as the shauri, and their shaky alliances with chiefs, such as Bùki. Despite the organization of Bùki's chieftainship provoking opposition among several bilolo, colonial administrators maintained their belief in it and him long after Louis Franck and Maurice Lippens had left office. Bùki's alliance in particular was crucial to incorporating the Luba in Kongolo into the political economy of the colonial state. Yet, although a diverse grouping of Luba and non-Luba peoples had technically been amalgamated under his rule, Bùki's authority was far from consensual. And aside from Bùki's chieftainship, the administration faced many contests for power in chieftainships meaning that as a whole Franck's vision only had a limited impact on Kongolo. The issue of the legitimacy of pre-existing chefs-médiallés, as well as those officials wished to instal, continued to prove a headache for territorial agents. Writing in 1926, the early optimism already seemed to be waning as the DC of Tanganika-Möero asserted that he was 'very much at the *middle* stage of preparation [my italics]' of amalgamating smaller polities into larger ones.[77] The Commissioner went on to suggest that the administration's only hope to bring stability to the chieftainships in Kongolo and in Tanganyika as a whole was to train and educate the younger generation of leaders: and in that endeavour the Church would be crucial.[78]

THE EXTENSION OF CATHOLIC AUTHORITY

The failure of the 'great' chieftainships to materialize and/or consolidate the power of paramount chiefs left the Catholic Church as *the* dominant political force in Kongolo even if missionaries still steered clear of the Bùki chieftainship for fear of another Luba rebellion or chiefly power struggle breaking out. For a while, Catholic power in the Congo as a whole was welcomed—not least because of its capacity to train local African leaders. Louis Franck's predecessor, Jules Renkin, had never been concerned about the relative weakness of chiefs vis-à-vis the out-stations because, as a Catholic himself, he was more than content to see the continued and widespread evangelization of the Congo. And, after having experienced a bruising and very public disagreement with Victor Roelens about the latter's belief that too many top jobs in the colonial judiciary went to Freemasons, Renkin feared antagonizing the Church any further than was necessary.[79] Yet Louis Franck, having never experienced such a public fall-out himself, wanted to reduce Catholic power over Belgium's largest colony and extend chiefs' powers at the same time. But in looking to scale back the Church's influence, the newly appointed Minister of the Colonies found it in an increasingly strong position. The 'republic' that Victor Roelens had sought to construct was taking shape after the First World War. The lack of great chieftainships fashioned according to secular, colonial law had allowed missionaries to become even more influential under indirect rule in the Congo.[80]

The missionaries constantly used the maxim from Luke 21:19 that: 'In patience possesses ye your souls' in their reports and it seemed that by the end of the War their patience was finally paying off.[81] The ending of wartime 'privations' had greatly intensified missionary activity.[82] The formation of 'native' clergies was even given Canon Law approval after the publication of Benedict XV's Apostolic Letter entitled *Maximum Illud* in 1919.[83] 'In this policy,' the pontiff stated, 'lies the greatest hope of the new churches.'[84] By 1932, Roelens opened the first meeting of the Ordinaires 'with a substantive report on how to build a *clergé indigène.*' In so doing, he publically articulated a policy that he had begun when he had first ordered the construction of a minor seminary in 1898.[85] As a result of the momentum that the idea of a local Catholic clergy had already accrued by the end of the War, as exemplified in the ordination of Stefano Kaoze, who became the first Congolese priest in 1917, a series of African catechists in Upper Congo carried the gospel ever further into the Congolese hinterland.[86] By 1919, clerics in the Lubunda complex, in northern Kongolo, could even afford to think about building a new seminary to house the converts they were amassing to prepare them for priesthood.[87] Lubunda was testament to the fact that the mission presence was unevenly spaced in Kongolo, though, not least given the travails that the White Fathers were experiencing in Sola. Lubunda excelled in a way that few other mission complexes did after the War even if most experienced more success after international hostilities ended in 1918.

The strengthening of Catholic mission presence took time to pose a problem for the Church's relations with the Belgian administration. As Crawford Young suggests, initially 'Louis Franck [noted] with approval that there were as many Catholic missionaries as functionaries (1800) and [described] their role as most useful.'[88] Despite being a strong advocate of secular education, he could simply not ignore the infrastructure that missionaries had constructed and the benefits it had already wrought for the state in terms of training African administrators. Even in his book, *Land En Volk*, Franck suggested that mission stations provided important training for those who wanted to become clerks for the colonial administration.[89] Although there were many who went to mission schools because they wanted to advance their faith, Franck claimed, many others wanted to advance their material concerns.[90] Put differently, mission schools provided the sort of social mobility that built an alliance between a growing African middle class and the colonial regime that in turn was important in sustaining Belgian rule in Tanganyika's hinterland.

As David Maxwell suggests, education was missionaries' major contribution in the twentieth-century and mission-educated, literate Africans were badly needed by an administration that had previously marched so many of them off to war.[91] Even as late as 1929, for example, Bùki's expansive chieftainship had no clerk.[92] The Vice-Governor of Katanga noted that while there might have been more European staff available to him after the War, their 'quality was questionable.'[93] In any case, the colonial administration was keener to employ Africans because it believed that it could pay them far less than Europeans. And it was not just African clerics and auxiliaries who needed training. As officials wanted to pass more of the administrative burden of colonial rule onto Africans, they needed a greater number of literate and numerate allied chiefs.[94] Bùki's son was just one of a number of examples of African elites educated in the Spiritan out-station in Lubunda.[95] Although the colonial administration subsidized Catholic education, missionaries managed and staffed them.[96] And their state-ordained duty to educate Africans was one enthusiastically embraced by Emilio Callewaert, the Apostolic Prefect (1911–1922) of the Spiritan vicariate on the left bank of Kongolo.[97] In 1921, he claimed that: 'The only way to save the black race from total destruction was through instruction.'[98] His bleak appraisal of pre-existing African cultures demonstrated that the views of senior Catholic clerics at the time often sat uneasily with the relatively progressive rhetoric Louis Franck promulgated.

Given the views of senior missionaries such as Emile Callewaert, it is not hard to see why 'while paying proforma homage to the role played by the missions, Franck was not pro-missionary.'[99] However, far from being hindered by the Church, Louis Franck's Governor-General, Maurice Lippens, published a circular on 25 January that was reprinted on 30 September 1922 in which he 'ordered … all native villages (including Christian villages) to be placed under the authority of local African chiefs.'[100] However, in Kongolo at least, his dictates fell on deaf ears and meant little when compared to those of the Church. The Songye chieftainship of Wangongwe in western Kongolo was illustrative of the ways in which Church power overcame that of the colonial state under Franck/Lippens' tenures. There, colonial officials believed they had found another potentially 'great' chieftainship and one that was suitable for consolidation along Franck and Lippens' lines. They understood Wangongwe as constituting a discreet cultural 'unit,' as evinced by their leaving it independent and unattached to Bùki's neighbouring polity. So it was not Bùki and his polyglot chieftainship that threatened to engulf Wangongwe. Rather, it was the Church that encroached onto Wangongwe's lands.

In 1922, administrators became increasingly concerned that the Spiritan faithful were 'passing the permitted limits of proselytism' in the

Songye chieftainship.[101] The DC went as far as to state that the spreading of the gospel message had destroyed chief Mobanga's authority.[102] Rather than following the chief's orders, catechists were loyal only to those propounded by their mission superiors. Colonial officials viewed the indifference with which Spiritan catechists greeted certain key precepts of 'customary law,' such as the obligation of subjects to obey their chiefs, as particularly troublesome given that Mobanga was 'one of the most devoted chiefs' in the territory [of Kongolo].[103] What is particularly interesting about this episode is that there is no evidence that the Belgian regime ever considered confronting the said catechist or the Church over this issue. Instead, in 1925, the Governor of Katanga considered paying Mobanga an indemnity to compensate him for the loss of land he experienced after the extension of a series of Christian villages in his domain.

Giving Mobanga financial compensation for the loss of his lands to the missionaries went far beyond the usual administrative protocol in the Belgian Congo. Likewise, Van den Boogaerde warned of the 'grave consequences' of allowing the mission to continue to outstretch its boundaries and the 'monstrous ingratitude' such an act would demonstrate.[104] In spite of Van den Boogaerde's concerns, though, very little was done to curtail the extension of Spiritan presence in Wangongwe or, for that matter, to deliver compensation to Mobanga for the loss of his land.[105] In 1923, an unnamed Spiritan father even struck Mobanga twice with a stick for refusing to give him the 'materials as [Mobanga's] father had done so as to finish the construction of his new house to be built further from the confines of the Christian village.'[106] Try as they might, TAs and DCs could not control the scope or the scale of mission presence in Kongolo. Although colonial officials were happy for Catholics to offer education, the consequences of the expansion of their presence were undermining the very system of indirect rule the administration was attempting to construct. Aside from the fundamental issue of land being expropriated from chefs-médaillés, the Catholic Church also wanted to impose its own legal system onto the lives of Africans in the 'great chieftainships.'

The ability to punish subjects and specifically the monopoly of legitimate violence is one of the most fundamental attributes of a modern state according to the German sociologist Max Weber.[107] So, the fact that the Spiritans established their own punishment regime was deeply troubling to the Belgian administration. Much like those of their secular counterparts, Callewaert's code of conduct seemingly included a variety of corporal punishments for those who transgressed them. And

Belgian functionaries were keen to remain in control of the use of corporal punishments, such as the whip, and for good reason. Recent scholarship has tended to emphasize the Belgian administration's 'total reliance on violence' without fully unpacking the precise ways in which it was deployed.[108]

The archival evidence suggests that Belgians thought about the symbolic aspects of the violence they meted out on Africans and believed that it should be carried out in precise and sometimes in discreet ways. One way to make their violence appear legitimate was to out-source it to African intermediaries and in so doing avoid being seen to flog colonial subjects. Belgian colonial violence was deeply inflected by the politics of race but this was managed by administrators far more than has previously been understood. Incredulously blind to their own use of systemic violence, territorial administrators felt threatened when other Europeans, which is to say Catholic missionaries, had, in their view, become unpopular with Africans as a result of inflicting cruelty on them. If Europeans as a whole got a bad reputation, so Belgian administrative thinking went, it would make the job of governing harder by stoking still more resentment against the colonial state. So, with no hint of irony, a territorial administrator wrote in 1921 that the Spiritans' apparent 'bad reputation among the [local people]' undermined European presence in Kongolo as a whole.[109]

How did the Spiritans get their 'bad reputation'? First, it should be noted that much of what we know about Spiritan involvement in Kongolo, in terms of their possible 'misdemeanors,' comes from the colonial archives and unsurprisingly not from those of the Society itself. Spiritan records themselves do not attest to their developing any kind of 'bad reputation' with the local populace. Rather, they repeatedly tell a far more triumphal story of mission popularity among African congregations. For example, when one of the founding fathers of the Spiritan mission in Kongolo, Joseph Ferry, left for Europe on 14 June 1926, the relevant mission diary indicated that 'all the black mission came to say goodbye to *Baba Mukubwa.*'[110] Ferry's African sobriquet, Bwana Mukubwa or 'Great Father' in Swahili indicated the respect that Spiritan diarists believed his congregants reserved for him. Admittedly, M(u) Kubwa was a term used on the eastern Savannah to describe Swahili 'big-man.' But given that in Ferry's case it was prefaced with 'Baba' ('father'), and the fact that Joseph Ferry never kept slaves, we can assume it was a reference to his high-status and not that of a slaver.

Yet it was not 'Baba Mukubwa' who gave rise to the Spiritans' 'bad reputation.' Rather, colonial reports accused Joseph Ferry's erstwhile Superior, Emilio Callewaert, of instigating a 'fierce disciplinary regime' that involved punishing those who transgressed his code with a hippopot-amus-hide whip known in the Belgian Congo as a *chicotte*.[111] According to Van den Boogaerde, Callewaert's use of the chicotte provoked 'serious tensions between civil and religious authorities.'[112] Although Callewaert's disciplinary regime had been in place for a decade, a lawsuit instigated by a European doctor in 1923 brought this controversy to light once again. By instigating a separate disciplinary regime that adhered to an identifia-ble internal logic, and one that clearly conflicted with that of the secular state, Callewaert directly challenged the administration's monopoly on legitimate violence. In fact, that the clergyman had indulged in independ-ent and public acts of violence against the wishes of the state was proba-bly why Van den Boogaerde termed it 'illegal' in the first place.

In an explicit demonstration of the weakness of his administration vis-à-vis the Church, Van den Boogaerde suggested that nothing would—or could—be done about Callewaert's actions because the cleric was simply 'unassailable.'[113] Rather than a relationship characterized by symbiosis, as Marvin Markowitz's model of Church-state relations would suggest, a spirit of competitive codependency had emerged within the colonial nexus.[114] And, rather than being increasingly constricted by the secu-lar regime as Louis Franck and his subordinates sought to consolidate 'great' chieftainships, missions became more powerful and more bull-ish as the 1920s progressed. The Spiritans as well as their White Father counterparts frequently involved themselves in chiefly succession dis-putes, which also undermined 'customary' law as this was supposed to be the preserve of the relevant notables and colonial officials.

On 28 September 1920, Gustave Motte, the superior of the Sola mis-sion, arbitrated a chiefly dispute that arose in the village of Kayungu, in the Hêmbá chieftainship of Bena Nkuvu.[115] With colonial agents nowhere to be seen, two rivals for the chieftainship of Bena Nkuvu had sent their children to Motte, presumably to become neophytes and thereby gaining the Church's favour in the process.[116] The incumbent chief, Kilala, had, ostensibly, already 'granted' one of his daughters to the mission station and therefore appeared to have been favoured in this arbitration. The outcome of this case was not noted in mission diaries but as 'the whole [of Motte's] voyage was blessed' we can assume that Kilala remained the chief. As well as intervening in chiefly succession disputes, missionaries also engaged in prohibiting unsupervised 'customary' dances. What is more, they also routinely intervened in 'customary' court procedures to diminish the punishments meted out to offenders.[117] The fact that chiefs could not have the final word on 'customary' law undermined their claims to sovereignty and by extension that of the colonial administration. While the Church was not hostile to the Belgian colonial project, its juridical powers were never meant to contradict those of its ally and certainly not to the extent that they did in Kongolo.

Not only was the Church gaining increasing power over the inter-war iteration of chieftainship, but it was also beginning to succeed in terms of its overall mission: that of conversion. Lavigerie's dream of a Christian state may have faded, and Joubert may have donned civil rather than military garb by the end of the First World War, but ever more Bena Nkuvu were coming to the biweekly catechism meetings in Sola. What is surprising, given the White Fathers' initial emphasis on converting young people supposedly orphaned by the Zanzibari slave trade, was that many elders were beginning to come to these meetings.[118] In a reversal of much of the White Fathers' thinking during the proto-colonial period, they now relied on the elders, who were typically male, to set 'a good example to the youth' of Bena Nkuvu.[119] Like many mission stations across Central Africa at the time, Van Acker, Vandermeiren and Motte's main concern was to bring women into the Church though. Yet even here, some progress was being made. Van Acker reported that some women swept the floor of the church in Sola. He also suggested that women contributed to the expenses of the church—though he did not specify how many women nor their origin in his reportage. Added to the beginning of their progress with women, the White Fathers church in Sola was completed around 1930 and this added to the out-station's sense of permanency (see Fig. 4.3).[120]

As powerful as the White Fathers became in Sola and the Spiritans were in Wangongwe, the Spiritans were even more influential in the Songye and Kusu chieftainship of Bena Lubunda. The success of the mission in terms of the numbers of converts and the physical presence of the out-station there was pronounced as the last chapter made clear. By the time the Depression struck Kongolo in 1931, 937 people lived in Bena Lubunda, which compared very favourably to the 1269 that lived in the 'indigenous city' (*cité indigène*) that had emerged out of the licencies the same year.[121] Eventually, the significance of the Lubunda mission became so pronounced that Edourd De Jonghe, a high-ranking Belgian official at the time, classed it as a separate enclave entirely when he reported on Congolese educational facilities in 1931.[122] By that time, the mission-polity played host to

Fig. 4.3   The White Fathers' Church at the Sola out-station, 2015

almost twice as many schools as the rest of Kongolo across almost every age group. The importance of Lubunda was also evinced by the impressive construction work that went on in the chieftainship, with one example being the church that was built there in 1925. The more the historical record at Lubunda is examined, the more examples one can find of mission power over the lives of their converts eclipsing those of local chiefs.

Given the strength of their presence in Lubunda, the Spiritans felt confident enough curtail many of the local expressive cultures in the chieftainship. So although the Spiritans found the resident Kusu there to be 'friendly,' they still prohibited their ritual dances if they found them to be distasteful even if they were simply performed to fertilize the land the Kusu farmed.[123] The colonial state never formally prohibited local dance cultures because it wanted to use tradition to secure the power of the African elites it enthroned. If it prohibited dances, it might undermine its allies' claims to be the custodians of their ancestral traditions and by extension their authority. As Bena Lubunda had had longer exposure to evangelism in Kongolo, missionaries ensured that fertility dances had lost much of the political and sexual overtones they believed they previous had. By the time the Great Depression arrived, therefore, missionaries had ensured that the dances in Lubunda were viewed mostly as entertainment events to an extent that they were not in most other chieftainships in Kongolo.

Despite the powers that missionaries had in the early interwar period, they were not an all-powerful Bula Matari-like force in the Kongolo bush even if they scored some notable successes. Jean and John Comaroff's model of the 'long conversation' still held true in one sense in that the White Fathers and the Spiritans did not believe that their project had been completed.[124] According to Mgr Huys, Jean Vandermeiren continued to lament the slow conversion rates in Sola.[125] Likewise, an in-house mission history written about Lubunda in the 1930s suggests that the 'population remained suspicious' of the Latin clerics until the mid-1920s and even beyond.[126] And an intriguing source, supporting the idea that unbelief was still a force to be reckoned with in Lubunda in the 1920s, comes in the form of possibly one of the earliest remaining examples of African catechist writing there. Penned in 1924, a letter, presumably to Father Luigi Lempereur, who took over the Prefecture of Katanga Septentrionale from Emile Callewaert in 1922, implies that there were still many unconverted locals in Lubunda. The letter was composed by someone called Antoine Philippe and was written in Swahili.[127] That the message was written in Swahili is one indication it was almost certainly the work of an African, as European missionaries nearly always wrote to their superiors in French. Philippe asked God to help Lempereur continue his work. But, tellingly, he went on to write: 'we pray for God … to save the pagans from savagery' (*Kuwokoa wapagani ku ushenzimi*).[128] Callewaert later echoed Antoine Philippe's acknowledgement of the strength of 'pagan' communities in a letter the Apostolic Vicar wrote to the Propaganda Fide.[129] He suggested that, although 'many men now begin to believe the truth,' '*many* are still in paganism [my emphasis].'[130] In short, Catholic presence did not mean ideological hegemony even if it meant institutional power over and above that of the 'great chieftainships.'

CONCLUSION

'Our Population Is Excessively Independent'

But there have been few if any missionaries in history who have not thought that there was more work to be done in their respective mission field(s). While Emile Callewaert believed that his missionaries had not yet succeeded in establishing the pristine Catholic communities that they had sought to engineer, they had come a long way. The expansion of Spiritan facilities, as well as the number of catechists, continued to mean that many Africans in Kongolo experienced the colonial occupation mainly through the prism of the Catholic Church. Although the state had established a number of chieftainships in Kongolo these were in a state of 'chaos' in the words of one DC.[131] Writing from his Sola out-station in the Hêmbá chieftainship of Bena Nkuvu, the Father Superior, Jean Vandermeiren, stated in his annual report for 1924 that: 'Our population is excessively independent ... No authority, and not even that of force, has persuaded people to accept the legitimacy of the chief [Mukelenge Tambwe] whose position they contest.'[132] Given Vandermeiren's observations, it was unsurprising that successive DCs lamented, first, the shortage of local tribunals in which those who disobeyed chiefs could be tried and, secondly, the lack of overall authority chiefs had in the eyes of their subjects.[133] If Louis Franck's 'great' chieftainships were supposed to tie down African societies and make their communities more 'legible' to colonial administrators it must be considered to have been at best only half-way successful in Kongolo.[134] The Belgian administration's failure to support chief Mobanga in Wangongwe was telling in this regard. Despite him being one of the state's major allies, they could not stop his maltreatment at the hands of a Catholic Church. Even when the Church did not have a base in a particular 'great' chieftainship, such as that ruled by Bùki, African leaders hardly welcomed their subordination to paramount chiefs.

The lack of state presence in Kongolo meant that forced cotton cultivation, which had been introduced to other areas of the Belgian Congo in 1917, was not a feature in the territory until 1933. Without reliable chiefs to carry out recruitment and enforce production, Belgian officials must have felt uneasy about introducing this most harsh and contentious of labour regimes despite the fact that it was introduced in other areas of the colony.[135] Instead, Africans continued to work in the CFL camp (see Fig. 4.4) or to be recruited to work for companies based in HKI when they were not labouring in the fields doing subsistence agriculture.

Kongolo's history indicates that Crawford Young's idea of interwar colonial consolidation in Africa needs to be revised for those areas that were peripheral to the political economy of the Belgian Congo. What marked Kongolo out from many other areas—both in the Belgian Congo and elsewhere—was the great extent to which the Church

Fig. 4.4   The CFL camp in Kongolo, 1930 (Royal Museum of Central Africa, Tervuren, AP.0.2.10323, Photo 1)

could capitalize on the weaknesses of secular state power and presence. It trained a number of Africans who went on to play various important roles within the administration. The turbulent careers of two colonial 'accommodators' in particular, namely Risaci Katore and Kalamba Sindano, chiefs of Bena Mambwe and Bena Nyembo respectively, feature strongly in the following chapter.

NOTES

1. Bogumil Jewsiewicki, 'Belgian Africa,' in Andrew Roberts (ed.), *The Cambridge History of Africa, Volume 7, c.1905–1940* (Cambridge: Cambridge University Press, 1986), p. 480.
2. F. Delicour, 'Jules-Laurent-Jean-Louis Renkin,' in *Biographie Coloniale Belge*, Tome IV, (1955), colons 747–753; Francis Marre, *Jules Renkin et la Conquête Africaine* (Bruxelles: G. Van Ouest, 1917).
3. Crawford Young, *The African Colonial State in Comparative Perspective* (New Haven: Yale University Press, 1994), p. 10.
4. A. F. G. Marzorati, 'The Political Organisation and Evolution of African Society in the Belgian Congo,' *African Affairs*, 53, 211 (1954), p. 104.
5. Bogumil Jewsiewicki, 'Belgian Africa,' p. 467.
6. Ibid.

7. Affaires Africains, Ministère des Affaires Etrangers, Bruxelles (AAB), Affaires Indigène et du Main-d'œuvre (AIMO), 1735, Rapport Annuel de l'Administration Générale (RAG), Tanganika-Möero, Première Trimestre, 1922, p. 3.

8. Archives Général des Missionnaires de l'Afrique, Rome (AGM), Auguste Van Acker, 'Rapport Annuel, 1918–1919' (Algiers: Imprimerie des Missionnaires d'Afrique, 1919), p. 164.

9. Michel Lwamba Bilonda, *Cours d'Histoire Politique du Congo de 1885 à nos Jours* (Lubumbashi: Centre d'Études et de Recherches Documentaires sur l'Afrique Centrale, Lubumbashi [henceforth CERDAC], 2008/9), p. 49.

10. Young, *The African Colonial State in Comparative Perspective*, p. 16.

11. Bogumil Jewsiewicki, 'The Formation of the Political Culture of Ethnicity in the Belgian Congo, 1920–1959,' in Leroy Vail (ed.), *The Creation of Tribalism in Southern Africa* (London: James Currey, 1989), p. 328.

12. Frederick Lugard, *The Dual Mandate in British Tropical Africa* (Edinburgh and London: William Blackwood and Sons, 1922). Louis Franck did publish an edited collection as well as *Land en Volk*, see: Louis Franck (ed.), *Le Congo Belge* (Bruxelles: Le Renaissance du Livre, 1928). However, like *Land en Volk*, *Le Congo Belge* was likewise more a collection of memoirs than a policy statement.

13. Louis Franck, *Congo, Land en Volk* (Bruxelles: Centrale Boekhandel, 1926).

14. Maurice Lippens, 'The Belgian Congo,' *Journal of the Royal African Society*, 38, 153 (1939), p. 421.

15. E. Van der Straeten, 'Maurice Auguste-Eugène-Charles, Marie-Ghislain, Lippens,' in *Biographie Belge d'Outre-Mer, Tome VI* (Bruxelles: Académie Royal des Sciences d'Outre-Mer, 1968), colons 664–672. Martin Rutten apparently took a keen interest in what were considered 'native affairs,' see: F. Dellicour, 'Martin Jean-Marie-René Rutten,' in *Biographie Belge d'Outre-Mer, Tome VI* (Bruxelles: Académie Royal des Sciences d'Outre-Mer, 1968), p. 714. The last Governor-General before the Depression was Auguste Tilkens (1927–1934) who happened to have been a former president of the CSK.

16. Unlike their subordinates, territorial officials, District Commissioners were the only officers endowed with the power to enthrone chiefs.

17. Boma was the capital of the Belgian Congo until 1926, when it was transferred to Leopoldville, now Kinshasa.

18. AAB, AIMO, 1735, RAG, Tanganika-Möero, Deuxième Trimestre, 1922, p. 3.

19. It was still being added to in 1929, see: AAB, AIMO, 1735, RAG, Tanganika-Möero, Première Semestre, 1929, p. 30.

20. AAB, AIMO, 1735, RAG, Tanganika-Möero, Deuxième Trimestre, 1926, p. 12.

21. Stannard, *Selling the Congo*, pp. 139–140.

22. Van der Kerken's successor, Joseph Van Den Boogaerde once summed up his thinking by quoting Virgil's *Georgics* (29 BCE): *Etsi parva licet componere magnis* ('If one may compare small things with great ones').

23. AAB, AIMO, 1735, Rapport Annuel de l'Administration Générale (RAG), Deuxième Trimestre, 1920, p. 9.

24. AAB, AIMO, 1735, RAG, Tanganika-Möero, Deuxième Trimestre, 1920, p. 9.

25. AAB, AIMO 1642, 'The Relegation of Kasongo Niembo, 1917–1921.'

26. Ibid.

27. AAB, AIMO, 1735, RAG, Deuxième Trimestre, 1920, p. 11.

28. Again, this is an odd comment given that Nyembo had just been responsible for a rebellion.

29. Terence O. Ranger, 'The Invention of Tradition in Colonial Africa,' in Terence O. Ranger and Eric Hobsbawm (eds), *The Invention of Tradition* (Cambridge: Cambridge University Press, 1983), p. 237.

30. AAB, AIMO 1735, RAG, Tanganika-Möero, Première Semestre, 1923, p. 8.

31. Ibid., p. 27.

32. AAB, AIMO 1735, RAG, Tanganika-Möero, Deuxième Trimestre, 1920, p. 11.

33. Ibid., p. 4.

34. The territory of Kongolo is on the margins of the Upemba Depression wherein the Luba were said to have emerged and so it is unlikely that the culture began in this location.

35. AAB, AIMO 1735, RAG, Tanganika-Möero, Deuxième Trimestre, 1920, p. 4.

36. Ibid.

37. Reefe, *The Rainbow and the Kings*, p. 132.

38. Ibid., p. 60. Thomas Reefe suggests that he could have had as many as four including Bùki.

39. AAB, AIMO 1735, RAG, Tanganika-Möero, Deuxième Trimestre, 1920, p. 4.

40. Karen Fields, *Revival and Rebellion in Colonial Central Africa* (Princeton: Princeton University Press, 1985).

41. AAB, AIMO 1735, RAG, Tanganika-Möero: Deuxième Trimestre, 1920, p. 1.

42. Ibid., p. 3.

43. Raymond Leslie Buell, *The Native Problem in Africa* (New York: The Macmillan Company, 1928), p. 484; AAB, AI 91, TRP, D-327, Maemans, Chefferie Bùki, Historique succinct, Novembre 1924, Bureau des affaires politiques, Province du Katanga, Dossiers des Chefs, p. 1.

44. Royal Museum of Central Africa (henceforth RMCA), Maemans (1924), 'Chefferie Bùki: Historique Succinct,' p. 2.
45. Michael Pesek, 'Cued Speeches: The Emergence of Shauri as Colonial Praxis in German East Africa, 1850–1903,' *History in Africa*, 33 (2006), p. 398.
46. Pesek, 'Cued Speeches: The Emergence of Shauri as Colonial Praxis in German East Africa, 1850–1903,' p. 398.
47. Bénédicte-Dembour, *Recalling the Belgian Congo*, p. 23.
48. AAB, AIMO 1735, RAG, Tanganika-Möero, Quatrième Trimestre, 1922, p. 2.
49. Connie L. Cartledge, Allyson H. Jackson, and Patrick M. Kerwin, 'Raymond Leslie Buell Papers: Finding Aid to the Collection in the Library of Congress' (Washington, DC, 2010), p. 3; Buell, *The Native Problem in Africa*, p. 484. The *Shauris* were eventually replaced with the Council of the Chieftainship, which performed almost exactly the same role of providing a forum in which territorial officials could meet notables and chiefs but it went under a different name.
50. AAB, L'Administrateur Territorial, 'Historique Succinct,' Territoire de Kongolo, Chefferie Bùki, 9 (Kongolo: novembre 1924).
51. RMCA, Maemans, 'Chefferie Bùki,' p. 1.
52. AAB, AIMO 1735, RAG, Tanganika-Möero, 1923, p. 8. This is not so dissimilar to the state sanctioned Kuba king, who also used the colonial administration to shore up his authority, see: Jan Vansina, 'Les Kuba et l'Administration Territoriale de 1919 à 1960,' *Cultures et Développement*, 4 (1972), pp. 275–298.
53. Hein Vanhee, 'Les Chefs Médaillés,' in Jean-Luc Vellut et al. (eds), *La Mémoire du Congo: le Temps Colonial* (Tervuren, 2005), pp. 79–82.
54. S. Terry Childs and Pierre de Marat, 'Re/Constructing Luba Pasts,' in M. Nooter Roberts and A. F. Roberts (eds), *Memory: Luba Art and the Making of Memory* (New York: Museum for African Art, 1996), p. 57.
55. David Gordon, *Invisible Agents: Spirits in a Central African History* (Athens: Ohio University Press, 2012), p. 33.
56. AAB, AIMO, 1579, 12, Coutumes Barbares—Luba (1918), p. 3.
57. David Cannadine, *Ornamentalism: How the British Saw Their Empire* (London: Penguin, 2001), p. 14.
58. Interview with Alexandre Bùki, Kongolo Town, 2 May 2009.
59. Joseph Schils, 'Histoire de Kongolo,' p. 5.
60. Jocelyn Alexander, *The Unsettled Land: State-Making and the Politics of Land in Zimbabwe, 1893–2003* (Athens: Ohio University Press, 2006), p. 5.
61. Nzongola-Ntalaja, *The Congo: From Leopold to Kabila*, p. 43. Nzongola-Ntalaja suggests that Lumungu was part of a primary rather than secondary resistance movement against Belgian rule although he may have been writing about Lumpungu I.

62. AAB, AIMO 1735, RAG, Tanganika-Möero, Deuxième Semestre, 1928, p. 33.
63. AAB, AIMO 1735, RAG, Tanganika-Möero, Première Semestre, 1929, p. 31; Interestingly the spread of sleeping sickness at the end of the 1920s and into the 1930s goes against the conclusions of Maryinez Lyons about Northern Congo when she observed that the disease was declining during this period, see: Lyons, *The Colonial Disease*, p. 230.
64. AAB, AIMO 1735, RAG, Tanganika-Möero, 1930, p. 25.
65. Ibid.; Bruce Berman, 'Ethnicity, Patronage and the African State: The Politics of Uncivil Nationalism,' *African Affairs*, 97, 388 (1998), p. 317.
66. Berman, 'Uncivil Nationalism,' p. 317.
67. Given that members of Bùki's family are still alive, I have not named my informants on this occasion for fear that they may suffer reprisals if their names are mentioned.
68. Indeed, so bad is Goy's reputation that no member of his family is allowed to hold office or even enter the Luba sector, see: Interview with informant A (anonymised due to sensitive nature of their comments).
69. Jewsiewicki, 'The Formation of the Political Culture of Ethnicity in the Belgian Congo, 1920–1959,' p. 328.
70. Vansina, *Paths in the Rainforests*, p. 242.
71. Archives Générales des Missionnaires d'Afrique, Rome (hereafter AGM), Bruges-Saint-Donat, Diaires, 1920, p. 99.
72. AAB, AIMO 1735, RAG, Tanganika-Möero, Deuxième Semestre, 1926, p. 37.
73. AAB, AIMO 1735, RAG, Tanganika-Möero, Deuxième Semestre, 1923, p. 6.
74. AAB, AIMO 1735, RAG, Tanganika-Möero, Quatrième Semestre, 1922, p. 2.
75. Archives Générales des Missionnaires de l'Afrique, Rome (AGM), Auguste Van Acker, 'Rapport Annuel, 1918–19' (Algiers: Imprimerie des Missionnaires de l'Afrique, 1919), p. 164.
76. Michael Meeuwis, 'The Origin of Belgian Colonial Language Policies in the Congo,' *Language Matters: Studies in the Languages of Africa*, 42, 2 (2011), p. 190.
77. AAB, AIMO 1735, RAG, Tanganika-Möero, Deuxième Semestre, 1926, p. 38.
78. Ibid., p. 37.
79. Mudimbe, *The Idea of Africa*, p. 115.
80. Rose-Hunt, *A Colonial Lexicon*, p. 163.
81. AGM, Auguste Van Acker, 'Rapport Annuel, 1919–1920' (Algiers: Imprimerie des Missionnaires de l'Afrique, 1920), p. 175.

82. Paul de Meester, *L'Eglise de Jésus Christ au Congo-Kinshasa* (Lubumbashi: Centre Interdiocésain de Lubumbashi, 1997), p. 245.
83. The policies of Benedict XV were continued with arguably even more vigour by his successor, Pius XI (1922–1939), see: Adrian Hastings, *The Church in Africa* (Oxford, 1994), p. 559.
84. Benedict XV, *Miximum Illud* (1919), p. 14.
85. Mudimbe, *The Idea of Africa*, p. 120.
86. Shorter, *African Recruits and Missionary Conscripts*, p. 110; Mudimbe, *The Idea of Africa*, p. 120.
87. However, these plans did not materialize until 1941, see: de Meester, *L'Eglise de Jesus Christ au Congo-Kinshasa*, p. 245. Catholic presence in northern Kongolo was furthered by the extension of the Kindu railway line to Lubunda in the mid-1920s, see: Meester, *L'Eglise de Jesus Christ au Congo-Kinshasa*, p. 4.
88. Young, *Politics in Congo*, p. 14.
89. Franck, *Congo: Land en Volk*, p. 279.
90. Ibid., p. 288.
91. David Maxwell, 'Christianity,' in Richard Reid and John Parker (eds), *The Oxford Handbook of African History* (Oxford: Oxford University Press, 2013), pp. 263–280; AAB, AIMO 1735, RAG, Tanganika-Möero, Premiere Trimestre, 1923, p. 5.
92. AAB, AIMO 1735, RAG, Tanganika-Möero, Première Semestre, 1929, p. 8.
93. AAB, AIMO 1735, RAG, Tanganika-Möero, Première Semestre, 1923, p. 2.
94. AAB, AIMO 1735, Lettre du Gouverneur, 2 décembre 1923, p. 5.
95. AAB, AIMO 1735, RAG, Tanganika-Möero, Première Semestre, 1929, p. 81.
96. Ndaywel é Nziem, *Histoire Générale du Congo*, p. 403. It is important to note that the state did not finance the schools whose character it deemed to be 'exclusively religious,' see: Ed. De Jonghe, *L'Enseignement des Indigènes au Congo Belge* (Bruxelles: Institut Colonial International, 1931), p. 167.
97. Callewaert's title (Apostolic Prefect) is important as it suggests that there were not yet enough Christians in Katanga Septentrional to warrant the creation of a separate diocese.
98. Emile Callewaert, 12 March 1921, quoted in Noël Perrot, *Eléments Pour l'Histoire de la Fondation du District de Kongolo au Congo-Kinshasa 1907–1927: Extraits de la Correspondance de Mgr Callewaert* (Self Published, 1997), p. 17.
99. Markowitz, *Cross and Sword*, p. 33.
100. Ibid.

101. AAB, AIMO 1735, RAG, Tanganika-Möero, Quatrième Trimestre, 1922, p. 4.
102. Ibid.
103. Ibid.
104. Ibid.
105. AAB, AIMO 1735, RAG, Tanganika-Möero, Deuxième Semestre, 1923, p. 6.
106. Ibid.
107. Max Weber (Translated by Talcott Parsons), *The Protestant Ethic and the Spirit of Capitalism* (New York: Dover Publications, 2003), p. 16.
108. Likaka, *Naming Colonialism*, p. 156.
109. AAB, AIMO 1735, RAG, Tanganika-Möero, Quatrième Trimestre, 1922, p. 22.
110. Archives Générales du Saint-Esprit, Paris (henceforth CSSp), 7J2.1b, Mission of the Sacred Heart, Kongolo, Journal de Kongolo, p. 1.
111. AAB, AIMO 1735, RAG, Tanganika-Möero, Première Semestre, 1923, p. 28.
112. Ibid., p. 28.
113. Ibid., p. 29.
114. Markowitz, *Cross and Sword*, p. 11.
115. AGM, Diaries, Sola: Bruges St. Donat (1904–1925), 28 September 1920, p. 98.
116. Ibid., p. 99.
117. Interview with Ngembwa Tambwe Norbert, Lubunda, 21 April 2009.
118. AGM, Auguste Van Acker, 'Rapport Annuel, 1919–1920' (Algiers: Imprimerie des Missionnaires de l'Afrique, 1920), p. 173.
119. Ibid.
120. AGM, Auguste-Léopold Huys, 'Rapport Annuel, 1929–1930' (Algiers: Imprimerie des Missionnaires de l'Afrique, 1920), p. 201.
121. AAB, AIMO 1735, RAG, Tanganika-Möero, 1931, p. 36.
122. Jonghe, *L'Enseignement des Indigènes*, p. 151.
123. Interview with Ngembwa Tambwe Norbert, Lubunda, 21 April 2009.
124. Jean Comaroff and John L. Comaroff, *Of Revelation and Revolution: The Dialectics of Modernity on a South African Frontier, Volume 2* (Chicago: Chicago University Press, 1997), p. 63.
125. AGM, Auguste-Léopold Huys, 'Rapport Annuel, 1928–1929' (Algiers: Imperimerie Des Missionnaires d'Afrique, 1929), p. 247.
126. CSSp, 'Historique de la Mission de Lubunda: Braine-L'Alleud St. Joseph,' p. 176.
127. CSSp, Boite 375, 7J1.1a8, Katanga Nord, Lubunda près MaKongolo, Lubunda, le 12.01.1924, Antoine Philippe.
128. Ibid.

129. CSSp, Boite 375, 7J1.1a8, Katanga Nord, Lubunda, Près Kongolo, Emile Callewaert, 'A Son Eminence le Cardinal Préfecture Apostolique du Katanga Septentrional,' 15 mars 1924, p. 1.
130. Ibid.
131. AAB, AIMO 1735, RAG, Tanganika-Möero, Deuxième Semestre, 1926, p. 37.
132. AGM, Bruges-Saint-Donat, Rapport Annuel, 1924–1925, p. 405.
133. There are many examples of DCs calling for more work to be done on local tribunals, see: AAB, AIMO 1735, RAG, Tanganika-Möero, Deuxième Semestre, 1926, p. 37; AAB, AIMO 1735, RAG, Tanganika-Möero, Première Semestre, 1924, p. 5.
134. James C. Scott, *Seeing Like a State: How Certain Schemes to Improve the Human Condition Have Failed* (New Haven: Yale University Press, 1998), p. 30.
135. For more details on cotton in the Belgian Congo, see: Likaka, *Rural Society and Cotton in Colonial Zaire.*

BIBLIOGRAPHY

Alexander, Jocelyn, *The Unsettled Land: State-Making and the Politics of Land in Zimbabwe, 1893–2003* (Oxford: James Currey, 2006).
Berman, Bruce, 'Ethnicity, Patronage and the African State: The Politics of Uncivil Nationalism,' *African Affairs*, 97, 388, (1998), pp. 305–341.
Bilonda, Michel Lwamba, *Cours d'Histoire Politique du Congo de 1885 à nos Jours* (Lubumbashi: Centre d'Études et de Recherches Documentaires sur l'Afrique Centrale, Lubumbashi, 2008/9).
Buell, Raymond Leslie, *The Native Problem in Africa* (New York: The Macmillan Company, 1928).
Cannadine, David, *Ornamentalism: How the British Saw Their Empire* (London: Penguin, 2001).
Cartledge, Connie L., Jackson, Allyson H., and Kerwin, Patrick M., 'Raymond Leslie Buell Papers: Finding Aid to the Collection in the Library of Congress' (Washington, DC, 2010).
Childs, S. Terry, and Marat, Pierre de, 'Re/Constructing Luba Pasts,' in M. Nooter Roberts and A. F. Roberts (eds), *Memory: Luba Art and the Making of Memory* (New York Museum for African Art, 1996), pp. 151–165.
Comaroff, Jean, and Comaroff, John L., *Of Revelation and Revolution: The Dialectics of Modernity on a South African Frontier, Volume 2* (Chicago: Chicago University Press, 1997).
Delicour, F., 'Jules-Laurent-Jean-Louis Renkin,' in *Biographie Coloniale Belge*, Tome IV (1955), colons 747–753.

Dellicour, F., 'Martin Jean-Marie-René Rutten,' in *Biographie Belge d'Outre-Mer, Tome VI* (Bruxelles: Académie Royal des Sciences d'Outre-Mer, 1968), p. 714.

Dembour, Marie-Bénédict, *Recalling the Belgian Congo: Conversations and Introspection* (New York: Berghahan Books, 2001).

Fields, Karen E., *Revival and Rebellion in Colonial Central Africa* (Princeton: Princeton University Press, 1985).

Franck, Louis, *Congo: Land En Volk* (Brugge: De Centrale Boekhandel S. V., 1926).

Franck, Louis (ed.), *Le Congo Belge* (Bruxelles: Le Renaissance du Livre, 1928).

Gordon, David, *Invisible Agents: Spirits in a Central African History* (Athens: Ohio University Press, 2012).

Jewsiewicki, Bogumil, 'Belgian Africa,' in Andrew Roberts (ed.), *The Cambridge History of Africa, Volume 7, c.1905–1940* (Cambridge: Cambridge University Press, 1986), pp. 460–493.

Jewsiewicki, Bogumil, 'The Formation of the Political Culture of Ethnicity in the Belgian Congo, 1920–1959,' in Leroy Vail (ed.), *The Creation of Tribalism in Southern Africa* (London: James Currey, 1989), pp. 324–349.

De Jonghe (ed.), *L'Enseignement des Indigènes au Congo Belge* (Bruxelles: Institut Colonial International, 1931).

Likaka, Osumaka, *Rural Society and Cotton in Colonial Zaire* (Madison: University of Wisconsin Press, 1997).

Lippens, Maurice, 'The Belgian Congo,' *Journal of the Royal African Society*, 38, 153 (1939), pp. 419–426.

Lugard, Frederick, *The Dual Mandate in British Tropical Africa* (Edinburgh and London: William Blackwood and Sons, 1922).

Lyons, Maryinez, *The Colonial Disease: A Social History of Sleeping Sickness in Northern Zaire, 1900–1940* (Cambridge: Cambridge University Press, 2002).

Markowitz, Marvin D., *Cross and Sword: The Political Role of Missionaries in the Belgian Congo, 1908–1960* (Stanford: Hoover Institution, 1973).

Marre, Francis, *Jules Renkin et la Conquête Africaine* (Bruxelles: G. Van Ouest, 1917).

Marzorati, A. F. G., 'The Political Organisation and Evolution of African Society in the Belgian Congo,' *African Affairs*, 53, 211 (1954), pp. 104–112.

Maxwell, David, 'Christianity,' in Richard Reid and John Parker (eds), *The Oxford Handbook of African History* (Oxford: Oxford University Press, 2013), pp. 263–280.

Meester, Paul de, *L'Eglise de Jésus Christ au Congo-Kinshasa* (Lubumbashi: Centre Interdiocésain de Lubumbashi, 1997).

Meeuwis, Michael. 'The Origin of Belgian Colonial Language Policies in the Congo,' *Language Matters: Studies in the Languages of Africa*, 42, 2 (2011), pp. 190–206.

Mudimbe, Valentine Yves, *The Idea of Africa* (Bloomington: Indiana University Press, 1994).

Ndaywel è Nziem, Isidore, *Histoire Général du Congo: De l'Héritage Ancien á la République Démocratique* [Préface de Théophile Obenga, Postface de Pierre Salmon] (Bruxelles: De Boeck & Larcier, 1998).

Nzongola-Ntalaja, Georges, *The Congo: From Leopold to Kabila: A Peoples' History* (London: Zed Books, 2002).

Perrot, Noël, *Eléments Pour l'Histoire de la Fondation du District de Kongolo au Congo-Kinshasa 1907–1927: Extraits de la Correspondance de Mgr Callewaert* (Self Published, 1997).

Pesek, Michael, 'Cued Speeches: The Emergence of Shauri as Colonial Praxis in German East Africa, 1850–1903,' *History in Africa*, 33 (2006), pp. 395–412.

Ranger, Terence O., 'The Invention of Tradition in Colonial Africa,' in Terence O. Ranger and Eric Hobsbawm (eds), *The Invention of Tradition* (Cambridge: Cambridge University Press, 1983), pp. 211–262.

Reefe, Thomas Q., *The Rainbow and the Kings: A History of the Luba Empire to 1891* (Berkeley: University of California Press, 1984).

Rose-Hunt, Nancy, *A Colonial Lexicon of Birth, Ritual, Medicalisation, and Mobility in Congo* (Durham: Duke University Press, 1999).

Scott, James C., *Seeing Like a State: How Certain Schemes to Improve the Human Condition Have Failed* (New Haven: Yale University Press, 1998).

Shorter, Aylward, *African Recruits and Mission Conscripts: The White Fathers and the Great War* (Rome: Missionaries of Africa, 2007).

Stannard, Matthew, *Selling the Congo: A History of European Pro-Empire Propaganda and the Making of Belgian Imperialism* (Nebraska: University of Nebraska Press, 2012).

Straeten, E. Van der, 'Maurice Auguste-Eugène-Charles, Marie-Ghislain, Lippens,' in *Biographie Belge d'Outre-Mer, Tome VI* (Bruxelles: Académie Royal des Sciences d'Outre-Mer, 1968), colons 664–672.

Sundkler, Bengt, and Steed, Christopher, *The History of the Church in Africa* (Cambridge: Cambridge University Press, 2000).

Vanhee, Hein, 'Les Chefs Médaillés,' in Jean-Luc Vellut et al. (eds), *La Mémoire du Congo: le Temps Colonial* (Tervuren, 2005), pp. 79–82.

Vansina, Jan, 'Les Kuba et l'Administration Territoriale de 1919 à 1960,' *Cultures et Développement*, 4 (1972), pp. 275–298.

Vansina, Jan, *Paths in the Rainforests: Toward a History of Political Tradition in Equatorial Africa* (Madison: Wisconsin University Press, 1990).

Weber, Max (Translated by Talcott Parsons), *The Protestant Ethic and the Spirit of Capitalism* (New York: Dover Publications, 2003).

Young, Crawford M., *Politics in Congo: Decolonization and Independence* (Princeton: Princeton University Press, 1965).

Young, Crawford M., *The African Colonial State in Comparative Perspective* (New Haven: Yale University Press, 1994).

CHAPTER 5

Missionaries and the Formation of Colonial Chieftainship, 1933–1939

The last chapter concentrated on the Luba and the Songye areas on the left bank of Kongolo whereas this one focuses more on the societies on the right bank of the Lualaba River and deals with the period from the Great Depression to the Second World War.[1] The chapter's concentration on the right bank is a result of the voluminous evidence available for social change there during the economic downturn, which overshadows that available for the left. Both sides of Kongolo, though, witnessed the Belgian administration's attempt to pass the burden of its debt onto African farmers during the 1930s.[2] In Kongolo, this meant that the colonial administration together with its concession allies tried to install a coercive cotton regime in chieftainships across the territory. To enforce its new labour regimen at the same time as cutting back on hiring expensive European officials, the Belgian administration increasingly relied on its emerging network of African chiefs. Yet Osumaka Likaka has suggested that chieftainship in Tanganyika was particularly turbulent and this observation is true of the polities of the Hêmbá groups and their neighbours in eastern Kongolo.[3] Many of the chiefs who had pre-colonial claims to legitimacy among the Hêmbá had been killed by Zanzibari slavers unlike Bùki and his family in the southern parts of the territory. So, the Belgian regime chose to experiment in some cases by installing chiefs who were loyal to them rather than because 'they fulfilled established regional criteria of leadership.'[4]

© The Author(s) 2019
R. A. Loffman, *Church, State and Colonialism in Southeastern Congo, 1890–1962*, Cambridge Imperial and Post-Colonial Studies Series, https://doi.org/10.1007/978-3-030-17380-7_5

This experiment meant that the colonial administration placed the chiefs concerned, namely Risaci Katore and Kalamba Lwamba Sunzu (Sindano) of Bena Mambwe and Bena Nyembo, respectively, in an invidious position because many of their subjects protested that they were illegitimate. Their alleged illegitimacy meant that Katore and Sindano came under added pressure as colonial officials expected them to enforce the hated cotton regime as well as contain the spread of Sleeping Sickness. To demonstrate that they were serious and authoritative figures, despite imposing forced labour conditions, Katore and Sindano undertook a witch-hunt known as *Kibangile* with brutal enthusiasm. While witch-hunting might have pleased those of their subjects who were not accused of wrongdoing, Katore and Sindano stepped outside the Church's moral economy. And so missionaries lobbied the colonial regime to dispense with them. Although colonial officials vacillated, the power that missionaries had accumulated since their arrival in Kongolo in 1909 meant that their counterparts in the Belgian administration eventually felt they had to listen to them. In so doing, the Church fleshed out the substance of chieftainship at least as much if not more so than the colonial administration as the expansion of the secular state into the hinterland faltered once again. Far from an era in which the colonial administration's reach grew, the contradictory demands it placed on chiefs and labourers to impose forced labour yet remain popular meant that the Church entrenched its power in the fiscally challenged years of the 1930s.[5]

COTTON AND THE HALTING CONSTRUCTION OF COLONIAL STATEHOOD IN EASTERN KONGOLO

Before the Great Depression, Belgian officials were still very much engaged in the process of tidying up the hinterland. As late as 1931, the frontiers of several chieftainships on the right bank, such as those of the Bango Bango ethnic group, a range of Hêmbá sub-groups, including the Bena Nkuvu, the Bena Nyembo, as well as Songye groups such as the Bena Kabishia and the Bena Kayungu still needed to be finalized.[6] Taken together, these chieftainships constituted the lion's share of land in this part of Kongolo. However, Belgian officials were impeded in their efforts to finalize these borders given that the administration had to lose staff during the Great Depression. The number of Belgian officials had been reduced as international demand for Congolese commodities, such as copper, fell on the world markets.[7]

To cope with these staffing shortages, Belgian rule quickly centralized and reduced the number of provinces and by extension their administrative teams.[8] In a pattern replicated across much of the Belgian Congo, in which territories were grafted onto one another to save administrative costs, Kabalo became part of Kongolo in 1932.[9] This expanded by six the number of chieftainships under the Kongolo team's jurisdiction. Altogether, then, the territory doubled in size to around 26,000 square kilometres and, even by 1940, there were only *seven* European agents charged with governing 59,791 African subjects (see Fig. 5.1).[10]

Fig. 5.1 Administrative map of Kongolo, 1932–1940

Kongolo's expansion put more pressure on the territory's already overstretched agents and meant that African chiefs played an even more unsupervised role in the administration. Chiefs' new powers were outlined in a new Decree that was enacted in 1933.[11] Yet, in spite of this Decree, the liberal District Commissioner of Tanganyika, H. L. Keyser, was concerned that the role of the chiefs upon which the administration would now place increased responsibility was still unclear. He worried that a number of chiefs were being placed under great pressure by 'unemployed workers,' who would only become more influential once the Depression struck, as well as by 'young men' in general.[12] Rather than simply enforcing colonial orders, therefore, chiefs in Tanganyika actually started to petition the Belgian administration on behalf of these disenfranchised yet restive groups. Keyser made it clear to his subordinates that chiefs were not the representatives of their people, however. Instead, it was the other way around. Chiefs were meant to be the administration's 'men on the spot.' It was into this ambiguous and volatile political environment that a brutal new cotton regime was rolled out across Tanganyika.

The cotton regime was nothing new to the Belgian Congo itself by the time it reached Kongolo. Edmund Leplae, a professor of agriculture at Leuven University, had already succeeded in getting the colonial government to instil cotton cultivation in the Congo as early as 1917.[13] His idea had been to transform what he considered to have been empty, unprofitable land into intensively farmed and lucrative agricultural plots that would promote the economic growth of the colony. The state would subsidize private concessions so that they could distribute free cotton seeds and employ people to teach African farmers how to grow cotton. Yet the administration would, at least in theory, recoup this initial investment because it owned shares in the aforementioned private companies and would therefore skew the market in their favour.[14]

The administration ensured that the concessions into which it had invested had the right to buy and sell all the commodities produced in the areas in which they operated. It also ensured that the companies it supported faced no formal competition for labour during key periods, such as harvest time. In addition, the state would use its supposed monopoly of legitimate violence against those deemed by company and colonial officials not to have produced enough cotton. To this end, the administration hired agricultural monitors whose job it was to ensure that farmers kept their fields tidy. Private firms followed suit and hired their own cotton monitors whose work broadly coincided with that of the agricultural monitors to ensure that there would be as few gaps in the surveillance of village farmers as possible.[15] Those farmers who fell behind in their cotton quotas were thus quickly identified and whipped and/or arrested.

Because Tanganyika had been so peripheral to the colonial economy for so long, the new cotton regime had not been introduced there immediately after it took root in the rest of the Congo. Rather, the Cotton Company of Tanganyika (Cotanga) was only established in 1933; it was in fact one of the last of the major colonial cotton concessions to be formed.[16] Yet it went to work quickly. By 1933, only the chieftainship of Bena Paye, which had formally been in the territory of Kabalo, did not cultivate cotton.[17] Cotanga purchased cotton mainly from the Kabalo, Manono, Mwanza and Kabongo territories in addition to Kongolo (see Fig. 5.1).[18]

Belgian officials and their company allies eventually expected people in these territories between the ages of fifteen and fifty to cultivate cotton. Much as elsewhere in the Belgian Congo, those who fell in this age category became known as *Hommes Adultes Valides* (HAVs).[19] As its name suggests, the HAV category was exceptionally gendered. As Karen Bouwer explains: 'although women, as was customary, continued to do the bulk of the agricultural work, they were excluded from wage-earning.'[20] Men and women suffered on the cotton fields but those who were less able to perform the labour as a result of injury or pregnancy particularly so. To try to prevent punishments being meted out on the less able-bodied, Hêmbá elders would call upon the labour of fellow kinspeople to help.[21] Before cotton production came into Tanganyika, elders hardly offered their kinspeople much compensation for the labour they requisitioned as their contribution was expected. However, after the introduction of cotton culture, those who came to the aid of their kinspeople routinely expected compensation.[22]

Aside from the backbreaking labour that cotton production demanded, and for which the infirm relied ever more on their kinspeoples' help to perform, it also 'interfered with food production.'[23] During harvest periods, the pressure on people to work on their cotton plots was immense, not least because of the punishments that could befall those who failed to meet their quotas, and these pressures detracted from farmers' efforts to grow their own subsistence crops. The amount of time used up trying to balance subsistence farming with cotton production resulted in far less people being willing to perform labour for those unable to undertake their duties as dictated by the colonial state. Even after cotton was harvested, many had to commute long distances transporting cotton crops in order to get to colonial markets.[24] Some of the only people who could requisition the necessary labour to till their fields no matter what other peoples' personal commitments were the chiefs, who in theory could mobilize the violence of the colonial state to call on reserves of collective labour.[25] Understandably, therefore, chiefs became objects of popular hatred and derision as social differentiation accelerated under the cotton regime. While before the introduction of cotton those forced to labour on a chief's plot would at least harvest or produce some commodities for the general good, under the cotton regime all produce grown on his land went on enriching the chief.

Why should someone be promoted to a position that would grant them guaranteed labour and higher rates of remuneration for the amount of cotton they harvested than others though? This question moved to the forefront of African subjects' minds as the cotton economy encroached into both the right and left banks. The unresolved question of what gave a chief their legitimacy to rule meant that pointed debates about who held authority that had been raging sporadically since the attempted Zanzibari colonization at the turn of the century resurfaced with renewed vigour. Even chiefs with pre-Zanzibari/Belgian claims to legitimacy, such as Bùki, struggled to maintain control during the imposition of cotton culture. But the situation was far worse for those who had no such pre-colonial claims to legitimacy. Rasaci Katore and Kalamba Sindano were two examples of chiefs who found themselves installed solely because they were literate and loyal to the Belgian regime. From having preferred indirect rule for so long, Belgian officials in Kongolo lurched towards a more direct style of rule based on selecting chiefs on the basis of their loyalty to their colonial overlords and on their educational background rather than their claims to pre-colonial legitimacy. The next section asks who these chiefs were and why the administration favoured them in particular.

BELGIUM'S NEW CHIEFS IN EASTERN KONGOLO

Before ascending to become chief of the Bena Mambwe, Risaci Katore, much like Kalamba Sindano, had been a servant, or 'boy,' living in the pay of an unnamed European(s) who had settled in the Belgian Congo 'for a period of twenty-five years.'[26] For a long time, the colonial category of 'boy' represented a 'diminutive, servile' male to many historians.[27] However, as Nancy Rose-Hunt suggests, '"boy" work seemed prestigious early in the [twentieth] century ... some no doubt were former slaves, honoured to locate to new patrons yielding access to a new social ladder ... Domestic service arrangements made economic sense.'[28] Regrettably, we do not know if Katore or Sindano were former slaves and thus proud of their work as a 'boys.' Yet the fact that they laboured in the very early twentieth century meant that their work as 'boys' was well before the job became less respectable after the Second World War, when other blue-collar jobs became more prestigious.

Whatever their opinions of their previous employment, all we can know about it is that it greatly endeared them to the colonial regime. After their work as 'boys,' Katore, for example, began to master French and so was able to act as a court translator in Kongolo as well as Albertville (now Kalemie). And so, even before he became a chief, Belgian officials described him as an *évoloué*, a colonial term for someone who had reached a relatively privileged position and had assimilated European customs.[29] Likewise, Keyser, who was Labrique's successor, described him as someone said to have been: 'entirely disengaged from fetishistic beliefs.'[30] Despite these claims, Labrique was more than a little nervous about Katore's investiture, which would be in his words 'an interesting experiment,' as the new chief had no local power base.[31] So began an experimental shift from genealogical to a more functional justification for holders of rural authority in Kongolo.

Colonial records do not describe Sindano as an évoloué and neither do they suggest anything about his mastery (or not) of French (or Dutch). But we do know that he took over as chief of Bena Nyembo in 1923 after the former chief, Bititi, had offered her resignation on the grounds that, according to colonial records, 'the functions [of chieftainship] are too difficult and thankless for a woman to perform.'[32] Bititi's words, as reported by the Belgian regime, indicate that, just as in cases across the colonial world, local intermediaries 'and the colonial state were mutually gendered' with Belgian officials and their African allies practising and performing 'the state as masculine.'[33] Bititi's story is intriguing in its own right, and has likely been distorted by a state that, in the historian David Maxwell's words, tried 'to sort out inconsistencies and anomalies such as female chiefs.'[34] Regrettably, accessing Bititi's own view of her resignation is unlikely because 'given the mutual construction of states and archives if ... women were largely excluded by state practices that exclusion would be reflected in the archive.'[35] Whatever the truth about Bititi's resignation, Sindano acceded to become chief immediately after she resigned. Despite being backed by the colonial regime, he soon faced a concerted revolt from a number of the local notables. By the end of 1924, a notable called Bibi Kayanza continued to oppose Sindano's rule and colonial officials confirmed that her 'baulking' at her new chief's authority would probably require 'firm action.'[36]

Although we do not know much about Sindano's background, we can assume from Bibi Kayanza's protestations that his claim to legitimacy was opposed—even at his own court—and so his authority required a good deal of colonial support to maintain. Like Katore, he was very much Belgium's 'man on the spot.' The annual territorial report that Reymenans, a territorial agent, compiled in 1933 noted that despite Sindano's activities as well as the intervention of the 'authorities' during the course of the year, 'almost nothing [had] been done' in [Bena Nyembo]. Given the efforts that Sindano must have expended to please his colonial masters, we can only assume not much was achieved because he simply lacked the authority to enact unpopular colonial orders. Although Bibi Kayanza had spoken up against Sindano's legitimacy, though, to all intents and purposes his rule seemed to be stable if one ignores the production levels in his chieftainship. Likewise, Katore's reign might have been blighted by drunkenness in the eyes of colonial officials but it was otherwise undramatic.[37] This official portrait of political stability in eastern Kongolo was to be shattered, however, at least in the eyes of the Catholic Church, on Thursday 19 April 1934.

Kongolo's New Chiefs and a New Witch-Finding Movement

On that Thursday, it became clear to the White Fathers based in Sola, the headquarters of Bena Nkuvu, that a violent witch-finding episode had begun and perilously close to their own out-station. Louis Verstraete, Joseph van den Tillaert and Friar Silvere heard that Sindano had adopted a witch-finding practice called *Kibangile*.[38] Having been on vacation from their studies there, a group of children returned from Sindano's court and told the three missionaries about this witch-hunt. They understood that it was not just Sindano leading efforts to hunt witches in eastern Kongolo but also that his friend, Risaci Katore, had joined him. Together, Katore and Sindano had put a number of their subjects through torture and poison ordeals in order to determine whether or not they were witches. On learning of these events, Joseph van den Tillaert went straight to Bena Mambwe to investigate.[39] Having arrived in Makutano, the headquarters of the chieftainship, he met with Katore in an effort to persuade him to stop witch-hunting. Yet Katore met the priest's requests with 'indifference' and continued in his efforts to rid his chieftainship of evil, known as *ulozi* in Hêmbá (and as well as in other languages across southern Africa).[40] Having failed to stop Katore's witch-hunt by petitioning the chief himself, van den Tillaert lodged a complaint with Reymenans in the hope of persuading the Belgian colonial forces to put an end to it.[41]

The colonial administration commissioned a medical study into Kibangile sometime around 30 April. Yet it was only on 16 May that Dr. Frederic Belhommet was given the unenviable task of examining the bodies of those afflicted by Kibangile-related ordeals. His testimony was grisly. It was likely compiled to assess whether or not Sindano's regime had become too violent even for the Belgian administration to tolerate— particularly given how self-conscious it was after the 'red rubber' atrocities committed by the Free State were exposed by the Congo Reform Association (CRA). Belhommet probably went to collect evidence in Bena Mambwe as well as Bena Nyembo though, unfortunately, there are no remaining medical reports from Katore's chieftainship. Instead, we only have the police report from Bena Mambwe. Nonetheless, Reymenans' subordinates found that witch-finding ordeals had been carried out in eight settlements across Bena Mambwe but that the vast majority, that is to say, 48%, had taken place in Makutano wherein Katore' s court was situated.[42]

Oral sources relating to Kibangile from Bena Nyembo support the supposition that the majority of these ordeals took place in open, publically visible spaces, such as a mount in Mbulula, the headquarters of Bena Nyembo, known locally as *Agulu-Abuti*.[43] Witch trials occurred in these public places because their whole existence was predicated on having an audience that could attest to the fact that Katore and Sindano's chieftainships were indeed being cleansed of ulozi. Instead of the sovereign, in this case the chief's, rule being breached by a subject breaking the law, in this case it was evil that threatened to undermine Katore and Sindano's power.[44] And so the chiefs involved in Kibangile had to show publically that they had triumphed over this outbreak of ulozi.[45] Nothing could be hidden from their victory over evil lest their Hêmbá subjects believe Katore and Sindano were not qualified to combat it or, worse still, had no interest in doing so. Yet their methods of dealing with alleged witches was alarmingly brutal.

Belhommet and van den Tillaert suggested that Kibangile confessions were extracted after suspected witches were strung upside down using vines and/or ropes that tied their limbs to two wooden poles approximately two and a half metres apart.[46] The mechanism was given the name *Kibangile* as were the prosecutors, in this case, Katore and Sindano, who became known as 'the men who made suffering.'[47] Failure to confess to involvement in witchcraft after being subjected to this torture mechanism resulted in a poison ordeal being administered in which suspected witches would have to drink a local concoction known as *mwavi*. Mwavi was a liquid made from boiling the bark of a tree known locally as *kihumi* and was potentially lethal.[48] If the person drinking mwavi survived, they were exonerated, if they died, they would be confirmed as witches. The use of mwavi poison is indicative of the trans-regional features of Kibangile and Hêmbá witch-finding in general. David Gordon even recorded its use in his work among the Bemba peoples in northern Zambia, for example, and it was also used by the Tabwa peoples in eastern Katanga.[49] Likewise, poison ordeals, like those employed in Kibangile, have a long history in Africa, and elsewhere.[50] What Katore and Sindano did that was different in the context of Kongolo, therefore, was to use a torture apparatus *alongside* the poison ordeal as both a litmus test and as a substance for spiritual purification.

Although Kibangile was unique in the history of witch-finding in Katanga up until that point, it was a fusion of local beliefs and outside methods and one which centred on the concept of kinship. In his path-breaking book *The Modernity of Witchcraft*, Peter Geschiere suggested that witchcraft was in fact the dark side of kinship or 'the frightening realization that there is jealousy and therefore aggression within the family, where there should only be trust and solidarity.'[51] Geschiere went on to write that '[witchcraft] is used ... to address modern changes [it is] the obvious discourse for attempts to relate new inequalities ... to the familiar world of kinship and relatives.'[52] Although Geschiere was writing about the post-colonial period and in a Cameroonian context, his argument sheds some light on what was happening in Kongolo in the early 1930s. The introduction of cash crops strained relationships as we shall see but kinship groups were held together to some extent by the way in which they understood evil. The idea of ulozi bound groups together because it abstracted jealousy and personal ambition to the spirit world and not that of the material one. It can be of little surprise, therefore, that few people actually died during the Kibangile outbreak given the way that evil was abstracted in Hêmbá societies.

Mission sources indicate that a man called 'Muti,' meaning 'medicine' in many African languages, had approached Sindano having just escaped being hanged by his village chief, Lengwe, for admitting being an *mlozi* (witch) and causing death by malevolent magic.[53] The village he escaped from was called 'Kibangule,' in what is now the Maniema Province, and it is from the name of this village from which the word Kibangile is in all probability derived.[54] Reymenans, then the TA of Kongolo, told a similar story of Kibangile being imported into the territory though with a different protagonist coming from a different location. According to Reymenans, someone called Kalukulu Lumande came to Kongolo from Nyunzu, Kongolo's eastern neighbour, to spread Kibangile on 18 April.[55] Reymenans' version of the origins of Kibangile in Kongolo mirrors some of those I came across during my own fieldwork in Kongolo. For example, Kitwanga Nzikala suggests that Kalukulu (or Katukulu as he described him) came from Nyunzu to spread Kibangile in Bena Nyembo.[56] Yet both versions suggest that Kibangile came from a town relatively far from Bena Nyembo and Bena Mambwe. Likewise, having arrived in Bena Mambwe, Muti (or Lumande) told Sindano that he could rid his chieftainship of ulozi presumably because he himself was a mlozi. Sindano took him seriously and so began to take steps to rid his own chieftainship of witchcraft in exactly the manner that his visitor had outlined. Having had a conversation with his friend Sindano, Katore adopted Kibangile soon afterwards. But why would Sindano wish to take this traveller's claim seriously in the first place? There are two mutually compatible possibilities.

Gender, Finance and the Social Politics of Witch-Finding

The first possible explanation for the outbreak of a witch-hunt in eastern Kongolo begins with an incident that occurred in Bena Nyembo in 1928 in which Kalamba Sindano wanted to marry a young girl who refused his hand. He allegedly summoned the girl's mother in an attempt to use parental pressure on the girl to secure his union with her. However, the girl's mother refused to allow her daughter to marry the chief. Upon hearing her dissent, Sindano hit the mother in question twelve times.[57] The twelfth time Sindano struck the women she fell to the floor at which point Sindano spat at her four times (*fruit de nez*) saying that his phlegm came from the female 'witch' herself. The people who witnessed this incident reportedly believed that the woman was a witch, at least according to van den Tillaert. Although the missionary's explanation seems plausible at first sight, we must treat it with caution because it draws heavily on the colonial stereotype of the brutal central African chief. Aside from using Sindano and Katore's inherent personal greed and lust for power as a vital explanation for Kibangile, Tillaert's account does not explain why the episode began in 1934 as opposed to, say, 1928, when Sindano had his request for marriage rejected. He might have argued that 1934 was the year that Sindano and Katore first learned of a new means of fighting witchcraft and imported the Kibangile witch finding apparatus/model from Muti or Lumande. But there were other ways in which the chiefs could have countered witchcraft *before* the arrival of Kibangile.

One of the most obvious readings of the failed marriage story is that Sindano had evoked witchcraft as a means of controlling bridewealth and by extension the control of young women. African men, especially elders, were concerned to control their female populations, first, because of their capacity for social reproduction and, secondly, to secure their domestic labour. Elders' accelerated their efforts to control young women during the Great Depression because many young men were arriving back into chieftainships, such as Mambwe, with cash that they had earned as mine workers in the central and southern regions of Katanga.[58] With their earnings, former mineworkers could afford to pay higher bride-wealth prices and marry far more easily thereby competing with their polygamous elders for women. Likewise, elders constantly suspected women of breaking with patriarchal conventions in a manner that facilitated their unions with younger men; for example by assembling at night without their husbands' or fathers' consent.

Given their ability to marry far more quickly than before, young men began to petition for increasingly large amounts of political power during the 1930s as Keyser had discovered. In Bena Nyembo, for example, a young man even petitioned to be recognized as chief after having returned to the chieftainship armed with the cash wages that he had saved from his old mining-work. That man was Augustin Luamba (Lwamba) and he had arrived back in Bena Nyembo after having served as a capita in the Great Lakes Rail Company (CFL) once his bosses had refused to renew his contract. To further his claims to chieftaincy, he sought to make the sub-chieftainship of Bena Honga, previously a part of Bena Nyembo, an independent, sovereign entity in its own right and with himself at the helm.[59] Luamba was clearly trying to appropriate the language of colonial chieftainship to advance his own power an authoritarian rural context. Despite his having clothed his claim in the garb of neo-traditionalism, the Belgian administration still dismissed them. Yet the failure of Luamba's claims to power did not mean that elders did not still regard controlling young men as vital to the propagation of their control over of colonial chieftainship. Given the insecurities of men whose claim to authority was based far more on 'custom' rather than wealth, it is potentially easier to understand why Sindano acted so violently towards a woman who dared to resist his control.

Alongside the witch-hunters' desire to control the circulation of women, Reymenans suggested that Lumande (who may well have been called Muti) 'shared his lavish profits' with Risaci and Sindano; though it is unclear if he meant his pre-existing profits or those he made from Kibangile. If Lumande did make a profit from witch-hunting, Reymenans did not explain how. Nonetheless, colonial officials were convinced that greed was at the root of the Kibangile outbreak.[60] That Katore and Sindano wanted a share of Lumande or Muti's profits explains in part why the witch-hunt began in 1934. But it does not explain why it did not continue when Sindano's request for marriage was first rejected in 1928. Nonetheless, there are potentially some reasons to take Reymenans seriously when he speaks of a material reward for initiating a witch-hunting episode. Risaci Katore had been fined a month's worth of wages for public drunkenness at some point in 1933.[61] Likewise, Kalamba Sindano had been fined three month's-worth of wages for engaging in an 'uncustomary act' during the same year. One could assume, therefore, that if someone were to come to both of these chiefs at around the time that their wages had been withheld offering 'riches' then Katore and Sindano would have been open to their suggestions.

But there are some important problems with Reymenans' early interpretation of the origins of Kibangile. First, Katore and Sindano might well have known the administration was of a secular persuasion and had little time for those who enacted violent witch-hunts given their time serving as clerks and translators in the late 1910s and the 1920s. So to risk their new-found authority for the sake of one or even three months wages appears an act of folly that would be beyond the intelligence that the regime had always attributed to these chiefs. What is more, Katore and Sindano governed two of the richest chieftainships in Kongolo and so would have been far better endowed financially than almost any of their peers, with the only possible exception being that of the Bùki chieftainship in southern Kongolo. There were 10,000 people living in Bùki in 1933, which compares favourably to the nearly 6000 people who inhabited Bena Mambwe alone—with many of them qualifying, no doubt, as HAVs. Colonial statistics, which admittedly always need to be treated with some degree of caution given how subordinates always wanted to impress their superiors, strongly suggest the cotton trade was booming in Bena Mambwe and Bena Nyembo. In Mambwe, for example, the state made 570 Francs net profit from its cotton trade in 1934.[62] And much of that money would have found its way into the hands of the chief.

THE SLEEPING SICKNESS FACTOR

The lure of easy money might or might not have tempted Katore and Sindano but, even if so, more important factors were at work in this outbreak of witch-hunting in eastern Kongolo. Oral sources pertaining to Kibangile are naturally difficult to find given that none of those who were cognizant of the episode as it unfolded are still alive. The closest we can get to contemporary oral sources are those recounted by people who were very young at the time and so had to learn about Kibangile from their kinfolk and neighbours. Muganza Walunga Augustin, the chief of Bena Mambwe in 2009 when I visited him, and an infant in 1934, was able to point to another reason why Kibangile could have started that year.[63] When asked why Kibangile began, he replied: 'at that time, perhaps there was an epidemic, sort of microbes, which killed people.'

On close inspection, the colonial record supports Augustin's supposition even if the way in which it does so warrants some explanation. The author of the colonial report that indicates Sleeping Sickness was a problem in Kongolo was René Wauthion, who had reprised his role as the head of the territorial administration of Kongolo in 1935 and so he wrote the annual territorial report for Kongolo for the year of 1934. Like any other TA, he was naturally under great pressure to emphasize the facets of the operations of the colonial state that reflected best on the job that he was doing.

As a consequence, he maintained that 'overall, there has been a marked reduction in suspected cases of Sleeping Sickness in the territory.'[64] Yet, on the very next page of his report, he admitted that there were in fact 165 'panics' about it in 1934.[65] Moreover, he complained that 'budgetary constraints,' unsurprising given the Depression context, severely curtailed his administration's efforts to fight the disease. He did not detail exactly where the 165 'panics' occurred but it would not be inconceivable that one or more could have happened in both Bena Mambwe and Bena Nyembo.

Mission sources corroborate the Wauthion's reporting on the prevalence of Sleeping Sickness in eastern Kongolo in the early 1930s. Not long after Kibangile ended, in June, missionaries in Bena Nkuvu had heard, via the colonial vet, Morandini, of eight cases of the disease in Sola alone.[66] The animal context is more important than it might first appear given that the African version of Trypanosomiasis (Sleeping Sickness) is capable of transferring from animals to humans in what is sometimes referred to as zoonotic infection. The concept of zoonotic infection was not known at the time but is relevant to the historian examining the Kibangile episode in retrospect because it supports the idea it was driven by Sleeping Sickness. Bena Nkuvu is also extremely close to Bena Nyembo—so much so the boundaries between the two polities were only just being finalized during the Depression. So, rather than placing Kibangile solely within a long history of elders trying to control women, this witch-finding episode might also be understood as an attempt to confront the 'evil' behind Sleeping Sickness.

As early as 1905, the Liverpool School of Tropical Medicine suggested that a Sleeping Sickness epidemic occurred in the Tanganyika district and subsequent colonial reports from there indicate that outbreaks of the disease continued in 1934 and beyond.[67] That Sleeping Sickness had a long-standing presence in Kongolo should also be no surprise given how extensively it had influenced the White Fathers' early mission encounters.[68] In fact, as the third chapter suggested, the reason that Roelens' missionaries moved to Sola in the first place was to avoid this deadly disease. That it should have been a long term factor in Bena Nyembo in particular, though, is evinced even by Sindano's name itself, which is a Swahili word meaning 'injection' in English. It is unlikely there would be any other reason why Kalamba would have been given the name 'Sindano' aside from his family's experience of injections carried out by the burgeoning number of colonial medical staff and their African intermediaries. By 1930, Maryinez Lyons observed that 'nearly

3,000,000 people annually' were being examined by colonial medics in the Belgian Congo, with a 'gradual evolution of a network of rural clinics, injection centres and hospitals.'[69] Although Sindano and his subjects may well have understood that 'microbes' caused some of the symptoms of Sleeping Sickness, like the peoples in the Uele region in the north east, the Hêmbá groups who inhabited Bena Mambwe and Bena Nyembo may well have ascribed 'most of the slower or chronic physical ailments ... to witchcraft.'[70]

The prevalence of Sleeping Sickness placed a greater onus on chiefs' ability to rid their chieftainship of ulozi. As Terence Ranger argued elsewhere, new religious movements often accompanied epidemics and Kibangile demonstrates this relationship albeit on a micro-scale.[71] With colonial officials keen to control African mobility as the boundaries of colonial chieftainships were being firmed up in Kongolo, African populations could not easily escape disease-infested homesteads. The increasing controls on their mobility added to the pressure felt by their chiefs that they should act to prevent such a clear and present danger to their subjects. Such controls on mobility took the form of subjects needing to get the written permission of their chief and territorial administrator if they wanted to leave a territory. Colonial subjects could be questioned by any authority figure about their movements and failure to show written permission for their travels could result in their imprisonment. At the same time, the colonial state's reliance on chiefs meant that their creativity, violent as it was, could thrive in a way it might not have done during the mid-1920s because of the shortage of European staff during the Depression.

A COMPARATIVE PERSPECTIVE: WITCHCRAFT IN THE BÙKI CHIEFTAINSHIP

Katore and Sindano both felt that they had to be seen to act against Sleeping Sickness given their lack of pre-colonial heritage. The actions of both Hêmbá chiefs is put into sharp perspective when compared to those committed by Bùki, who had pre-colonial heritage, in his 'great' chieftainship in southern Kongolo. In the late 1920s, Bùki's domains had been subjected to what Labrique called 'chickenpox epidemics' that may not have been as serious as those of Sleeping Sickness but were nonetheless a debilitating.[72] Despite the prevalence of this disease in southern Kongolo, there was no evidence of a witch-hunt nor of a chiefly-directed campaign against evil in Bùki at this time. The fact that Bùki had pre-colonial heritage, which dovetailed with discourses of Luba cosmology, meant that he was not as insecure in his position as his Hêmbá colleagues—not that his subjects always believed that Bùki always adhered to the moral precepts of Luba kingship of course.

Alongside Bùki's pre-colonial pedigree, a different but complementary explanation for the lack of a witch-hunt in his chieftainship in the 1920s and early 1930s lies in the fact that the colonial state made every effort to combat Sleeping Sickness there. Before the Depression, state coffers were considerably fuller than they would be afterwards and so they could support more extensive vaccination projects. Labrique, reflecting on his administration's programmes to tackle Trypanosomiasis during the 1920s, suggested that they were 'unfavourable to supporting tribal custom but this was inevitable ... the epidemic diseases that occur periodically in [Tanganyika] and that have taken many lives this year make [Africans] increasingly appreciate our medical care.'[73] Bùki, for one, though, did not appreciate these efforts because he believed that they undermined his claims to legitimacy as he did not direct them personally and so was seen not to have had control over this fundamental aspect of the daily life of his subjects. In the Bùki case, as in many others, colonial officials cordoned off parts of the chieftainship, re-grouped African villages and built stations for officials to monitor the disease and inoculate Africans. The colonial administration, both in Bùki's chieftainship and others, exercised a very visible public power, over and above that of the chief, which Belgian agents were still aware undermined the authority of the self-same intermediaries they chose to execute their orders.

The state's effective yet deeply intrusive response to Sleeping Sickness in his chieftainship meant that Bùki felt that his struggle for legitimacy was one waged far more between him and the colonial administration than one in which he and his followers were pitted against some sort of spiritual adversary. Conversely, Katore and Sindano's battle was very much to secure their subjects' loyalty and in a context in which the secular administration had arguably made too *little* effort to prevent Sleeping Sickness in their chieftainships. The lack of large-scale colonial vaccination programmes undertaken in eastern Kongolo in the early 1930s must ranks, therefore, as one of the most important reasons why Kibangile emerged when it did.

Although Bùki did not engage in a top-down movement like Kibangile, and witch-hunting episodes in general were rare in his chieftainship in the early 1930s, the same was not true of the later part of that decade.[74] Belgian officials identified a semi-secret society known as *Mama Ukanga*, meaning 'the mother of all charms,' in and around Bùki in 1937 after it had first reached the Tanganyika province in 1928. The word Ukanga itself, though referring to the word 'charm' in the singular, in reality probably meant a series of objects sold by a hierarchically ordered group of adepts. It is likely that these charms served a variety of purposes depending on the specificities of the local milieu in which Mama Ukanga operated. Yet much of what we know about Mama Ukanga comes from the scribblings of colonial officials who were groping for answers as to the social movements that seemed to surround them.

As in many cases involving semi-secret societies, colonial officials had conflicting interpretations Mama Ukanga. First, Belgian agents believed that a selection of workers recruited by the Katangese Labour Exchange had adopted it because they believed that it fought witches.[75] Unlike the Kibangile case, if the accused survived a poison ordeal, they were thought to have been witches but if they died they were believed to have been innocent. Later on, however, many of those selfsame colonial officials came to think that Mama Ukanga was in fact a means of seeking protection from the labour demands of the colonial state. Belgian officials working in Katanga claimed that it sprang from 'those who worked for Europeans' in Elisabethville and made its way into Kongolo in 1936.[76] According to them, a retired soldier, presumably an African, had spread it across Katanga via the sprawling railway network. The colonial state identified Joseph Bandela, a CFL labourer, for example, as a leading adept in Kongolo.[77] Having begun elsewhere, therefore, Mama Ukanga started to take root in Tanganyika. Yet it was likely that, due to the time it took to get there, it was only branded a 'secret society' by the Belgian administration 1930s.[78] Unlike Kibangile, Mama Ukanga was closer to witchcraft beliefs than to witch-hunting even if it did involve the latter on occasion.

In 1937, Keyser alerted the TA in Kongolo to the existence of Mama Ukanga in the chieftainship of Kanunu, which was located within the former territory of Kabalo.[79] He ordered that the organization be 'constantly surveyed.' And, as was usual when a so-called 'subversive' society was discovered, a prolonged study was commissioned to investigate its character. Following the completion of this study, the TA decided that

Ukanga was, indeed, a 'xenophobic and subversive' group.[80] The leading advocates of Mama Ukanga in Kongolo were therefore rounded up and jailed so as to prevent its spread across the territory. In 1937, the state accused Kiambilwa, Kasuku, Mwamba and Kibakazi of belonging to the sect.[81] The abovementioned adepts came from different villages but they all lived in Bùki or Kanunu. For example, Kasuku was from the village of Zefu in Bùki as was Kiambilwa. Mwamba was from the village of Kabobe in the Kiambilwa as well while Kibakazi was from Kienge in Kanunu. What these adepts shared in the eyes of the state, aside from the fact that they lived in southern Kongolo, was their use of Mama Ukanga to avoid obligatory labour.

State fear of this new movement was only increased by the proximity of so many adepts to the cotton plantation at Katompe, again in the former Kabalo territory.[82] For example, Mulonda, one of the most active Mama Ukanga adepts, had been caught looking for what was known as 'the dowry of Ukanga' in the Katompe region. The presence of Mama Ukanga in Katompe, in the Paye chieftainship, was entirely unsurprising, though, as it was famed for HAV resistance against the newly ensconced cotton industry.[83] Despite widespread propaganda efforts by the state, the local populations could not be persuaded to stop farming subsistence foodstuffs such as maize, peanuts and palm oil instead of cotton.[84] Although its adepts were placed under close state surveillance, Mama Ukanga was not easy to expiate because it supposedly offered over-burdened farmers a means of avoiding cash-crop production and substituting it with subsistence farming. Keyser stated that there 'was no ... Ukanga activity' in 1938 but he was forced to record a resurgence of the group in 1940.[85] In that year, seventeen adepts were convicted as a result of Katanda Goy, then the chief of Bena Nyembo, alerting the state to their presence.[86]

Mama Ukanga was a movement that had followed the penetration of Belgian colonial concessions into the hinterland and could adapt to whichever aspect of labour was prevalent in the milieu into which it was introduced. In Elisabethville, it had been a means of avoiding servile labour just as in Katompe it was a means of avoiding cotton production. Just as relations of governance had been contested and re-made under Kibangile so were relations of labour through Ukanga. While Ukanga outlived Kibangile, not least because it was related not to the personal career of a chief but to the colonial political economy, it was eventually suppressed. Outright contestation of cotton labour relations was not to be tolerated as the colonial state passed the burden of the Depression onto Congolese farmers.

Rural radicalism would be tackled by a range of institutions, including a police force dedicated to ensuring that no more movements like Mama Ukanga would emerge in Tanganyika. But unlike most other areas of Kongolo, mission presence was still barely noticeable in Bùki and this greatly impeded the state's knowledge of the occult and by extension its ability to deal with it there. The only mission presence in Bùki was a short-lived Seventh Day Adventist (SDA) mission. Bùki had let them stay in his chieftainship but the state had asked them to leave again in the late 1920s and so they had moved to Bigobo in Bena Nyembo.[87] The sparse mission presence in Bùki contrasted sharply with that in eastern Kongolo where as much as missionaries tried to stop witch-finding they also indirectly spurred it on.

MISSION INTRUSION AND KIBANGILE

At first, it seems counterintuitive to write that Catholic missionaries, who viewed witch-finding with the deepest distain, could have indirectly helped to propel it. However, the evidence in Kongolo points to mission encroachment as being a factor in Katore and Sindano's occult activities. To understand why, Joseph van den Tillaert's meeting with Katore on 11 May 1934, which he convened to try to restrain the chief once again, is instructive. During this meeting, Katore declared himself to be 'invulnerable' because he was the 'God' of the region (with 'region' presumably meaning Bena Mambwe) (*il declare être invulnerable et être le "dieu" du pays*).[88] But why, one might reasonably ask, would Katore wish to articulate his secular powers in such a spiritual way?

In one of African history's many enduring ironies, David Gordon has argued that mission penetration of the African hinterland catalyzed instances of witchcraft accusation because missionaries 'proclaimed the pervasiveness of sin,' one of the most important manifestations of witchcraft, yet prohibited Africans from hunting those responsible for propagating evil.[89] By asserting that he was 'God,' Katore may thus have been reacting to the pervasiveness of sin, as preached by a steadily encroaching White Fathers' mission, and, further, that he and he alone could cleanse his chieftainship as a result of his deistic powers.

The White Fathers' presence in Bena Mambwe was slight but tangible. There was already a small chapel there by the 1930s and more facilities followed after the Second World War.[90] Katore would have noticed the small chapel as well as the missionaries who came and went as a result of its construction. What is more, in 1931, three years before the Kibangile outbreak, Joseph van den Tillaert made a good deal of progress in converting Kayanza Mutoke, a prominent notable in Bena Mambwe who would become regent-chief after Katore was eventually deposed for his witch-finding in the summer of 1934.[91] And, to add insult to the injury of anyone fearing the extension of Christian modernity into Bena Mambwe, people started to leave/lose interest in the local *Bambudji* chapter.[92]

Bambudji was a Hêmbá iteration of the Luba society of the same name (*Bambudye* in Luba).[93] It provided many functions for Hêmbá societies, not least in terms of its members' knowledge of local therapeutic practices. But it owed its continuing existence in a large part to the friendly and supportive relationships that they established between the matrilineal and patrilineal affiliations in Hêmbá villages.[94] In short, the Bambudji chapter in Bena Mambwe would have been the foundation of much of the social and political organization of villages in the chieftainship, involving itself in matters ranging from healthcare to the mediation of political authority. To see it undermined by missionaries who viewed it as a superstitious practice, and who were gaining notables as converts, threatened the coherence of pre-existing kinship relations.[95]

While the physical and spiritual intrusion of European missionaries into Bena Mambwe was not indicative of a popular following among those who inhabited the chieftainship, it was very public. Thus by asserting that he 'was God,' Katore might well have been uttering a defiant statement against this increasing power missionaries had over space and souls in his chieftainship. Although the grammatical phrasing of the sentence as reported in the mission diaries suggests it was not spoken to van den Tillaert alone, Katore purposefully made this comment in front of him. This supports the point that Katore was suggesting that *he* was God and not the Christian God and/or his mission representatives. Our efforts to understand what Katore meant by declaring himself 'God' are frustrated by the fact that we do not know if he used the French, Swahili or Hêmbá word for God. For example, the Hêmbá term for 'God,' *vilinyambi*, implies a very immanent God that does not exist in most Christian theologies in which the main deity is more distanced from the material world.[96] The most likely interpretation, though, is that Katore was referring to a local earth spirit of the sort associated with therapeutic societies of which Bambudji could have been one. Yet as much as Katore might have thought he was a God, or an Earth spirit, his witch-hunting had ultimately alienated him from the missionaries whose intrusion may have displeased him but was to prove significant in his undoing.

MISSION PRESSURE, ADMINISTRATIVE DELAY AND THE ENDING OF KIBANGILE

Despite being initially favoured by Belgian officials, after prolonged mission lobbying for them to take action against Kibangile, they did eventually arrest Katore and sent twenty soldiers into Bena Nyembo on 17 May 1934 to do the same to his co-conspirator Sindano.[97] On 3 July 1934, both Katore and Sindano were brought before the territorial court to account for what in the minds of the colonial state and their mission allies were their crimes.[98] Unfortunately for them, they had tested the boundaries of colonial law and were told they had overstepped the mark. Katore had his chieftainship revoked on 16 December 1934 and was swiftly replaced by Holela Sylvestre.[99] Sindano had his chieftaincy withdrawn on 15 December 1934 and Kayanza Mutoke acted as 'chief-regent' before a long-term replacement could be found.[100] The two chiefs also found themselves being sentenced to 'relegation,' which meant being internally exiled from their own chieftainships. Once in prison in Albertville, they were only allowed back 'home' at the discretion of the Belgian administration, which ended up incarcerating them until the early 1950s.[101] With its two chief protagonists exiled and imprisoned, Kibangile quickly drew to a close in Kongolo.

Although colonial reports betrayed more than a little anxiety over its possible return, they do not cite anyone attempting resurrect Kibangile anywhere in Kongolo. One of Tanganyika's most dramatic witch-hunts was thus concluded. Set alongside other witch-finding episodes, though, Kibangile does not appear to be particularly devastating in terms of the loss of life it caused. According to Reymenans, only one woman actually died from being accused of witchcraft in the whole of Bena Mambwe despite a total of twenty-four being put through the poison ordeal and thirteen having been subjected to the torture method. It is therefore conceivable that Kibangile appealed to the chiefs concerned in part not *because* it killed women but rather because it *saved* them from the poison ordeal if they confessed to being witches after being tortured. So, in the largely patriarchal worldview of Hêmbá chieftainship under Belgian rule,

Kibangile spared a precious source of labour in the form of women yet simultaneously expiated evil.

Despite Kibangile's end appearing to be easier to explain than it's beginning, all is not necessarily as clear as a standard colonial intervention might suggest. As much as the colonial administration did ultimately bring an end to Kibangile, it is intriguing that it took it so long to do so. Having started in mid-April, it was only on 17 May 1934 that Katore was arrested and those twenty colonial soldiers went to Bena Mambwe to stop Sindano's witch-hunt after it had been going on for around a month.[102] Despite initially claiming that the administration managed to stop Kibangile promptly, the annual territorial report from 1934 did acknowledge that the slow pace of the Belgian response to the atrocities 'still left too many victims.'[103] Admittedly, there are some minor discrepancies between mission accounts of Kibangile and that of the colonial state in terms of the timing of the colonial response. Yet even despite these discrepancies, we know that the Belgian officials waited for some time to intervene and the crucial question for our purposes is why. The answer to this question goes to the heart of the relationship between the Belgian agents and their African allies and provides further evidence of how much this relationship meant to both parties during the Depression.

One important explanation for their delayed response to Kibangile is that the colonial regime simply did not care about the excesses of its allied chiefs until the White Fathers forced their hand. Karen Fields argued much the same in the context of chiefly led witch-hunting episodes in British central Africa.[104] Accordingly, while Kibangile was underway, one White Father, most likely Tillaert, lamented in the out-station journal: 'is the authority of Sindano and Katore so precious that colonial officials wish to turn a blind eye to their atrocities?'[105] In short, the answer was mostly yes. In the context of the Great Depression, that colonial administrators chose to turn a blind eye to the excesses of its allies and this is easy to understand. Given that chiefs had to oversee a more exploitative system of labour than the ones that had prevailed during the 1920s, and because Belgian officials sought to pass the financial burdens of the Depression onto their subjects, the colonial state installed a series of chiefs who had consistently demonstrated their allegiance to it. Likewise, there were simply not many literate and numerate replacements for Katore and Sindano available and so deposing them would create as many problems as it would solve. Firing Katore and Sindano would open up a power vacuum in already turbulent pair of chieftainships, therefore.

Colonial officials had known for some time that both Katore and Sindano were resorting to increasingly violent means of shoring up their rule yet did nothing to rein in their authoritarianism—even though the legislation was in place for them to have done so. For example, Kibangile took place at a time when the colonial regime acknowledged that African intermediaries in the territorial court were 'rebelling' against Belgian prohibitions outlawing what they deemed 'uncivilized customs,' such as witchcraft, as well as other offences, such as slavery.[106] In Nyunzu, Kongolo's eastern neighbour, over 400 people were imprisoned by the colonial state for witch-craft alone.[107] Other people, therefore, were being punished for crimes related to the occult. Writing in 1934, Wauthion told his superiors that there 'were six cases' in which African intermediaries (who were not chiefs) had practiced 'customs' he considered 'barbaric' and so they were dispensed with. Yet, despite noting that a number of African 'customs' remained, as well as its desire to extinguish them, the administration delayed in its response to Kibangile. In so doing, they allowed what they called Katore's fiercely autocratic regime in Mambwe to continue.[108] For his part, colonial officials described Sindano's character as 'brutal' and believed him to be a 'drunkard,' though this description came only after his Kibangile activities.[109] In Katore's case, and very probably in Sindano's too, a measure of brutality towards their subjects was tolerated, potentially even encouraged. Although Sindano was seen as a brutal drunk, he was 'their' brutal drunk who rendered a reasonable service to the colonial administration.

CONCLUSION

As the state tried to expand its brutal cotton regime, it relied increasingly heavily on its intermediaries. But it was at pains to try to identify these intermediaries and define what exactly their role was. While Bùki in southern Kongolo had claims to pre-colonial legitimacy, the situation was very different in the east—where most Hêmbá leaders with pre-colonial heritage had been killed by the various convulsions that had occurred in the region during the turn of the century. As an experiment, the local Belgian administration had decided to install two chiefs, namely Katore and Sindano, who had no real pre-colonial claims to power and were both fiercely opposed by their subjects. Although for much of the 1920s these chiefs had given the administration the impression that their rule was stable, they could not do likewise during the 1930s. Mission intrusion, the outbreak of a Sleeping Sickness episode as well as the exigencies of the new cotton industry meant that they were under increasing pressure to legitimize themselves. So, they enthusiastically embraced a witch-finding movement known as Kibangile which had been introduced to them by an outsider, be they from Maniema or Nyunzu.

At first, the secular administration was at a loss to know what to do about Katore and Sindano. While there was legislation in place against witchcraft, Belgian officials were reluctant to use it given that there were no obvious replacements for their former allies should they be relegated. It is telling that a medical study into Kibangile was commissioned in the first place because this might well have been a delaying tactic designed to specifically stall a decision about Kibangile. While the state dithered, the Church, in the form of Joseph van den Tillaert, took a strong stand against Katore and Sindano. Although he had tried to restrain Katore in particular, the chief had not listened to him—going so far as to claim that he was God in the missionary's presence. Van den Tillaert eventually led to this local deity's fall from colonial grace, however, by lobbying the Belgian regime consistently to dethrone him. In so doing, the Church shaped the trajectory of chieftainship on the right bank by helping to remove two of the secular state's most trusted allies there. The values held by the Catholic Church held sway, therefore, over the administration's desire to see the consolidation of its allies' power come what may.

NOTES

1. This chapter is based on: Reuben Loffman, '"An Interesting Experiment": Kibangile and the Quest for Chiefly Legitimacy in Kongolo, Northern Katanga, 1923–1934,' *International Journal of African Historical Studies*, 50, 2 (2017), pp. 461–477.
2. Matthew G. Stannard, 'Interwar Crisis and Europe's Unfinished Empires,' in Nicholas Dumas (ed.), *The Oxford Handbook of European History, 1914–1945* (Oxford: Oxford University Press, 2016), p. 230.
3. Likaka, *Rural Society and Cotton in Colonial Zaire*, p. 95.
4. LaGamma, *Heroic Africans*, p. 267.
5. Ibid., p. 270.
6. AAB, AIMO, 1735, RAG, 1931, p. 24.
7. Ch. Didier Gondola, *The History of Congo* (Westport: Greenwood Press, 2002), p. 86.
8. Though the provinces went from 4 to 6 as Kasai and Orientale were split in two and these provinces were highly centralised and run via the colonial capital, Leopoldville.

9. According to John Higginson, 'between 1933 and 1934 the number of territorial agents in Katanga went from 81 to 66' see: Higginson, *A Working Class in the Making*, p. 130.

10. AAB, AIMO 115, RATK, 1940, p. 37.

11. Vellut, *Guide de l'Etudiant en Histoire du Zaïre*, p. 125.

12. Likaka, *Rural Society and Cotton in Colonial Zaire*, p. 27.

13. Gann and Duignan, *Colonialism in Africa, 1870–1960*, p. 176.

14. Ibid., p. 177.

15. Likaka, *Rural Society and Cotton in Colonial Zaire*, p. 50.

16. Ibid., p. 20.

17. AAB, AIMO 114, Rapport sur la Territoire du Kongolo (RATK), 1933, p. 51.

18. Likaka, *Rural Society and Cotton in Colonial Zaire*, p. 22.

19. Karen Bouwer, *Gender and Decolonization in the Congo: The Legacy of Patrice Lumumba* (London: Palgrave Macmillan, 2010).

20. Bouwer, *Gender and Decolonization in the Congo*.

21. Likaka, *Rural Society and Cotton in Colonial Zaire*, p. 50.

22. Ibid.

23. Ibid., p. 4.

24. Interview with Kimoto Mulongoy Alphonse, Kongolo, 11 April 2009.

25. Likaka, *Rural Society and Cotton in Colonial Zaire*, p. 4.

26. AAB, GG 13 157, 'Katore,' 1934; AGM, Bruges-Saint-Donat Diaries (1934), p. 340.

27. Rose-Hunt, *A Colonial Lexicon*, p. 130.

28. Ibid., p. 136.

29. Some Congolese did learn Dutch, the other official language of the Belgian Congo. Congolese often learnt Dutch specifically to undermine colonial officials, many of whom were required in theory to learn Dutch but did not know it. Congolese would then learn Dutch and say whatever they wanted to Francophone officials they knew could not speak the language.

30. AAB, GG 13 157, 'Dossier de Révocation et de Relégation du Chef Risaci Katore,' p. 2. Katore was very much an *évolué Avant la lettre* as the title was much more prominent after 1947, with the introduction of the carte du merité civiqué. Colonial identification of Katore as an *évolué* suggests that the epithet was ambiguous and given in unofficial circumstances related to the perceived allegiance of the African in question.

31. AAB, AIMO 1935, 'Rapport Annuel de l'Administration Générale: Premier Semestre' (1924), pp. 11–12.

32. AAB, AIMO 1735, 'Rapport sur l'Administration Générale: Premier Semestre' (1923), p. 8.

33. Jonathan Saha, 'The Male State: Colonialism, Corruption, and Rape Investigations in the Irrawaddy Delta c.1900,' *Indian Economic Social History Review*, 47 (2010), p. 344.

34. David Maxwell, 'The Soul of the Luba: W. F. P. Burton, Missionary Ethnography and Colonial Science,' *History and Anthropology*, 19 (2008), p. 330.

35. Saha, 'The Male State,' p. 345. The elite oral archive that is often our only way of finding out about the trajectory of court politics is also heavily androcentric though the oral record outside of this might divulge a more gynocentric view.

36. AAB, AIMO 1735, 'Rapport sur l'Administration Générale: Premier Semestre' (henceforth RAG), 1924, pp. 9–10. We are not told what this 'firm action' would be though.

37. AAB, AIMO 114, RATK, 1933, p. 21.

38. Joseph De Jaeger, *Bahemba: Etude Ethnologique* (Bukavu, 1987), p. 210. Archives Générales de la Société des Missionnaires de l'Afrique, Rome (AGM), Bruges-Saint-Donat, Diaries, 1926–1938, 19 April 1934, p. 340.

39. Archives Africaines, Ministère des Affaires Etrangers, Bruxelles (AAB), Gouverneur-Général (GG) 13, 537, 'Dossier de Révocation et de Relégation du Chef Risaci Katore' (1934), p. 4.

40. We must be careful, as Allen F. Roberts suggests with this term *ulozi*, it is dangerous to reductively translate it as witchcraft, certainly in the context of the Tabwa much as the Hêmbá, because it can be interpreted in a number of different ways depending on the everyday context, but in this context it is nearly beyond doubt that it meant evil see: Roberts, *A Dance of Assassins*, p. 8. The Tabwa are a peoples situated to the East of Lake Möero on the bank of Lake Tanganyika and many reside in what is now Kalemie.

41. De Jaeger, *Bahemba*, p. 211. For the clearest rendition of the Belgian colonial hierarchy, see: Dembour, *Recalling the Belgian Congo*, p. 19. Although this table is for the period 1947–1960, there was not a great deal of change from 1929–1947.

42. These were: Makutano, Kafiye, Bugana Mwehu, Kisiba, Kalimba, Kahanga, Kalombo, and Kabulo.

43. The precise translation of Agulu-Abuti is unclear. 'Agulu' might derive from the Swahili verb 'aguliwa,' to 'predict,' while 'abuti' might come from 'mabutu' or 'stump.' Altogether the literal translation could be something like 'prediction stump.' It should be noted that 'buti' is 'boot' in Swahili, though this complicates the translation and I suspect is not a likely rendering of 'agulu-abuti' given the context. Mbululà is 'une variété de mouche a miel,' see: Avermaet et Mbuyà, *Dictionnaire Kiluba-Français*, p. 360.

44. Michel Foucault (Translated by Allan Sheridan), *Discipline and Punish: The Birth of the Prison* (London, 1977), p. 48.
45. Regrettably, we do not know how many people would have actually witnessed the torture of suspected witchcraft.
46. De Jaeger, *Bahemba: Etude Ethnologique*, p. 210.
47. Ibid.
48. Ibid., p. 208.
49. Gordon, *Invisible Agents*, pp. 61–62. Mwave was also used in Malawi during the Mchape witch-finding episode, see: John McCraken, *A History of Malawi, 1859–1966* (Oxford: James Currey, 2012), p. 210.
50. Vansina, *Being Colonized*, p. 51; Gloria Waite, 'Public Health in Precolonial East-Central Africa,' in Steven Feierman and John M. Anzen (eds), *The Social Basis of Health and Healing in Africa* (Berkeley, 1992), p. 218; and A. J. H. Latham, 'Witchcraft Accusation and Economic Tension in Pre-colonial Calabar,' *Journal of African History*, 13 (1972), pp. 249–260.
51. Peter Geschiere, *The Modernity of Witchcraft: Politics and the Occult in Post-colonial Africa* (Charlottesville: University of Virginia Press, 1997), p. 11.
52. Geschiere, *The Modernity of Witchcraft*, p. 11.
53. SMA, Bruges-Saint-Donat, Diaries, 1926–1938, 19 April 1934, p. 340.
54. There is also a Kibangule in western DRC that was entirely unconnected from these events. Mission diaries seem to suggest that Lengwe and Muti came from a Báhêmbá-like culture through their association of the word 'lozi' with the origins of *Kibangile*, I am not sure the extent to which Maniema contained groups affiliated to the Báhêmbá.
55. AAB, AIMO 114, RATK, 1934, p. 4. Reymenans' version of the origins of *Kibangile* means that we need to be relatively circumspect about the extent to which a trans-regional culture of witch finding existed. I find Reymenans' account more likely given that there are a number of linguistic similarities between Kongolo and Nyunzu-based Báhêmbá groups.
56. Interview with Kitwanga Nzikala, Mbulula, Bena Nyembo, 2 May 2009.
57. De Jaeger, *Bahemba: Etude Ethnologique*, p. 210.
58. AAB, AIMO, 114, RATK, 1934, p. 4.
59. Ibid., p. 12. The CFL existed from 1902 to around 1962/3 as a private company under Baron Edouard Empain. Relatively shortly after independence it was nationalised and became the *Société Congolaise des Chemins de Fer des Grands Lacs*.
60. Anjali Arondekar, *For the Record: On Sexuality and the Colonial Archive in India* (Durham: Duke University Press, 2009), p. 13.
61. AAB, AIMO 114, RATK, 1933, p. 21.

62. AAB, AIMO 114, RATK, 1934, Tableau Annexe: Model 12, p. 2.
63. Interview with Muganza Walunga Augustin, Makutano, Bena Mambwe, 15 April 2009.
64. ABB, AIMO 114, RATK, 1934, p. 75.
65. Ibid., p. 76.
66. AGM, Bruges-Saint-Donat, Diaries, 1926–1938, 15 May 1934, p. 344. Sleeping sickness spreads via the Teste fly and those exposed to cattle are particularly at risk. So, the animal–human connection in this instance is valid.
67. Lyons, *The Colonial Disease*, p. 93.
68. See, for example: Roelens, *Notre Vieux Congo*.
69. Lyons, *The Colonial Disease*, p. 103.
70. Ibid., p. 171.
71. Terence Ranger, 'Plagues of Beasts and Men: Prophetic Responses to Epidemics in Eastern and Southern Africa,' in Terence Ranger and Paul Slack (eds), *Epidemics and Ideas: Essays on the Historical Perception of Pestilence* (Cambridge, 1996), pp. 241–268.
72. AAB, AIMO 1735, RAG, Deuxième Semestre, 1928, p. 1.
73. Ibid.
74. AAB, AI 1397, Dossier Sectes, Rapport PCE, Elisabethville, 1936, p. 23.
75. AAB, Affaires Indigènes (henceforth AI) 1397, Dossier sectes, Province Orientale, Maniema, Territoire de Kasongo, A. T. Wynants, 'Secte de l'Ukanga,' p. 1.
76. Thomas Turner suggests that Ukanga first originated among the Tetela group situated in 'the savanna of Lusambo,' see: Thomas Turner, *Ethnogenese et Nationalisme en Afrique Centrale: Aux Racines de Patrice Lumumba* (Paris, 2000), p. 215. It is possible, though, that it started in Lusambo and transferred to Elisabethville afterwards.
77. AAB, AIMO 114, RATK, 1936, p. 33.
78. AAB, AI, 1397, A. T. Wynants, 'Secte de l'Ukanga,' p. 1. And it was not until 22 June 1951 that the Belgian authorities actually passed a Decree explicitly prohibiting Ukanga, which by then was identified as an iteration of a wider movement known as *Muyaka*, see: Jean-Pacifique Balaamo Mokelwa, *Eglises et Etat en République Démocratique du Congo: Fondements Juridiques et Jurisprudence, 1876–2006* (Paris, 2009), p. 182. Mokelwa suggests that there were a number of other names for Ukanga, including: Shukunda, Kishieta and Punga.
79. AAB, AIMO 114, RATK, 1937, p. 7.
80. Ibid., p. 32.
81. Ibid., pp. 32, 33.
82. Ibid., p. 33.
83. AAB, AIMO 114, RATK, 1936, p. 6; Likaka, *Rural Society and Cotton in Colonial Zaire*, p. 27.

84. AAB, AIMO 114, RATK, 1936, p. 6.
85. AAB, AIMO 171, RADT, 1938, p. 2; AAB, AIMO 171, RADT, 1940, p. 19.
86. AAB, AIMO 171, RADT, 1940, p. 9.
87. AAB, Missionnaires (henceforth M) 641, Les Adventistes du 7° Jour, p. 2.
88. AGM, Bruges-Saint-Donat, Diaries, 1926–1938, 19 April 1934, p. 343.
89. Gordon, *Invisible Agents*, p. 60.
90. AGM, Bruges-Saint-Donat, Diaries, 1926–1939, p. 149.
91. Once Kayanza Mutoke died, her young son inherited the chieftainship, see: AAB, AIMO 114, RATK, 1935, p. 19; AGM, Bruges-Saint-Donat, Diaries, 1926–1939, p. 149.
92. In the diaries, *Bambudji* is spelt *Bambuli*.
93. Blakely and Blakely, 'Ancestors, "Witchcraft," and Foregrounding the Poetic,' p. 401.
94. Ibid., p. 402.
95. LaGamma, *Heroic Africans*, p. 270.
96. In French, God is *dieu*, in Swahili, this is *mungu*, and in Kíhêmbá this is *vilinyambi*. I have taken the Kíhêmbá word for God from: Johannes Fabian, *Ethnography as Commentary: Writing from the Virtual Archive* (Durham, 2008), p. 85.
97. AGM, Bruges-Saint-Donat, Diaries, 1926–1938, 19 April 1934, p. 343. There was anti-witchcraft legislation in Northern Rhodesia as early as 1914, with the passing of the Witchcraft Ordinance during that year, see: Gordon, *Invisible Agents*, p. 11.
98. AAB, AIMO 115, RATK, 1934, p. 5.
99. AAB, AIMO 114, RATK, 1935, p. 19.
100. It is likely that the colonial regime felt that because Kayanza Mutoke was a woman she was *en stage* before a man could be found to replace her but colonial reports do not make this explicit even if it is implicit.
101. Kalamba Sindano did eventually come back to Bena Nyembo in 1953.
102. AGM, Bruges-Saint-Donat, Diaries, 1926–1938, 19 April 1934, p. 343
103. AAB, AIMO 115, RATK, 1934, p. 5.
104. Fields, *Revival and Rebellion*, p. 73.
105. AGM, Bruges-Saint-Donat, Diaries, 1926–1938, 19 April 1934, p. 343.
106. AAB, AIMO 114, RATK, 1933, p. 3.
107. AGM, Kabalo Diaries, Volume 1, 1934–1939, 18 September 1935, p. 41.
108. AAB, GG 13.537, H. L. Keyser (16 Juillet 1934) Rapport spécial appuyant les décisions du Conseil des notables de la chefferie des Bena Mambwe – et motivant la révocation du Chef Risaci Katore, p. 2.
109. AAB, AIMO 114, RATK, 1934, p. 12.

BIBLIOGRAPHY

Arondekar, Anjali, *For the Record: On Sexuality and the Colonial Archive in India* (Durham: Duke University Press, 2009).

Blakely, Pamela, and Blakely, Thomas, 'Ancestors, "Witchcraft," & Foregrounding the Poetic: Men's Oratory & Women's Song-Dance in Hêmbá Funerary Performance,' in Thomas Blakely, Walter Van Beek, and Dennis Thomson (eds), *Religion in Africa: Experience & Expression* (James Currey: London, 1994).

Dembour, Marie-Bénédict, *Recalling the Belgian Congo: Conversations and Introspection* (New York: Berghahan Books, 2001).

Fabian, Johannes, *Ethnography as Commentary: Writing from the Virtual Archive* (Durham: Duke University Press, 2008).

Foucault, Michel (Translated by Allan Sheridan), *Discipline and Punish: The Birth of the Prison* (London: Allen Lane, 1977).

Gann, Lewis H., and Duignan, Peter, *Colonialism in Africa, 1870–1960* (Cambridge: Cambridge University Press, 1975).

Geschiere, Peter, *The Modernity of Witchcraft: Politics and the Occult in Post-colonial Africa* (Charlottesville: University of Virginia Press, 1997).

Gondola, Ch. Didier, *The History of Congo* (Westport: Greenwood Press, 2002).

Gordon, David M., *Invisible Agents: Spirits in a Central African History* (Athens: Ohio University Press, 2012).

Higginson, John, *A Working Class in the Making: Belgian Colonial Labor Policy, Private Enterprise and the African Mineworker, 1907–1951* (Madison: University of Wisconsin Press, 1989).

Jaeger, Joseph De, *Bahemba: Etude Ethnologique* (Bukavu: Centre Interdiocésain de Pastorale et de Catéchèse, 1987).

LaGamma, Alison, *Heroic Africans: Legendary Leaders, Iconic Sculptures* (New Haven: Yale University Press, 2011).

Latham, A. J. H., 'Witchcraft Accusation and Economic Tension in Pre-colonial Calabar,' *Journal of African History*, 13 (1972), pp. 249–260.

Likaka, Osumaka, *Rural Society and Cotton in Colonial Zaire* (Madison: University of Wisconsin Press, 1997).

Loffman, Reuben, '"An Interesting Experiment": Kibangile and the Quest for Chiefly Legitimacy in Kongolo, Northern Katanga, 1923–1934,' *International Journal of African Historical Studies*, 50, 2 (2017), pp. 461–477.

Lyons, Maryinez, *The Colonial Disease: A Social History of Sleeping Sickness in Northern Zaire, 1900–1940* (Cambridge: Cambridge University Press, 2002).

McCraken, John, *A History of Malawi, 1859–1966* (Oxford: James Currey, 2012).

Mokelwa, Jean-Pacifique Balaamo, *Eglises et Etat en République Démocratique du Congo: Fondements Juridiques et Jurisprudence, 1876–2006* (Paris: L'Harmattan, 2009).

Ranger, Terence, 'Plagues of Beasts and Men: Prophetic Responses to Epidemics in Eastern and Southern Africa,' in Terence Ranger and Paul Slack (eds), *Epidemics and Ideas: Essays on the Historical Perception of Pestilence* (Cambridge: Cambridge University Press, 1996), pp. 241–268.

Roberts, Allen F., *A Dance of Assassins: Performing Early Colonial Hegemony in the Congo* (Bloomington: Indiana University Press, 2013).

Roelens, Victor (ed. N. Antoine), *Notre Vieux Congo 1891–1917, Souvenirs du Premier Evêque du Congo Belge* (Namur: Editions Grands Lacs, 1948).

Rose-Hunt, Nancy, *A Colonial Lexicon of Birth, Ritual, Medicalisation, and Mobility in Congo* (Durham: Duke University Press, 1999).

Saha, Jonathan, 'The Male State: Colonialism, Corruption, and Rape Investigations in the Irrawaddy Delta c.1900,' *Indian Economic Social History Review* 47 (2010), pp. 343–376.

Stannard, Matthew G., 'Interwar Crisis and Europe's Unfinished Empires,' in Nicholas Dumas (ed.), *The Oxford Handbook of European History, 1914–1945* (Oxford: Oxford University Press, 2016), pp. 223–240.

Turner, Thomas, *Ethnogenese et Nationalisme en Afrique Centrale: Aux Racines de Patrice Lumumba* (Paris: L'Harmattan, 2000).

Vellut, Jean-Luc, *Guide de l'Étudiant en Histoire du Zaïre* (Kinshasa: Centre de Recherches Pédagogiques, 1974).

Waite, Gloria, 'Public Health in Precolonial East-Central Africa,' in Steven Feierman and John M. Anzen (eds), *The Social Basis of Health and Healing in Africa* (Berkeley: University of California Press, 1992), pp. 212–231.

A Marriage of Convenience: Church and State in the Late Colonial Period, 1940–1956

Drawing on a thawing of relations that had begun during the Depression, the Church became more amenable to the Belgian administration in Tanganyika during the late colonial period. Victor Roelens died in 1947, having retired in 1941, and Emilio Callewaert had also long since passed on by the 1940s.[1] Their deaths in many ways facilitated the solidification the trinity of institutions that Crawford Young suggested comprised Belgian rule, namely the Church, the administration and industry.[2] A new generation of Catholic missionaries, with no lived experience of the proto-colonial period, came to Tanganyika to take over the running of the Church in southeastern Congo. While they often shared in Roelens' and Callewaert's uncompromising attitude to proselytization, missionaries such as Joseph De Jaeger had no aspirations of establishing a theocracy or a close approximation to one. And, while Church–state relations might have suffered at the end of the 1950s, with the colonial state attempting to sideline mission schools in the Congo in favour of state ones, they were cordial during the 1940s and early 1950s.[3]

Alongside the changing of the mission guard, and the missionary-centric reasons for a change in the Church–state relationship more generally, there were some more state-orientated ones too. First, the Church helped Belgian officials survey what they regarded as potentially subversive groups present in Kongolo's hinterland. This chapter will concentrate primarily on a group called Wazungu Wejusi, which

© The Author(s) 2019 189
R. A. Loffman, *Church, State and Colonialism in Southeastern Congo, 1890–1962*, Cambridge Imperial and Post-Colonial Studies Series, https://doi.org/10.1007/978-3-030-17380-7_6

was not a proto-nationalist group but nonetheless the state evidently feared that it was and the Church helped colonial officials understand its operations. Secondly, the Church helped to educate Africans who went on to work within the institutions that comprised the late colonial state. Church education was particularly important given the expansion of the colonial state's technocratic agricultural ambitions. This chapter will not only look at Church education of those who directly facilitated the state's agricultural plans, but also other Africans who played an important part in post-war colonial modernity. Some Church-educated Africans mediated labour relations, for example, with some even entering the colonial administration itself later on.

While Crawford Young projected the relatively strong post-war Church–state relationship backwards through time, this chapter argues that it was in reality the product of a complex range of contingent historical circumstances. Put simply, the strong post-WWII Church–state relationship was not in fact an inevitable part of Belgian rule in Central Africa in spite of what Leopold II had envisaged when he first instigated the creation of the Free State in the late nineteenth century. As previous chapters have suggested, the Church was often at loggerheads with the administration during the proto-colonial period. Its proximity to the state during and after the Second World War proved its undoing once decolonization began in 1960, though. Far from remembering the Church's hostility to the state in the early colonial period, many Africans born during and after World War Two associated the Church with the colonial state. Consequently, militant nationalists targeted missionaries in Kongolo during decolonization as they saw them as a fifth column for the Katangese secession that they believed to have been the continuation of colonial rule. Many of the Church's achievements in the late colonial period were rent asunder as many congregations fled Kongolo and some of the buildings that had taken the missionaries so long to construct were gutted.

MISSION EDUCATION AND THE LATE COLONIAL STATE

By the 1940s, Lavigerie's and Roelen's dream of establishing a Christian kingdom in Central Africa was a distant memory. Instead of building a theocracy set apart from the flow of Belgian administration, the Church found a place as an ideologically distinct institution *within* the framework of colonial rule. Following the Great Depression, many of the boundaries of Kongolo's chieftainships, as well as those of the Church's own infrastructure, had been confirmed. Although Kongolo and its southern neighbour, Kabalo, were detached in 1947 this did not require any changes to chieftainship boundaries. What is more, there are few if any records of chiefs opposing the construction of out-stations on their land in marked contrast to the 1920s. We can only speculate as to why this may have been the case but the absence of Louis Franck's 'great chieftainship' policy must have helped—chiefs no longer had the political muscle to think they could challenge the Church. Likewise, the benefits of mission schooling were doubtless becoming more evident. Many of the most high-profile public figures in Kongolo in the post-war period were Church educated. Rather than the era of the 'customary' chief, the 1940s and early 1950s was one dominated by literate and numerate Africans who had precious few claims to any kind of 'traditional' or 'customary' authority.

A new generation of missionaries also came to Tanganyika to take over Victor Roelens' work after he died in 1947 while a similar process had already long since begun in the Spiritan case after Callewaert died in 1938. While the new generation of missionaries, such as Joseph De Jaeger, were in many ways just as uncompromising about the kind of Catholicism they pro-offered as Callewaert and Roelens had been, they did not see the Church as a rival to the state in any meaningful sense. This is not to say that there were no Church–state conflicts. Rather, the state sometimes bemoaned the dire state of some of the mission schools it subsidized. Yet, overall, the Church and the state worked together much better in the late colonial period than before. One of the most obvious manifestations of the link between the Church and state were the Church schools themselves and by extension the educated cadres of Africans who went on to play important roles in public life in Kongolo in the post-war period. The schools that the Catholic Church built in the early colonial period, as well as the ones it constructed during the later one, were vital in ensuring a ready supply of qualified Africans to take up work that was directly and indirectly relevant to the state's modernization plans.

While the missionaries had always taught as many Africans as they could, the scope of their educational ambitions broadened during the late colonial period. The White Fathers in particular expanded their network of schools further after the turbulence of the First World War and the Depression had passed. As a result, new White

Fathers out-stations, which included schools, were built in Mbulula, in Bena Nyembo, and Makutano, in Bena Mambwe. These new out-stations gave a number of rural Africans living in Kongolo access to mission education that many would simply not have got otherwise. Away from Kongolo's hinterland, the Spiritans also opened schools mainly in the city centre during the post-war period, with the most notable being a girls' school in 1946.[4] Alongside the girls school, the Spiritans expanded into Katea in 1950, in southern Kongolo, in a bid to, in brother Leuck's words, 'deliver a knockout blow' to Protestants' who drew close to Kongolo, such as the Congo Evangelistic Mission (CEM).[5] Not only that, but the older mission complexes, not least the Spiritans' facilities in Lubunda, continued to attract students not only from Kongolo but increasingly from across the Belgian Congo as a whole.

As a result of the spate of the proliferation of older out-stations as well as the spate of building activities the Church engaged in, the number of pupils attending the Catholic schools within the mission out-stations grew rapidly during the late colonial period. While mission figures can never be taken completely at face value, given their methodology was based largely informal head counting at best or simple guesstimates at worst, the figures from the Sola mission, as an example, are nonetheless illuminating. The school in Sola supposedly had 160 catechist pupils whereas before the Second World War there were only ninety-two catechists in total.[6] Naturally, there are no pre-War numbers for Makutano given that the station did not exist before 1939 and, unfortunately, the Church did not seem to record the number of baptisms during the 1940s and the 1950s in Makutano.

So famous were Kongolo's Catholic mission schools, and the social mobility they offered, that Africans from outside the territory migrated there to enrol in them. Ihunga Marcel was an example of an itinerant student who travelled to Kongolo during the late colonial period. In 1940, he finally arrived in Lubunda having walked barefoot all the way from Kabambare, which was at least one-hundred kilometres to the north of Kongolo.[7] In 1942, he was baptized and so became a member of the Spiritan congregation in the chieftainship of Wangongwe. He spent three years with the Spiritans in Lubunda before becoming one of the first teachers to welcome pupils to a school in central Kongolo, which was called Saint Augustine's, in 1946. Pupils from this school came mostly from the Hêmbá chieftainships of Bena Nkuvu and Bena Mambwe but some came from the CFL camp nearby. Having spent two years as a teacher at Saint Augustine's, he then went on to teach in Libermann, which he called the *Ecole d'Apprentissage Pédagogique* (EAP).[8] In Georges Balandier's words, Marcel became part of an 'administrative bourgeoisie' that emerged in Kongolo during the 1940s.[9] The high concentration of mission schools in Kongolo that had been constructed from the early twentieth century meant that this 'administrative bourgeoisie' grew roughly in proportion to them.

The growing middle class in Kongolo undertook a wide variety of roles within the context of the late colonial state. Some, like Ihuna Marcel, served as teachers, yet mission-trained Africans also went on to participate directly in agricultural projects. One of the best examples of such a student was Kilonda Sylvestre. He was born in the village of Kisompa in the chieftainship of Bena Nyembo and he finished his primary schooling in Sola in 1949, having been trained by the White Fathers in their out-station in the town. After completing his primary schooling, he went to Tongoni, in Maniema, to learn how to be an agricultural monitor. A number of years later, he graduated and began working back in Kongolo in 1956.[10] He served for a number of years as an agricultural monitor. While agricultural monitors like Sylvestre had existed during the Depression and even before, their numbers swelled during the late colonial period. For example, Kilonda Sylvestre would have known Bruno Muyumba (head of agricultural school leavers) as well as Grégoire Kitumbagani (head of agricultural non-school leavers) even if their careers did not entirely overlap chronologically.[11] Sylvestre therefore had an important stake in the agricultural modernity given that it was his job to promote the colonial state's version of it alongside Kitumbagani and Muyumba.

While some Church-trained students went on to work directly for the state's agricultural projects or to teach those who would eventually work in them, others participated in colonial modernity in a wider variety of ways. One example was to be found in the life of Tambwe Benoit Abati. He left his natal village, Kihonga, to go to the teacher-training school (*école normale*) in Lubunda just after the Second World War.[12] Although he was not among the majority of his peers in going to secondary school, he was hardly alone in doing so. He had been able to go to Lubunda as a result of doing particularly well during his years in his local primary school in Mbulula, the headquarter-town of Bena Nyembo.[13] Not only would Abati have had the opportunity to go to school in Mbulula, and so benefit from the 1940s expansion of the White Father mission stations, but he would have seen different White Fathers missionaries working there. Joseph Van Den Tillaert died in 1948 and Jean Vandermeiren, who had been so instrumental in helping the White Fathers understand Hêmbá, had also passed away.[14] So instead, Abati was taught by missionaries such as Joseph De Jaeger.

Having studied with the White Fathers in one of their new primary schools, Abati travelled out of eastern Kongolo to study with their Spiritan counterparts in the north of the territory.[15] Those who studied in the *école normale* could expect to become primary school teachers and some might have even harboured ambitions to teach in Lubunda itself; though competition was fierce given the few places available. Whatever their ambitions, studying at Lubunda was intense for the students involved given that they took maths, history, geography, psychology as well as actual teacher-training courses during their time there.[16] Abati's efforts were rewarded when he eventually succeeded in becoming a qualified teacher and went on to practise in a college colloquially known by Africans as 'Mwamba' but that the Spiritans had actually named after one of the founders of their Society: Libermann. As Libermann was the biggest college in Kongolo, at least according to Abati, teaching there was considered a very respectable occupation. Likewise, some of Abati's students went on to become university professors once institutions of higher education opened just before independence.

Having worked in Libermann College for a number of years, Abati swiftly rose to the upper echelons of Kongolo's post-war colonial society. It is difficult to cite a middle-class institution that Africans could take part in that Abati did not lead at one time or another. One of the most important, though, was Kongolo's chapter of the Confederation of Congolese Christian Syndicates (*Confédération de Syndicat Chrétiens du Congo*) (CSCC). The CSCC was a colony-wide organization that got started in Leopoldville shortly after the Second World War, with individual syndicates having been organized in most territories in the Congo by the 1950s.[17] The CSCC lobbied for workers' rights in the colony and in many ways mirrored the function of a trade union. The first CSCC emissaries arrived in Kongolo in 1956 and invited Africans employed in various trades in the territory to organize elections and create a leadership committee. Abati, one of the first African Libermann-trained teachers in Kongolo, was soon elected President of the local branch of the CSCC. As President, he organized CSCC meetings with the most significant employers in Kongolo, namely, first, the CFL railway company and, secondly, the cotton giant, Cotanga.[18] He remembered that Monsieur

Virguens led the CFL during his tenure as president of the CSCC and so if a grievance arose within the CFL, Abati would typically have a meeting with him and his senior colleagues. Afterwards, he would go back to the CFL workers to let them know what he had permission to tell them about the deliberations that had taken place in camera.

By the time Abati became the elected President of the CSCC in Kongolo, he estimated that there were around half a million CFL workers from across northern Katanga and even beyond. While he surely exaggerated the size of the labour force in the CFL camp in Kongolo, he did speak on behalf of a significant number of people. During one of the many conversations we had, Abati spoke proudly of his achievements as a representative of the CSCC as well as the labour discussions he convened. He recalled a triumphant labour negotiation in one of his interviews with me that still gave him a considerable amount of pleasure even decades after the event.[19] His local popularity and enabled him to eventually get elected onto the consultative Territorial Council once these institutions had been established in 1957. While Territorial Councils made precious little differences to colonial policy, his place on it put him in a strong position to eventually become the first African leader of the territorial administration in Kongolo just before independence arrived. So, Abati's career straddled the worlds of labour and politics during the late colonial period. While his labour activities placed him in opposition to the industrial parts of the colonial trinity, his rise through the ranks of local politics in Kongolo meant that he mediated many of the institutional changes at this time.

While Abati's activities were concentrated in the labour and political realms of the colonial state, other graduates of Church schools worked in the medical profession. An important example of such a student was Muhiya Musafiri from the chieftainship of Bena Mambwe. He trained as a doctor and worked in the health facilities of Kongolo. The earliest mention of a hospital in the state archives comes from 1920 and was where Musafiri worked.[20] This, the first hospital constructed by the colonial state in Kongolo's town centre, was a medical facility used for the treatment of Africans and Musafiri spent a large part of his adult working life working there.[21] It is worth noting in passing that territorial agents built another hospital exclusively for European use in the 1930s, though, after initially using unoccupied government 'dwellings' for this purpose.[22] In any case, the Church's training of nurses such as Musafiri was vital in ensuring that Africans could access Western biomedicine. Not only that, but the pharmacies that the White Fathers established in their out-stations, particularly in Sola, were vital in complementing the state's efforts to securing the demographic growth of the African population after the violence of the early colonial period. Aside from pharmacies, the Daughters of the Cross (of Liège), who had been working with the Spiritans since the 1920s, were providing an ever increasing number of consultations to pregnant mothers and new parents in the early 1950s in Keba, in Bena Yambula, and Kongolo's town centre. In 1954, for example, they oversaw the safe delivery of over 1000 babies and so helped to decrease infant mortality in the places in which they worked and, at the same time, increase the population of Kongolo territory as a whole.

In short, a wide range of Church-trained administrative elites arose to take up important positions in nearly every sphere of late colonial life in Kongolo. The colonial state's projects could not have survived had it not have been for agricultural monitors such as Sylvestre, nurses such as Musafiri or for administrators such as Abati. The gendered nature of the education system, with African women in Kongolo's town centre largely confined to learning about tasks that were defined by white Belgian middle class ideas about domesticity, is worth remarking on however. I could find few women who had careers in public life such as Abati. Aside from the acutely gendered nature of the late colonial state, I do not mean to argue that the state universally lauded Church education as we shall see in the next chapter. Even before the so-called 'School Wars' of the late 1950s, state agents complained that many of the schools that had been subsidized by the regime were actually being run down by negligent missionaries.[23] Moreover, the Belgian territorial administration of Kongolo also accused the White Fathers of forcing young girls into boarding schools in Mbulula in December 1945.[24] But the very public altercations between Victor Roelens and the colonial administration that had been such a feature of the former's reign over Tanganyika were not a characteristic of the late colonial period.[25] And the schools that the Church had built, both before and during the 1940s and 50s, were indeed generally supported and lauded by Belgian colonial officialdom.

The State and Church's Struggle Against 'Traditional Disorder'

Rather than seeing themselves as surveying and sometimes disciplining the Belgian administration's African intermediaries, as it did in the last chapter, missionaries saw local expressive cultures as being among its most potent enemies during this period alongside Protestants. In one report on the Baudouinville Vicariate, the author wrote as follows: 'At the same time, everywhere, there is a return to the old pagan ways. The wizards and soothsayers are becoming more numerous as there is money coming into the countryside now and so superstition and pagan practices continue to exercise a great attraction for our Christians.'[26] The Church was not alone in its pessimism and even paranoia about what was happening in rural Kongolo. Indeed, the Church and the state both developed an interest in challenging what they saw as potentially subversive African groups even if somtimes they did not fear the same groups. Put differently, the state sometimes pursued groups that missionaries believed were less of a threat to the conversion of local communities while the Church often pursued groups the state viewed as less of a threat. There were times, however, when the two interests conjoined.

It is worth beginning to explain the overlap between the state and the Church's agendas with regard to these groups by outlining why the Church in particular was so keen on extinguishing them. The fact that Sola and Makutano in particular were on the fringes of the White Father's network of out-stations meant that annual reports consistently complained of 'pagan rites' continuing in Kongolo.[27] Such pessimism was rarely expressed in the White Fathers' reports about Baudounville, which was at the centre of Roelens' old Christian 'kingdom' (or 'republic' as he always liked to refer to it) for example.[28] Likewise, the Spiritans were optimistic about their conversions given that Kongolo was increasingly occupying an important position within its own network of out-stations not least Lubunda. Indeed, from their bases in Kongolo, the Spiritans fanned outwards and were able to found missions in Kindu (1956) and had helped missionaries in Manono convert around 10,000 by the end of the late colonial period if mission figures are to be believed.[29] A sign of the devotion of at least some of these converts is to be found in the fact that the Spiritans ordained many more African priests than the White Fathers during the late colonial period. One example of an African priest trained by the Spiritans was from Lubunda and comes in the form of Jean-Louis Lambert.[30] For the Spiritans, the late colonial period was a time of great consolidation even if the White Fathers often struggled to keep up with them in this period.

The White Fathers' fears about the commitment of their Christians to the religious life was perhaps best expressed in an annual report written in 1949, which is worth quoting directly. It claimed that, in Makutano: 'The

Christians, comprised largely of young converts, are still the minority and are surrounded by imposing blocks of adult pagans.'[31] The author goes on to state that, probably in reference to their congregations' faith: 'some Christians, on the other hand, grow tired and weak.'[32] While Makutano was an out-station that was only built after the Second World War, and so it is natural to expect that relatively few would have been converted by 1949, the White Fathers made very similar complaints about the conversion process in Sola. The author of the 1949 annual report noted that: 'many of the old Christians live in disorder and have even returned to pagan practices. This is the fate awaiting the half-converted.'[33] The process of conversion, as the White Fathers noted, was far from a linear process— very much as Jean and John Comaroff found was the experience of the Baptists who worked among the Tswana in South Africa.[34]

The White Fathers identified a number of what they liked to call 'sects' or even 'evil sects' that were, at least in their minds, manifestations of paganism and continued to attract initiates. These so-called sects included many of the institutions that were so instrumental in the functioning of the Luba monarchy, described in the second chapter, which had later been translated into Hêmbá contexts, such as *Bambudye* or *Bambudji*.[35] Yet many of the European White Fathers believed that to break the hold of pre-Christian traditions, such 'sects' needed to be dissolved. Much like their Protestant counterparts, such as William Fredwick Padwick Burton of the CEM, the White Fathers were structural functionalists who saw pre-Christian thought as something structurally opposed to Christianity.[36] One of the White Fathers who was at the forefront of engaging with the so-called 'sects' was Joseph De Jaeger and his approach to conversion in Sola is illustrative of many of the paradigms outlined out in this paragraph so far. Like many of his fellow White Fathers in the late colonial period, De Jaeger believed his struggle was with local traditions and not the colonial state. He saw a range of 'sects' as hampering conversion in Sola and was keen to act against them and by force if necessary.

De Jaeger enlisted the help of a catechist called Petro Malazi to help him identify and research the 'evil sects' that he believed plagued the Hêmbá parts of Kongolo.[37] Malazi grew up in eastern Kongolo and so was both fluent in Hêmbá as well as French but he was also willing to act on De Jaeger's behalf to drive out the local manifestations of the Equatorial tradition.[38] Not only that, but Malazi was also even a former member of some of the groups he helped De Jaeger to survey. And so, through his collaboration with Malazi, De Jaeger wrote extensive notes about the Hêmbá that he would eventually publish as an ethnography in 1990.[39] In an interview with me, the current chief of the Bena Mambwe, Muganza Walunga Augustin, recounted his experience of being taught by De Jaeger and he remembered that the missionary did not speak Hêmbá and so must have relied quite heavily on Malazi to do his research into what he described as 'evil sects.'[40] Just like William Burton, De Jaeger might have been suspicious of African expressive cultures but he nonetheless built up good relations with local people. Augustin remembered him as a good man (*bon monsieur*), for example, and that he gave out bicycles to some of his congregants.[41] It was through his congregants, such as Malazi, that De Jaeger heard about some of the societies that would later form part of his 1990 ethnography.

Missionaries would sometimes approach these supposedly subversive groups and try to break them up in order to curtail their influence over local cultures. Yet while the White Fathers succeeded in curtailing their activities to some extent, they did not extinguish them completely and this was a source of constant frustration for them. As well as more long-standing groups, the White Fathers also believed that they needed to confront other ones that, unbeknown to them at the time, drew directly from the growth of the late colonial state. An important example of such a group is *Wazungu Wejusi*. The anthropologist Nicholas Argenti observed that theatrical groups, such as Wazungu, were: 'not monolithic or unidimensional … but undetermined, conflicted and heteroglossic.'[42] Much like the Cameroonian masquerade groups that feature strongly in Argenti's work, Wazungu Wejusi was a highly nuanced social phenomenon that sought to tell stories that its participants were not able articulate in words. And, much like all texts, it was 'marked out for attention and made repeatable or detachable from the immediate context.'[43] But what exactly was Wazungu Wejusi and what did it set out to do? Some answers to these questions can be deduced by examining its very name.

The franchise was recorded by the White Fathers and Belgian officials simultaneously as *Wazungu Wejusti* and/or *Wazungu*. Unfortunately, it is not exactly clear what the name 'Wazungu Wejusti' or 'Wazungu' actually means or meant and, at least to some extent, the etymology of this phenomenon has now been lost: much as we saw in the case of *Kibangile* in the previous chapter. Before proceeding by suggesting what Wazungu Wajusti might have meant, though, it is important to note that Tambwe Abati referred to the group as Wazungu *Wajusi* and not

Wazungu *Wajusti* and I will explain Abati's version before the colonial one for reasons that will soon become clear. The word that both Abati and the colonial regime agreed on, though, was *Wazungu* which means 'stranger' in Swahili but it is commonly used to denote white foreigners in particular. *Jusi* means 'lizard' in Swahili. So, altogether, *Wazungu (Wa)Jusi* probably meant 'white lizards.' Immediately, therefore, those who sat down to watch Wazungu would have been alerted to the bitingly satirical nature of the franchise.

Missionaries and colonial officials were well aware of the negative associations that were implied in the name 'Wazungu Wejusi.' So, colonial officials in particular sought to distort the name for their own purposes in a manner that broadly coincided with the Belgian penchant for reshaping African idioms that occurred across colonial Congo.[44] Rather than referring to the phenomenon as 'Wazungu Wejusi' colonial officials changed it in their reportage to 'Wazungu Wajusti.'[45] The subtle name change might seem insignificant but in fact means that 'jusi' (lizard in Swahili) becomes similar to the French for 'just' (*juste*) (as in virtuous). In colonial parlance, the name 'Wazungu Wajusi' thus became 'Wazungu Wajusti' ('Just Whites'). Colonial officials thus sought to project their own power onto and through Wazungu. What is interesting about the colonial name change, though, was that one Swahili word was not replaced with another but rather a Swahili word was replaced by a Swahili-inflected French one, *justi*. Belgian agents simply may not have known enough Swahili or Hêmbá to have made an effective distortion of the word *Wajusi* in those languages. Or, they might have felt that the most important people on whom to project their new name were the French-speaking *évolués* who may have attended these performances and were potentially best placed to organize and publicize anti-colonial politics. Unfortunately, the evidence that exists only allows us to speculate on this matter.

If Wazungu's name was indeed changed to appeal to the more urbanized *évolués*, the artistic form that it took drew heavily on rural influences. During one of my interviews with Benoit Tambwe Abati, he indicated that Wazungu performances, together with the dances that accompanied them, were an iteration of a pre-existing tradition of 'tambourine dance(s)' (*mucheza wa tambour*) in the north-eastern parts of Kongolo and southern Maniema.[46] Given that Europeans, probably missionaries, introduced the tambourine to Hêmbá groups it is difficult to imagine that the mucheza wa tambour tradition pre-dated the colonial regime. Unlike its Tanzanian contemporary, the *Beni Ngoma*,

Wazungu was a distinctly colonial *not* pre-colonial product.[47] Like the Beni Ngoma, though, performances of this genre of satirical theatre were highly gendered, with men playing the instruments, in this case the tambourine, though in Wazungu's case women danced in order to accompany performances rather than setting up their own society altogether.[48]

While Wazungu was initially more popular in the Hêmbá chieftainships of Kongolo, particularly Bena Nyembo, Bena Nkuvu and Bena Mambwe, my interview with Abati, who witnessed it, suggested that it rapidly spread to other areas, such as the southern parts of the territory.[49] It is likely that Wazungu began in Hêmbá populated areas simply because they were the closest to Maniema, the province from which the colonial official Lebrun believed it had started.[50] We cannot say for sure why Maniema first innovated Wazungu but one of the most likely explanations is that it was again an import from Eastern Africa and potentially even a version of the Beni Ngoma.[51] In any case, Wazungu must have been a very protean movement because it was able to draw on the traditions of its host society with relative ease. For example, one of the main dances performed by the Hêmbá during Wazungu, the *Bulamba*, had apparently been part of the group's cultural repertoire for quite some time before becoming incorporated into Wazungu.

Like the colonial hierarchy they mimicked, Wazungu was also hierarchical. The White Fathers reported that a large meeting had been held in 1947 in which the performers and their audience appointed a 'Kaiser' or 'big chief.'[52] Aside from the 'big chief' themselves, Abati remembered that Wazungu performers represented nearly every echelon of the colonial hierarchy. There would be someone playing a territorial agent, such as Lebrun, right up to royalty, such as Leopold III or Baudouin I. Someone called 'Bendera,' who came from the Hêmbá village of Kahenga in Bena Muhona, for example, usually performed as the Belgian king in eastern Kongolo.[53] In keeping with his regal role, Bendera sometimes entered Wazungu performances on a *tipoyi* (or a *Kípoyo* in Hêmbá). If Lebrun, or any other colonial agent, tried to address him he would simply ignore them because he was not permitted to speak to royalty being only a humble agent. Instead, Lebrun had to content himself with addressing the person who was known to play the role of an agent, usually Makelele Leopard.[54]

The usurpation of colonial hierarchies of race and rank irked Lebrun, as well as some of his peers, and made him even more determined to monitor the phenomenon. In this way, colonial responses to Wazungu were an important part of the performance overall not least for the amusement they provided and to test how faithfully European hierarchies were represented. At times, though, the Wazungu joke wore too thin for the Belgian administration and Abati recalled that some Wazungu performers were imprisoned. As their attempt to distort the name of Wazungu noted above suggested, colonial officials had been apprehensive of it ever since Lebrun first noted its existence in June 1947.[55] On hearing about it, he had made every effort to investigate its 'aims.' To help him understand it, he contacted the White Fathers, which was unsurprising given that the Society had had prolonged contact with many of the Hêmbá peoples involved and not least with the Bena Nkuvu. Much like their colonial counterparts, the White Fathers' diaries betray a very hostile attitude to the 'sect' because they saw it as yet another obstacle to their proselytizing—and mission hostility to Wazungu doubtless fired Lebrun's own anxiety about the franchise.[56]

In one of his own territorial reports, Lebrun initially couched the theatre group firmly within the phraseology that his predecessors had used to describe the illegal 'secret societies' they encountered during the 1920s and the 1930s. Lebrun also used the word 'adept' to describe Wazungu performers, which was a term officials employed in association with members of these supposedly secret groups.[57] Yet as Douglas Johnson reminds us, 'secret' societies were not really secret at all given that they often performed, as Wazungu did, in the open. Johnson instead used the term 'closed associations' to describe such groups and this is more apt in the Wazungu case. Lebrun himself expressed considerable doubt over whether Wazungu could in fact be classed as a '*secret* society' [my emphasis] given that 'adepts [readily] made themselves known to territorial officials' with no need for interrogation.[58] It is Lebrun's doubt about how dangerous Wazungu was that means we cannot bracket it as a simple resistance movement. Had it caused the regime serious concern, there is no doubt that such a votary of colonialism as Lebrun would have had little hesitation in mobilising the violence of the state against it. As it was, Wazungu was allowed to continue.

Despite doubting if it could be categorized in the same bracket as, say, Watchtower, Lebrun still erred on the side of caution in his dealings with it. His fear emanated from the fact that he believed its 'adepts': 'made no effort to hide their contempt for the colonial regime.'[59] Its rapid spread was another source of colonial concern. It was clearly a trans-regional movement as it had been imported from outside Kongolo. It was able to come from Maniema and spread largely because troupes were organized between different villages in a manner Lebrun feared could facilitate class consciousness and even nationalist resistance. Members of one village invited those from another to join them in purpose-built 'hangars' for a theatrical performance and, later, a feast. J. M. M. Geerts, one of Lebrun's successors, echoed many of his predecessor's observations in his own territorial report of 1951.[60] He suggested that most of those who took part in Wazungu performances were 'young' people who would 'binge drink' until long into the evening. Yet despite its usurpation and satire of the colonial hierarchy, Geerts, like Lebrun before him, did not prohibit Wazungu in and of itself even if he did blame it for what he described as 'laziness' on the part of the African audience the day after a performance. For their part, Tambwe Abati suggested that the Africans who attended the performances enjoyed them as satire and entertainment.

Geerts' response to Wazungu suggests that the phenomenon had a considerable leisure component to it that was perhaps as much if not more threatening to the 'cult of productivity' that Vellut noted was so important to Belgian officialdom in this period.[61] It would be easy to cast Wazungu as an underground hotbed of rural proto-nationalism but its leisure component, for one, means that such as interpretation would be to misrepresent the revelry that was so important during and after performances. This observation is not made as a retrograde means of reviving Eric Hobsbawm's argument that phenomena, such as Wazungu, were simply 'primitive' and 'inarticulate' forms of protest awaiting the intervention of urban-based nationalists to give them a political language with which to resist more articulately.[62] In fact, Wazungu performers were, I suggest, highly articulate given that their satire was understood by any and all who saw it. The colonial insistence on the 'Wajusti' appellation is a sign that Belgian officials understood only too well what was being said and purposefully tried to distort the message.

In all, Wazungu demonstrated how the Church's war against groups it believed to have been non-Christian or even anti-Christian coincided with colonial officials' need to survey groups they believed to have been subversive. Both the colonial administration and the Church were glad to see Wazungu fade away in the mid-1950s. Although the state had invested more in seeing off Wazungu, at least during the start of its appearance in Kongolo in its incarceration of certain adepts, the Church also resented the group's presence in its domains. For the Church, Wanzungu was but one more sign, along with other groups such as

Bambudji, of rural peoples' decadence and neglect of Catholic discipline. Given that the colonial state, in Crawford Young's words, demanded only obedience its interest in the group waned once it discovered it was not a proto-nationalist outfit.[63] Wazungu was not viewed in and of itself as an existential threat to the Church either—far from it—but was none-theless a sign that more work needed to be done to ensure a pristinely Catholic Christian hinterland.

THE INTENSIFICATION OF AGRICULTURE AND THE EXPANSION OF THE LOCAL COLONIAL STATE

Missionaries also benefitted from the fact that colonial officials wanted to transform the Congolese hinterland during the 1940s and the 1950s both to stave off uncontrolled urban migration but also to make the hin-terland more profitable. The historian Bruce Fetter, for example, wrote that from 1945–1957, Elisabethville's 'population grew from 70,000 to 170,000, a rate of approximately 8 per cent per year.'[64] The expanding nature of Elisabethville—as well as other cities in Katanga—was viewed as a problem both by the state *and* the Church. For its part, the Church wanted to maintain the rural communities it had worked so hard to establish during the early twentieth century. Missionaries did not want to see their catechists leave the hinterland for promise of better pay in cities such as Elisabethville, as well as in some cases Albertville and even Leopoldville. This last substantive section outlines the ways in which the Belgian administration, as opposed to the Church, sought to remake the Congolese hinterland in the late colonial period before turning later on to consider how the Church thrived within the framework of the state's modernization drive.

The colonial state's desire to transform the hinterland was not solely a product of the late colonial period but had been an ongoing concern. Given that there were few minerals in Tanganyika, particularly when compared to the HKI to the south, agriculture became a mainstay in the district's colonial economy after the First World War. However, the colonial state's desire to transform the hinterland in a way that would halt rural–urban migration had largely failed by time the Second World War broke out. As chapter four argued, Louis Franck's 'great' chieftain-ships policy did not substantively transform Kongolo and so it did not act to stem emigration. In spite of these past failures, the colonial state still wanted to turn the Congolese hinterland into, first, a breadbasket capable of providing both food for the Congo's rapidly growing cities and, secondly, into somewhere where cash crops could be cheaply produced for global markets. And, rather than the pessimism that had been preponderant during the Depression, the late colonial period saw a profound sense of optimism develop among cadres of Belgian officials. Officials saw a historic increase in state spending that served to support their ambitions that was predicated in part on the fact that Belgium slowly abandoned its commitment to a colonial budgetary surplus.[65]

By the 1950s, state development projects were supported under the aegis of the First Ten Year Plan (FTYP) that saw 'almost $1 billion [invested in] the Congo.'[66] The FTYP provided the funds for an agricultural scheme that had been developed by the colonial state during the Depression era. Following his extensive tour of the Belgian Congo, Prince Leopold, the future King Leopold III (1934–1951), wanted to reshape colonial agriculture to offset some of the worst aspects of Western capitalist exploitation there.[67] His wish for the wholesale reform of Congolese agriculture was inspired in part by the extent of the economic downturn whose effects were so visible during his tour in 1933 and which had devastated much of the colony.[68] Later that year, he gave a controversial speech in Brussels arguing that Africans needed to be given titles to their farmland in a scheme known as *Paysannat* ('farmer').[69] Although Leopold's plan caused considerable discomfiture in certain metropolitan quarters, not least because it privileged African agriculture above European concessions, it did eventually take hold.[70] In 1936, the colonial administration began its first experiments with Leopold's Paysannat plan.[71] But rather than giving titles only to individuals, the first one was given to a man *and* his family in a place called Gandajika in the south-central province of Kasaï.[72]

The initial Paysannat experiment proved successful in that the family concerned produced enough food to feed themselves with a surplus left over that they could then sell on the open market. In this way, the most important iteration of Paysannat, *Paysannat Indigène* (PI), was born. PI involved giving titles to family groups just as the first experiment had done rather than to just one person to maximize production and in so doing taking advantage of economies of bulk. Given the success of the initial PI venture, it was extended to six other families shortly afterwards.[73] While it had been developed during the Depression, PI was only rolled out nationally after the Second World War.[74] Fearing that soil erosion due to overuse threatened their entire industry, cotton companies were at the forefront of attempts to transform PI from a marginal policy into a mainstream one. The Congolese Cotton Company (*Compaigne Cotonnière Congolaise*) (Contonco) persuaded the *Insitut National pour l'Etude Agronomique du Congo Belge* (National Institute for the Study of Agriculture in the Belgian Congo) (INEAC) to extend its experiment over an area of nearly 7000 square kilometers with this expansion involving nearly 50,000 inhabitants.[75]

Like PI, INEAC was a product of the 1930s, but INEAC was responsible for the promotion of PI as well as its development. What is more, INEAC was invested with a special responsibility to oversee agronomists' work and that of their subordinates. And, by 1947, INEAC and its colonial partners had begun to impose PI on the territory of Kongolo.[76] Once there, PI tended to involve forcibly resettling around ten to twenty families at a time onto areas that colonial officials deemed the most fertile and away from places that the families concerned had farmed before.[77] Africans were made to farm a portion of land in shared allotments (*lotissements*) whose locations were determined by the relative ease of irrigating them and their ability to support the use of mechanical equipment such as tractors.[78] And, rather than nuclear families, allotments in Kongolo were populated by 'clans' that were defined in Belgian colonial thinking as *extended* kinship groups with these in turn tending to be identified by elders and colonial officials. Even children under ten years old were tasked with helping their families in the cotton industry during key moments such as during harvest time.[79]

Much like the early twentieth century, official thinking with regard to the identification of clans derived in the most part from old, functionalist beliefs about anthropology that relied heavily on the idea of reified segmentary lineages. Even as Belgian officials were eschewing the hereditary inheritance of *chiefly* power; kinship, narrowly defined, was still the most important way in which groups of farmers in Kongolo were identified so as to be resettled onto PI allotments. Although farmers worked on the land that was held collectively under the rubric of the clan, 'exploitation of the crop … was on an individual basis and the harvested crops were individually owned.'[80] In other words, clans' allotments were subdivided into individually farmed fields with the exact dimensions of the whole allotment being contingent on the place they identified. Allotments were harvested on a rotating basis once or twice a year. Farmers usually planted their cotton seeds before their own cassava ones. The cassava remained in place for a number of months, which supposedly allowed farmers to harvest it as and when they needed to but *only* if they had grown the requisite quota of cotton. After the cotton and cassava had been harvested, the allotments were allowed to lie fallow to recover their fertility. If an allotment proved successful, and there was the space to extend it, the administration did not hesitate to do so. For example, in Kongolo in 1953 '150 farmers were moved to an area that had increased from 242 hectares to 382.'[81]

While it drastically altered the local landscape—and hardly ever through genuinely consensual means—PI met with positive approval in some quarters. Unsurprisingly, the colonial state and its operatives were among its most fervent believers. The former agronomist of the Tanganyika district as a whole, René Chambon, remembered PI in a particularly positive light. In a book he published before I met him, he argued that this experiment in collectivization 'allowed increased acreage to be placed under cultivation due to the mechanisation of labour.'[82] He went on to write that the implementation of PI was 'done with great enthusiasm' by all those involved, be they officials from the Tanganyika Cotton Company (*Cotonnière du Tanganika*) (Cotanga) or those in the territorial service.[83] Likewise, PI scored some very big successes by the end of the colonial period. In 1959, colonial officials reported that the district of Tanganika as a whole exported 20,000 metric tons of food-stuffs to Upper Katanga.[84] Under PI, Kongolo intensified the produc-tion of a number of cash crops of which the most important were cotton, groundnuts and palm oil. Hêmbá groups in the eastern parts of Kongolo predominantly specialized in palm oil while cotton had been slowly introduced to most if not all societies there by the end of the 1930s.

The production of cash crops was accelerated by a new generation of seeds that were grown in an experimental out-station in Kaseya, in southern Kongolo, after 1955. The experiments conducted in Kaseya had ramifications for the whole of Katanga as seeds produced there were exported well beyond Kongolo itself. Kaseya was integral to Kongolo's status as a territory that was on the vanguard of an agricultural revolu-tion that occurred in the Belgian Congo in the post-war period.[85] The agricultural innovations PI offered, as well as the production figures it boasted, meant that far from remembering the episodic violence that accompanied the installation of PI, Jonas Mwilambwe Mukalay and André Kalenga, writing as late as 2007, suggested that: 'it is unfortu-nate that the [PI] that was practiced in Kongolo was not extended to Ankoro.'[86] Even one of the most ardent critics of Belgian colonial agricultural policies, the historian Osumaka Likaka, suggests that 'peasant household income increased significantly ... under the paysannat scheme in the 1950s.'[87] But while PI had some notable benefits, there were clearly substantial downsides.

If one reads René Chambon's memoirs closely, for example, a far more nuanced picture emerges than that of the coming of a tranquil and bucolic, colonial modernity. He observed that during: 'the important moments of clearing, planting and processing crops [Cotanga agents, agronomists, territorial officials, African subordinates (*animateurs autochtones*)] roamed the villages at dawn, knocking on doors, encouraging people to go to the fields ... the villages were usually only constituted of old people and children ... did the adults not realise the benefit of living and working in peace?' Chambon's writing evokes two main questions; though more, of course, could be added. First, what happened if Africans did not heed the agents' 'knock at the door'? Secondly, and arguably more importantly, why were there so few working-age people in the villages? Belgian coercion forms a large part of the answer to both of the above questions though unsurprisingly the 'colonial library' is unforthcoming about the details about it.

In an interview with me, Mouthedba Lambert, who was trained as an agricultural monitor, said that chiefs were required to rubber-stamp agronomists' plans before colonial agents were officially able to create an allotment.[88] Local leaders would be asked several times if they agreed to PI being imposed among their people and, if they refused, they would simply be asked until they accepted.[89] Exactly as Marie-Bénédicte Dembour suggests, chieftainship councils in general, which consisted of colonial officials, notables and the relevant chief, was not a forum for meaningful deliberations and dialogue between equal parties.'[90] Nonetheless, some chiefs needed less 'persuasion' to adopt PI than others. For example, the chief of the Bena Nyembo, Lubembe Lambert, was supposedly open to it whereas many of his peers were less so.[91] According to Mouthedba Lambert, Lubembe Lambert went to a mission school whereas a number of other chiefs had not received much of an education; hence a possible reason why Lubembe Lambert was more open to PI than many of his peers.[92] While Lambert consented to PI, there were a number of Africans who were more sceptical about its installation on their land and it is still unclear as to exactly how the administration dealt with those who, no matter how many times they were asked, still refused to take part in PI. Unsurprisingly, the colonial

archives in Brussels are rather coy when it comes to referencing the violence that occured when colonial officials could not overcome Africans'
verbal disagreement to their plans.

The word that was typically employed by the administration when
it referenced violence in its reports was *persuasion*.[93] Henri Headrick,
a colonial agent working in 1946, used this word when he was
writing about bringing Africans back to seven key villages that year.[94] His
example did not refer directly to PI but gives an indication of the way
in which violence was euphemized in the territorial reports. Typically, it
is also difficult to tie any colonial official to any act of violence in these
documents. One example of convenient omission is in another territorial report written in 1946 in which the author, unnamed of course,
acknowledges that 'since the natives do not wish to regroup voluntar-
ily, which would be better, it is in their own best interest to *force* them
to do so' [my emphasis].[95] From having spoken to at least one Belgian
agronomist involved in PI, the forced relocations did inspire violence as
some Africans struggled to resist them. Likewise, African women such as
Mwanga Luzinga Florentine, also remember rural violence in the post-
war context in Bena Mambwe in particular.[96] Yet these incidents hardly
appear in the relevant archives.[97] We do know that the patterning of
forced relocations was uneven and staggered. The result was that there
was no sudden shock of colonial violence that affected every community and all at the same time. Instead, PI was 'drip-fed' into communities
and consequently never inspired a concerted proto-nationalist revolt in
Kongolo.

Whether drip fed or otherwise, the state grew its staff substantially
to identify areas that could be used for PI and to ensure PI allotments
would be profitable. Previously, members of the territorial service toured
villages to 'reinforce' chiefs' authority, collect the taxes their African allies
had taken and preside over judgements of customary law.[98] Following
the War, a new cohort of Belgian agricultural specialists surveyed African
farmers' work and helped monitors to 're-group' them. The colonial
administration in the Tanganyika district had, therefore, to promote the
intense 'cult of production and performance' that emerged in the late
colonial period.[99] The administration that took shape after the Second
World War came the closest any in the Belgian Congo ever would do to
the 'Bula Matari' type transformative model that Crawford Young argued
typified it throughout the colonial era.[100] Gone was the age of the lonely
territorial occasionally being carried about the bush on his *tipoyi* and in

came another that involved colonial officialdom incorporating a far larger and more professionalized constituency than before. While PI was the most obvious manifestation of the expansion of the colonial state, it joined a pre-existing group of institutions that also thrived in the 1940s and early 1950s such as the CFL and the state-run hospital in Kongolo's town centre.

In order to aid its modernist projects, the state took every opportunity it could to ensure it supported and installed reputable and effective African allies in the hinterland. One of their most important allies, Bùki, who had ruled much of southern Kongolo, died in 1947. While the aging chief had often disagreed with the Belgian administration, he united a polyglot series of polities whose scale would, in the post-war period, make PI easier. Unsurprisingly, therefore, colonial officials working in Kongolo wanted to make Bùki's former domains into a sector.[101] Making southern Kongolo into a sector would mean, as chapter four suggested, that an outsider who was literate and numerate would become chief rather than someone who had inherited power. The advantages of a well-trained chief coming to power in southern Kongolo, particularly in a time when the state was intensely pursuing PI, were clear for the colonial state. The Belgian's preferred choice of chief was a man called Kilombo. While Kilombo was from the Luba ethnic group, he was not related to Bùki and this fact irked the former paramount chief's surviving relatives. Despite their protestations, however, Kilombo was installed as chief of the new Bùki-Kiloshi sector in 1949.[102]

At first it might seem as though such an intense administrative push into the hinterland would compromise the Church's efforts to evangelize yet this was not the case. There is every indication that missionaries expanded along with the needs of the late colonial state as previously indicated. Indeed, a White Fathers report written in 1950 suggested that the colony was developing 'rapidly,' for example, and this meant that the missionaries had to work to produce 'new constructions'—which mainly meant schools.[103] The White Fathers' problem was not opposition from state officials during this time but, rather, as the Annual Report from 1950 suggests, they had trouble finding enough missionaries to build fast enough to accommodate the state's appetite for mission-trained Africans.[104] The Missionary Sisters of Our Lady Of Africa or the 'White Sisters,' who had arrived in Kongolo shortly after the White Fathers, were also scoring success too. Having struggled initially to get girls and women into the Sola mission station, by 1946 the White Sisters were frequently giving classes to girls from Bena Nkuvu that attempted to impose middle-class Belgian ideas of domesticity onto them. Young men were approaching the girls and women in such classes to propose to them and as such more Christian families were being created in eastern Kongolo. In 1947, the state also created the Native Welfare Fund or the *Fond du Bien-Être Indigène* (FBEI). The FBEI provided significant monies for the Church to construct the schools it wanted to build in its post-war expansion efforts. The first classrooms of a teacher-training school on the right bank of the Lualaba River, for example, were completed with FBEI funds in Sola by 1954.[105]

Conclusion

Far from continuing the acrimonious and fractious relations that defined the proto-colonial and even the early colonial periods, the Church and state drew much closer together in the post-war period. Rather than being a natural manifestation of Belgian rule, though, the close proximity of the Church and state was the product of a range of historical circumstances that had their roots in the Depression era but crystallized in the post-War period. Such factors included the state's need to use the Church's expertise on local social phenomena such as Wanzungu in addition as to its need for schools that was propelled in part by the PI schemes it ran. The Church thus built a range of educational facilities during the 1940s and beyond that enabled an administrative African bourgeoisie to emerge in Kongolo. This administrative bourgeoisie both directly and indirectly facilitated colonial modernity. Kilonda Syvestre was the best example in that he directly participated in PI but there were a number of other school leavers, such as Tambwe Benoit Abati, who played an indispensable role in Kongolo's public life during the post-War period. While the state often believed that the Church did not properly maintain its schools or even forced Africans to attend schools, the territorial administration clearly recognized the contribution the Church made to its plans. At the same time, the Church was becoming increasingly identified with the state in the minds of many Africans and this would have severe consequences later on once decolonization arrived.

NOTES

1. Valentine Yves Mudimbe, *The Idea of Africa* (Oxford: James Currey, 1994), p. 114.
2. Crawford Young, *Politics in Congo: Decolonization and Independence* (Princeton: Princeton University Press, 1965), p. 10.
3. Patrick M. Boyle, 'School Wars: Church, State and the Death of the Congo,' *Journal of Modern African Studies*, 33, 3 (1995), pp. 451–468.
4. CSSp, 'Kongolo,' *Bulletin Officiel*, Numéro 592–593 (1946), p. 230.
5. CSSp, 7J2.1b, Journal du Communauté, Kongolo, Journal du 14 juin 1926 au 19 aout 1950, p. 291.
6. AGM, 'Rapport Annuel, 1946–1947' (Algiers: Imprimerie des Missionnaires de l'Afrique, 1947), p. 336; AGM, 'Rapport Annuel, 1938–1939' (Algiers: Imprimerie des Missionnaires de l'Afrique, 1939), p. 215.
7. Interview with Ihunga Mundaza Marcel, 10 April 2009, Mission Quarter, Kongolo.
8. Ibid.
9. I have quoted Georges Balandier, *Sociologie de Brazzaville Noires* (Paris: Librairie Armand Colin, 1955), p. 123 from Young, *Politics in Congo*, p. 197.
10. Interview with Kilonda Kisangani Komombo Sylvestre, Bel Air, Lubumbashi, 24 March 2009.
11. Chambon, *Le Coton du Tanganika*, p. 30; Interview with Kilonda Kisangani Komombo Sylvestre, Bel Air, Lubumbashi, 24 March 2009.
12. Interview with Benoit Tambwe Abati, Mampala, Lubumbashi, 20 March 2009.
13. Reuben Loffman, 'On the Fringes of a Christian Kingdom: The White Fathers, Colonial Rule, and the Báhêmbá in Sola, Northern Katanga, 1909–1960,' *Journal of Religion in Africa*, 45 (2016), p. 17.
14. Archives Générales des Missionnaires de l'Afrique, Rome (AGM), Auguste-Léopold Huys, 'Rapport Annuel, 1935–1936' (Algeris: Imprimerie des Missionnaires de l'Afrique, 1936), p. 273.
15. Interview with Benoit Tambwe Abati, Mampala, Lubumbashi, 20 March 2009.
16. Ibid.
17. Guy Bernard, 'Perspectives pour une Sociologie Dialectique de la Décolonisation du Congo,' *Journal of Canadian African Studies*, 5, 1 (1971), pp. 33–43.
18. Interview with Benoit Tambwe Abati, Mampala, Lubumbashi, 20 March 2009.
19. Ibid.

20. Archives du Ministère des Affaires Etrangers, Bruxelles, AIMO 1735, Rapport sur l'administration Générale: Second Trimestre 1920, p. 20.
21. Ibid.
22. AAB, AIMO 1735, Rapport Annuel du Territoire de Kongolo, 1931, p. 56.
23. AAB, AIMO 115, Henri Hendrick, Rapport Annuel de Territoire du Kongolo, p. 13. In some ways this criticism was unfair since many of the White Fathers outstations suffered from a lack of resources during the Second World War period, see: AGM, Rapport Annuel, 1939–1945 (Algiers: Imprimerie des Missionnaires de l'Afrique, 1945), p. 480.
24. AGM, Bruges-Saint-Donat, Diaries, Décembre 1945, p. 525.
25. See for example: A. M. Delathuy, *Missie en Staat in Oud-Kongo, 1880–1914: Witte Paters, Scheutisten en Jezuïeten* (Bercham: EPO, 1992), pp. 66–79.
26. AGM, 'Rapport Annuel, 1953–1954' (Algiers: Imprimerie des Missionnaries de l'Afrique, 1954), p. 314.
27. Loffman, 'On the Fringes of a Christian Kingdom,' pp. 279–306.
28. See for example: AGM, 'Rapport Annuel, 1948–1949' (Algiers: Imprimerie des Missionnaires de l'Afrique, 1949), p. 255.
29. CSSP, 'A Travers le Monde,' *Bulletin Officiel*, Numéro 675 (1957), p. 25.
30. CSSP, 'Nouvelles des Communautés,' *Bulletin Officiel*, Numéro 666 (1956), p. 200.
31. AGM, 'Rapport Annuel, 1948–1949,' (Algiers: Imprimerie des Missionnaires de l'Afrique, 1949), p. 254.
32. Ibid.
33. Ibid.
34. Jean and John Comaroff, *Of Revelation and Revolution: The Dialectics of Modernity on a South African Frontier* (Chicago: University of Chicago Press, 2009), p. 49.
35. Thomas Q. Reefe, *The Rainbow and the Kings: A History of the Luba Empire to 1891* (Berkeley: University of California Press, 1981), p. 47.
36. David Maxwell, 'The Soul of the Luba: W. F. P. Burton, Missionary Ethnography and Belgian Colonial Science,' *History and Anthropology*, 19, 4 (2008), pp. 325–351.
37. AGM, Joseph De Jaeger traduit des notes du Petro Malazi, Mauvaise Sectes de la Mission du Makutano (Pères Blancs: Baudouinville, 1948), p. 1.
38. De Jaeger traduit des notes du Petro Malazi, Mauvaise Sectes de la Mission du Makutano, p. ii.
39. Joseph De Jaeger, *Bahemba: Etude Ethnologique* (Bakavu: Centre Interdiocésain de Pastorale et de Catéchèse, 1990).
40. Interview with Muganza Walunga Augustin (in Lubumbashi) with the present author (in Folkestone) by telephone, 10 October 2018.
41. Ibid.

42. Nicolas Argenti, *The Intestines of the State*, p. 4.
43. Barber, *The Anthropology of Texts*, p. 33.
44. Likaka, *Naming Colonialism*, pp. 136–156.
45. Interview with Tambwe Benoit Abati, Mampala, Lubumbashi, 28 March 2009; AAB, AIMO 115, RATK, 1947, p. 3.
46. Interview with Tambwe Benoit Abati, Mampala, Lubumbashi, 28 March 2009. The tambourine is called the *ngoma* in Kíhêmbá. The word *ngoma* is suggestive of the military brass-band, a parade style performance that was popular across eastern Africa from the 1890s to the 1960s, see: Terence O. Ranger, *Dance and Society in Eastern Africa, 1890–1970* (Berkeley: University of California Press, 1975).
47. Ranger, *Dance and Society in Eastern Africa, 1890–1970*, pp. 6–7.
48. Ranger, *Dance and Society in Eastern Africa*, pp. 12, 168.
49. Interview with Tambwe Benoit Abati, with Deogratias Symba, Mampala, Lubumbashi, 28 March 2009.
50. Ibid.
51. Ranger, *Beni Ngoma*.
52. AGM, Bruges-Saint-Donat Diaries, 1948, p. 604.
53. Interview with Tambwe Benoit Abati, Mampala, Lubumbashi, 25 March 2009.
54. Women did not perform in *Wazungu* as females played such a small part in colonial hierarchies.
55. AAB, AIMO 115, RATK, 1947, p. 3.
56. AGM, Bruges-Saint-Donat Diaries, 1947, p. 2.
57. AAB, AIMO 115, RATK, 1947, p. 3.
58. Ibid., p. 9.
59. Ibid., p. 3.
60. AAB, AIMO 116, RATK, 1951, p. 30.
61. Vellut, 'Hégémonies En Construction,' p. 330.
62. Eric J. Hobsbawm, *Primitive Rebels: Studies of Archaic Forms of Social Movement in the Nineteenth and Twentieth Centuries* (London: W. W. Norton, 1965), p. 2 quoted in Glassman, *Feasts and Riot*, p. 16.
63. Crawford Young, 'The End of the Post-colonial State in Africa? Reflections on Changing African Political Dynamics,' *African Affairs*, 103, 410 (2004), p. 34.
64. Bruce Fetter, *The Creation of Elisabethville, 1910–1940* (Stanford: Stanford University Press, 1976), p. 174.
65. Vanthemsche, *Belgium and the Congo, 1885–1980*, p. 163.
66. Bogumil Jewsiewicki, 'The Formation of the Political Culture of Ethnicity in the Congo, 1920–1959,' in Leroy Vail ed., *The Creation of Tribalism in Southern Africa* (Berkeley, 1991), p. 333; V. Drachoussoff (Translated by Bruce F. Johnson), *Agricultural Change in the Belgian Congo, 1945–1960* (Stanford, 1965), p. 188.

67. Piet Clement, 'Agricultural Policies and Practices in the Congo: The Origins and Implementation of the Indigenous Peasantry Scheme, 1917–1959,' Paper presented to KAOWARSOM conference entitled: The Belgian Congo in between the Two World Wars' (2016), p. 6.
68. Clement, 'Agricultural Policies and Practices in the Congo,' p. 6; Vanthemsche, *Belgium and the Congo, 1885–1980*, p. 54.
69. Clement, 'Agricultural Policies and Practices in the Congo,' p. 6.
70. Ibid.
71. Ibid.
72. Ibid., p. 11.
73. Ibid.
74. Ibid., p. 13; Likaka, *Rural Society and Cotton in Colonial Zaire*, p. 39.
75. Clement, 'Agricultural Policies and Practices in the Congo,' p. 13.
76. Loffman, 'An Obscured Revolution,' p. 430; Clement, 'Agricultural Policies and Practices in the Congo,' p. 11.
77. Loffman, 'An Obscured Revolution,' p. 430.
78. Drachoussoff, *Agricultural Change in the Belgian Congo, 1945–1960*, p. 155. While farmland was by far the most important form that PI took, it is worth noting that pisciculture was also significant in Kongolo. Fish farming was practiced in small, purpose-built ponds in the chieftain-ships of Bena Nkuvu and Bena Muhona, see: AAB, AIMO, 116, RATK, 1952, p. 53. According to David Gordon, ponds were not individually owned but were common property, see: David Gordon, *Nachituti's Gift: Economy, Society, and Environment in Central Africa* (Madison: University of Wisconsin Press, 2006), p. 125.
79. Interview with Kitungwa Lwenye Jules, Chef de Bena Nyembo, Mbulula, 14 April 2009.
80. Drachoussoff, *Agricultural Change in the Belgian Congo, 1945–1960*, p. 155.
81. Loffman, 'An Obscured Revolution,' p. 430.
82. Chambon, René, *Le Coton du Tanganika: Souvenirs et Projets* (Schepdaal, 2003), pp. 30–31.
83. Chambon, *Le Coton du Tanganika*, pp. 30–31; Likaka, *Rural Society and Cotton in Colonial Zaire*, p. 85.
84. Loffman, 'An Obscured Revolution,' p. 430.
85. An author cited as 'G. B. M.' declared that: 'The Belgian Congo is a rising star of the first magnitude' in relation to its agricultural devel-opment in 1950, see: G. B. M., 'The Agricultural Development of the Belgian Congo,' *The World Today*, 6 (1950), p. 348.
86. Jonas Mwilambwe Mukalay and André Kalenga, *Ankoro (Katanga): Notre Village* (Paris, 2007), p. 48.
87. Likaka, *Rural Society and Cotton in Colonial Zaire*, p. 89.

88. Interview with Moutheba Gwaboundi Jean Lambert, Ruishi Quarter, Lubumbashi, 18 March 2009.
89. Ibid.
90. Dembour, *Recalling the Belgian Congo*, p. 24.
91. Interview with Moutheba Gwaboundi Jean Lambert, Ruishi Quarter, Lubumbashi, 18 March 2009.
92. Mouthedba Lambert went on to say that Kalamba Sunzu, Lubembe Lambert's predecessor, had not been open to state-run cotton being imposed in his chieftainship as he feared 'the destruction of traditions.' Interview with Moutheba Gwaboundi Jean Lambert, Ruishi Quarter, Lubumbashi, 18 March 2009.
93. Loffman, 'An Obscured Revolution,' p. 431.
94. Ibid.
95. Ibid.
96. Interview with Mwanga Luzinga Florentine, Lubumbashi, 20 May 2009.
97. Loffman, 'An Obscured Revolution,' p. 431.
98. Dembour, *Recalling the Congo*, p. 89.
99. Jean-Luc Vellut, 'Hégémonies En Construction: Articulations Entre Etat Et Entreprises Dans Le Bloc Colonial Belge (1908–1960),' *Canadian Journal of African Studies*, 16, 2 (1982), p. 330.
100. Young, *Politics in Congo*; Young. *The African Colonial State in Comparative Perspective*.
101. AAB, AIMO 115, RATK, 1947, p. 4.
102. AAB, AIMO 115, RATK, 1949, p. 13.
103. AGM, 'Rapport Annuel, 1949–1950' (Algeris: Imprimerie des Missionnaires de l'Afrique, 1950), p. 267.
104. Ibid.
105. AGM, 'Rapport Annuel, 1953–1954' (Algeris: Imprimerie des Missionnaires de l'Afrique, 1954), p. 316.

BIBLIOGRAPHY

Argenti, Nicolas, *The Intestines of the State: Youth, Violence and Belated Histories in the Cameroonian Grassfields* (Chicago: University of Chicago Press, 2007).
Austen, Ralph A., 'Colonialism from the Middle: African Clerks as Historical Actors and Discursive Subjects,' *History in Africa*, 38 (2011), pp. 21–33.
Balandier, Georges, *Sociologie de Brazzaville Noires* (Paris: Librairie Armand Colin, 1955).
Barber, Karin, *The Anthropology of Texts, Persons and Publics* (Cambridge: Cambridge University Press, 2007).

Bernard, Guy, 'Perspectives pour une Sociologie Dialectique de la Décolonisation du Congo,' *Journal of Canadian African Studies*, 5, 1 (1971), pp. 33–43.

Beurden, Sarah van, *Authentically African: Arts and the Transnational Politics of Congolese Culture* (Athens: Ohio University Press, 2016).

Chambon, René, *Le Coton du Tanganika: Souvenirs et Projets* (Schepdaal, 2003).

Clement, Piet, 'Agricultural Policies and Practices in the Congo: The Origins and Implementation of the Indigenous Peasantry Scheme, 1917–1959,' Paper presented to KAOWARSOM conference entitled: The Belgian Congo in between the Two World Wars' (2016).

Davidson, Basil, *Modern Africa: A Social and Political History* (London: Routledge, 2014).

Dembour, Marie-Bénédict, *Recalling the Belgian Congo: Conversations and Introspection* (New York: Berghahan Books, 2001).

Drachoussoff, V. (Translated by Bruce F. Johnson), *Agricultural Change in the Belgian Congo, 1945–1960* (Stanford: Stanford University, 1965).

Fabian, Johannes, *Language and Colonial Power: The Appropriation of Swahili in the Former Belgian Congo, 1880–1938* (Berkeley: University of California Press, 1991).

G. B. M., 'The Agricultural Development of the Belgian Congo,' *The World Today*, 6 (1950), pp. 348–354.

Glassman, Jonathan, *Feasts and Riot: Revelry and Rebellion on the Swahili Coast, 1856–1888* (Oxford: James Curry, 1995).

Gordon, David, *Nachituti's Gift: Economy, Society, and Environment in Central Africa* (Madison: University of Wisconsin Press, 2006).

Higginson, John, 'Steam without a Piston Box: Strikes and Popular Unrest in Katanga, 1943–1945,' *The International Journal of African Historical Studies*, 21, 1 (1988), pp. 97–117.

Hobsbawm, Eric J., *Primitive Rebels: Studies of Archaic Forms of Social Movement in the Nineteenth and Twentieth Centuries* (London: W. W. Norton, 1965).

Jewsiewicki, Bogumil, 'Political Consciousness among African Peasants in the Belgian Congo,' *Review of African Political Economy*, 9, 19 (1980), pp. 23–32.

Jewsiewicki, Bogumil, 'The Formation of the Political Culture of Ethnicity in the Congo, 1920–1959,' in Leroy Vail ed., *The Creation of Tribalism in Southern Africa* (Berkeley: University of California Press, 1991), pp. 324–349.

Lemarchand, René, *Political Awakening in the Belgian Congo* (Berkeley: University of California Press, 1964).

Likaka, Osumaka, *Rural Society and Cotton in Colonial Zaire* (Madison: University of Wisconsin Press, 1997).

Likaka, Osumaka, *Naming Colonialism: History and Collective Memory in the Congo, 1870–1960* (Madison: University of Wisconsin Press, 2009).

Loffman, Reuben, 'An Obscured Revolution? USAID, The North Shaba Project and the Zaïrian Administration, 1976–1986,' *Canadian Journal of African Studies*, 48, 3 (2014), pp. 425–444.

Loffman, Reuben, 'On the Fringes of a Christian Kingdom: The White Fathers, Colonial Rule, and the Báhêmbá in Sola, Northern Katanga, 1909–1960,' *Journal of Religion in Africa*, 45 (2016), pp. 279–306.

Markowitz, Marvin D., 'The Missions and Political Development in the Congo,' *Africa: Journal of the International African Institute*, 40, 3 (1970), pp. 234–247.

Mukalay, Jonas Mwilambwe, and Kalenga, André, *Ankoro (Katanga): Notre Village* (Paris: L'Harmattan, 2007).

Nzongola-Ntalaja, Georges, *The Congo from Leopold to Kabila: A Peoples' History* (London: Zed Books, 2002).

Ranger, Terence O., *Dance and Society in Eastern Africa, 1890–1970* (Berkeley: University of California Press, 1975).

Renton, David, Seddon, David, and Zeilig, Leo, *The Congo: Plunder and Resistance* (London: Zed Books, 2007).

Rose-Hunt, Nancy, 'Domesticity and Colonialism in Belgian Africa: Usumbura's Foyer Social, 1946–1960,' *Signs*, 15, 3 (1990), pp. 447–474.

Samarin, William J., 'Protestant Missions and the History of Lingala,' *Journal of Religion in Africa*, 16, 2 (1986), pp. 138–163.

Scott, James C., *Seeing Like a State: How Certain Schemes to Improve the Human Condition Have Failed* (New Haven: Yale University Press, 1998).

Vanthemsche, Guy, *Belgium and the Congo, 1885–1980* (Cambridge: Cambridge University Press, 2012).

Vellut, Jean-Luc, 'Hégémonies En Construction: Articulations Entre Etat Et Entreprises Dans Le Bloc Colonial Belge (1908–1960),' *Canadian Journal of African Studies*, 16, 2 (1982), pp. 313–330.

Vinck, Honoré, 'Carte du Mérite Civique,' *Aequatoria*, 11, 3 (1948), pp. 103–105.

Young, Crawford M., *Politics in Congo: Decolonization and Independence* (Princeton: Princeton University Press, 1965).

Young, Crawford M., *The African Colonial State in Comparative Perspective* (New Haven: Yale University Press, 1994).

CHAPTER 7

Religion, Class and the Katangese Secession, 1957–1962

The last chapter argued that an important switch in Church–state relations occurred during the late colonial period. Rather than being at loggerheads, the Church and the state—at least in Kongolo—became far closer despite the occasional conflicts that arose between them. Several major points about the Church's close relationship to the state are worth recapitulating from the previous chapter so as to take the argument forward. First, there was nothing inevitable about the close Church–state relationship in the late colonial period. The cordial Church–state relationship in the 1940s and the 1950s was not the natural consequence of Leopoldian imperialism. Despite Leopold II's desire to see missionaries work with his nascent polity, the close Church–state relationship in the post-war period was the product of the state's heightened need for Church education as it stepped up its modernization plans. The Church's ethnographic expertise in the African societies that inhabited the hinterland was also useful to colonial officialdom as it sought to survey what it regarded as potentially subversive groups. The fact that a close Church–state relationship was not to be taken for granted was graphically and brutally brought home to the former by the post-independence state in the Congo, which would militarily confront the Church—even killing many missionaries in the process.

This, the final substantive chapter, finishes the story of the Church–state relationship in the Belgian Congo by explaining why it was targeted by militant African nationalists during decolonization. Rather than

© The Author(s) 2019   219
R. A. Loffman, *Church, State and Colonialism in Southeastern Congo,*
1890–1962, Cambridge Imperial and Post-Colonial Studies Series,
https://doi.org/10.1007/978-3-030-17380-7_7

foregrounding ethnicity in splitting Kongolo during independence, this chapter suggests that religion—and specifically mission education—was a key determinant in the divisive politics that took root in southeastern Congo during the early 1960s. The chapter begins by suggesting that the Church-educated Africans who featured so strongly in the last chapter often sided with a conservative brand of Congolese nationalism during decolonization as advocated by the Confederation of Katangese Tribes (Conakat). Conakat eventually sought secession from the Congolese state in what many militant nationalists, notably Jason Sendwe, a Luba activist, saw as the simple continuation of colonial rule. Yet the President of Conakat, Moïse Tshombe, was unmoved by such criticism. He had enjoyed a successful career in business before assembling an unwieldy coalition of political parties in Katanga. As well as taking advantage of the cross-party appeal to Katangese nationalism, Conakat appealed to voters in the Congo in part because it had strong links with mining concessions such as the UMHK. Those who had risen in company hierarchies, such as Benoit Tambwe Abati, therefore believed that their futures would be secure under Conakat in a way that they would not be under leftist leadership of Patrice Lumumba, the first Congolese Prime Minister. The Church never openly endorsed Conakat but mission diaries suggest missionaries were sympathetic to the party's cause—with one Kongolo Spiritan, Jules Darmont, even giving homilies to the Katangese army.

Given Conakat's popularity among the administrative class, it would be easy to posit a traditional model of decolonization in which Kongolo's elites shepherded a group of impressionable and uneducated farmers towards their own opinions.[1] However, while urban leaders persuaded many, Conakat's message of continuity would not have resonated had most people in the hinterland wanted a more radical alternative. Instead, an increasing number of Africans living in rural Kongolo fought hard to get their children into mission schools rather than to overturn the colonial state in its entirety. By the time decolonization arrived, many in Kongolo, like Kibondo Katumbo, were learning to be literate *not* with the intention of printing radical nationalist pamphlets but in order to become clerks, for example.[2] At times, struggles for resources were articulated in nativist terms but importantly rural elites were not all ethnic entrepreneurs. Instead, Conakat supporters used a range of discourses to persuade their compatriots of their cause; including references to colonial law. In short, while Conakat activists did persuade some in rural Kongolo to side with Tshombe, the power of conservative African nationalism in the territory came more from the fact that both urban elites and the farmers of the hinterland believed the continuation of Euro-centric capitalism was in their best interests.

THE COLONIAL ENDGAME

Congolese decolonization caught many, not least in Kongolo, by surprise with few enjoying much if any time to consider the fast-moving events that would shape their futures. Even today, it still seems like the colonial 'trinity' in the Congo broke down in an unfathomably short amount of time.[3] Historians naturally have differing views about why it ended so quickly.[4] But most agree that the system began to fall apart by the late 1950s. Given the power it accrued in the colony, scholars have traditionally given a lot of credit to the role of the Catholic Church in triggering decolonization.[5] While this book has suggested that the Church had a *competitively co-dependent* relationship with the state, its at least remaining in a relationship with the administration was important. Missionaries had access to many Africans through their hospitals and schools, for example, and so it could try to dissuade them from rebellion should the need have arisen. However, relations between the Church and the state began to sour in Brussels significantly during Auguste Buisseret's tenure as Minister of the Colonies (1954–1958).

As the historian Patrick Boyle notes, Bruisseret believed that missionaries had 'scant competence to organize and teach all the Congolese want to learn.'[6] Such remarks, written in the context of a report on Congolese education, were leaked to the public shortly after Bruisseret had made them in 1954.[7] As could be expected, these comments angered many Catholic missionaries in the Congo because they stood in stark contrast to their view of themselves as sacrificing much of their time and efforts for the greater Congolese good. Matters only got worse in late 1954 as the 'colonial administration announced that it would have to reduce subsidies for African teacher salaries and for boarding school operations.'[8] Boyle suggests that this statement provoked the Congolese episcopacy to give Bruisseret an ultimatum.[9] Léon Pétillon was told that Bruisseret's policy would necessitate the closure of all Catholic schools because it violated a 1952 Convention that promised 'a real equity between government and mission education.'[10] To calm the situation, a deal was offered whereby Catholic schools got 45% of state subsidies and state ones got the same—with Protestants left with 10%.[11] Despite this compromise, however, Church–state relations never recovered to their 1940s and early 1950s peak. Rather, both the Church and the colonial administration wanted to show that they had the authority to dictate matters of education to the Congolese in the late 1950s. So, in 1956, Guy Mosmans, who was to become the secretary of the Congolese episcopacy, 'publically advocated the complete disassociation of the Catholic Church from the colonial administration and its policies.'[12] As Boyle suggests, the Church began to side more closely and openly with African populations than with the colonial administration.[13] And, in 1956, the Vatican joined the Congolese episcopacy in realigning its policy 'toward the acceptance of political independence in Africa.'[14]

The distinction between Church policy—both in and outside of the Congo—before and after 1956 was subtle but significant. It meant that whereas before Churchmen and women might have actively intervened— or at least felt some obligation to intervene—to stop African discussions of nationalism, they would now have far more leeway to allow them if they so wished. This hardly meant that Catholic mission schools became hotbeds of nationalism overnight—they hardly ever did as Kongolo's experience demonstrates. And most of the most radical nationalists were Protestants, such as Jason Sendwe, in any case even if, like Joseph Kasa-Vubu, the first President of the independent Congo, they converted after having attended Catholic schools. What the Church's political shift did mean, however, was that in theory the Belgian administration could be rhetorically challenged in public and by one of its most important institutional allies. Not only that, but given that both the Church and the state courted African favour, the Congolese were beginning to appreciate the fissures in Belgian society first-hand.[15]

Just like many of the Congolese, big businesses in the Congo were astonished to see the Church and state at odds with one another so publically even if the debate was conducted much more in Belgium than in the Congo. Initially, the majority of industries wanted to prevent decolonization given that whatever would replace it was unclear but, with the Church's increasing indifference to Belgian rule, businesses found it hard to cling to what by the late 1950s seemed like a dying edifice.[16] What is more, as part of the liberal reforms Buisseret brought forth, the state allowed for the creation of cultural associations in Congo—including trade unions— thereby opening up the Congo to outside influences that only accelerated the rate of political change.[17] Big businesses, along with the colonial administration, thus continued to lose their ability to shield the colonial administration in the Congo from outside influences and by extension what remained of its political hegemony.

Yet it should still be noted that in most cases discussions involving the question of Congolese independence were considered academic. Most commentators envisaged independence as something that was going to happen well after the duration that Professor J. J. 'Jeff' Van Bilsen had outlined in his thirty-year plan decolonization plan in 1955.[18] What changed the concept of independence from being a mere academic discussion to one of profound political urgency were the Leopoldville Riots that took place on 4, 5 and 6 January 1959.[19] The history of the Riots has been examined at some length and so I will not go into comprehensive detail here.[20] Briefly, though, when an Abako demonstration was prohibited by colonial police, many of its members gathered anyway and contrary to the wishes of Joseph Kasa-Vubu, their ponderous and pragmatic President.[21] When the day of the meeting came, Kasa-Vuba came to the scene to urge his supporters to disband fearing that the gathering would be broken up by force.[22] Kasa-Vubu was correct in his belief that colonial police did break up his party's meeting. But neither he nor the Belgians, it would seem, anticipated that the ending of a football match nearby that would result in around **20,000** people arriving at the scene to shore up Abako's numbers.[23]

With the angry Abako supporters having been joined by a large gathering of football fans, the situation in Leopoldville snowballed rapidly out of the control of the local colonial authorities and resulted in around three days of looting and violence. That there were Belgian snipers on the roofs of some of Leopoldville's buildings meant that the scenes became eerily reminiscent of other conflicts that occurred elsewhere in Africa at the same time—not least those in the large settler colonies of Algeria and Kenya.[24] While the scale of the violence that accompanied the Leopoldville Riots was in fact largely coincidental, that the disturbances occurred after independence was pronounced as a formal Abako policy gave at least some company directors pause. More than this, many began to question just how long Belgian rule in the Congo would and could last. As the scholar Herbert Weiss suggests, there was little appetite in the Belgian metropole for a war to keep hold of the Congo.[25] Even the Belgian administration itself now seemed to doubt its own resolve or at the very least it commissioned a report into what remedial steps could possibly be taken to calm the situation.

Even before this government report into the Riots was published, Baudouin I, the reigning Belgian monarch, made a policy statement on 13 January 1959 in which he stated that the Congo was to become an independent state and this would happen more quickly than Van Bilsen had suggested.[26] After the study into the Leopoldville Riots was published shortly after the King's pronouncement, which euphemistically suggested that the Congo needed a greater degree of 'internal autonomy,' two Round Tables were hastily organized in January and February 1960. Despite the Round Tables having been convened, Belgian leaders still hoped that the Congolese leaders would arrive disunited and independence could be stalled. However, the Congolese presented a united front demanding independence at the earliest possible juncture.[27]

That the Congolese succeeded in broking an early independence was in many ways remarkable since political parties had been legal in the Congo for only a little over two years by 1960. Many of the old so-called 'cultural associations,' groups formed to protect their traditions, such as Abako, had been turned into political parties almost overnight in late 1957/early 1958. The unity that the Congolese displayed in Brussels was also somewhat surprising given how many different political parties the delegates represented. In fact, there were too many to survey here. However, a few stood out as being particularly influential. While the Abako party was important as far as the Lower Congo was concerned, the Congolese National Movement (*Mouvement National Congolais*) (MNC) gained the most seats in the general election in May 1960. Founded in 1958, the MNC was one of the only parties with a genuinely national following as opposed to solely a regional or ethnic one. Most of the literature on decolonization has therefore tended to focus on the national elections in May and the MNC's role in them, often as part of a Lumumba hagiography.[28,29]

However, local electoral politics and campaigning in the context of the Belgian Congo has almost always been ignored—even in mineral-rich Katanga.[30] The local picture in Kongolo in fact runs starkly counter to the MNC triumphalism that is present in many historical accounts of Congolese decolonization. While MNC candidates did get votes in Kongolo, they were far from the majority there even if they were able to gain the majority of votes in other territories outside Katanga. Rather than Patrice Lumumba's MNC, it was Tshombe's Conakat that got the majority of votes in the territory in the May elections.[31] But what, in fact, did Conakat stand for, how did it originate and what impact did the party have on Kongolo once it was elected? The Conakat party was formed in the midst of a number of political divisions in Katanga with one of the most important being demonstrated in a series of local elections that took place in December 1957.[32] These elections were not part of the independence process but were instead instigated primarily to muffle demands for decolonization. Yet, in these polls, the Luba from Kasaï won a number of important municipal elections in Elisabethville and that in turn prompted a significant amount of resentment among those who considered themselves native to Katanga.[33] The Kasaïan Luba were related to the Katangese Luba, incidentally, but they had settled further west than the latter. After 1935, as the Congo began to recover from the Depression, Luba from Kasaï were recruited by the state and migrated of their own volition to work in the mines of Upper Katanga.[34]

During the cusp colonial period, the Luba from Kasaï looked to many of their Katangese brethren that they were displacing them from public political offices across Katanga. Most of the cultural associations in Katanga that had sprung up in the 1950s flocked to federate themselves to Conakat so as to prevent the Kasaïan Luba's rise to power in Elisabethville and beyond.[35] One of the most important of these groups was the Baluba Association of Katanga (Balubakat), who joined Conakat in February 1959, and which was led by Jason Sendwe.[36] Sendwe was not schooled in one of Kongolo's Catholic schools but in one run by American Methodists who were based to the south of Kongolo in Katubwe, Western Kasaï. Ironically, given where Sendwe was trained, Balubakat was formed largely to advocate for the rights of the Luba of Katanga as opposed to those of Kasaï.[37] However, as Erik Kennes and Miles Larmer suggest, the relationship between Balubakat and Conakat was always strained and for a number of very important reasons.[38]

Conakat increasingly viewed Katangese independence as the only way to stop the influx of Luba-Kasaï workers—and their political influence—coming into Elisabethville. At the very least, the party argued for a strongly federalist system in the run-up to the May elections. While Balubakat at most accepted a very weak form of federalism to prevent Luba-Kasaïan migration, they were not at all in favour of Katangese independence. At first, Conakat and Balubakat's differing ideas about Katangese independence were irrelevant, though, since not even

Conakat advocated the independence of Katanga when it was formed in 1958. Yet Conakat's staunchly federalist agenda steadily shifted towards independence for Katanga during the decolonization process. In late 1959, realizing that Conakat were increasingly inclined towards independence, Balubakat declared that it could no longer be part of the Confederation.[39]

The Balubakat–Conakat relationship was not only threatened by the possibility of an independent Katangese state, though. Sendwe's Balubakat were also hostile to the pronounced European influence present in Conakat.[40] This is not to say that Balubakat had no European support. After all, the European settlers, or the *colonat*, had provided some limited funds to Sendwe's party too.[41] However, Sendwe and his followers believed that the colonat's support of Conakat went *far beyond* the odd donation here and there. Rather, the colonat were an *integral* part of the Conakat machine and not in any way peripheral to it. The colonat's agricultural work was not especially profitable, but the significant sums of money that had been spent on subsidising them, such as the 72 million Francs the CSK invested in the early 1940s, boosted the capital available to them.[42] At the same time, the differences between Conakat and Balubakat only became more pronounced after the latter split from the former in 1959. For Balubakat supporters, Moïse Tshombe soon became the embodiment of everything they despised, someone in the pay 'of the whites,' and intent on derailing the success of an independent Congolese state for the sake of his wealthy backers who wanted to secure Katangese minerals.[43]

Once the Congo became independent on 30 June 1960, the new Prime Minister, Patrice Lumumba, made a number of miscalculations that gave Moïse Tshombe every opportunity to garner support for and rationalize secession, at least to his followers. When Lumumba's MNC took power after independence on 30 June 1960, one of his first orders of business was to give nearly every civil servant a pay rise—yet the Force Publique was not included in it.[44] So, on 5 July, the country's soldiers mutinied in Leopoldville and the unrest quickly spread throughout the rest of the newly independent country. White Fathers diaries in Sola demonstrate that the revolt even spread into the hinterland in a way that scholars have not fully appreciated hitherto.[45] The Mutiny lasted nearly a week and did much to damage Lumumba's early tenure as PM.

Having destabilized much of the Congo, both rural and urban, the Mutiny of the Force Publique gave Tshombe exactly the excuse he needed and he declared that he was 'seceding from chaos' on 11 July 1960.[46] Thereafter, the Congo was plunged into what scholars have subsequently called the 'Congo Crisis.'[47] Lumumba repeatedly tried to recapture Katanga along with the United Nations (UN), which launched several operations against Tshombe's army. Moreover, after Tshombe's declaration of Katangese independence, Tanganyika as a whole became bitterly and militarily divided between those who agreed with Conakat's agenda and those who did not. Kalonda Sylvestre, who was elected to the Provincial Assembly during the May 1960 general election, told me much about the excesses of the violence that occured after Tshombe's declaration of independence.[48] The next section examines these stories and asks how and why Kongolo sided with Tshombe when those territories that surrounded it did not and what their support for him meant for Kongolo.

A LONE CONAKAT TERRITORY IN TANGANYIKA PROVINCE

In the early days of 1960, René Chambon was busily working on the *Paysannat* fields of the kind described in the last chapter. On one particular day that year, he remembered that the sun was shining and life in the colony seemed entirely normal. Yet this colonial 'normality' was soon to be interrupted by the sound of his crackling two-way radio. Upon answering its call, he was told that the Congo was going to become independent on 30 June. Like many of his colleagues then working in Katanga, he was perplexed by this news. While he understood that the Leopoldville riots had profoundly disrupted Belgium's plans to extend independence indefinitely, these disturbances had had little effect on southeastern Congo up to this point. Likewise, although some politicians, most famously Joseph Kasa-Vubu and Patrice Lumumba, had cried out for immediate independence—many had not yet done so. And even if they had, Chambon never believed that they would persuade the resident colonial powers that independence would be as immediate as 30 June. How would a government be formed by that time? Who would administer the policies the government enacted in a state that boasted barely more than a handful of university graduates?[49]

Part of the answer to the above questions, particularly the question about who would govern the Congo when Belgian rule finished, was that national elections would be held in 1960. As the general election loomed, Tambwe Benoit Abati busied himself campaigning for the local branch of the Conakat party. Abati became a member of Tshombe's party nearly from its inception in 1958 in Bena Mambwe.[50] He had initially joined the *Association des Hêmbá du Katanga* (Alibakat), yet after Alibakat federated itself to Conakat he played a more active role in promoting the latter.[51] Before the May 1960 elections, Moïse Tshombe had arranged a meeting with all the presidents of the parties affiliated with Conakat to ensure that they were on 'on message.'[52] Abati could recall nearly word for word what Tshombe had said to him that day and it bears repeating as it clearly reinforced his opinion that secession was necessary.[53]

According to Abati, Tshombe believed that Katanga had hardly if ever been part of the Belgian Congo or, for that matter, of the Free State.[54] As the first two chapters of this book explained, this belief was seductive in large part because it contained more than a grain of truth. The Katanga Company (CK) had indeed been created as a largely—but not completely—separate entity from the Free State just as the CSK had also enjoyed a large degree of autonomy.[55] Abati claimed that Tshombe had given him a copy of a letter that suggested a Belgian monarch (Abati did not say which) went to Elisabethville to ask for money for the central state. Nevertheless, the history that he recited, which in turn drew on Tshombe's, was interesting in terms of what it emphasized and what details were missing. Abati did not mention most of Katanga's history from the Great Depression onwards, for example, when it was integrated far more thoroughly into the central state bureaucracy. Rather, it was the *early colonial period* in which he suggested that the fundamental law of the colony was made in which Katanga would always be separate from the rest of the Congo.[56]

Some explanation of the term 'fundamental law' is required in order to properly understand the point Abati made with regard to Katangese independence. Unlike in many democratic countries, in which any law can theoretically be appealed should elected representatives decide to do so, Abati suggested that in the Belgian Congo there were some laws that could never be amended and these were called 'fundamental laws.'[57] These laws could not be altered at the behest of the colonial government of the day nor can they be amended. The legislature and executive must let these laws stand as they are considered 'fundamental' to the existence of the Belgian Congo—independent or otherwise. According to Abati, the Colonial Charter that was signed in 1908 outlined some of these laws.

Yet, Article 22 of the Colonial Charter, which decreed that the Katangese administration was placed 'in the hands of the CSK,' was not a fundamental law as Abati would have defined the term.[58] But in Abati's view the integration of the CSK into the Belgian Congo that occurred in 1910 was illegal and unconstitutional. The early colonial history of Katanga, and in particular its early legal history, was therefore paramount in Abati's mind as he went about Kongolo trying to mobilize the territory's electorate. Just as in any interview, however, the present loomed over my conversation with Abati when he talked to me about why Katanga should have been a separate nation state. In 2009, he suggested that 40% of Katanga's tax revenue went straight to Kinshasa and never comes back and the situation was similar in the colonial days.[59] For Abati, then, as much as Conakat's Katangese nationalism was a legal rectification of past wrongs, secession was also a present financial necessity.

As much as it was unsurprising that Abati was influenced by the present, what might strike a reader as more surprising about my interviews with him was that he was not greatly influenced by the pre-colonial period. Given the attention to pre-colonial symbolism that Tshombe gave to his version of Katangese nationalism, not least in his inclusion of the copper ingots M'Siri used as currency on his flag, one might have expected Abati to have referenced it more frequently. Likewise, it would have been good, particularly in a period of intense nationalist fervour, to make the case that there was a pan-Katangese state of sorts *before* the arrival of the KC. As the first two chapters made clear, mostly by conscious omission of the topic, Kongolo was never a part of M'Siri's domains and so in many ways it was in some respects in fact unsurprising that Abati based his claim that Katanga was and always had been an independent state *entirely* on the early colonial period.

The only passing reference Abati made to the pre-colonial period in fact had more to do with the Congo's eastern neighbours, Rwanda and Burundi, than it did to Kongolo itself. He said that Rwanda and Burundi were two different kingdoms before they were occupied, first, by the Germans and, after the First World War, by the Belgians.[60] When the Germans occupied Rwanda and Burundi at the end of the nineteenth century, they became conjoined under a colony called Ruanda-Urundi.[61] Yet the Belgians planned to make them independent as separate countries. Abati claimed that if the Belgians were talking about letting Rwanda and Burundi become separate states once they became independent, then why not make Katanga a separate state also?[62] But to make this argument properly, Abati had to argue

Kongolo was part of M'Siri's pan-Katangese state and this would not resonate with people in the territory who knew better.

Despite their weaknesses, the arguments that Abati had outlined for me during my interviews with him clearly swayed his fellow Church-trained friends Kilonda Sylvestre and Raymond Munganga. Just as Abati had done, Munganga and Sylvestre campaigned for Conakat when the Congolese general elections were held on 20 May 1960.[63] Afterwards, they joined Abati as Conakat representatives in the newly created Katangese Provincial Assembly that was convened after the May elections.[64] Altogether, Conakat won 3171 votes in Kongolo, which was enough to see a clean Conakat sweep of the territory.[65] This was not the case in Kongolo's neighbouring territories, though, which by and large did not support Conakat. Kongolo's eastern neighbour, Nyunzu, for example, voted for the MNC.[66] Likewise, Manono, the territory to the south of Kabalo, voted for Balubakat. Kabalo voted for what was known as the 'Cartel' that was a political alliance that was constituted mainly of Balubakat sympathisers.

The upshot of the May elections was that the Conakat territory of Kongolo was completely encircled by territories that had not voted the same way as so much of its populace had done. Many of the areas that had supported Conakat mapped directly onto those that had had more experience of the mission encounter. For example, the eastern areas of the territory, which were predominantly Hêmbá and that had witnessed the expansion of the White Fathers' schools after the Second World War, voted for Conakat. However, the non-Catholic Luba areas, in which people professed Protestantism or retained their belief in the Luba cosmological world, in the west of the territory, often voted for the Cartel or the political association most closely related to Balubakat. Although there were Catholic mission stations in territories aside from Kongolo that voted for more left-leaning parties during the May elections, David Maxwell has written in detail about the significant Protestant activity in the Luba heartlands, such as Kabongo, which potentially served to override the influence of more moderate Catholics there.[67] This is not to say that the material conditions under which various populations laboured did not matter. Rather, radical activists often—though not always—came from cotton-producing areas.

But the density of Catholic schools—and in particular primary schools—on the right side of the Lualaba River and the relative lack of them on the left side meant that, in Crawford Young's words, there were 'differentials in access to [colonial] modernity' in Kongolo.[68] What is more, all the Conakat provincial deputies had been trained, first, by the White Fathers and, secondly, by the Spiritans. It would be tempting to think, particularly given the existence of Alibakat, that people tended to vote along strict ethnic lines and this was certainly Gérard Jacques' view when he toured the territory at the time as a Belgian official.[69] Yet in addition to the Hêmbá, who voted Conakat in Kongolo, the Bango Bango population in the extreme north of the territory also did. And Conakat as a whole was quite literally a *confederation of different ethnicities*—a position that ironically in part elevated it above ethnic feuds until Balubakat's split. Likewise, the Songye voted for the Cartel alongside their Luba-Katanga brethren. Politics in Kongolo was therefore not wholly a matter of ethnic blocks voting for a particular party solely on the basis of its appeal to ethnicity. Rather, the Church history and that of the early colonial occupation also played a major, if indirect, role in the outcome of the elections in May 1960. But how did the Church-trained, administrative class get their message into the hinterland and, if they did not, how did Conakat gain the votes it did there?

THE CHURCH AND THE POST-WAR STRUGGLE FOR RESOURCES

A struggle for mission resources intensified in Kongolo during the lead up to independence and it was increasingly being debated through the language of ethnicity. In other words, nativist discourses became important as competition for scarce mission resources took hold. The evidence that mission diaries and reports provide is patchy. But, all the documents produced by missionaries working in Kongolo at the time indicate, first, that there were ever more people trying to get their children into the White Fathers' school in Sola and, secondly, that there were not the funds available to match the demand. Not only were funds to expand pre-existing schools not available, at least according to the missionaries themselves, but even maintaining the existing infrastructure also proved difficult for the White Fathers as independence approached.[70]

The sorry state of some of the mission schools was interpreted by many local residents as a sign of the White Fathers' neglect of the African population rather than as an indication of a group of missionaries simply struggling to cope with the demand for their services. On 6 October 1957, the superior of the Sola out-station found hostile letters in his post-box, for example. The White Fathers diarist described the author as a 'well-educated person' who must therefore have had a good deal of experience with the missionaries.[71] They contended that, by taking tithes without delivering opportunities for local people, the White Fathers were doing 'the devil's work.'[72] Worse still, the accuser argued that they were actually stealing Francs from the congregation. The letter went on to conclude that the White Fathers were simply not doing enough to enlarge the school in Sola.

A distinctly nativist tone steadily became apparent in African discourse in the Sola out-station as Africans lobbied missionaries to do more to ensure that the chieftainship of Bena Nkuvu 'evolved,' in the words of one local resident. For example, on 17 March 1959 a frustrated student of the White Fathers suggested that the Society was not from the locality and so 'should go home.'[73] Mukelenge Tambwe, the chief of the Bena Nkuvu, mused on the question of the loyalty not of the White Fathers' leadership but more of their African congregants. He thought that as many of them were not from the chieftainship, they did not have its best interests at heart. It was not only the congregants in the Sola out-station whose heritage began to become a matter for speculation for the Bena Nkuvu residents. The White Fathers' diaries suggested that some agricultural monitors from the chieftainship worried that there were 'alien' elements among their number.[74] One supposed example of such an 'alien' was a monitor called Gaston Ngongo yet he protested angrily about this belief.[75]

Despite the nature of the increasingly fraught contests for resources, Chief Mukelenge Tambwe wisely retained a veneer of politeness in his dealings with the missionaries themselves. When he worried that there were not enough medical staff in the chieftainship to accommodate the pressures that an increased birth rate had on maternity wards, for example, he stated simply that 'there is no-one with a medical diploma in the ward.'[76] In Tambwe's mind, the only solution to the problems that his chieftainship was experiencing, be they medical or agricultural, was for missionaries to build a sixth grade school in Sola. Yet the threatening letters in the mission post boxes meant that he found himself in a position where he had to at least be seen to mediate increasingly strained Church relations with his subjects. So, he organized a meeting that took place on 7 July 1959. While Tambwe was pleased that a meeting between his court and the missionaries had been scheduled, he would not be content at its outcome. Rather than delineating plans for expansion, the Church and its representatives simply tried to explain that their finances could not keep pace with the rapid growth of demand they were experiencing. So, it is not hard to see how pressured the missionaries' resources were. What is more, the White Fathers often had to choose only thirty postulates from at times as many as three hundred applicants. Mukelenge Tambwe was also far from the only local chief petitioning the White Fathers to extend their infrastructure into their domains at this time. The chief of Bena Nyembo, Lubembe Lambert, was also lobbying the missionaries hard to try to expand their facilities in his capital of Mbulula.[77] Even if missionaries had the funds to expand, therefore, the White Fathers excitedly reported in their internal correspondence that many in Bena Muhona 'seriously wanted to convert.'[78] Tambwe, therefore, was in something of a queue for mission resources.

Dissatisfied with the outcome of his big tent meeting with the White Fathers on 7 July, Tambwe went to the colonial administration to complain that he did not have the clerks he needed to administer his domain. Gérard Jacques, one of the functionaries in Kongolo at the time, seemed as unforthcoming with the resources Tambwe asked for as the missionaries had been. However, it bears repeating that Jacques did not have a mandate to increase expenditure on schools. As the pressure on resources was felt by many of the Hêmbá populace, overarching political identities began to form a more prominent part of public discourse. Even in 1959, though, the label of 'Hêmbá' was still not the only political rallying cry, particularly as many felt that inter-Hêmbá competitions for resources were more significant than Hêmbá-Luba conflicts for example.

Rather than rallying around ethnicity per se, many in Kongolo's hinterland campaigned actively and explicitly around the issue of resources. One of the clearest examples of such campaigning comes from a series of territorial elections that were held in December 1959. To explain, these elections were held as part of the state's plans to control the trajectory of independence by giving a measure of power to local African elites who the administration hoped would be sympathetic to Belgium after independence. In and of themselves, these contests meant relatively little as those elected did not have the kind of executive powers that Belgian provincial governors enjoyed. However, they were important, first, in giving a public voice to the resource competitions that were coming to the fore and, secondly, by beginning the processes of political mobilization that would be so important later on in May 1960.

One of the most high-profile political parties in Kongolo in the 1959 local elections was *Faida ya Muhona* (Benefit Muhona). As its name suggests, *Faida* was formed to lobby specifically for the development of the chieftainship of Bena Muhona and not as an inter-Hêmbá ethnic party. That no out-station had been built in Bena Muhona was a constant source of frustration to Faida's members who saw their party as a means to lobby both the White Fathers and the colonial administration on their behalf. Yet although *Faida* did very well in the local elections, Moïse Tshombe's Conakat party did better, especially in the Hêmbá chieftainships, and this provides some evidence that the Alibakat group was already formed by that time and had allied itself to Conakat. 1959 therefore probably represented the start of the explicit use of the Hêmbá identity as a means of gaining resources and its more widespread public use continued well into 1960. The first time that the word Hêmbá appears in the Sola mission record was in reference to another big-tent meeting on 20 March 1960 that involved all the Hêmbá chiefs, many notables and as well as a smattering of agricultural monitors and that gathering was called to address the resource shortages in their respective chieftainships.[79]

Not only was there a meeting of the Hêmbá in general at this point but the White Fathers diarist in Sola also stressed that this was also explicitly 'a political meeting.'[80] If Alibakat was not formed by the 1959 elections, then it was almost certainly a product of this meeting. Whenever the first use of Hêmbá as an outright political term actually was, what was important about those who used it was that they clearly allied themselves to the Conakat cause very early on. There are several reasons why Alibakat affiliated itself to Conakat and not to other parties, such as the Cartel. First, it would not have made much sense for them to join the Cartel because of their opposition to European capitalism, of which missionaries were an intrinsic part—knowingly or otherwise. If Alibakat sided with militant nationalists then they would endanger their access to Church resources given Balubakat's hostillity to European Catholic missionaries. The Hêmbá's struggle was not wholly or potentially even in part to overthrow Belgian rule but to gain the resources necessary to expand mission education under it. Hêmbá ethnic mobilization was therefore ambiguous, far from hegemonic and only just beginning to bubble to the surface by the time that the 20 May 1960 elections arrived.

Rather than being driven by urban elites desperate for votes, inasmuch as it existed by May 1960, Hêmbá ethnic mobilization was very much a 'bottom up' affair or at least the little evidence we have suggests as much. The model of Hêmbá mobilization conforms to a large extent with John Lonsdale's idea of *moral ethnicity* in which local people hold their leaders to account using ethnic identity rather than to a top-down model in which elites use the language of tribalism to galvanize followers. For example, in the eyes of colonial subjects in eastern Kongolo, a good Hêmbá chief became someone who would be an effective lobbyist for his people and gain resources on their behalf.[81] This is not to argue that chiefs were saints who had their subjects in mind at all times, this book has hopefully observed the reverse in many chapters, it is merely to say that they clearly felt a good deal of pressure from them to lobby whomsoever they felt could deliver resources and wherever possible. But much as the overwhelming majority of voted Conakat-affiliated delegates onto territorial councils were Hêmbá, theirs was not the only ethnic identity to side with the more conservative nationalists. The Bango Bango group, frequently identified by the Hêmbá as their ethnic 'cousins,' were also Conakat stalwarts in Kongolo.[82] Indeed, Ihunga Mundaza Marcel, who featured in the last chapter, was from this group.[83] Like Tambwe Benoit Abati, whose early life history was also detailed in the fifth chapter, he voted for Conakat and did not wish to see the Cartel or any of its constituents gain power in 1959 or for that matter in 1960.[84]

In sum, there was a strong correlation between the availability of mission resources, notably those pertaining to education, and the way that people in Kongolo voted during the 1960 elections. At times, Conakat mobilization seemed to follow ethnic lines, for example in the Hêmbá's overwhelming vote in favour of Conakat and the Luba's overwhelming rejection of Tshombe's party. However, such an analysis would be misleading given that Conakat was popular among a range of ethnic constituents in addition to the Hêmbá, such as the Bango Bango. As much as Abati and Marcel were two natural examples of Conakat voters, the Luba, Songye and Kusu peoples also voted Conakat though not, perhaps, in the same numbers as their Bango Bango and Hêmbá counterparts. Moreover, some Luba and Songye commuted to the Lubunda educational facilities as well as, on rare occasions, to the White Fathers out-stations on the right bank of the Lualaba River. Ethnic identities sprung largely from competition over resources, therefore, and not from some distant primordial past that, as the second chapter made clear, did not lead to the creation of discreet, coherent and monolithic ethnicities. Rather than depending on the voting processes, most if not all of my informants saw ethnic tension as something that happened only *after* 30 June and not before it.[85]

The Church and the Cusp Colonial Period

The Church found itself markedly less able to respond to requests for resources as decolonization approached yet the political pressure on it to do so were unrelenting. From playing a major part in Kongolo's colonial history, the violence that overtook Kongolo during decolonization left European missionaries in particular increasingly on the periphery of Congolese politics. The most important reason for the Church's rapid marginalisation from local politics in Kongolo was the hostility of a minority in Kongolo—but many more from outside the territory—who did not want to see Tshombe's secession become a legal and political reality. As the last section suggested, most of Kongolo's neighbouring territories voted for radical leftist political parties both in the 1959 local elections and those in May 1960. This section explains why, despite the fact that many in Kongolo voted for Tshombe's party, the Church found itself in such perilous position after the declaration of independence. In the end, it would be dealt such a severe blow that it would take over a generation for it to recover.

Even before Moïse Tshombe's declaration of independence on 11 July 1960, the security situation in Kongolo had been rocked by the mutiny of the Force Publique. The fact that the military could not be counted on to maintain the peace, such as it was, provided missionaries with serious pause for thought. At the very least, the threat of violence from the rebelling Force Publique meant that a significant number of Europeans began to leave Kongolo much as they did elsewhere in the colony.[86] At worst, this meant that hostility grew between those members of the gendarmerie in Kongolo who were loyal to the Leopoldville administration and those who were not. More work needs to be done on what precisely defined this division and presently it is unclear why certain battalions supported the rebellion while others did not. Nonetheless, not only was anger solely directed from the Force Publique to Europeans but violence also erupted the other way around, e.g., between Europeans and the rebel members of the Force Publique. In Sola, this resulted in the death of a member of the gendarmerie who tried to stop Europeans leaving and was shot as he did so.

From the peaceable elections in May 1960, the situation in Kongolo now grew increasingly violent. Tshombe's declaration of independence on 11 July was met with disbelief by many from Jason Sendwe's party who were becoming increasingly militant in their opposition to Conakat. Rather than side with Elisabethville, Sendwe and many of his supporters now wanted to unite with the new Leopoldville government. The mechanisms for doing this remained unclear, though, and a period of profound uncertainty followed Tshombe's declaration. What exactly happened after 11 July in Kongolo, aside from the skirmishes that occurred outside mission stations in the east of the territory, remains unclear to this day. What is certain is that at some point in late July or in early August, Balubakat activists began what the scholar Joshua Forrest describes as a movement for 'separatism-within-the-secession.'[87] What is more, British governmental documents from 1960 indicate that Sendwe had helped to mobilize a significant number of Balubakat militants and these fighters began to rebel against the Katangese state but crucially not the Leopoldville one.[88] Rather, in their struggle, Balubakat wanted to forcibly attach Tanganyika, including Kongolo, to the rest of the Congolese state but never wanted outright secession.

It would be a mistake to assume that an army of Balubakat militants instantly arose in Kongolo and elsewhere in Tanganyika. In fact, the Balubakat 'rebellion,' if an opposition against a state whose existence was not condoned by any other international states can be so called, got going slowly.[89] Likewise, Kongolo exhibited rather less Balubakat fervour than the Luba heartlands of Kabalo and Manono. Sources from the Great Lakes Railway Company (CFL) indicate that there were looting sprees being carried out in Kongolo's town centre but it was not at all clear who was responsible for these acts of violence and pillage. Likewise, the Company was nervous of those in the workers' camp in Kongolo who they identified as Luba. Aside from the skirmishes that broke out in Kongolo's town centre in August 1960, though, there is very little evidence of much violence during the immediate aftermath of independence nor of widespread mobilization on the part of Balubakat. This is not altogether unsurprising given that the majority of Jason Sendwe's supporters came from other provinces. It was Manono, and not Kongolo, which became the de facto capital of the Balubakat resistance even if, by September 1960, Tanganyika was still technically part of Tshombe's independent Katanga. In some ways, it was not surprising that the Lualaba Province was not based in Kongolo. As David Maxwell suggests, as opposed to the Congo Evangelistic Mission (CEM), who worked in the more central areas of Katanga, the Spiritans did not 'produce an extensive vernacular literature and sought to raise a French-speaking, cosmopolitan-minded Luba elite.' Much the same could be

said of the White Fathers.[90] Given that many territories to the south of
Kongolo were predominantly Luba, and they tended to have a great deal
more Protestant presence than Kongolo, the translation of Luba ethnicity into a political project could be achieved despite the more cosmopoli-
tan influences of the Catholic missionaries working in the region—even if
it was admittedly not entirely a linear process.

Conflict between Balubakat sympathisers and whose they considered
their enemies intensified in October 1960, when Luba activists officially
declared their allegiance to the Congolese state and their opposition
to the secession by starting to form the Lualaba Province.[91] Balubakat
had therefore taken control of much of Tanganyika and in doing so
had attempted to make incursions into the Hêmbá heartlands in eastern Kongolo. On 24 October, many Hêmbá houses had been set on
fire by Balubakat forces. And on 4 November, *L'Essor* printed an article authored by a group that claimed to be the 'Voice of the Hêmbá.'[92]
It suggested that should Balubakat forces continue to make incursions
into Hêmbá lands then Hêmbá militias would organize to repel them.
Even before this article went to press, the then Director of the CFL in
the Tanganyika province, Edouard Bruart, suggested that the Hêmbá
had already 'given the Luba a bloody nose.' So there was clear Hêmbá
support for Conakat in Kongolo and this was perceived as such by both
Conakat and their opponents.

Around November, Moïse Tshombe visited Kongolo and declared
that Balubakat were pursuing 'the politics of suicide.'[93] In many ways,
the Conakat President had a point. The methods through which
Balubakat governed the lands that its activists had so rapidly taken over
were, by all accounts, extremely violent. Given that they lacked the
arms that the Katangese army had, the most important weapon they
deployed in the northern Katangese Luba campaigns was arguably the
fear they inspired on the part of their enemies through rumous of the
gruesome punishments they meted out on them.[94] The journalist Smith
Hempstone, who travelled near to but not necessarily *into* Tanganyika
at this time, chronicled some of the Balubakat atrocities.[95] The idea of
Balubakat 'savagery' in particular subsequently took hold and Europeans
often contrasted it to the supposedly more targeted actions of the
Katangese army if they wanted to justify the secession.[96] Even acknowl-
edging the bias of the remaining evidence, though, it is clear that life was
particularly difficult for those living under Balubakat rule in late 1960.
Remembering that time, Ihunga Marcel looked at me during one of

our many interviews and said simply 'you must have fear, you must have fear.'[97] There were many reasons why Marcel said what he did to me. A large part of the reason why residents of Kongolo were afraid was because their daily habits became the object of constant suspicion. Alongside the Balubakat activists, who policed as much of Kongolo's infrastructure as they could, people had to be careful exactly what they said in the territory's bars.[98] Ihunga Marcel remembered having to watch what he said all the time. Likewise, he recalled how people who became indiscreet after a few drinks met with very grave consequences afterwards if they suggested they had ties to Tshombe's Elisabethville regime.[99] Ethnicity—and in particular language—also formed part of the ways in which Balubakat supporters attempted to identify their Conakat counterparts. For example, if one were to run into Balubakat militants crossing a bridge from eastern to western Congo you might have been asked pointed questions in the Luba language.[100] Failure to answer or, worse still, failure to even understand what was asked could result in an immediate and extra-judicial death sentence.

Viewed in this light, Balubakat activists seemed to be in the process of creating an ethno-polity, a Luba quasi-state, though still linked to the central state in Leopoldville (hence the *quasi* appellation). Ethnicity therefore appears to be the main driver of the violence behind what was happening in Kongolo in late 1960 but it was one of many factors that combined to accelerate the violence in Kongolo in 1960. For example, many Songye also joined Balubakat in their opposition to the secession much as the Bango Bango joined the Hêmbá in siding with Conakat. Likewise, language was only one of a range of ways in which loyalty to the Balubakat regime was tested. Aside from what people, Luba or otherwise, said in bars, if people living in Kongolo or elsewhere were caught with what were thought to have been western commodities then their lives were also in danger.[101] Balubakat militants believed that any commodities that were not native to northern Katanga were flown in from Elisabethville and therefore those who enjoyed them had a connection to Tshombe's nascent Katangese state. So, not only did people need to speak Luba to survive in increasingly large parts of Kongolo, but they also needed to ensure they were not seen with the wrong commodities. It is not surprising that the Church used many of the commodities the Balubakat troops identified as coming from Elisabethville, not least pencils, paper and even bottled beer, with this usage serving to underline what Balubakat later saw as its sympathy with the secession.[102]

The violent skirmishes between those who opposed the secession, and so supported Balubakat, and those who supported Conakat intensified as 1960 wore on and this began to have consequences for the Church in Kongolo. The White Fathers' mission diaries in particular increasingly began to tell a story of a group of Europeans who were not in control of their environment and who were repeatedly being asked to leave for their own safety by the Katangese army.[103] While they stayed as long as they could, the Sola diary ends abruptly in 1961 and it may be that it does not continue because many of the European White Fathers felt forced to leave or at least go to Belgium for a short time to avoid the worst violence at that point.[104] Likewise, the Spiritans diary from Kongolo town centre also runs out in 1961. This is not to say that the Spiritans left the territory; indeed many of the European Fathers stayed on.

Jean-Marie Godefroid, who had only arrived in Kongolo on 30 June 1960, said that he could carry on teaching in the minor Spiritan seminary 'as if nothing was happening.'[105] But soon afterwards it was clear that insecurity was intensifying. The question of whether or not the European Spiritan Fathers should leave only became more urgent as time went on and the violence intensified. For a period, it looked as though the Katangese army was on the ascendency and Jean-Marie Godefroid's assessment might have turned out to be right. Tshombe's army had taken territory, for example, and attempted to cut off northern Katanga's key lines of communication to Elisabethville. It had also begun to fight back against the Lualaba Province.[106] It had taken Tshombe and his administration some time to assemble an army capable of repelling the Balubakat forces but, by late 1960, this had finally happened.

Miles Larmer and Erik Kennes suggest that, much like the Balubakat forces, the Katangese army used very brutal tactics to ensure that northern Katanga was 'pacified.'[107] In fact, the violence got so bad that the UN, which had since entered the conflict, felt compelled to create 'neutral zones' on 17 October 1960.[108] Rather than a stepping stone to peace, though, both the Katangese army and Balubakat activists simply used this time to regroup. If the Lualaba Province was not officially declared by the Balubakat leadership in October 1960, then it was by the time that Patrice Lumumba was brutally assassinated on 17 January 1961.[109] This assassination enraged Balubakat activists who very reasonably blamed it on Tshombe's government. *The Economist* newspaper suggested that soon after Lumumba's assassination, on 21 January 1961, Lumubist troops declared the existence of the Lualaba Province with Manono as its capital.[110] Whatever the true date of the declaration of the Lualaba Province, what is clear is that Balubakat activists, and their young counterpart: Jabakat, intensified their violence after Patrice Lumumba's death.

Just as Balubakat were regrouping using the time that the UN peace keeping plans bought them, so had the Katangese army. At the beginning of 1961, Tshombe's forces launched three military successful operations, namely Banquise, Mambo and Lotus, 'which reduced the territory held by Balubakat.'[111] Only the rebel's stronghold of Kabalo remained under their control, which meant that Balubakat forces in Kongolo had also been reduced to near insignificance. This gave the Church in Kongolo at least some breathing space as, again, the Spiritans relied on the Katangese army to protect them from the increasingly anti-clerical Balubakat forces. One priest in particular, Jules Darmont, even worked as a chaplain for Tshombe's troops at this time.[112] Likewise, the White Fathers' Sola diaries reported that they were able to get supplies not only into their out-station in Bena Nkuvu but those across eastern Kongolo as the Katangese army launched their anti-Balubakat operations.[113]

As much as the summer of 1961 proved a time of relief for the Church in Kongolo as a whole, the troubled peace was altogether fleeting. National and international opinion turned rapidly against the secession towards the end of 1961. The main reason why the secession proved difficult to maintain in a national context was that Antoine Gizenga, who had formed a breakaway government in Stanleyville following Lumumba's death, had been placed under house arrest by Cyrille Adoula and so he was unable to maintain his breakaway Stanleyville province.[114] Gizenga's arrest therefore meant that Tshombe faced a national governmental opposition that was not simultaneously fighting Stanleyville for the first time since he declared independence. The Force Publique, now having Africanized its command and going under the name of the *Armée Nationale Congolaise* (ANC), rapidly mobilized whatever resources it could to stop the secession.

Outside of the Congo, the international community had been shocked by Patrice Lumumba's death and this outrage resulted in the UN passing Security Council Resolution 161 in February authorizing the use of force as a last resort to 'prevent the occurrence of civil war in the Congo.'[115] Driven on by their new mandate, and by the unification of the Leopoldville and Stanleyville governments, the UN launched a major operation to reintegrate the fragmented Congolese state. In April 1961, the UN began offensives in northern Katanga and by August it had expelled 338 'mercenaries' and 443 Belgian political 'advisors' who were essential to the day-to-day functioning of the Katangese state.[116] Later that year, the UN launched Operation Rumpunch with Operation Morthor following hot on its heels in September 1961.[117] Having 'succeeded in militarily defeating the Balubakat revolt, the Katangese army held out as much as they could against the UN onslaught' but their resources would only take them so far.[118]

Even as late as August-September, there were around 535 soldiers from the Katangese army stationed in Kongolo.[119] But the UN pressured these troops to leave the Congo if they were not from the country. By November 1961, the presence of the UN force meant that many of the Katangese army units, at least in Kongolo, began to leave. Along with the UN, the ANC was also beginning to mount a campaign against the Katangese army in Tanganyika by the end 1961. While they were leaving, the Katangese army made increasingly urgent appeals to the European priests working for both the White Fathers and the Spiritan missionaries to leave their mission fields and return to their homes.

As missionaries debated whether to stay or leave Kongolo in the winter of 1961, many Africans' minds were already made up and they began to flee in anticipation of a hostile ANC-Balubakat takeover. The refugees in question came from all across Kongolo and not just those Hêmbá on the right bank. What was so tragic for the missionaries was that many of these refugees were precisely those people they had trained in their out-stations, who now felt far too insecure to continue living in their homes. While some of the refugees took shelter in the Spiritan's mission facilities in Kongolo's town centre, many continued their journey out of the territory to get anywhere they felt that they would be safe. Jules Darmont's fear that everything his congregation had spent fifty years working towards would be eviscerated in a short space of time was beginning to become a reality.[120] By 1962, UN intervention put the Katangese army on the back foot once again and so they began to withdraw from the Tanganyika district. Soon after, the Lualaba Province reconquered lands from which it had been forced to retreat in 1961.

The Kongolo Massacre and the Post-Independence Church

Although a number of nationalist leaders, such as Jason Sendwe, advocated moderation in public, in practice their followers, particularly the Jebakat, simply ignored these pleas and occasionally did target priests and other European civilians in eastern Congo. Many European missionaries feared that they may be targeted by the Jebakat militias once the Katangese army had left. And their fears were well-founded. Many of those who had fought for the central state and the Lualaba/North Katanga province strongly identified the Church with Tshombe's secessionist regime and therefore believed that it needed to be expunged as quickly as possible. During the time, when the Katangese army had been able to shield them from the dangers of the Jabakat, missionaries had gone about their business as normal. Yet without the Katangese army to protect them, fears grew among the missionaries that they would be the subject of violence on the part of Jebakat activists.

One of the most important examples of violence directed against missionaries in the aftermath of independence affected the Spiritan missionaries working in the centre of Kongolo. By the time the Katangse army had left Kongolo in 1961, there were twenty Spiritan missionaries based in the seminary in the mission quarter of town. Some, such as Jules Darmont, had been there for over a decade, while others, such as Walter Gillijns, had only been there for a short amount of time. Gillijins had only arrived in Kongolo on Independence Day, for example.[121] The missionaries knew that they may be a target both of Jebakat as well as ANC activists who joined them to crush the Katangese secession. One of the most powerful demonstrations of the kind of violence the ANC meted out was the killing of a number of Italian airmen working for the UN in Kindu on 11 November 1961.[122] It is unclear exactly if this Massacre was ordered and, if so, who ordered it. Whatever the truth of the chain of command that day, it demonstrated explicitly to the Europeans still present in southeastern Congo that they could be the target of attacks no matter what their profession. The Spiritans and their sister order, The Sisters of the Immaculate Heart of Blessed Virgin Mary of Kongolo or 'CIMKO' for short, convened an extraordinary general meeting to address the question of what they should do.[123] The option of leaving was very unpopular with most of the missionaries given that their buildings were providing shelter for many of the refugees fleeing the violence of the ANC/Jebakat forces. Likewise, the Spiritans were reluctant to leave a place they had spent over fifty years working.

Mission hesitation to leave Kongolo, understandable though it was, was to prove fatal given that it meant that as the ANC/Jebakat forces entered Kongolo, the missionaries could do little else but sit tight and wait to see what would happen to them. There was no option of ordering a plane to take them out of Kongolo given that the Kongolo airstrip might be taken by the leftist forces at any moment. And if the missionaries decided to leave with the wave of refugees fleeing Kongolo, Father José Vandamme said that the remaining Spiritans 'will still be taken and be in the same dangerous position.'[124] So the Spiritans had to sit and eventually accept whatever fate awaited them. At 5.30 p.m. on 31 December 1961, ten militant nationalists burst into the Grand Seminary where the Spiritans were gathered.[125] After demanding to see their passports in the mistaken belief this might prove or disprove whether the missionaries were working for the Katangese army, the ANC/Jebakat forces took the missionaries to the military camp outside Kongolo.

It is unclear whether the militants who captured the missionaries wanted to kill them from the outset and it is more than likely that there was disagreement among them as to what course of action to take. One option was to try to get information out of the missionaries relating to the whereabouts and strategy of the Katangese army. However, other witnesses suggest that there was never a question of whether or not the militia intended to kill the priests.[126] It is very clear, however, that the missionaries were beaten and brutalized in a manner that reversed patterns of colonial violence because the infamous hippopotamus-hide whip, the *chicotte*, was used on Europeans as opposed to Africans. The next day, New Year's Day 1962, the Spiritans were taken one by one from their cells in the military camp and shot and killed on the banks of the Lualaba River. Worse still, at least two of the student Congolese seminarians, who had been dragged from the surrounding seminaries, were forced to dump the bodies of their co-religionists into the Lualaba River.[127]

Even today, it is not known who exactly was responsible for the violence. At first, the commander of the ANC forces, Victor Pakassa, was implicated. But Jules Darmont himself was very quick to exonerate the general from international suspicion saying that he could not imagine him killing priests. What is more, Pakassa rescued three confrères, André Remy, Maurice Seyssens and Jean-Louis Lambert, who were hiding in Lubunda.[128] Blame for the Massacre fell instead on wayward and largely intoxicated Jebakat soldiers. The narrative of young soldiers being responsible for the Massacre worked conveniently to exonerate those in the high command of the ANC, such as Laurent Kabila, who may themselves have faced awkward questions about the Massacre. And given that most of the Jebakat forces died during the period from 1960 to 1964, the excesses of the post-independent state could be pinned on the deceased rather than the living.

Widely condemned by politicians across the political spectrum, this episode later became known as the 'Kongolo Massacre.'[129] But general condemnation of the Massacre did not change the fact that a number of Church buildings in Kongolo had been gutted and—more important-ly—a lot of missionaries had been killed. Remarkably, though, the struc-tures of the buildings that Emilio Callewaert, Auguste Van Acker and other early Catholic pioneers had built remained intact. Darmont was only half right, therefore, when he said that all the work that had been done by the Church in fifty years in Kongolo would be destroyed. Not only were the physical buildings still intact after the ANC/Jebakat vio-lence, but many of the same missionaries were still alive even if they had had to flee to Belgium during the Katangese secession. Joseph De Jaeger, for example, continued to work in Kongolo for many years following the early 1960s.[130] De Jaeger called the Congo 'a boiling pot' during the 1960s yet wrote that he was prepared to die there if necessary.[131] Death was seldom far from De Jaeger during decolonization. In Kalemie on 11 November 1964, he saw Fathers Lenaerts and Stove killed in front of him.[132] And so it is easy to understand why De Jaeger did go on retreat to Belgium on occasion during the 'Congo Crisis.'

Even then, the Church still needed to take stock after such a pro-nounced period of violence and the trauma that this period of militancy had imposed. Much as elsewhere in the newly independent Congo, it relied in part on African clergy to support its reconstruction efforts. The most important figurehead in this regard was Monseigneur Jérôme Nday. Nday took over as the Spiritan Bishop of the then elevated Kongolo dio-cese on 16 January 1971 after his predecessor, Gustave Bouve, resigned his post citing the toll that the political tumult there had taken on him as the main reason.[133] Although the gap between the early 1960s and 1971 at first seems relatively large, in fact Bouve moved quickly to remove himself from most of the responsibilities involved in his post during the mid-1960s. In a letter that resembled Tennyson's *Ulysses*, he wrote to the Prefect of the Propaganda Fide in 1966 saying that: 'There is no longer that momentum of the past which would be necessary amidst the present difficulties, after five years of troubles and rebellions, to reconstruct and reorganize the diocese.'[134] He thus wanted to be relieved of a number of duties, namely, first, his regular visits to congregations dotted around the vast Kongolo diocese; secondly, his training of young Christians; and, finally, the administration of the sacrament.[135] So while the Kongolo diocese was nominally under European rule until 1971, in fact much of the daily administration was already being carried out by Africans after 1966. Even as early as 1964, Nday was one of the only priests actually left in Kongolo given the troubles that had overtaken the territory during the tenure of the First Republic.[136]

CONCLUSION

It has now become commonplace to remark on the importance of the Church's spat with the state during the late 1950s as helping to trigger decolonization. Yet few scholars have set this significant institutional debate into the wider history of Church–state relations in southeastern Belgian Congo. Setting the 'School Wars,' as Patrick Boyle calls them, and their ramifications into a longer historical context—both local and national—serves once again to highlight just how contingent the close relationship between Church and state in the late colonial period actually was and how much effort had to go into holding this fragile alliance together. As old conflicts, such as those between a theological or vocational education, resurfaced, the colonial trinity unravelled in the face of a rapidly industrializing colony.

But emphasizing the 'School Wars' at the same time as suggesting that the Church and the state were identified by many African nationalists as one and the same thing is to a great degree to identify a paradox. How could the Church be both the enemy of the colonial administration while at the same time as being identified so closely with it? It is precisely this paradox that this chapter—as well as the previous one—has sought to interrogate and the focus on the local milieu is at the core of the answer here. The fierce 'School Wars' were in many ways a phenomenon confined to urban areas, whether to Brussels in Belgium or to cities in the Congo such as Leopoldville. In Kongolo, missionaries continued to dominate the educational sphere much as they had done before the 'School Wars' broke out. Local disagreements over the poor state of some of the mission schools in Kongolo, while indicative of an uneasy collaboration, did not produce the stark Church-state division that the 'School Wars' did. As such, a close relationship between the Church and the state in the late colonial period, furthermore, was all that most young Africans knew if they had been born in the 1940s. And young Africans were precisely those who filled the ranks of the Jebakat militias—even if not many of them actually came from Kongolo. To be sure, vocational colleges emerged, even in Kongolo, but these in no way carried the same level of prestige nor commanded the same widespread popularity as the Catholic schools in Lubunda, Kongolo or Sola did. At a local level, therefore, not much appeared to change in the local context in terms of the Church–state relationship in the late 1950s.

Yet decolonization presented the Church with an immediate crisis that it ultimately took decades to resolve at least in the context of Kongolo. To understand the depth and significance of this watershed, it is instructive to reflect on the early history of the Church–state relationship. After the rancour of the early colonial period, Roelens, Callewaert and Bouve, for example, had begun to work within the framework of Belgian rule even if they hated some of the legislative imperatives they felt were imposed upon them and their congregations. It is true that Urbain Morlion of the White Fathers and Gustave Bouve of the Spiritans, who steered the Church during decolonization, faced a similar challenge to Victor Roelens and Emile Callewaert. Neither knew, for example, exactly what kind of state would emerge during the time that they led the Church in southeastern Congo. But unlike Roelens and Callewaert, the rules of the game were far less clear given that who would ultimately end up in charge of the Congo seemed to change on a near monthly basis.

The violent political oscillations between capitalist and communist regimes, which was only accelerated by the Cold War context, meant that how exactly the Church—and European missionaries in particular—should adapt was distinctly unclear. As Chris Bayly suggested, for example, the 'vicissitudes of Lumumba's rule in the Congo were part of [an] international struggle' between the capitalist US and the Communist USSR.[137] Both superpowers weighed into the political situation in the Congo and exacerbated tensions, with Nikita Khrushchev providing military equipment to Lumumba's government and the US, conversely, actively plotting to eliminate the late first Congolese Prime Minister and his government.[138] There was no clear sense, therefore, of what kind of state missionaries during the late 1950s or early 1960s should have been adapting to. From the few remaining sources pertaining to this turbulent time, the Church pinned its hopes on the Katangese secession protecting them from the Lumumbist tidal wave that was crashing down over eastern Congo. As Tshombe's regime was increasingly pushed back in 1962, though, the Church leadership struggled to find an alternative. But it is key to point out that the Church did remain in the Congo as the Belgian administration left. The fact the Church stayed on is demonstrative of the contingency of their relationship with the colonial state and in a local context. The Church was a competitive collaborator with the state and so not bound to it come what may, despite the protection that the Belgian administration occasionally offered it.

In many ways, this chapter has conformed to a familiar—if potentially peculiarly dramatic—narrative of the Catholic Church struggling to cope with decolonization.[139] Likewise, the fact that the Church felt threatened by Lumumbist nationalist forces is perhaps hardly surprising. Where this chapter has added to the literature, though, is by placing the Church–state relationship in the context of the Katangese secession. As its history in Katanga suggests, the Church was not opposed to African nationalism *tout court* and there is every indication that it could have accommodated the independent Katangese state. It could even have worked with a more moderate state governed by Joseph Ileo or Cyrille Adoula, who succeeded Lumumba as Prime Ministers of the Congo. And even the most hardened left-leaning nationalists, such as Victor Pakassa, worked to save European missionaries. So, there was nothing inevitable about the Kindu or Kongolo Massacres. Likewise, as David Maxwell suggests, the Church led the way in terms of Africanizing its hierarchy.[140] Jérôme Nday might not have been promoted to being a bishop until the 1970s, but he enjoyed a particularly privileged status in Kongolo during decolonization given that Bouve frequently went to Belgium to recover from the events that had befallen the Spiritan congregation. Instead of the Church's failure to adapt to decolonization, its successful resilience to a range of competing groups during the early 1960s would be what would eventually bring it once again in conflict with the Congolese state. The Church often stood firm in its competition against Joseph Mobutu's cult of personality, for example, and in particular the presence of Catholic schools undermined Mobutu's plan to achieve cultural hegemony over the Congolese peoples. The presence and political influence the Church has enjoyed in the post-colonial Congo is, of course, though, due to a wide range of factors that are beyond the scope of this book to explore. But the fact that the Church saw itself as operating independently from Belgian rule during its tenure in the Congo, while at the same time competitively collaborating with it during the early twentieth century, allowed it to stay on after 1960 and renew its commitment to continue the work that Roelens and Callewaert had started all those years ago.

NOTES

1. Thomas Hodgkin, *Nationalism in Colonial Africa* (London, 1956), p. 18, quoted from Kate Skinner, *The Fruits of Freedom* (Cambridge: Cambridge University Press, 2016), p. 17.
2. Interview with Kibondo Katumbo, Kongolo town centre, 24 April 2009.
3. Frederick Cooper, *The Past of the Present: Africa Since 1940* (Cambridge: Cambridge University Press, 2002), p. 164.
4. Jean-Phillipe Peemans, 'Imperial Hangovers: The Economics of Decolonisation,' *Journal of Contemporary History* 15 (1980), pp. 257–286.
5. Peemans, 'Imperial Hangovers,' p. 270; Jean-Luc Vellut, 'La Belgique et la Préparation de L'indépendance du Congo,' in *La Belgique et L'Afrique Centrale: De 1960 á Nos Jours*, Olivier Lanotte, Claude Roosens, and Caty Clement (eds) (Bruxelles, 2000), p. 85.
6. Patrick M. Boyle, 'School Wars: Church, State, and the Death of the Congo,' *The Journal of Modern African Studies*, 33, 3 (1995), p. 458.
7. Ibid., p. 459.
8. Ibid., p. 460.
9. Ibid.
10. Ibid., p. 461.
11. Ibid.
12. Ibid., p. 462.
13. Ibid.
14. Peemans, 'Imperial Hangovers,' p. 270.
15. Boyle, 'School Wars,' p. 463.
16. Peemans, 'Imperial Hangovers,' pp. 270–271.
17. Ibid., p. 269.
18. Even many Europeans thought that 'Jeff' Bilsen's plan was pure fantasy, see: Theodore Trefon, 'The Political Economy of Sacrifice: Kinois and the State,' *Review of African Political Economy*, 29, 93–94 (2002), pp. 481–498.
19. M. Crawford Young, 'Background to Independence,' *Transition*, 25 (1966), pp. 34–40.
20. Marjory Taylor, 'The Belgian Congo Today: Background to the Leopoldville Riots,' *The World Today*, 15, 9 (1959), pp. 351–364.
21. Martin Thomas, Bob Moore, and L. J. Butler, *Crisis of Empire: Decolonization and Europe's Imperial States* (London: Bloomsbury, 2015).
22. Theodore Trefon, *Reinventing Order in the Congo: How People Respond to State Failure in Kinshasa* (London: Zed Books, 2004), p. 137.
23. Nzongola-Ntalaja, *The Congo*, p. 85.
24. Daniel Branch, *Defeating Mau Mau, Creating Kenya: Counterinsurgency, Civil War and Decolonization* (Cambridge: Cambridge University Press, 2009); Rabah Aissaoui and Claire Eldridge (eds), *Algeria Revisited: History, Culture and Identity* (London: Bloomsbury, 2017).

25. Herbert Weiss, 'The Congo's Independence Struggle Viewed Fifty Years Later,' *African Studies Review*, 55, 1 (2012), p. 112.

26. Nzongola-Ntalaja, *The Congo: From Leopold to Kabila*, p. 86; Leo Zeilig, *Patrice Lumumba: Africa's Lost Leader* (London: HopeRoad, 2012), p. 76.

27. Weiss, 'The Congo's Independence Struggle Viewed Fifty Years Later,' p. 113.

28. Georges Nzongola-Ntalaja, *Patrice Lumumba* (Athens: Ohio University Press, 2014).

29. Zeilig, *Lumumba*.

30. For an example of a Lumumba hagiography, see: Zeilig, *Patrice Lumumba*. Some scholars have focused on the local elections at this time, though, see: Erik Kennes and Miles Larmer, *The Katangese Gendarmes in Central Africa: Fighting Their Way Home* (Bloomington: Indiana University Press, 2016), p. 40.

31. Omasombo et al., *Tanganyika*, p. 210. Omasombo has Benoit Tambwe Abati as working for a party that was not Conakat during the independence era but from my interviews with him this seems to be wrong, he was in fact a Conakat activist.

32. Lemarchand, *Political Awakening in the Congo*, pp. 72–73.

33. Kennes and Larmer, *The Katangese Gendarmes in Central Africa: Fighting Their Way Home*, p. 158.

34. Jewsiewicki, 'The Formation of the Political Culture of Ethnicity in the Belgian Congo, 1920–1959,' p. 333.

35. Young, *Politics in Congo*, p. 493.

36. 'Sendwe' means an artisan or a man of merit in Kiluba, see: Van Avermaet et Benoît Mbuyà, *Dictionnaire Kiluba-Français*, p. 591.

37. Young, *Politics in Congo*, p. 493.

38. Kennes and Larmer, *The Katangese Gendarmes in Central Africa: Fighting Their Way Home*, p. 53.

39. Sendwe warned against the secession of Katanga saying on 24 December 1959 that 'the Congo does not want to be mutilated,' see: Jules Gérard-Libois, *Katanga Secession* (Madison: University of Wisconsin Press, 1966), p. 306.

40. Kennes and Larmer, *The Katangese Gendarmes in Central Africa: Fighting Their Way Home*, p. 37.

41. Ibid., p. 39.

42. Bogumil Jewsiewicki, 'Le Colonat Agricole Européen au Congo Belge, 1910–1960: Questions Politiques et Economiques,' *The Journal of African History*, 20 (1979), p. 564.

43. *L'Essor du Congo*, 'Le Conakat Reçoit les Chefs Coutumières,' 2 novembre 1959, p. 2; *L'Essor du Congo*, décembre 1959, 'Les Elections au Katanga,' p. 11.

44. Nzongola-Ntalaja, *The Congo: A Peoples' History*, p. 98.
45. Archives Générales de la Société des Missionnaires de l'Afrique, Rome (AGM), Diaries, Sola, July 1960, p. 980.
46. Josiah Brownell, 'Diplomatic Lepers: The Katangan and Rhodesian Foreign Missions in the United States and the Politics of Non-recognition,' *International Journal of African Historical Studies*, 47, 2 (2014), p. 209.
47. Alan James, *Britain and the Congo Crisis, 1960–1963* (London: Springer, 1996); Kevin A. Spooner, *Canada, the Congo Crisis, and UN Peacekeeping, 1960–1964* (Toronto: UBC Press, 2009).
48. Interview with Kilonda Kisangani Komombo Sylvestre, Lubumbashi, 24 March 2009.
49. Young, *Politics in Congo*, p. 96.
50. Interview with Muhiya Musafiri, Klubwe Quarter, Lubumbashi, 24 May 2009
51. David N. Gibbs, *The Political Economy of Third World Intervention: Mines, Money and US Policy in the Congo Crisis* (Chicago: University of Chicago Press, 1991), p. 84.
52. Interview with Tambwe Benoit Abati, Mampala, Lubumbashi, 1 April 2009.
53. Ibid.
54. Ibid.
55. Simon Katzenellenbogen, *Railways and the Copper Mines of Katanga* (Oxford: Clarendon Press, 1973), p. 28.
56. Interview with Tambwe Benoit Abati, Mampala, Lubumbashi, 1 April 2009.
57. R. C. van Caenegem, *An Historical Introduction to Western Constitutional Law* (Cambridge: Cambridge University Press, 1995), p. 198.
58. Kennes and Larmer, *The Katangese Gendarmes in Central Africa: Fighting Their Way Home*, p. 24.
59. Interview with Tambwe Benoit Abati, Mampala, Lubumbashi, 1 April 2009.
60. Ibid.
61. William Roger Louis, *Ruanda-Urundi, 1884–1914* (Oxford: Clarendon Press, 1963).
62. Interview with Tambwe Benoit Abati, Mampala, Lubumbashi, 1 April 2009.
63. Interview with Kilonda Kisangani Sylvestre, Bel-Air, Lubumbashi, 24 March 2009.
64. Omasombo et al., *Tanganyika*, p. 210.
65. Ibid.
66. Ibid.

67 David Maxwell, 'The Creation of Lubaland: Missionary Science and Christian Literacy in the Making of the Luba Katanga in Belgian Congo,' *Journal of Eastern African Studies*, 10, 3 (2016), pp. 367–392.

68. Young, *Politics in Congo*, p. 263.

69. Jacques, *Lualaba*.

70. AGM, Journal de la Communauté, 1954–1960, p. 913.

71. Ibid.

72. Ibid.

73. Ibid., p. 944.

74. Ibid., p. 954.

75. Ibid.

76. Ibid., p. 940.

77. Ibid., p. 903.

78. Ibid., p. 916.

79. Ibid., p. 974.

80. Ibid.

81. John Lonsdale and Bruce Berman, *Unhappy Valley: Conflict in Kenya and Africa, Book Two: Violence and Ethnicity* (Oxford: James Currey, 1992), p. 466.

82. Interview with Tambwe Benoit Abati, Mampala, Lubumbashi, 1 April 2009.

83. Interview with Ihunga Mundaza Marcel, Kongolo Mission Quarter, 10 April 2009.

84. Ibid.

85. Interview with Kilonda Kisangani Sylvestre, Bel Air, Lubumbashi, 24 March 2009.

86. Kennes and Larmer, *The Katangese Gendarmes in Central Africa: Fighting Their Way Home*, p. 44.

87. Joshua Forrest, *Subnationalism in Africa: Ethnicity, Alliances, and Politics* (London: Lynne Rienner Publishers, 2004), p. 111.

88. The National Archives, Kew (TNA), Foreign Office (FO), 37/146650/1015/400, Jason Sendwe, Leader of the Katanga Opposition to Mr. Tshombe, 1960.

89. Emmanuel Gerard and Bruce Kuklick, *Death in Congo: Murdering Patrice Lumumba* (Harvard: Harvard University Press, 2015), p. 132.

90 David Maxwell, 'The Creation of Lubaland: Missionary Science and Christian Literacy in the Making of the Luba Katanga in Belgian Congo,' *Journal of Eastern African Studies*, 10, 3 (2016), p. 382.

91. Kennes and Larmer, *The Katangese Gendarmes in Central Africa: Fighting Their Way Home*, p. 48.

92. *L'Essor du Congo*, 4 novembre 1960, 'La Voix du Bahemba du Katanga: Ultimatum aux Baluba,' 33: 204, p. 6.

93. *L'Essor du Congo*, 1960, 'M. Tshombe Fait une Importante déclaration á la Suite de son Voyage au Nord du Katanga,' 33: 217, p. 1.

94. Kennes and Larmer, *The Katangese Gendarmes in Central Africa: Fighting Their Way Home*, p. 48.

95. Smith Hempstone, *Katanga Report* (London: Faber, 1962).

96. Ibid.

97. Interview with Ihunga Mundaza Marcel, Kongolo Mission Quarter, 10 April 2009.

98. Ibid.

99. Ibid.

100. Ibid.

101. Ibid.

102. Anti-Catholicism was prevalent among many left-leaning groups during the early 1960s, for example Pierre Mulele, who was Minister for Education in 1961, wanted to nationalise the Catholic schools that had been constructed in the colonial period, see: Kennes and Larmer, *The Katangese Gendarmes in Central Africa: Fighting Their Way Home*, p. 49.

103. AGM, Bruges-Saint-Donat Diaries, July 1960, p. 982.

104. AGM, Bruges-Saint-Donat Diaries, January 1961.

105. 'RP Jean-Marie Godefroid,' online at: http://spiritains.forums.free.fr/defunts/godefreu.htm (consulted on 20 October 2015).

106. Kennes and Larmer, *The Katangese Gendarmes in Central Africa: Fighting Their Way Home*, p. 48.

107. Ibid.

108. Conor Cruise O'Brien, *To Katanga and Back: A UN Case History* (London: Faber and Faber, 2011), p. 122.

109. Donatien Dibwe dia Mwembu, 'L'Epuration Ethnique au Katanga et l'Ethnique du Redressement des Torts du Passé,' *Canadian Journal of African Studies*, 33 (1999), p. 488.

110. *The Economist*, 'The Black Man's Burden: Events in the Congo Move on, Presenting the West with a Challenge Which It Has yet to Find a Way of Facing,' 21 January 2916, p. 229.

111. Kennes and Larmer, *The Katangese Gendarmes in Central Africa: Fighting Their Way Home*, p. 49.

112. P. Jules Darmont, online at: http://users.skynet.be/kongolo/MASSATEM08.htm (consulted on 6 November 2015).

113. AGM, Journal de la Communauté, 1954–1960, p. 1003.

114. Jean Mpisi, *Antoine Gizenga: Le Combat de l'Hériter de Lumumba* (Paris: L'Harmattan, 2008), p. 13.

115. Kennes and Larmer, *The Katangese Gendarmes in Central Africa: Fighting Their Way Home*, pp. 50–51.

116. Ibid., p. 51.

117. O'Brien, *To Katanga and Back*, p. 139.
118. Kennes and Larmer, *The Katangese Gendarmes in Central Africa: Fighting Their Way Home*, p. 56.
119. Ibid.
120. Jules Darmont, 'Les Évènements du 1 Janvier 1962' (consulted on 6 April 2015).
121. Reuben Loffman, 'Same Memory, Different Memorials: The Holy Ghost Fathers (Spiritans), Martyrdom and the Kongolo Massacre,' *Social Sciences and Missions*, 31 (2018), p. 11.
122. Ibid., p. 13.
123. Ibid., p. 14.
124. Ibid., p. 15.
125. Ibid., p. 16.
126. Ibid., p. 17.
127. Ibid.
128. Ibid.
129. Bernard Slevin, *The Kongolo Massacre: The Supreme Achievement* (Bickley: Paraclete Press, 1962).
130. AGM, *Petit Écho des Missions d'Afrique (P.B.)*, 'Nos Defunts: Père Joseph De Jaeger, 1919–1997,' 86, 892 (1998), pp. 297–300.
131. Ibid., p. 297.
132. Ibid.
133. Catholic Hierarchy, 'Kongolo,' available at: http://www.catholic-hierarchy.org/diocese/dkngl.html [accessed 12 February 2017]. Olivier Nkulu Kabamba, *Monseigneur Nday Jérôme: Kongolo et les Spiritans* (Louvain-la-Neuve: L'Harmattan, 2015).
134. CSSp, Monseigneur Gustave Bouve, Lettre á le Cardinal-Préfet de la Sacrée Congrégation 'di Propaganda Fide,' le 26 décembre 1966, p. 1.
135. CSSp, Gustave Bouve, Lettre á le Cardinal-Préfet de la Sacrée Congrégation 'di Propaganda Fide,' p. 1.
136. Kabamba, *Monseigneur Nday Jérôme*, p. 51.
137. C. A. Bayly, Remaking the Modern World 1900–2015: Global Connections and Comparisons (London: Wiley-Blackwell, 2018), p. 145.
138. Sergei Mazov, Soviet Aid to the Gizenga Goverment in the Former Belgian Congo (1960–1961) as Reflected in Russian Archives, 7, 3 (2007), p. 428.
139. David Maxwell, 'Decolonisation,' in Norman Etherington (ed.), *Missions and Empire* (Oxford: Oxford University Press, 2005), p. 287.
140. Ibid., p. 292.

BIBLIOGRAPHY

Aissaoui, Rabah, and Eldridge, Claire (eds), *Algeria Revisited: History, Culture and Identity* (London: Bloomsbury, 2017).

Balandier, *Sociologie de Brazzaville Noire* (Paris: A. Colin, 1955).

Bayly, C.A. 2018. *Remaking the Modern World 1900–2015: Global Connections and Comparisons*, 145. London: Wiley-Blackwell.

Boyle, Patrick M., 'School Wars: Church, State, and the Death of the Congo,' *The Journal of Modern African Studies*, 33, 3 (1995), pp. 451–468.

Branch, Daniel, *Defeating Mau Mau, Creating Kenya: Counterinsurgency, Civil War and Decolonization* (Cambridge: Cambridge University Press, 2009).

Brownell, Josiah, 'Diplomatic Lepers: The Katangan and Rhodesian Foreign Missions in the United States and the Politics of Non-recognition,' *International Journal of African Historical Studies*, 47, 2 (2014), pp. 209–237.

Caenegem, R. C. van, *An Historical Introduction to Western Constitutional Law* (Cambridge: Cambridge University Press, 1995).

Catholic Hierarchy, 'Kongolo,' available at: http://www.catholic-hierarchy.org/diocese/dkngl.html [accessed 12 February 2017].

Cooper, Frederick, *The Past of the Present: Africa Since 1940* (Cambridge: Cambridge University Press, 2002).

Edgerton, Robert, *The Troubled Heart of Africa: A History of the Congo* (London: Palgrave Macmillan, 2002).

Fabian, Johannes, *Language and Colonial Power: The Appropriation of Swahili in the Former Belgian Congo, 1880–1938* (Berkeley: University of California Press, 1991).

Fanon, Frantz, *The Wretched of the Earth. Translated from the French by Richard Philcox with Commentary by Jean-Paul Sartre and Homi Bhabha* (New York: Grove Press, 1963).

Forrest, Joshua, *Subnationalism in Africa: Ethnicity, Alliances, and Politics* (London: Lynne Rienner Publishers, 2004).

Gerard, Emmanuel, and Kuklick, Bruce, *Death in Congo: Murdering Patrice Lumumba* (Harvard: Harvard University Press, 2015).

Gérard-Libois, Jules, *Katanga Secession* (Madison: University of Wisconsin Press, 1966).

Gérard-Libois, Jules, and Verhaegen, Benoit, *Congo 1964: Political Documents of a Developing Nation* (Princeton: Princeton University Press, 2015).

Gérard-Libois, Jules, and Verhaegen, Benoit, *Congo 1965: Political Documents of a Developing Nation* (Princeton: Princeton University Press, 2015).

Gibbs, David N., *The Political Economy of Third World Intervention: Mines, Money and US Policy in the Congo Crisis* (Chicago: University of Chicago Press, 1991).

Gondola, Ch. Didier, *The History of Congo* (Washington, DC: Greenwood Publishing Group, 2002).

Hempstone, Smith, *Katanga Report* (London: Faber, 1962).

Hodgkin, Thomas, *Nationalism in Colonial Africa* (London, 1956).

Jacques, Gérard, *Lualaba: Histoires de l'Afrique Profonde* (Bruxelles: Éditions Racine, 1995).

James, Alan, *Britain and the Congo Crisis, 1960–1963* (London: Springer, 1996).

Jewsiewicki, Bogumil, 'Le Colonat Agricole Européen au Congo Belge, 1910–1960: Questions Politiques et Economiques,' *The Journal of African History*, 20 (1979), pp. 559–571.

Jewsiewicki, Bogumil, 'The Formation of the Political Culture of Ethnicity in the Belgian Congo, 1920–1959,' in Leroy Vail (ed.), *The Creation of Tribalism in Southern Africa* (Berkeley: University of California Press, 1989), pp. 324–349.

Kabamba, Olivier Nkulu, *Monseigneur Nday Jérôme: Kongolo et les Spiritans* (Louvain-la-Neuve: L'Harmattan, 2015).

Katzenellenbogen, Simon, *Railways and the Copper Mines of Katanga* (Oxford: Clarendon Press, 1973).

Kennes, Erik (en collaboration avec Munkana N'Ge), *Essai Biographique sur Laurent Désiré Kabila* (Tervuren, Institut Africain-CEDAF, 2003).

Kennes, Erik, and Larmer, Miles, *The Katangese Gendarmes in Central Africa: Fighting Their Way Home* (Bloomington: Indiana University Press, 2016).

Kisangani, Emizet F., *Civil Wars in the Democratic Republic of the Congo, 1960–2010* (London: Lynne Rienner Publishers, 2012).

Lemarchand, René, *Political Awakening in the Congo* (Berkeley: University of California Press, 1964).

Loffman, Reuben, 'An Obscured Revolution? USAID, The North Shaba Project and the Zaïrian Administration, 1976–1986,' *Canadian Journal of African Studies*, 48, 3 (2014), pp. 425–444.

Loffman, Reuben, 'Same Memory, Different Memorials: The Holy Ghost Fathers (Spiritans), Martyrdom and the Kongolo Massacre,' *Social Sciences and Missions*, 31, 3–4 (2018), pp. 217–250.

Lonsdale, John, and Berman, Bruce, *Unhappy Valley: Conflict in Kenya and Africa, Book Two: Violence and Ethnicity* (Oxford: James Currey, 1992).

Louis, William Roger, *Ruanda-Urundi, 1884–1914* (Oxford: Clarendon Press, 1963).

Lovell, Bill (ed.), 'History in Pictures of United Methodist Missionaries and Congolese Leaders Who Worked to Build the United Methodist Church in Central Congo,' available at: https://www.scribd.com/doc/167701380/100th-Anniversary-of-United-Methodism-in-Central-Congo-1912-Present [accessed 13 July 2017].

Maxwell, David, 'Decolonisation,' in Norman Etherington (ed.), *Missions and Empire* (Oxford: Oxford University Press, 2005), pp. 285–306.

Maxwell, David, 'The Creation of Lubaland: Missionary Science and Christian Literacy in the Making of the Luba Katanga in Belgian Congo,' *Journal of Eastern African Studies*, 10, 3 (2016), pp. 367–392.

Mazov, Sergei. 2007. Soviet Aid to the Gizenga Goverment in the Former Belgian Congo (1960–1961) as Reflected in Russian. *Archives* 7 (3): 428.

Mpisi, Jean, *Antoine Gizenga: Le Combat de l'Hériter de Lumumba* (Paris: L'Harmattan, 2008).

Mudimbe, Valentine Yves, *The Idea of Africa* (Oxford: James Currey, 1994).

Mwembu, Donatien Dibwe dia, 'L'Epuration Ethnique au Katanga et l'Ethnique du Redressement des Torts du Passé,' *Canadian Journal of African Studies*, 33 (1999), pp. 483–499.

Nzongola-Ntalaja, Georges, *The Congo: From Leopold to Kabila: A Peoples' History* (London: Zed Books, 2002).

Nzongola-Ntalaja, Georges, *Patrice Lumumba* (Athens: Ohio University Press, 2014).

O'Brien, Conor Cruise, *To Katanga and Back: A UN Case History* (London: Faber and Faber, 2011).

Omasombo, Jean, Kisonga Kasyulwe, Désiré, Léonard, Guillaume, Zana, Mathieu, Simons, Edwine, Krawczyk, Joris, and Laghmouch, Mohamed, *Tanganyika: Espace Fécondé Par Le Lac et Le Rail* (Tervuren: Musée Royale de l'Afrique Centrale, 2014).

Peemans, Jean-Phillipe, 'Imperial Hangovers: The Economics of Decolonisation,' *Journal of Contemporary History* 15 (1980), pp. 257–286.

Skinner, Kate, *The Fruits of Freedom* (Cambridge: Cambridge University Press, 2016).

Slevin, Bernard, *The Kongolo Massacre: The Supreme Achievement* (Bickley: Paraclete Press, 1962).

Spear, Thomas, 'Neo-traditionalism and the Limits of Invention in British Colonial Africa,' *The Journal of African History*, 44, 1 (2003), pp. 3–27.

Spooner, Kevin A., *Canada, the Congo Crisis, and UN Peacekeeping, 1960–1964* (Toronto: UBC Press, 2009).

Spritians, 'P. Jules Darmont,' online at: http://users.skynet.be/kongolo/MASSATEM08.htm (consulted on 6 November 2015).

Spiritans, 'RP Jean-Marie Godefroid,' online at: http://spiritains.forums.free.fr/defunts/godefreu.htm (consulted on 20 October 2015).

Taylor, Marjory, 'The Belgian Congo Today: Background to the Leopoldville Riots,' *The World Today*, 15, 9 (1959), pp. 351–364.

The Economist, 'The Black Man's Burden: Events in the Congo Move On, Presenting the West with a Challenge Which It Has yet to Find a Way of Facing,' 21 January 2916, p. 229.

Thomas, Martin, Moore, Bob, and Butler, L. J., *Crisis of Empire: Decolonization and Europe's Imperial States* (London: Bloomsbury, 2015).

Trefon, Theodore, 'The Political Economy of Sacrifice: Kinois and the State,' *Review of African Political Economy*, 29, 93–94 (2002), pp. 481–498.

Trefon, Theodore, *Reinventing Order in the Congo: How People Respond to State Failure in Kinshasa* (London: Zed Books, 2004).

Van Avermaet et Benoît Mbuyà, *Dictionnaire Kiluba-Français: Exposant le Vocabulaire de la Langue Kiluba tell qu'elle se Parle au Katanga* (Bruxelles: Ministère des Colonies de Belgique, 1909).

Vellut, Jean-Luc, 'La Belgique et la Préparation de L'indépendance du Congo,' in *La Belgique et L'Afrique Centrale: De 1960 á Nos Jours*, Olivier Lanotte, Claude Roosens, and Caty Clement (eds) (Bruxelles, 2000).

Weiss, Herbert, 'The Congo's Independence Struggle Viewed Fifty Years Later,' *African Studies Review*, 55, 1 (2012), pp. 109–115.

Young, Crawford M., *Politics in Congo: Decolonization and Independence* (Princeton: Princeton University Press, 1965).

Young, Crawford M., 'Background to Independence,' *Transition*, 25 (1966), pp. 34–40.

Zeilig, Leo, *Patrice Lumumba: Africa's Lost Leader* (London: HopeRoad, 2012).

CHAPTER 8

Conclusion

This book has challenged the conventional 'seamless' model of Church–state corporation in the Belgian Congo that scholars such as Crawford Young and Wamu Oyatambwe advanced.[1] More recently, David Van Reybrouck was more ambiguous than above authors, describing the Church–state relationship as simply 'mammoth' to indicate that it was important. But his observation does not do justice to the complexities that sustained it in the Congo and, in the end, which shattered it.[2] Rather than being content merely with the observation that the Church–state relationship was important or indeed with adopting Young and Oyatambwe's seamless model of Church–state relations, this book has instead advocated a model of *competitive co-dependency*. It has argued that the Church harboured state-like ambitions in the proto-colonial period that, even when these gradually faded in the 1920s and the 1930s, meant that missionaries believed they had the authority to interfere in chiefly politics in a way that frequently overshadowed what David Northrup described as its secular protectors.[3] This is not to overturn the general perception of close Church–state in the context of Belgian rule. Rather, it is to suggest that, when properly scrutinized, there were serious disagreements at times between the two institutions—both at the metropolitan and local levels—that gave rise to important patterns of historical change and continuity in southeastern Congo. The Church-state relationship in the Belgian Congo was at some remove from the extremely close relationship Catholic

© The Author(s) 2019   259
R. A. Loffman, *Church, State and Colonialism in Southeastern Congo,*
1890–1962, Cambridge Imperial and Post-Colonial Studies Series,
https://doi.org/10.1007/978-3-030-17380-7_8

missionaries with the state in the Portuguese colony of Angola during the early modern period, for example.

For most of its time in the Belgian Congo, the Church held the upper hand in the competitive collaboration it entered into with the state and its allies in southeastern Congo. Although the colonial state and industrial concessions, for example, acted unilaterally and in transformative ways on occasion, notably in its pursuit of PI projects, they rarely boasted enough staff or even political will to alter Church practice in Kongolo. The Church's ability to pursue conversion irrespective of state restrictions was great and particularly visible in the cracks in the state's system of indirect rule as Nancy Rose-Hunt suggests.[4] The most visible demonstration of Church power was in the built environment or the out-stations it was able to construct in towns such as Sola and Makutano, which dwarfed the territorial administration's own meagre construction efforts. Thereafter, the Church began to project its influence through a network of schools, pharmacies and maternity wards. Missionaries also interfered with chiefly politics even in the more direct version of Belgian colonial governance, such as in Bena Mambwe and Bena Nyembo in the 1930s. The Belgian regime's new men, Riscasi Katore and Kalama Sindano, for example, found that the violence that they had imposed on their domains ran contrary to the moral economy of the Catholic White Fathers' vision of chieftainship. So, despite the territorial administration's initial reluctance to do so, the missionaries successfully lobbied the colonial administration to de-throne them.

The significant extent of Church influence over the colonial construction of chieftainship can be explained in the first instance by the fact that state officials and their commercial allies had neglected Kongolo during the crucially important initial phase of proto-colonial expansion. Victor Roelens had sought a Christian 'republic' and although he did not get this he and his missionaries were able to enjoy considerable political power during the proto-colonial period. Furthermore, during the turn of the century period, the colonial administration had given the Church the chance to establish an enormous infrastructure not just in Kongolo but in Tanganyika as a whole. At times, such as the 1920s, Church policies competed directly with and disrupted the state's plans. Aside from the demission of Katore and Sindano, there were numerous other examples of such concessions, such as the chief of Wangongwe being deprived of land on account of the Church's desire to build on it instead. Likewise, of all the continuities involved in the history of Kongolo from the pre-colonial to the post-colonial era, of which there were a number, the arrival and popularity of the Church was one of *the* major changes in the early twentieth century.

As opposed to the administration, colonial capitalism admittedly sometimes influenced the patterning of Church infrastructure. Most obviously, the CFL rail network provided the transit arteries that allowed Catholic missionaries to enter (and exit) Kongolo. Yet, as they developed, the CFL camps were a consistent thorn in the side of missionaries who saw them as bastions of consumer capitalism and union organization. But despite the impact that the CFL and cotton companies had, they did not shatter the Church's out-stations. As the penultimate substantive chapter indicated, colonial capitalism could in fact work to missionaries' advantage. Outside of the CFL complexes, the implementation of PI on behalf of Cotanga meant that the colonial state continued to act to prevent Congolese mobility in order to keep them in the cotton plots. Such an emphasis on preventing rural–urban migration suited the Church because it could continue to try to build the pristine Christian communities that it had begun in the early twentieth century. In short, even during the post-war boom, missionaries were able to work with the forces of capital rather than against it even if they continued to be frustrated by the CFL camps.

Likewise, alongside the administration, the Church was able to keep Protestants missionaries, such as the Congo Evangelistic Mission (CEM) and the Seventh Day Adventists to the periphery of Kongolo. The CEM boasted only a small presence on the edges of the Bùki-Kiloshi sector while the SDAs were confined to the outskirts of Bena Nyembo. Victor Roelens and Emilio Callewaert had largely seen through their religious-political visions on the Katangese hinterland not just to counter European proletarianization but also, crucially, to prevent what they saw as a rising tide of Protestantism in the Congo. Callewaert also knew that the Spiritans were at a comparative disadvantage to Protestant missionaries given that the Spiritans had been asked to leave the Congo Free State. There was every incentive, therefore, for his missionaries to build and convert with haste. Roelens, also, wanted to prevent any Protestant encroachment and, in the case of Kongolo, particularly from the SDAs. The fact that the SDAs were sponsored mainly by Americans meant that the White Fathers' desire that they should be undermined dovetailed with state suspicions of Anglophone missionaries more generally. As a result, even today, the SDAs form a negligible presence in the religious life of Kongolo.

The observation that the Catholic Church wielded considerable power relative to other colonial institutions in the Belgian Congo corresponds in part with Jules Marchel/A. M. Delathuy and Marvin Markowtiz's work, which emphasizes missionaries' contribution to colonial state-building. Yet these authors concentrated largely—even if not wholly—on the metropolitan angle of the Church–state relationship instead of the local, Congolese one. Alternatively, this book emphasized the need to examine the local historical dynamics rather than simply analyzing the metropole. For example, the rancour between the Church and the colonial state's representatives in Brussels did not translate into open competition between the two institutions in Kongolo. Instead, while the Church faced increasing competition from vocational schools, it developed a close relationship with the state in the late colonial period that would haunt it as decolonization approached. Rather than being seen as an enemy of the colonial state, militant African nationalists, often from outlying territories and not Kongolo itself, saw the Church and the state as the same thing. Rather than fighting the Church, in Kongolo itself, many parents fought to get their children into mission schools and nativist discourse began to appear as a means of competing over scarce educational resources.

Chapters 5 and 6 emphasized that the mission encounter in Kongolo was unevenly patterned, though, with communities on the right bank of the Lualaba River tending to host a greater Catholic mission presence than those on the left. Given their unequal access to mission schooling, and exactly as Crawford Young's model suggests, African communities in Kongolo had differing encounters with colonial modernity.[5] The Hêmbá, for example, generally had a more successful experience under colonial rule than their Luba counterparts. This book has argued that the social mobility that the Church afforded individuals, not least Benoit Tambwe Abati, influenced his and his peers' choices during the crucial May 1960 elections. Rather than voting for forms of socialist nationalism, such as the MNC, many chose to vote for a party that would maintain the socio-economic structures put in place by the departing colonial regime. Indeed, this book concentrated on Kongolo in part because the province was the only one in Tanganyika to vote for Conakat during the decolonization process. Throughout, it has maintained that the density of Church infrastructure there, particularly with regard to education, was central to this trend.

Nationalist histories, as well as popular literary works such as Aimé Césaire's *A Season in Congo*, have tended to characterize the secession chiefly as the product of imperial intrigue while downplaying the importance of African agency within this history.[6] In the popular imagination, those Western interests who owned stocks in the UMHK used Tshombe and his Conakat party as puppets through which they could stop the nationalization of their assets. There was certainly some truth in this portrayal of the secession. For example, René Clemens, a Professor from Liège University, was instrumental in writing the Katangese Constitution.[7] Recently, though, Miles Larmer and Erik Kennes have done much to draw attention to the role that Africans played during the secession.[8] Rather than marionettes who served ambiguous and sinister imperial ends, Tshombe and his interior minister, Godefroid Manongo, had their own agendas at stake in Katangese independence. Larmer and Kennes concentrated on southern Katanga and emphasized the importance of the transnational precolonial Lunda state as a factor in Tshombe's motivation to push for secession.[9] This book has complemented their research by concentrating on the north of the Katanga province and focusing on the Church. In Kongolo, those who voted for Conakat during the secession believed that under Tshombe's stewardship the schools that missionaries had jealously guarded from the state could be preserved. Likewise, the secular arguments propounded by leading politicians such as Patrice Lumumba did not resonate with many in Kongolo given the importance of Catholic spirituality in the territory.

Although there are many clashes between Church and nationalist perspectives, there are many areas in which the two can usefully speak to each other. Most significant nationalist figures were trained in Church facilities at one time or another in their lives, for example. Can it be a coincidence that some of the leading radical nationalist figures, such as Jason Sendwe, spent more time in Protestant schools than Catholic ones? As such, did they feel more distanced from the Belgian Congo and its administration than figures who ended up embracing the US during the Cold War such as the Catholic schooled Joseph Kasa-Vubu given that they were educated by those who did not have state patronage? The important Protestant presence in areas outside Kongolo in the Tanganyika district may well have served to propel the militant Lualaba province in the face of less radical, Catholic-trained catechists in territories such as Manono. In any case, these are topics for future biographers to answer in more detail but they are, I think, worth asking and point to areas in which both ecclesiastical and more secular histories can usefully enter into a dialogue with each other. Other authors have done precisely this in other contexts. Stephen Ellis and Gerrie ter Haar, for example, have noted how the first President of Congo-Brazzaville, Abbé Fulbert Youlou, was a Catholic priest before embarking on his political career.[10] More generally, Kate Skinner, in her book *Fruits of Freedom*, argued that the Presbyterian Church stimulated Ewe ethnic nationalism in the Ghana–Togo borderlands.[11] Church schools in the Ghana–Togo context, while they were often Protestant and not Catholic ones, served as a core strategy for upward social mobility, much like they did in the Congo, as well as avenues into paid work.

Despite the Church's powerful political position in the Katangese hinterland as independence approached, little could have prepared it for what would happen during the tumult that accompanied decolonization. The Massacre of twenty missionaries in January 1962 was a hammer blow. Coming just under three years after Kongolo was elevated to a diocese, the local Church faced an immense challenge to recover from this atrocity. In many respects, the violence of 1 January 1962 brought the mission encounter between Europeans and Congolese people to a bloody climax. But there were nonetheless some important continuities. Monseigneur Gustav Bouve, a European, continued in his role as Bishop of Kongolo after the Massacre. Likewise, although militant nationalist could wield the power of transformative violence in the hinterland, they ended up offering few institutional alternatives to the network of pharmacies and schools erected by their Catholic opponents. The survival and experience of the Church in the post-colonial period warrants further study. Suffice to say here, though, that Roelens and Callewaert's legacy was substantial enough not to be entirely stripped away in the violent years proceeding independence. What is more, the fact that the Church stayed on in the Congo after 1960 is to some extent indicative of its own institutional indentity and one that could function independently of the Belgian colonial administration. After 1960, the Church's competitive collaboration with the colonial state was over as it sought to navigate its relationship with its successors.

In their long-standing pursuit of pristine Catholic Christian communities under Belgian rule, though, this book has also noted that Roelens and Callewaert, along with their successors such as Huys and Morlion, promoted a dogmatic form of Catholicism in Kongolo. The version of Catholicism that emerged in Kongolo exhibited far less interest in forms of African religious thought than many of its contemporaries. It is telling, for example, that Roelens' magnum opus *Instructions aux Missionnaires*

Pères Blancs du Haut Congo, was an *instruction* manual rather than a philosophical tract that engaged with African thought in the mold of Placide Tempels' *Bantu Philosophy*.[12] Roelens did not strive to create an elite, literate class of converts either—four years of basic schooling was generally enough in his eyes. While he was happy to sponsor Stefano Kaoze's passage to priesthood, he stopped short of incorporating African idioms into the Catholicism he espoused in Kongolo and Tanganyika as a whole. Catholic out-stations were not spaces of intellectual dialogue but more of rote learning. From the archives from them that are open, we can know that the Propagande Fide rarely had a problem with the doctrine that Roelens espoused and this was not a coincidence.

Even if catechists were trained to be able to explain the catechism, Roelens never meant for the theology behind it to be influenced by Hêmbá cosmological thought. It is harder to get a general sense of how Emilio Callewaert conceived of his mission work since he never published as extensively as Roelens. However, there is little to suggest Callewaert took a different approach from his White Fathers colleagues. From what little of his correspondence remains to us, it is clear that he was deeply hostile to African thought and concerned to struggle against it rather than incorporate aspects of it into his own thinking about the gospels. This book has therefore departed from the majority of scholarship on the mission encounter that has examined how African thought influenced Catholic theology in various colonies across the continent. What is more, it has suggested that the Comaroff's model of conversion, which was top-down in the main, was the aim of the vast proportion of high-ranking clerics even if the mission diaries show clearly that neither the White Fathers nor the Spiritans ever fully colonized the consciousness of the Congolese.

Notes

1. Crawford Young, *Politics in Congo: Decolonization and Independence* (Princeton: Princeton University Press, 1965); Wamu Oyatambwe, *Eglise Catholique et Pouvoir Politique au Congo-Zaïre* (Paris: L'Harmattan, 1997); and David Van Reybrouck, *Congo: The Epic History of a People* (London: Fourth Estate, 2013).
2. Reybrouck, *Congo*.
3. David Northrup, 'A Church in Search of a State: Catholic Missionaries in Eastern Zaïre, 1879–1930,' *Journal of Church and State*, 30, 2 (1988), p. 312.

4. Nancy Rose-Hunt, *A Colonial Lexicon of Birth Ritual, Medicalization and Mobility in Congo* (Durham: Duke University Press, 1999), p. 165.
5. Northrup, 'A Church in Search of a State,' p. 246.
6. Aimé Césaire, *A Season in Congo* (London: Seagull Books, 2010).
7. Tukumbi Lumumba-Kasongo, 'Why Katanga's Quest for Self-Determination Failed,' in Redie Bereketeab (ed.), *Self-Determination and Secession in Africa: The Post-colonial State* (London: Routledge, 2014), p. 174.
8. Miles Larmer and Erik Kennes, 'Rethinking the Katangese Secession,' *The Journal of Imperial and Commonwealth History*, 42, 2 (2014), pp. 741–761; Miles Larmer and Erik Kennes, *The Katangese Gendarmes and War in Central Africa: Fighting Their Way Home* (Bloomington: Indiana University Press, 2016).
9. Larmer and Kennes, 'Rethinking the Katangese Secession,' pp. 741–761
10. Stephen Ellis and Gerrie ter Haar, *Worlds of Power: Religious Thought and Political Practice in Africa* (Oxford: Oxford University Press, 2004), p. 68.
11. Skinner, *The Fruits of Freedom in British Togoland*, pp. 33–80.
12. Victor Roelens, *Instructions aux Missionnaires Pères Blancs du Haut-Congo par son Excellence Monseigneur Roelens, Vicaire Apostolique du Haut Congo Belge* (Baudouinville: Vicariat Apostolique du Haut Congo, 1938); Placide Tempels, *La Philosophie Bantoue* (Elisabethville, 1945).

BIBLIOGRAPHY

Césaire, Aimé, *A Season in Congo* (London: Seagull Books, 2010).
Comaroff, Jean, and Comaroff, John, *Of Revelation and Revolution, Volume 2: The Dialectics of Modernity on a South African Frontier* (Chicago: University of Chicago Press, 2009).
Ellis, Stephen, and Haar, Gerrie ter, *Worlds of Power: Religious Thought and Political Practice in Africa* (Oxford: Oxford University Press, 2004).
Hiribarren, Vincent, *A History of Borno: Trans-Saharan African Empire to Failing Nigerian State* (London: Hurst and Company, 2015).
Larmer, Miles, and Kennes, Erik, 'Rethinking the Katangese Secession,' *The Journal of Imperial and Commonwealth History*, 42, 2 (2014), pp. 741–761.
Larmer, Miles, and Kennes, Erik, *The Katangese Gendarmes and War in Central Africa: Fighting Their Way Home* (Bloomington: Indiana University Press, 2016).
Loffman, Reuben, 'On the Fringes of a Christian Kingdom: The White Fathers, Colonial Rule and the Báhêmbá in Sola, 1909–1960,' *Journal of Religion in Africa*, 45 (2015), pp. 279–306.

Lonsdale, John, and Berman, Bruce, 'Coping with Contradictions: The Development of the Colonial State in Kenya, 1895–1914,' *The Journal of African History*, 20, 4 (1979), pp. 487–505.

Lumumba-Kasongo, Tukumbi, 'Why Katanga's Quest for Self-Determination Failed,' in Redie Bereketeab (ed.), *Self-Determination and Secession in Africa: The Post-colonial State* (London: Routledge, 2014).

Markowitz, Marvin D., *Cross and Sword: The Political Role of Christian Missions in the Belgian Congo, 1908–1960* (Stanford: Hoover Institution Press, 1973).

Northrup, David, 'A Church in Search of a State: Catholic Missionaries in Eastern Zaïre, 1879–1930,' *Journal of Church and State*, 30, 2 (1988), pp. 309–319.

Oyatambwe, Wamu, *Église Catholique et Pouvoir Politique au Congo-Zaire* (Paris: L'Harmattan, 1997).

Roelens, Victor, *Instructions aux Missionnaires Pères Blancs du Haut-Congo par son Excellence Monseigneur Roelens, Vicaire Apostolique du Haut Congo Belge* (Baudouinville: Vicariat Apostolique du Haut Congo, 1938).

Skinner, *The Fruits of Freedom in British Togoland* (Cambridge: Cambridge University Press, 2016).

Tempels, Placide, *La Philosophie Bantoue* (Elisabethville, 1945).

Van Reybrouck, David, *Congo: The Epic History of a People* (London: Fourth Estate, 2013).

Young, Crawford M., *Politics in Congo: Decolonization and Independence* (Princeton: Princeton University Press, 1965).

Correction to: Church, State and Colonialism in Southeastern Congo, 1890–1962

Correction to:
R. A. Loffman, *Church, State and Colonialism*
in Southeastern Congo, 1890–1962, **Cambridge Imperial**
and Post-Colonial Studies Series,
https://doi.org/10.1007/978-3-030-17380-7

Belated corrections have been made by the author to the Front Matter and Chapters 1, 2, 3 and 4. The original version of the book has been updated with these changes.

The updated version of the book can be found at
https://doi.org/10.1007/978-3-030-17380-7

© The Author(s) 2019   C1
R. A. Loffman, *Church, State and Colonialism in Southeastern Congo,*
1890–1962, Cambridge Imperial and Post-Colonial Studies Series,
https://doi.org/10.1007/978-3-030-17380-7_9

INDEX